The Tourism and Travel Industry in Ireland

Denise Guiney

D1437947

Gill & Macmillan

Gill & Macmillan Ltd
Hume Avenue
Park West
Dublin 12
with associated companies throughout the world
www.gillmacmillan.ie

Contents

Part 2: The tourism industry

Part 3: Geographical tourism

Foreword

The Tourism and Travel Industry in Ireland is designed to cover tourism modules in FETAC and third level college courses. The tourism industry operates in a changing world, and students must be aware of these changes and be able to adapt to them.

The 1900s were a period of unprecedented investment in the industry and tourist numbers grew without a break for the six years to 2001. During the Spring of 2001 foot and mouth struck, and as the tourism industry began to recover from this, the events of 11 September occurred. Tourism numbers fell by seven per cent and tourism revenue decreased by one per cent, a blow to an industry which expected at least five per cent growth each year. Investment in marketing has been increased in order to reverse this trend, but it will have to cope with many problems that are beyond Ireland's control.

The events of September 2001 had major implications for those in the airline business. Most airlines serving the USA have had to cut staff and operations, and have sold off aircraft. Security at airports has increased which has resulted in higher costs. Airlines like Swiss Air collapsed, while Aer Lingus' position has changed greatly since 2000. Low cost airline traffic is growing. Ryanair has expanded its routes and Aer Lingus has now entered this market. As airlines change, the operations of Irish Airports and Aer Rianta will be forced to modify the way they carry out their business.

The tourism industry is a major player in Ireland's economy and has contributed much to the economic success of the late 1990s. Although the industry will face many challenges in the future, it must learn to overcome all obstacles that are put in its way. It is only in this way that the industry can continue to create jobs and earn foreign revenue. Some of the tourism businesses that opened during the 1990s failed to realise their full potential, and have closed or moved to better locations. In a more competitive world tourism businesses will have to improve the delivery of their product in order to survive and grow.

The Government is planning to make changes in the way it organises the tourism industry. Both CERT and Bord Failte are due to change in the near future. Changes after general elections in the past led to alterations in the names of government departments; this may occur in the future and students must ensure that they are aware of this.

Students are supplied with references at the end of each chapter in order to help them investigate any subject to which the tourism industry is linked. These may be useful for essays, assignments and projects.

Acknowledgments

This book could not have been written without the help of many businesses and organisations within the Irish tourism industry. I wish to thank all of these organisations for their help in providing information and illustrations. These include the Department of Public Enterprise, Department of Heritage, Arts, Gaeltacht and the Islands, Department of Tourism and Sport, Bord Failte, the Northern Ireland Tourism Board, CERT, the Irish Hotel Federation, Ireland West, Shannon Development, Coras Iompair Eireann, Dúchas, the Irish Farmhouse Association, Irish Town and Country Homes Association, Jurys Doyle Hotels, Aer Lingus, Budget Travel, *The Irish Times*, UCD Folklore Department, ENFO, Ballyhoura Failte Society, Silverdale's Ireland, and Clans of Ireland. In particular I would like to thank those people who went out of their way giving me their time and advice, these include Rosemary O'Neill, Ciara Gallagher and Leo Ganter of Bord Failte, Gerry Weir of Aer Rianta, Margaret Cronin of Cronins Coaches, Colette Pearson of Pearson Travel, Don Moore of Irish Ferries, Nuala White of the Cassidy Clan, Rebecca O'Carroll, Tom Conway, Detta Melia, and Katie Dowling. I wish to thank the staff at Gill & Macmillan who gave me advice during the writing of this book. I wish also to thank my husband John who provided me with the information on the Smyth family, and who helped with the proof reading.

Denise Guiney

The Publishers are grateful to the following for permission to reproduce material used in the book:

Bord Failte; Ordnance Survey Ireland; The National Museum of Ireland; The Board of Trinity College, Dublin; The National Gallery of Ireland; Northern Ireland Tourist Board.

Part 1
Economic Aspects
of the Industry

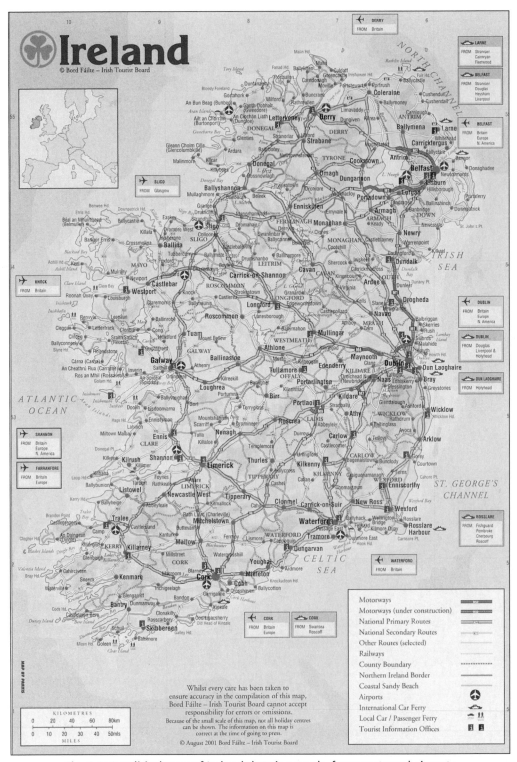

Fig. 1.1: A political map of Ireland showing roads, ferry ports and airports

12

CHAPTER I

Introduction to the Tourism Industry

DEFINITION OF A TOURIST

Tourism and tourists have been defined in different ways. In 1937, the League of Nations defined a tourist as a person who travelled away from home for more than twenty-four hours, and travelled for a range of reasons, such as business, pleasure, and health, or on a cruise trip. Professors Hunziker and Krapf of Berne University in Switzerland, described tourists in 1942 as 'people who travelled, and stayed away from home on a temporary basis, but were not earning money.' In 1963 the World Tourism Organisation (WTO) broadened this definition further and included the terms visitor and excursionist. It was agreed that a visitor was someone who stayed away at least twenty-four hours and who travelled either for leisure or business purposes, while the excursionist travelled for less than twenty-four hours. In 1991 the WTO stated, 'Tourism comprises the activities of persons travelling to and staying in places outside their usual environment for not more than one consecutive year for leisure, business and other purposes.'

This development of the definition of what a tourist is tells us that tourism has three main elements:

1. A tourist moves away from his or her main home; this can mean that he or she has gone to stay with relations, or in a hotel, in a mobile home for a weekend or a month, or on a day trip.
2. The journey is only for a short time, for the day, weekend, week, or month.
3. There is a particular reason or purpose for the trip, for example holidays; but there can be many other reasons.

The tourism industry provides the services for the tourist; these include transport, accommodation and other facilities. Within this definition of tourism we also find that there are two types of tourists. These are domestic or national tourists, and overseas or international tourists. A domestic tourist is someone who travels within his or her own country. For instance, a Dublin family who go to West Cork for two weeks to stay in a rented house are described as domestic tourists. An international tourist is one who travels abroad. International tourists are of two types: (a) inbound tourists and (b) outbound tourists. Inbound tourists are American, British and European tourists who travel to Ireland on holidays. The German couple who come to Ireland and spend a week on the River Shannon in a cabin cruiser are inbound international tourists. Inbound tourists bring large amounts of foreign revenue and create tourism jobs in Ireland, and it is this group of tourists that the tourism industry is most concerned with. Irish people who stay in Ireland on holidays also contribute to the Irish tourism industry. Outbound tourists are Irish people who go abroad on holidays; for example Irish students on holiday in Ibiza. An outbound tourist makes little financial contribution to the Irish tourism industry. Excursionists are often referred to as day-trippers, and include school students making day trips during the year to visit historical and other sites.

Tourists can come either on inclusive tours or as independent tourists. An inclusive tour is also known as a package tour. This is a holiday that is organised by a tour operator, who puts together transport, accommodation, and other services such as food, visits to places of interest and entertainment. The tour operator then sells the package to the tourist at an 'all in' price. Often tourists who come on coach tours of Ireland for a week or fortnight are on package tours. The price of their holiday has included the flight to Ireland, a coach trip around Ireland's most popular tourist attractions, such as Killarney Lakes and Kilkenny Castle, entrance fees to these attractions, hotel accommodation and meals in the hotels, and entertainment at night which might include a medieval banquet or traditional Irish music. Independent tourists are those who book their own airfare and perhaps car hire, or their ferry trip from England; they will then organise their own B&B, meals and entrance into historical attractions and other sites as they travel around the country at their own pace.

THE PURPOSE OF TOURISM

There are three main categories of tourism:

1. Leisure
2. Business
3. Visiting friends and relations (VFR).

Within each of these categories there are sub-categories that go a long way to explaining the different types of tourism.

1. Leisure

(a) Holidays. There are three types of holidays. Recreation and relaxation holidays appeal to tourists who spend their time at the beach or seaside resort. Here the people are looking for sunshine, sea and sand, and as long as they have days of sunshine then they are happy. The traditional seaside resort, for example Tramore and Kilkee, provided this type of holiday in Ireland until the 1960s and 1970s, but now most who want this type of holiday go abroad. This has meant a decline in many of our seaside resorts. Cultural holidays appeal to the tourist who wants to travel and see new things. This type of holiday involves visiting historical buildings, seeing new scenery, or going to festivals. Often people on this type of holiday are also touring the country, staying at different hotels each night. Activity holidays involve tourists going on holidays to participate in their hobby, or interest. This could mean going on a walking or cycling holiday. It may mean that as they stay in their hotel, they make use of the leisure-centre attached, going swimming, using the gym, or golfing. The main point of their holiday is that they participate in activities, rather than just sitting back and doing nothing. Ireland is very well suited both to cultural and activity holidays.

(b) Education is another reason that people travel, whether it is Irish students going to the Gaeltacht to learn Irish, or foreign students coming to Ireland to learn English. Apart from the actual classes that these students attend, they also participate in a range of cultural activities. They visit historical and scenic sites close by, and they go to Irish cultural events. The students who travel to Ballyvaughan to learn how to paint, or to Miltown Malbay to play the fiddle, are tourists who are travelling for educational purposes.

(c) Sport is another type of tourism. Sport attracts large numbers of tourists. Many Irish people travel to England each weekend to see their favourite team play in the Premiership. During the months of February and March thousands of rugby fans travel to Ireland to watch their teams play in Lansdowne Road, Dublin. In September each year thousands of people from all over Ireland travel to Croke Park in Dublin to watch the all-Ireland hurling and football finals.

(d) Religion is another reason why people travel, and over the last thousand years people have gone on pilgrimages all over the world. The year 2000 was designated as a Holy Year in Rome, and millions of Catholics visited Rome during that year. The main Irish pilgrimage centres are Knock and Croagh Patrick, both in Co. Mayo. Abroad, Catholic pilgrims travel to Lourdes and Fatima, amongst other destinations, and Moslems to Mecca in Saudi Arabia.

(e) Health is another type of tourism. This includes people who travel to health spas, and health farms. Health spas are very important on the Continent, with thousands of people visiting them each year. Most of the original tourist towns were health spas. Health tourism is one area that the Irish Government has tried to develop since 1994. There have been a number of new health farms opened in Ireland since 1990.

(f) Shopping attracts large numbers of tourists to Ireland each year. These people come because Ireland has favourable prices for a range of goods. Icelandic tourists, for example, come for this reason. Until relatively recently, many Irish people travelled to London to shop, but with the arrival of English high-street shops in Irish cities, this is no longer necessary. The downside of the new type of shops is that many towns have a similarity about them, and Irish towns are no longer unique for shopping.

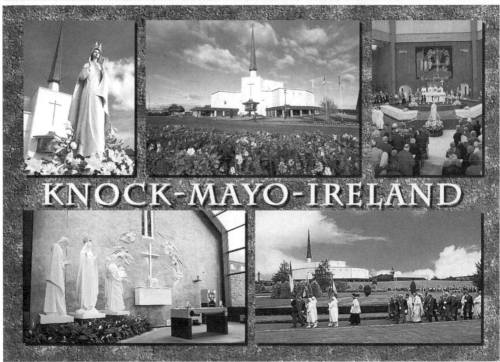

Fig. 1.2: Knock Basilica

2. Business tourism

(a) Meetings are often scheduled for business people in other cities and countries; because they travel to these meetings they are classified as tourists. Every morning hundreds of Irish business people, all involved in a variety of meetings, travel from Dublin Airport to London, making this the busiest airline route in Europe.

(b) Conferences attract large numbers of people, and these are also classified as business tourists. Trade unions, political parties and professional bodies all hold conferences each year. They attract large attendances, and this is an important source of tourism revenue.

(c) Exhibitions and trade fairs are held all year round in Dublin and other cities. The favourite venues are currently the RDS and the Point Depot. Such exhibitions are attended by a large number of companies which provide services for this particular business, in the hope of attracting new buyers. In January the Holiday eXperience is held in Dublin, Belfast, Cork and Galway.

3. Visiting friends and relations

This includes people who travel to visit family who live in Ireland. These may be people who travel for a wedding or a funeral. It may be someone who is coming to

Ireland to visit his or her pen friend of many years. Generally VFRs don't spend as much money on accommodation as other tourists, because in many cases they will be staying with their friends and relations, but they will use other tourist products and services.

REVISION EXERCISES

Explain what kind of tourists each of the following are:

1. A group of girl friends at a health farm for the weekend
2. An Irish student in the Gaeltacht for three weeks
3. A day at the beach with your family
4. A French couple on a coach tour of Kerry
5. A young boy visiting his uncle in London to go to a football match
6. A school trip to Newgrange, Co. Meath
7. A Japanese businessman visiting his Irish factory
8. A schoolteacher attending a trade union annual conference in Killarney over Easter.

Tourism industry components

There are eight different sectors within the tourism industry offering a range of products to the visiting tourist. These are:

1. Accommodation, which includes hotels, guesthouses, hostels, self-catering accommodation – cottages and apartments, caravan and camping sites.
2. Catering; this includes a range of different types of restaurants, fast food outlets, cafés, take-away outlets, and pubs that serve food.
3. Transport; this includes air, sea, rail, road (coach, car hire, bike hire) and inland waterways.
4. Natural resources such as beaches, cliffs, mountains, lakes and rivers.
5. Tourist attractions; these include historical buildings, museums, interpretive or visitor centres, gardens, art galleries, and ancient monuments.
6. Leisure facilities; these include marinas, swimming pools, golf clubs, equestrian centres, nature reserves and national parks.
7. Entertainment; this includes night clubs, theatres, concerts, pubs, festivals, arcades and parks.
8. Information; this includes Bord Fáilte, tourism information offices, maps, guide books.

All these sectors provide the tourist with the facilities that make holidays enjoyable. While not everyone will use all of these facilities they will make use of most of them. Each sector contributes to the economy, i.e. in revenue and job creation. The tourism industry earned £3 billion (€3.8 billion) in 1999. Nearly 138,000 jobs were created in the tourism industry, that is one job in every twelve in the country. These jobs and this wealth were not concentrated in one region, but were spread throughout the country.

The **hospitality** of the Irish people is legendary with their 'Céad míle fáilte'. This is not just among those who are involved in the tourism industry; more importantly, it is in the attitudes of the Irish people. It is the smile that makes people feel welcome. It is the helping hand that the locals provide to the tourists, giving them directions when they are obviously lost. It is the relaxed way of life that our tourists love; this allows the natives the time to talk to tourists, whether in the street, in a shop or in the pub. Tourists come to Ireland because of the friendliness of the people. The advent of the Celtic tiger is putting all this friendliness and relaxed way of life under threat. People are in such a hurry they cannot help others out. The ugly head of racism is threatening. This can be seen in people's attitudes to Spanish students, to coloured people, and to people who do not speak English. Some of these attitudes are creating the climate where people are being harassed and physically attacked; this will end up affecting the Irish tourism industry. Irish people need to be aware of this threat; it needs to be counteracted by all, but particularly by those within the industry, because in the end they will have the most to lose. The Irish Tourism Industry Confederation is trying to encourage Irish people to continue to be friendly towards tourists with their 'People and Places' programme.

Customer care refers to the quality of the service provided to tourists. The tourism industry is a service industry, and has the following distinguishing factors:

- Perishability: this refers to the fact that the industry's products cannot be stored. Bedrooms must be filled in hotels every night, tables filled in the restaurants, airline seats on each flight, because if they are not, they cannot be stored for some time in the future.
- Heterogeneity of tourism personnel: this is where the level of service varies or is not uniform. Because the industry depends on people, the way everyone in the industry treats every customer may not be of the same high standard every time. It is very difficult to monitor quality control in the tourism industry. Every time a waitress serves a table, she must be smiling, friendly and efficient, and if she is not then the level of service that she provides to each customer is not of the same high standard.
- Intangibility: this means that the product cannot be actually seen before you buy it. This makes it difficult, for both the service provider and the customer, to understand the quality of the product. The customer expects a high standard, regardless of the price they are paying; so it is up to the producer to reach this standard
- Inseparability of consumption: when hotels and restaurants provide the service, and the tourist stays on the premises to enjoy the product.
- Interdependence: occurs particularly when package holidays are involved. This

is because a number of different tourism providers are involved and for tourists to have a successful holiday, all the parts of the holiday (airlines, accommodation, coaches, etc.) must work together.

These are the problems that the tourism industry faces. In order to overcome them, a high level of training must be provided for all within the industry. The emphasis is always to provide a friendly, efficient service and make every customer feel special. The growth of the Irish tourism industry in Europe and Japan has created a need for workers in the industry to speak foreign languages; training needs to be provided for this. Labour shortages in the industry have led many hoteliers to bring in Europeans to work in their hotels and restaurants. Some Europeans need training in the English language and in customer care so that they provide the same level of service as their Irish counterparts. Those who are in constant contact with the tourists need to be well informed about tourism facilities in their local area, and any general information that a tourist might require.

TOURIST CHOICE

The type of holiday that each tourist selects depends on interests, background, financial position, age and sex. Different types of holidays appeal to different people. This can be seen in the following examples:

- Sporting holidays appeal mainly to men, e.g. rugby weekend trips.
- Shopping holidays appeal mainly to women.
- In the past men took business trips, but this trend is changing because more women are involved in senior management.
- Cultural holidays tend to be more attractive to the well-educated tourist.
- Recreation and relaxation appeal to people who want to have a good time on holiday.
- Activity holidays appeal to those who are more energetic, and probably young.

Those involved in the tourism industry need to know what makes tourists choose a particular type of holiday, so that they can develop their product, price and promotion policies to meet the needs of that tourist. This allows them to decide whether they want to appeal to the mass market, to a small segment of the market, or to a niche market. The factors that need to be studied are: 1. Economic and social class, 2. Demographic characteristics, 3. Geographical characteristics

1. Economic and social class

People involved in marketing have divided society into different social classes based on different incomes, jobs, and level of education. This is because marketers believe that these influence people's purchasing behaviour. A typical social grading definition is as follows:

Social Class	Status	Typical Jobs	Percentage Population (approx)
A	Professionals	Owners of business of medium Co., Top managerial/company directors of large companies, Senior civil servants, Professionals – doctors, solicitors	Under 3%
B	Managerial	Managers, journalists, senior teachers, accountants, army captains, chemists	Under 14%
C1	White Collar Workers	Junior managers, civil servants, bank workers, nurses, office workers, social workers	27%
C2	Skilled Workers	Electricians, carpenters, bus/train drivers, printers, gardaí, army, foremen	25%
D	Unskilled Workers	Bus conductors, shop workers, labourers, fishermen, postmen	20%
E	Others	Pensioners, unemployed, casual labourers, anyone living on state assistance.	12%

Table 1.1: Social grading definitions Source: JICNARS National Readership Survey

This social structure was developed about 1950 and was applied to the earnings of males. While it is outdated, it gives some idea of the groups who have the largest disposable income to spend on holidays and those who have very little. Generally speaking at the turn of this new century most people try to go on holidays, but those in social class E find it the most difficult to afford holidays. Different social groups in general look for different things out of their holidays. The better educated look for a lot more than just sitting on the beach and cultural holidays appeal to this group, while other groups with less money will look for destinations that offer them good value for money, where food, drink and accommodation are cheap.

Different social groups will behave differently. The very wealthy tend to be conservative in their tastes. Many of these will spend their holidays in Ireland, perhaps in their holiday home; abroad they might stay in a friend's villa. The managerial and professional classes on the other hand often go to destinations where they will be seen; they go to the top hotels around the country. White-collar workers are more interested in value for money, so they are attracted to special offers, such as good value package holidays. Skilled workers earn good money so they can afford to go on the same or better holidays than the white-collar workers, but different types of facilities will attract them. In general Irish holidays do not appeal to unskilled workers.

Each year as part of Bord Fáilte's survey of overseas travellers, an analysis of tourists is carried out under the headings of age, social class and party composition. In 1999 the findings were as follows:

Table 1.2: Analysis of tourists in 1999 Courtesy of Bord Fáilte		
Age	**Social Class**	**Party Composition**
Under 25 19%	AB Managerial/Professional 37%	Couple 44%
25–34 24%	C1 White Collar 46%	Alone 19%
35–44 18%	C2 Skilled Worker 13%	Family 16%
45 + 39%	Unskilled Worker 4%	Other Adult Group 21%

This shows that Ireland is most popular among the middle class of society rather than other groups; this is perhaps because of the types of holidays we have to offer – cultural and activity holidays – and the high cost of holidaying in Ireland.

2. Demographic characteristics

Included in this are family life-cycle, age, and sex. The first of these is important because at different stages of a family's development there are different demands on the family's finances.

Table 1.3: Family life-cycles Source: D. Reynolds and W. Wells, Consumer Behaviour		
Age	**Stage of development**	**Family cycle**
18–30	Early adulthood	People are young and single Couples with no children Couple with young children
30–54	Middle adulthood	Couple with dependent children
55 +	Later adulthood	Empty nest – children have left Retired couple Widow/widower

At each of these stages people have different demands on their incomes. People who are young and single have no call on their money, so they have a lot of disposable income to spend on holidays and leisure activities; they may go away for weekends to festivals, or abroad on package holidays. Some may be students, and have a lot of time to travel but little money to spend, and may use economy-style accommodation, for instance hostels or camping.

As single people become couples and get older they have extra expenses, such as setting up house. This involves high rents or high mortgages; either way they have less money to spend on holidays, and may cut back on this area, becoming domestic tourists for a while. Young children bring extra expenses, either crèche costs, or a parent job sharing, or giving up work. This forces the family to go on cheaper self-catering holidays, or on VFRs. As time passes, house expenses generally go down as a percentage of income, so the family has more disposable income. They spend some of this on holidays, choosing perhaps package or touring holidays, but they do not choose the same destinations as they did when they were young.

After the family have left home, the family income is now at one of its highest levels. The older couple now has a larger disposable income, and can afford many expensive holidays. As people retire, they have less income but unless they are solely dependent on state pensions, they will still have enough to travel. There are many cheap holidays during the low season; these appeal to the retired tourist who has the time to enjoy them. Later on, as pensioners get older there may not be the opportunity to travel and many again may revert to visiting friends and relatives.

Only 16 per cent of overseas holiday-makers to Ireland are families; this may be due to the cost of accommodation, cost of access, or the type of holidays on offer. Our climate is not suitable for beach holidays which young families often prefer; a good climate is guaranteed at continental resorts. Many tourists come to Ireland on touring holidays, which are not the most suitable for families.

Age also influences the type and place of holidays that people choose. Young children love the beach, while teenage children prefer activities to keep them busy. Young adults have a preference for plenty of night entertainment, pubs, clubs etc. When children appear, it is back to the family holiday at the beach. Only when the family have gone, and the couple are older do they choose quiet resorts, or hotels. There are hotels and tour companies that offer special holidays for the over fifty-fives; these include Ryan Hotels' Golden Holidays, and the tour company Saga. While most holidays appeal to both sexes, some sporting and shopping holidays may appeal to one. While all age groups come to Ireland on holidays, the largest group are in the forty-five plus age group (39 per cent). This suggests that the type of hotel accommodation and facilities that we offer to tourists has greater appeal to this age group.

3. Geographical characteristics

Different nationalities behave in different ways; they expect different things from their holidays. Europeans like Ireland because of its unpolluted countryside, little traffic on the roads, good seafood, clean comfortable accommodation and its cultural heritage and entertainment, while Americans look for good quality hotel accommodation, good transport facilities, city tours, Irish souvenir shops, and the forty shades of green. Irish domestic holiday-makers look for self-catering accommodation that is reasonably priced, activities for children, good entertainment at night, cheap restaurants or take-away food outlets, and baby-sitting facilities. Overseas tourists of Irish descent are often interested in tracing their family roots, and this is why many Australians and Americans come to Ireland.

The Irish tourism product has changed over the years to meet the demands of tourists. These changes have occurred in the areas of accommodation, where it is now the norm to have ensuite bathrooms even in guesthouses. Heritage centres have been developed to cope with the demands of ethnic tourists. Leisure centres are attached to hotels to provide for the increasing demands of more health-conscious tourists. The success of Irish culture abroad, with such groups as the Chieftains and Riverdance, means that there is a demand for traditional music entertainment.

A multitude of different factors are at play in defining a tourist, therefore those in the tourist industry must decide what kind of tourist they are going to satisfy and then aim their product at that particular market.

REVISION EXERCISES

Using the following information, taken from brochures produced by the Northern Ireland Tourist Board, answer these questions.

1. Classify the information into the eight component areas of the tourist industry.
2. Decide on the tourist profile that is most suited to these tourism products.

The Causeway Coast: Co. Antrim and Derry

This area of Northern Ireland has a wide range of tourist attractions and facilities. These include:

- Giant's Causeway with its basalt columns that rise up out of the sea, forming cliffs
- The Glens of Antrim which offer scenic views with their steep-sided valleys
- The Carrickarede rope bridge that swings eighty feet above the sea
- Dunluce Castle, the Norman castle that is situated on the top of cliffs
- Carrickfergus Castle which dates from the twelfth century
- Old Bushmill Distillery which is the oldest licensed whiskey-distillery in Ireland, and was founded in 1608. Tourists learn how whiskey is produced and are able to sample it
- Glenariff Forest Park which has lots of walks through woodlands
- Route 93 which is part of the network of cycle routes that goes around Whitepark Bay, close to the Giant's Causeway
- Rathlin Island with its large colonies of seabirds on its cliffs
- Orchard Arts and Craft Centre in Ballymoney which allows tourists to create crafts and to buy copper-craft, sculpture, timber and ceramics
- Ballycastle's blue flag beach which offers sandy beaches and shallow, safe waters
- Portrush with its blue flag beaches, water world, and amusement park
- Benone tourist complex which has an adventure playground, heated splash pools and golf ranges

- Causeway Coast hotel, and Magherabuoy Hotel in Portrush
- Scuba diving off Rathlin Island
- Carrickfergus Marina
- Surf-riding along the north coast
- Salmon and trout fishing in the rivers Bann, Bush and Roe
- The special atmosphere of Lughnasa Fayre in Carrickfergus, and the ancient Ould Lammas Fair in Ballycastle
- The beautiful Antrim Castle gardens.

Assignments

1. Look at the tourist attractions in your own local area, city or county:
   (a) Decide the age and family cycle that these tourist attractions target.
   (b) Decide the socio-economic groups they are aimed at.
   (c) Classify the attractions according to their product type.
   (d) Identify any area that you feel is not catered for.
   (e) Compare and contrast your own area with another area of your choice.
2. Research the ITIC's 'People and Places' programme, and debate 'The importance of Irish hospitality to the Irish tourism industry'.

Fig. 1.3: Map of north Antrim coast (above) and list on pages 23-24 courtesy of Northern Ireland Tourist Board

References and further reading:

Bord Fáilte's *Ireland Guide.* Gill & Macmillan, 2000.

Bord Fáilte, *Link* magazine.

Davidson R., *Tourism,* Pitman, 1989.

Holloway J.C., *The Tourism and Travel Industry.* Longman, 1998.

NITB: *The Causeway Coast Brochure and Glens Brochure*, 2000.

CHAPTER 2

Historical Development of Tourism

EARLY TOURISM IN EUROPE AND ENGLAND

Historically the growth of the tourism industry has been linked to two main factors: the development of transport, and accommodation and catering facilities. As these have improved, so the numbers of tourists have grown. The earliest tourists were mainly religious and business tourists. The **Greeks** as early as 600 B.C. travelled to their sacred sites such as Delos and Olympia. From about 31 B.C. **Roman** administrators and traders travelled through the Empire, which stretched from England to the Middle East. Travelling by sea was safe, as Roman patrols guarded against pirates. Latin was spoken throughout the Empire and Roman coins were accepted everywhere, making it easy for people to travel. The wealthy of Rome had their holiday homes in the Bay of Naples. Romans built roads wherever they went and they also built taverns, encouraging people to travel.

Later, after the decline of the Roman Empire (in the fifth century), tourism also declined. War raged throughout much of Europe. Roman roads deteriorated and were soon of poor quality. Few people travelled far from their homes. Travel by ship was the fastest and easiest way to travel around Europe, because of the poor condition of the roads. During this time, 'holy days' or holidays developed. The eves of 'holy days' became a time of celebration, a time to break from work. There were many such 'holy days', sometimes up to thirty in the year. In the Middle Ages (thirteenth century), monasteries offered hospitality to travellers. Apart from businessmen, other travellers went on **pilgrimages**, going to such famous centres as Canterbury in England, and Santiago de Compostela in Spain. The abolition of monasteries during the Reformation (sixteenth century) ended the availability of this type of accommodation. Castles and manor houses provided refuge for travellers. Only small numbers travelled at this time; most people never travelled more than ten miles from their homes during their lifetime.

Until the sixteenth century travellers went on foot, on horseback, or were carried in a litter, or wagon. Horse-drawn carriages were not sprung, so they were very uncomfortable. The roads were pot-holed, and during winter were churned up by wagons into a sea of mud. They were also unsafe, with the threat of highwaymen always present. Improvements were made in coach transport during the 1600s, when Hungarian sprung coaches came to England. During the seventeenth century

stage-coaches were set up between all the major cities in England and in Ireland. An inn was built at each stage which provided food and accommodation for the passengers on the coach and allowed horses to be changed. With new sets of horses every few miles, journeys could be completed in much shorter times. Coaches averaged forty miles per day; it took six days to travel between London and Holyhead, and then a sea journey to Dublin. In 1815 tarmacadam was discovered, and this greatly improved the quality of roads. Stage-coaches were able to go at much greater speeds; for example, journeys that in the past had taken three days now took only twelve-and-a-half hours.

In the early seventeenth century the wealthy began to travel to the Continent on the **Grand Tour**. This was an educational tour, when they visited such important cultural cities as Florence, Venice and Paris. There they learned about art and architecture. Later these trips became more of a social occasion. Travel was inconvenient at this time, as it was mainly by coach on muddy roads. The Napoleonic wars at the end of the eighteenth century stopped all travel to Europe for about thirty years. Visiting health **spa resorts** became popular. The most fashionable of these in England were Bath and Leamington Spa, and in Ireland Lucan and Mallow. The motivation for these trips was to improve a person's health, soon replaced by pleasure as these resorts became centres of social life for the wealthy. Fashionable houses were built around the spas, which people purchased or rented for the season, and assembly rooms were also built where concerts and entertainment were staged. Some of the resorts, like Bath, developed Pump Rooms where the curative waters could be sampled. At first only the very wealthy went to health spa resorts; later the gentry were replaced by the professional and merchant classes and these places declined as resort towns. Many of these towns still retain their Georgian attractions, and remain tourist destinations because of them.

In the eighteenth century, **seaside resorts** began to develop because people believed that sea-water had many curative properties similar to the mineral waters of health spas. They originally drank the water but later discovered that they could achieve the same effect by bathing in it. The development of bathing machines meant that bathers did not have to expose their bodies to the public. The first popular seaside resort in England was Scarborough, which was also a health spa. Brighton and Blackpool also grew to become important seaside towns. The long distances, poor quality of roads, and high cost meant that it was still only the wealthy who could travel to these destinations. For example it took two days and six weeks ' wages to go the sixty miles from London to Brighton. Steamboats began to link cities to seaside resorts, and this is why piers were built at the resorts. Steamboats reduced both the cost and time it took to get to the seaside. Later the piers became important social centres for the resorts, for example Brighton Pier. In 1761 steamboat services began to link England to France, and resorts along the north French coast were developed for English tourists. The Napoleonic wars interrupted this tourism, but after it resumed, by 1820, over 150,000 English tourists visited French resorts each year.

The industrial revolution resulted in new types of transport. **Canals** were first developed in 1762 by the Duke of Bridgewater to carry goods between Manchester and the port of Liverpool. Later they were used to carry passengers. A large network of canals was developed throughout England. The development of railways led to the decline of canals for passenger transport, but they continued to carry freight. Today many canals are used for pleasure craft. George Stevenson developed **railways** in England in 1825. They were originally built to carry goods, but were soon used for passenger travel. They provided cheap, fast transport, which encouraged many people to travel. From 1830 there were many rail services connecting all the major cities. Cities were soon linked to coastal resorts; for example London to Brighton, Dublin to Bray.

Entrepreneurs like **Thomas Cooke** organised day trips to the seaside for the members of his temperance club. In 1841 he brought 570 people from Leicester to Loughborough for one shilling each (7 €cent). Within four years he was organising these trips as a business. He then set about providing holidays within England, and from England to Ireland, to visit the Dublin Exhibition. The railway companies themselves began promoting such trips in the 1850s by offering special fares, such as for day trips or weekends. In 1855 Thomas Cook organised his first package holiday to the Continent to visit the Paris Exhibition. He was a successful tour operator and he had good contacts with the railway companies, shipping companies and hotels. He ensured a good quality service at the cheapest rates, and he personally escorted his customers on these trips, making sure they felt safe. With the development of steamships, he organised trips to Europe and across the Atlantic.

As seaside resorts became popular and large numbers flocked to them, there was a great need for accommodation. The railway companies built many of these new hotels. Along with the new hotels came the family entertainment that was associated with Victorian seaside resorts; this included Punch and Judy shows, donkey rides, seaside piers for boat rides, band performances. Seaside resorts close to cities became the destination of day-trippers, while resorts further away had a more exclusive clientele. Later as steamships replaced sailing ships, the Continent became more available and popular with the wealthy, who visited Biarritz, Deauville and Monte Carlo. Expensive, exclusive trains, like the Orient Express that linked Paris to Constantinople, were developed for these wealthy customers. The Rhine and Switzerland appealed to those who sought outdoor activities. Mountaineering holidays in Switzerland became popular in the 1860s and skiing in the 1890s (although skiing originated in Norway in the seventeenth century).

THE HISTORICAL DEVELOPMENT OF TOURISM IN IRELAND

Travel in Ireland before the eighteenth century was mainly by water because the roads were generally of poor quality. Most early Irish settlements were located along the coast, for example Wexford, or close to rivers, for example Clonmacnoise. During the eighteenth century major advances in transport took place, i.e. canals and coach transport. In Ireland the Grand Canal was built between 1756 and 1805, which linked Dublin with Shannonbridge. Five hotels were built along the canal, in which the passengers stayed overnight; only two of these remain today at Robertstown, Co. Kildare, and at Portobello in Dublin. Ten passenger barges operated on the Grand Canal and Barrow Navigation. It took sixteen hours to travel by barge from Dublin to Shannonbridge in 1818. Later the Royal Canal was built, also linking Dublin with the Shannon, but on a more northerly route via Mullingar. They had four passenger barges. Travel by canal was comfortable, but slow and expensive.

Fig. 2.1: Robertstown on the Grand Canal

In 1803 Sir John Carr wrote of his experiences travelling by canal between Athy and Dublin.

> Precisely as the clock struck one, the towing horse started, and we slipped through the water in the most delightful manner imaginable, at the rate of 4 miles an hour. The boat appeared to be about 35 feet long, having a raised cabin, its roof forming a deck to walk upon. The cabin was divided into a room for the principal passengers, having cushioned seats and a window on each side, and a long table in the middle of the room, another room for the servants of the vessel and pantry: the kitchen was in the steerage. From Athy to Dublin by water is 42 miles: and the setting off and arrival of the boats are managed with great regularity: the passage money is ten shillings and ten pence (€0.70). The day was very fine, and the company very respectable and pleasant. We had an excellent dinner on board, consisting of boiled mutton, a turkey, ham, vegetables, porter, and a pint of wine each at four shillings and ten pence a head ... Our liquid road led through a very fine country, adorned with several noble seats ... We slept at Robertstown, where there is a noble inn belonging to the Canal Company, and before daylight we set off for Dublin, where after descending a great number of locks, and passing through a long avenue of fine elms, we arrived about 10 o'clock a.m. All the regulations of these boats are excellent. I was so delighted with my canal conveyance, that if the objects which I had in view had not been so powerful, I verily think I should have spent the rest of my time in Ireland in the Athy canal boat.

Canal transport lasted only seventy years, but in that time it was profitable for the canal companies and pleasurable for the passengers. Today these canals form a large network for pleasure craft, canoes, cruisers and sailing boats, and are a major resource for the tourism industry.

Until the nineteenth century road transport was poor. At the beginning of the nineteenth century Charles Bianconi, an Italian immigrant, set up his stagecoaches to service the Clonmel area. Later he expanded his network of coaches, to cover most of the south and mid-west of the country and by 1830 he had 100 vehicles on the road providing transport between the towns of Ireland. His long cars could carry fifteen passengers each, and they provided a fast (eight miles per hour), cheap (one-and-a-half pence a mile (€0.1)), and efficient service. The service was used by a wide variety of travellers. After the development of the railways Bianconi continued to provide a service to the railway towns, until the 1860s when there was a good network of trains all over the country.

In 1834 the first **railway in Ireland** was built between Dublin and Kingstown. The train travelled at twenty miles per hour, and it cost between 1 shilling (6 €cent) for first class seats, and 6d (3 €cent) for third class seats. Ten years later there were only forty-five miles of railway, between Portadown and Belfast, and Dublin and Drogheda, but within a few years hundreds of miles of railway were built. The railway was very successful, and led to investment by thirty other railway companies in Ireland. William Dargan was one of the main railway engineers in Ireland, and he built the Boyne viaduct near Drogheda, and the Glanmire tunnel near Cork City. The main railway companies involved in building railways in Ireland were The Great Northern (Dublin–Belfast), The Midland Great Western (Dublin–Galway), The Great Southern and Western (Dublin–Cork, Limerick). Dublin was soon linked to Donegal via Belfast, and it was possible to reach Donegal from London in about fourteen hours. Before the advent of the railway it had taken several days. The railway linked Dublin to Killarney by 1853, and helped make it the premier tourist resort in the country. Soon trains linked all of the major cities. Many smaller lines in Donegal, Connemara, through Clare and south Kerry, were built during the 1880s and 1890s with Government help; regrettably these were all closed down in the 1950s and 1960s as the railways could not compete with road transport. The advent of trains changed Irish people's attitudes to travel.

- Trains encouraged poorer people to travel, helped in their migration to cities and abroad.
- Goods could now be transported cheaply all over the country, giving a wider range of products.
- Seaside resorts like Bray developed and this provided holidays for the middle classes.

Hotels began to emerge in the late 1780s. Most of these were large houses which had been converted into hotels and the majority were in Dublin. They were located near College Green and Temple Bar. When coach transport was popular many hotels were used as departure points, like the Royal Hibernian in Dawson Street, and many provincial hotels served a similar purpose, for example Cruises Hotel, Limerick. When the gentry came to Dublin after 1800, they required accommodation and more hotels were developed to meet this need. Among the earliest hotels in Dublin were the Gresham, built in 1817, the Shelbourne in 1825 and Jury's in Dame Street in 1830. These attracted the aristocracy, military, and businessmen. They provided a high standard of food and service, and these standards have stood the test of time.

Some of the great hotels from the nineteenth century remain with us. These include the hotels that the railway companies developed, and these were later known as the Great Southern Hotels. They were all located in scenic areas that were often at the end of the railway lines, like Parknasilla (1895), Killarney (1854), Kenmare and Caragh Lake (1890s), all in Kerry. These were built to the best Victorian designs, were famous for their wine and food, and for their fishing facilities. They appealed to the very wealthy. Other hotels were situated in Galway and Sligo, at Mulrany in Co. Mayo, and at Bundoran in Co. Donegal, which was part of the Great Northern Railway. Only one new hotel was located in Dublin, and that was The North Wall, which was built in the 1880s to serve cross-channel passengers. At the other main railway stations smaller hotels developed for tourists.

During the 1960s there was major hotel building in Ireland. Among the main builders was Dermot Ryan who started off in the car rental business. He opened Ryan Hotels in Killarney, Limerick, Rosses Point Sligo, and Galway. These hotels were aimed at budget travellers from Britain and Ireland, and they provided basic bedroom and ensuite bathroom accommodation and restaurants. P.V. Doyle built his first hotel in Stillorgan in the 1960s, which he later sold to Ranks. He then built his larger 200-bedroom hotel, the Montrose, opposite University College Dublin. Both hotels were aimed at the mid-market, and consisted of bedrooms with ensuite bathrooms, a trend that was to become the norm. P.V. Doyle went on to build a number of hotels, located along major routes into Dublin City, all of which were successful. Later he built five-star hotels, for example the Berkeley Court. The troubles in Northern Ireland affected tourism to Ireland in the 1970s, forcing the closure of some hotels, and causing the failure of some hotel companies, including the near collapse of Ryan Hotels.

Seaside resorts were developed during the nineteenth century, providing holiday accommodation for the needs of the middle classes, and day excursions for the workers. Resorts like Bray, Co. Wicklow, Youghal, Co. Cork, Tramore, Co. Waterford, Kilkee, Co. Clare and Salthill in Galway all developed from about this time. Hotels and boarding houses were built for guests. The beach supplied entertainment during the day. The promenade provided a walking area to get the sea air, and the bandstand offered entertainment in the afternoons and evenings. These resorts first appealed to the wealthy classes, but as transport improved, especially rail links, many of the wealthy left and were replaced by the families of the middle classes. Gradually over time, these resorts lost their appeal to the middle classes and became the resort of the working class. New entertainment was added like amusement parks, bumper cars, and slot machines. Cheaper holidays abroad in the 1960s led to the decline of many of these traditional resorts. Recent Government financial packages have encouraged investment in these towns, leading mainly to the provision of holiday homes.

Touring resorts like Killarney, Co. Kerry, Enniskerry, Co. Wicklow and Glengarrif, Co. Cork have been popular destinations for tourists since the nineteenth century. These were areas of great scenic beauty and attracted tourists even before the coming of the railways.

Until the twentieth century the only way to reach Ireland was by sea. The Vikings set up our earliest towns along the coast. During the twelfth century trade was developed with the ports of England (Bristol) and France (Bordeaux). Ports like Kinsale developed in the years that followed. The journey between Dublin and Wales took two days and, apart from bad weather, pirates were also a problem. For example, the *Margaret* was plundered by pirates in 1581 as it travelled between Dublin and Holyhead. During the eighteenth century a regular service was set up between Holyhead and Dublin. It ran three days a week and carried mail; its vessels were known as 'mail packets'. The cost of travelling from Holyhead to Dublin in

1747 was 10 shillings and 6 pence (66 €cent), and it took twenty-six hours at sea. In 1768 the number of sailings doubled each way.

Henry Bell developed **steamships** in 1812, in Scotland. The first steamship was called the *Comet*, and by 1815 the *Argyll* was linking the *Clyde* with London. In 1816 the *Hibernian* steamship began to operate on the Howth–Holyhead route (later this company joined B&I). Steamships soon reduced the time between England and Ireland to just eight hours. They were also more reliable and were not as badly affected by the weather. The number of crossings increased, and passengers were offered greater comfort. The British and Irish Steam Packet Company operated services between Kingstown/Dun Laoghaire and Holyhead from 1836 and carried passengers, freight and livestock. They did not face any competition until 1919, when the forerunner of Stena began to provide services between Queenstown/Cobh and Holyhead. The first steamship to cross the Atlantic was the *Sirius* in 1838, but steamships were not very popular on the ocean routes until the development of iron ships. For the next thirty years wooden sailing ships dominated the Atlantic routes between Ireland and America. They often carried 2,000 passengers on their two-month journeys across the Atlantic. Poor sanitation and food often led to deaths on these ships, which became known as coffin ships. The development of steel-hulled, steam-powered ocean liners provided quicker journeys (half the time), and far more comfort. Wealthy Americans started to visit Europe, and do a Grand Tour. Their first stopping-off point was Queenstown, Co. Cork. Harland and Wolff in Belfast built many of these new ships, including the ill-fated *Titanic* which sank on its maiden voyage across the Atlantic in 1912, with the loss of 1,500 lives.

Air transport first began when Wilbur and Orville Wright in 1903 recorded the first flight by an aircraft. Six years later the first flight in Ireland took place at Hillsborough, Co. Down. In 1912 Denys Corbett Wilson made the first crossing of the Irish Sea by air. During the First World War Foynes in Co. Limerick was used by seaplanes. Later, Rineanna was developed into Shannon Airport. Alcock and Brown made the first transatlantic flight in 1919; they flew from Canada to Clifden. The first flight from east to west across the Atlantic took place from Baldonnel, Co. Dublin to Greenly Island off the coast of Canada in 1923; it took thirty-five hours to make the 2,270 mile journey. Air transport provided fast and comfortable services. Sea transport could not compete. Aer Lingus was founded in April 1936 and it played a major role in the development of air transport in Ireland.

The ownership of **motor cars** provides tourists with flexibility and independence. Improved ferry services allow tourists to bring their cars with them on holidays. Routes were developed between Ireland and France in the early 1970s, and these encouraged continental tourists to come to Ireland. In the 1990s the Channel Tunnel improved access from the Continent via England and Wales to Ireland.

Case study: Bray, Co. Wicklow, a Victorian seaside resort

In 1750 Bray was just a small village on the lowest bridging point of the river Dargle and consisted of a few houses, a mill, a church, and a barracks. There was also a row of small fishermen's cottages along the sea front. Shortly afterwards it developed into a market town, and a fashionable centre for touring the surrounding area. William Quin owned a hotel on Main Street, and it was one of the best in the area; it had sixty bedrooms, provided good food and wine, and fresh horses for coaches. The fashion for sea bathing became popular in the early nineteenth century and by 1838 Bray had acquired a number of large villas and lodging houses. These villas could be hired for the season by the wealthy, for a mere £100 (€127). During the 1840s the Lord Lieutenant spent the summer season in Bray.

In 1854 the first train from Dublin came to Bray. The engineer William Dargan decided to develop Bray into a fashionable resort like Brighton in England. The railway station was located between the main street and the beach. An esplanade was built facing the beach, along with Turkish baths and the Carlisle Grounds. In the 1860s new hotels were built; these were Breslin's Royal Marine Hotel, Brennan's International Hotel and Lacy's Bray Head Hotel. Quin's hotel was extended and renamed the Royal Hotel. In 1864 the Turkish baths were changed into Assembly Rooms; these were used to provide a range of entertainments, including concerts. Sea baths were also built at Naylors Cove beneath Bray Head. Many events took place during the summer months along the promenade, including band concerts, regattas, and in the Carlisle Grounds cricket, croquet matches and athletic competitions. The town was a popular destination for excursionists: it had 4,000 visitors on the Easter weekend in 1861.

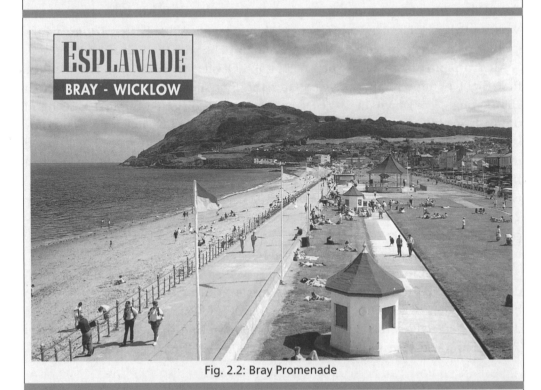

Fig. 2.2: Bray Promenade

New terraces and villas were also built. As a result, the town doubled in size between 1850 and 1901. Other facilities were developed including the public park, market house and town hall. Constant flooding along the beach in the 1880s forced the building of a sea wall that later became the promenade. All this rapid growth caused a number of problems, including an inadequate water supply, poor sewerage, and lack of public lighting. The town sought investment, but never got enough to make it as popular and successful as the seaside resorts in England. Attempts were made by the Improvement Committee to provide more entertainment and to build a pier, but while they were successful in organising many events, they never raised enough money to build the pier. In the first years of the twentieth century Bray was a popular destination for the middle classes; it still had four hotels, nine private hotels along the esplanade and 147 guesthouses, with many others involved in providing a range of activities for tourists. The esplanade had no shopping facilities for tourists.

The First World War brought about the end of expansion in Bray, and the beginning of its gradual decline. The Marine Station Hotel was burnt down in 1916 and was never rebuilt. The International Hotel was used as a hospital. There was no investment in the properties along the sea-front. At the end of the First World War most English tourists went to English seaside resorts instead of visiting Bray. The War of Independence, followed by Civil War, caused a period of unrest in Ireland between 1919 and 1923, and this did not encourage tourism. Any building that did take place was in suburban housing, and this did not improve the town as a seaside resort. Over time Bray attracted less well-off clients, and it became less attractive as a major seaside resort. It became more important as a destination for excursionists. Bray was never as successful as Brighton because it faced competition from other beaches and resorts around Dublin Bay.

MASS TOURISM

Development of the tourism industry in the twentieth century was not continuous, as the two world wars interrupted travel. Major improvements in the development of air transport during both wars had an impact on the tourist industry. Soldiers got a taste for travel. Motorised transport took off after the First World War, with the development of charabancs, which were a type of primitive coach and were used for excursions to the seaside. Later, luxurious coaches were developed for this purpose. The invention of the 'Model T' in 1904 by Henry Ford made cars cheap enough for large numbers of people to buy them. In the 1920s the middle classes started using cars. This affected the use of railways by domestic tourists, but tourists to the Continent continued to use trains. Railway companies were forced to merge. Later after the Second World War (1939–45) most railways in Europe were nationalised because they were unprofitable.

In the 1930s holiday camps were developed to provide holidays for the low-income market and to cope with poor summer weather. They were aimed at those who had previously stayed in guesthouses in seaside resorts. They offered a range of entertainments, child-minding services, accommodation and catering. Billy Butlin set up his first holiday camp in Skegness in 1936 and other companies like Pontins were also set up about the same time. There were similar holiday camps in France and Germany. In Ireland the earliest and only real holiday camp (until winter 2000) was Butlin's at Mosney, Co. Meath; Trabolgan in Cork was not set up until the 1980s by a Dutch company and is now under Pontins' management. Hotels copied the 'all in' entertainment, and built attached leisure-centres. These were done in the 1930s in the USA, but not until the 1990s in Ireland. In 1931 the Youth Hostel Association (An Óige) was set up to make cheap accommodation available for the young while they participated in outdoor activities.

The years immediately before and after the Second World War were the years when domestic seaside holidays were at their peak. The introduction of paid holidays in 1939 meant that most people went on annual holidays for the first time. People went to the seaside because it was good for their health; it offered leisure activities, and they could acquire a sun-tan. Most people stayed in guesthouses or hotels, and the traditional resorts developed a range of activities to keep their tourists happy. The French Riviera began to attract wealthy tourists from the 1920s, and the development of package holidays to destinations in Spain became popular in the 1960s.

Long-distance commercial flights were developed across the Atlantic immediately after the Second World War. These involved a number of stops between England and New York. The airports of Shannon, Gander in Newfoundland, and Boston USA all developed as re-fuelling stops for these flights. After the war there were many surplus aircraft, which were sold off to charter and private airline companies. After 1958 new jet airliners gradually replaced the older propeller aircraft. The new jets were able to achieve high speeds, over 800 kilometres per hour, and in 1957 for the first time more tourists travelled by air than by ocean liners.

Governments began to realise the potential value of tourism, as a source of revenue, employment, and earner of foreign currency to pay for imports. The setting up of Bord Fáilte to promote Ireland as a tourist destination is an example of the Irish Government involving itself in the development of the industry. Unfortunately this was their only major involvement until 1987, but the development of the Operational Programmes for tourism followed.

Since 1960 **mass tourism** has evolved as a result of a number of factors:

1. **Increased prosperity**. The levels of prosperity people now experience were unknown in the past. Most people are no longer living from day to day; they have a disposable income, which they can spend on luxuries like leisure and holidays.
2. **More leisure time**. The working week has come down to thirty-nine hours, and people work a five-day week. Until the 1970s many jobs involved a five-and-a-half or six-day week. There are more bank holidays, giving more long weekends in the year.

3. **Higher standards** of education and greater curiosity about other cultures. People stay in school longer, and receive more formal education. They also get a lot of information from newspapers, books, television and the Internet. This has created a curiosity about different cultures and countries, and is responsible for an increase in overseas travel.

4. **Annual paid holidays**. In 1939 paid holidays were introduced for the first time. This was for a one-week holiday. It allowed many working people go away on vacation for the first time. Paid leave has been increased over time, first to 10 days paid leave, then in 1973 to 15 days paid leave, and this has now been increased to a minimum of 20 working days in the year.

5. **Air transport** has become cheaper, more comfortable and faster. People now travel long distances, whereas in the past they would not have travelled far. For example, the Mediterranean is only three hours away, while America is five hours. Since 1990 there has been growth in the long haul market to South East Asia and Australia where flights take from fifteen to twenty-two hours.

6. **Package holidays**. Tour operators developed these to mainland Europe in the 1960s. They provided cheap holidays to industrial workers in northern Europe. Since then these have expanded to many exotic destinations all over the world. Package holidays offer an easy means of visiting foreign destinations, where there are language difficulties, and where people have neither the time nor inclination to organise such a trip themselves.

7. **Tourism marketing** has improved greatly over the years. Hotels, access, facilities and service have all improved. We now know more about holiday destinations because of holiday programmes on the television, holiday magazines, newspaper articles, brochures, holiday fairs. Governments have also became involved in expanding tourism facilities, and marketing, because they realise that tourism brings in revenue and taxation, and creates jobs.

8. **Attitudes to tourism have changed**. People no longer consider holidays a luxury; instead they see them as a necessity. The pace of life has become faster and people believe that they have earned the right to get a rest and re-charge their batteries. Most people go on holidays, even if it is only a weekend away.

These factors have led to major growth in tourist numbers.

The first charter flight and package holiday was organised by Horizon Holidays to Corsica in 1950. Its success was repeated by many other companies including Tjaereborg Travel in Denmark in 1962, Thomson's in the UK, TUI in Germany, and subsequently by Irish companies like Joe Walsh Tours. The favourite destination was the Mediterranean region, where the three summer months had little rainfall and lots of sunshine and high temperatures. Spain was the most popular destination. It offered cheap food and drink along with the sunshine. Controls on foreign currencies in the UK and other European countries meant that people were limited in the amount they could take away with them (£50 i.e. €63). Currency control ended in

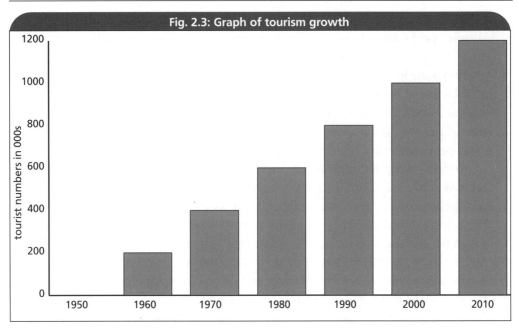

Fig. 2.3: Graph of tourism growth

England in 1970, but still existed later in France. Prepaid package holidays got around the controls, so more people availed of these. After 1970 with the introduction of longer holiday entitlements (from 10 to 15 working days), winter holidays either on the ski slopes or in sun destinations were developed. Larger aircraft like the Jumbo/Boeing 747 meant that the price of flights fell and this encouraged people to go on long-haul flights to Miami or the Caribbean. All of this was good for countries which offered guaranteed sunshine, but less so for countries like Ireland.

Cultural and touring holidays developed during the 1970s but they generally appeal to a smaller number of tourists. Like sun destinations, cultural holidays were put together into packages. Most American tourists who come to Ireland come on organised tours, many as part of a tour to a number of European countries. From the mid 1980s there has been major growth in short-break holidays to city destinations and Dublin benefited from this during the 1990s. Fear of the effects of sun burn and the growth of activity holidays has encouraged many people to move away from sun destinations as their main holiday and to move to temperate holiday destinations like Ireland.

Since the 1950s there has been a growth in the ownership of cars. This has affected tourism in a number of ways, as increasingly tourists bring their cars on holiday. Public transport (like trains and coaches) has been unable to compete with the flexibility that a car gives to a holiday. There has been a growth in the number of caravan and camping holidays. However, there are fewer benefits from these than from other types of tourists, because they have their own accommodation and often bring their own food. Along motorways, particularly in England and on the Continent, motels have been built for transit tourists; but there are few of these motels in Ireland because distances are quite short. Tour operators have developed 'Fly-drive holidays' for those who want the flexibility of a car on holiday; these are popular with tourists coming to Ireland. There has been increased demand for car hire but in the past there have been some problems with this in Ireland. There has been major growth in ferries to facilitate motorists.

The tourism industry is changing all the time and those involved in the industry must be aware of this. The 1990s have seen the following changes:

- Special-interest holidays have become popular particularly among the young and health conscious. These include a range of activities from walking to bungee-jumping.
- Self-catering has become very popular as people look for better value for money.
- More people own properties abroad like apartments, time-shares, villas etc. This has created a demand for 'seat only' packages as people travel all year round to their homes abroad.
- The short-break market has increased enormously; most people take these holidays as well as their main summer holiday. This is very important for Dublin, particularly in the low season.
- There has been growth in the long-haul market, as incomes rise and the cost of air fares drop. South-east Asia, Africa and America are popular destinations from here, while Ireland is a popular destination for Americans, Australians and Japanese.
- The over-fifties are a growing end of the market. In the UK, 40 per cent of the population are over fifty and they own 60 per cent of the wealth. They are interested in a range of holidays including cruising, long-haul and short-break holidays.
- Tailor-made holidays for the consumer have also developed; these can include expensive hotels and activities or cheap B&B accommodation with expensive restaurants. This is a move away from package holidays having a similar quality and standard.
- All-inclusive holidays are on the increase. Every aspect of the holiday is provided for: accommodation, food, entertainment, alcoholic drinks, water sports etc are pre-paid. These are growing in popularity because the tourist knows exactly what all the costs are and need not bring much spending money. Club Med and Sandals both have developed these types of resorts in the Caribbean, and in the Mediterranean.

IRISH GOVERNMENT PLANNING FOR THE TOURISM INDUSTRY

While tourism grew dramatically since 1960 both worldwide (500 per cent) and in Europe (420 per cent), in Ireland it grew more slowly (150 per cent) and in fact as a percentage market share, Ireland's tourism industry fell from 2 per cent to 1 per cent between 1960 and 1990. There were many problems with the industry, including the troubles in Northern Ireland, seasonality, regionalism, poor product range and quality, under-utilisation of facilities, expensive transport to the country, little investment in the industry and little Government planning for the industry. There was not even a dedicated Department of Tourism until 1977. In the mid 1980s a number of events took place that were to have a major impact on the development of the tourism industry.

- In 1985 a White Paper on Tourism Policy was published by the Government. It looked at the problems facing the industry and set about establishing the broad objectives of tourism policy. These included the promoting and developing of tourism in order to create jobs, help the regions to develop, preserve Ireland's culture, and preserve the environment. While the Government set objectives, it did not develop a strategy to achieve them, and did not invest any money in the industry.
- Liberalisation of the air transport industry reduced the cost of access to Ireland, first from the UK and the USA, and later from Europe. Lower prices led to an increase in the numbers of tourists using air transport, and boosted the tourism industry.
- In 1987 a number of reports on the industry were published including 'Improving the Performance of Irish Tourism', which was acted on by the Government who set out targets for the period 1988–92. This was known as the Programme for National Recovery and it was the first time targets had been set for the tourism industry in Ireland.

The targets set were as follows:

1. Double the numbers of tourists visiting Ireland over the next five years, to reach four million.
2 Double the revenue earned from tourism to £500 million.
3. Create 25,000 new jobs in the tourism industry, an annual increase of 15 per cent.

The Operational Programme for Tourism 1989 – 1993

This provided EU funding for the development of the tourism industry. The strategy involved:

1. Developing new products in the areas of specialist activities – golfing, fishing and other sports, genealogy and language learning; cultural and heritage products like heritage towns, historic houses and gardens; new leisure- and health-centres; business- and conference-centres. Training was also provided to give the highest quality of service in these new businesses.

2. Improving competitiveness in the industry in the areas of quality and price. Cheaper flights into Ireland helped improve our competitiveness.
3. Promoting Ireland as an attractive holiday destination. Increase the number of holidaymakers coming here and move into new markets like Japan and Scandinavia.
4. Developing package holidays for distribution through travel agents abroad. Gulliver was developed to have online booking and to provide information about Ireland to tourists.

The Operational Programme (OP) for Tourism did not work in isolation; it worked with the OP for Peripherality which improved roads, ferry ports and airports, and the OP for Rural Development which helped clean up pollution threats from farming and develop rural tourism. Local authorities were also involved in investing in new sewage treatment plants, water supplies and urban renewal. This work was also of great importance to the tourism industry.

Public investment during this period resulted in a large number of tourism products being developed. These included: Shannon Erne Waterway, nineteen national walking routes, a new caravan park in Clondalkin, Co. Dublin, national computerised genealogical network, all-weather leisure facilities like the Aquadome in Tralee, Brú na Bóinne visitor centre. Private investment increased the number of cruiser fleets on the River Shannon. Seven marinas were provided round the coast like the one at Kilrush. Twenty-seven new golf clubs were developed for tourists. English language schools were upgraded and health farms developed. Investment in training involved CERT spending £300 (€375) million for the tourism industry. This was to ensure that the highest possible level of service was given to our tourists. These investments led to growth in the tourism industry; for example:

1. Foreign earnings rose from £841 (€1,045) million in 1988 to £1,367 (€1,680) million in 1993, a growth rate of 102 per cent.
2. The number of overseas tourists increased from 2,345,000 in 1988 to 3,330,000 in 1993, a growth rate of 74 per cent.
3. Jobs in the tourism industry grew from 67,600 to 91,000, a growth of 98 per cent.
4. Investment occurred in every region of Ireland, and earnings were also spread throughout the country.

The Operational Programme for Tourism 1994–1999

The aim was to increase tourism revenue from £1,367 (€1,710) million to £2,250 (€2,810) million, a growth rate of 65 per cent, to create employment for another 35,000 people, and to reduce seasonality. Again a large percentage of EU money was used to finance this investment and the emphasis was on four main areas.

1. Product development included large-scale national and regional projects like the National Conference Centre, and a dedicated Family Holiday Park and Health Tourism Centre; restoration of historic buildings like Castletown House, Co. Kildare; eighteen new heritage towns and nature reserves like Clara Bog; angling development; special-interest holidays, and specialist accommodation with conference and leisure facilities. Most private investment was channelled into special-interest holidays and specialist accommodation.
2. Cultural institutions like the National Museum and National Gallery were improved and expanded; art galleries, theatres and arts festivals around the country and Temple Bar cultural centre in Dublin were developed.
3. Marketing involved the development of new markets, getting access to Ireland, niche marketing for special-interest activity holidays, and extending the season.
4. CERT was to provide training for the unemployed and for early school leavers.

Like the earlier Operational Programme for Tourism this was also linked with improving roads, sanitary services and urban renewal. Cross-border co-operation in marketing, training and cultural development was also encouraged.

Again this was a very successful Operational Programme for Tourism. Tourism numbers have increased, jobs have been created and revenue has increased. The real benefit of this growth in the tourism industry is that 90 per cent of all of these earnings remain within the country, very little is spent on imported products, and since most of the businesses are small or medium-sized and Irish-owned, no profits are sent abroad. Another major benefit is that 55 per cent of earnings went to the western region; this is unlike other industrial development. Not all of the projects actually took place. For example by 2001 the National Conference Centre had still not been built.

The Strategy for Tourism Development 2000–2006

The aim of this plan is to make Ireland a 'desirable holiday destination for discerning, high-spending international tourists'. This will be achieved by:

1. Increasing foreign earnings to £3.4 (€4.3) billion, a growth rate of 6 per cent per annum
2. Creating 50,000 more jobs
3. Growth in the shoulder and low season
4. Sustainable tourism development
5. Improving the quality of Irish tourism.

EU investment will be less than in the past and only applies to developing and underdeveloped regions. There will be more investment from private tourist interests than in previous programmes. Four areas are being developed:

1. Product development will be in projects that are not already being provided for in the region, in other words where obvious gaps in the market exist.
2. Marketing will play a much greater role in this programme, with the emphasis on bringing tourists here in the low season and all-Ireland marketing. Direct marketing will only occur for new products.
3. Training will be limited to the unemployed, early school-leavers and women returning to work. The industry will have to pay for its own training and not rely on EU funding to pay for it.
4. Access transport needs will be improved, especially direct sea transport from the Continent.

These are the areas of development that the Government and tourism interests are going to concentrate on in the future.

During the 1990s £1 (€1.25) billion was invested in the Irish tourism industry. Between 1986 and 1996 overseas visitors to Ireland increased by 150 per cent. Revenue increased in the same period by £1.3 (€1,625) billion. There were nearly 100 new hotels, there was a 40 per cent increase in rooms, and occupancy levels in hotels increased particularly in the shoulder and low season. Profits in four-star and five-star hotels averaged 15 per cent, while it was less in lower-grade hotels. Visitor numbers at tourist attractions grew by 68 per cent during this period. This was a good period for the tourism industry; it is now up to those in the industry to continue to invest in new products and to invest in marketing and training in order to sustain this growth into the future.

REVISION EXERCISES

1. List with their dates the main developments in transport, and developments in tourism in Europe.
2. Create a table as follows and fill in the main information.

Date	Developments in World Tourism	Developments in Irish Tourism

3. Explain the main influences on the development and decline of Bray as a seaside resort.
4. Describe the three main types of holidays that were popular in the twentieth century.
5   Give five reasons why mass tourism has developed.

6. Explain the effect of the motor car on the tourism industry.
7. Describe five changes that are occurring in the tourism industry worldwide.
8. Outline the role of Government planning in the development of the Irish tourism industry.

Assignment

Look at a range of tourism products in your local area, and discover the improvements that have taken place since 1989, as a result of investment made from the three Operational Programmes for Tourism.

References and recommended reading:

B. O'Connor and M. Cronin, eds, *Tourism in Ireland: A Critical Analysis.* Cork University Press, 1993.

J. O'Sullivan, T. Dunne and S. Connor, *The Book of Bray.* Blackrock Teachers' Centre, 1989.

Bord Failte, *The Failte Business* 1997.

Bord Failte, *The Failte Business 2000: The Role of Tourism in Economic Growth*, Millennium Issue.

F. Corr, *Hotels in Ireland.* Jemma.

Holloway, *The Business of Tourism.* Longman 1998.

Department of Tourism and Transport, *Improving the Performance of Irish Tourism.* Government of Ireland, 1987.

Department of Tourism and Transport, *Investing for Tourism in Ireland.* Government of Ireland.

Department of Tourism and Transport, *Operational Programme for Tourism 1989-94.* Government of Ireland, 1989.

The Stationery Office, *Operational Programme for Tourism 1994-99.* Government of Ireland, 1994.

Department of Tourism and Sport, *Strategy for Tourism 2000-2006.* Government of Ireland, 2000.

CHAPTER 3

The Structure of the Tourist Industry

THE GOVERNMENT'S ROLE IN TOURISM

There are three departments of Government that are heavily involved in the tourism industry. These are the Department of Tourism, Sport and Recreation The Department of Arts, Heritage, Gaeltacht and the Islands, and the Department of Public Enterprise.

THE DEPARTMENT OF TOURISM, SPORT AND RECREATION

This plays a major role in the development of the tourist industry in Ireland. Since the setting up of the first Department of Tourism, the department has been linked with many other departments, but since 1997 it has been linked with Sport. The Department has three sections: Tourism, Sports and Recreation, and Local Development.

The aim of the Department of Tourism is to develop a tourism policy that will increase earnings from overseas tourists, and create employment in the industry. The tourism industry in the twenty-first century will be more environmentally sensitive. This will be achieved through five major strategies:

- Implement the present Strategy for Tourism, 2000–2006. This policy is being complemented with the work of the Irish Tourism Industry Confederation's People and Places Policy, and Bord Fáilte's Business Plan for Irish Tourism Marketing 1988–2003. The Strategy will be monitored and analysed over its lifetime by the Department of Tourism. The signing of the Good Friday Northern Ireland Peace Agreement led to the establishment of a new all-Ireland tourism marketing body to promote Ireland abroad as one destination. Bord Fáilte is carrying out a review on the role played by the Regional Tourism Authorities in the development and marketing of tourism in Ireland.
- Develop future tourism strategies beyond 2006. This will involve reviewing the tourism situation in Ireland, and how best to improve growth in the future.
- Preview the use of public funds for the marketing of tourism through Bord Fáilte. This involves looking at the work of the Overseas Tourism Marketing Initiative which had a budget of £32 (€40) million in 1999, and the Marketing Management Board which had a similar budget but which was given to

individual tourism businesses as a grant to help them with marketing. Reviews of different marketing initiatives have been undertaken by the Department, for example the German market, golfing holidays. The effectiveness of Tourism Brand Ireland has also been reviewed. The performance of these three types of marketing initiatives allows the Department to make decisions on future marketing policies.

- Look at the role of CERT, and ensure that this body is making the best use of public money in recruiting and training staff for the tourism industry. At present the extraordinary growth of the industry has caused a demand for skilled labour, which cannot be filled from Ireland. This means that CERT will have to look to new areas to seek workers for the industry, and this will mean that they will have to develop new training methods. They will have to ensure that those in the industry will maintain high standards, even with the difficulties that they face in attracting workers to their businesses.
- Give attention to the Border regions and the implementation of INTERREG programmes, the International Fund for Ireland, the Special Programme for Peace and Reconciliation, and North/South Bodies, for example Waterways Ireland, in order to develop the tourist industry in these areas (see chapter 5).

Bord Fáilte is the main body that carries out the Government's policy on tourism.

THE DEPARTMENT OF ARTS, HERITAGE, GAELTACHT AND THE ISLANDS

The aim of this Department is to 'enrich the quality of life and sense of identity of all our citizens and to preserve their inheritance for present and future generations.' More than 50 per cent of the Department's brief is related to areas that come into direct or indirect contact with tourists. The Department deals with the following areas:

1. The arts: This is an area that has expanded rapidly since 1985. The quality and range of the arts have improved, and the numbers attending arts events have grown. This sector is trying to encourage people all over the country to attend such events; in order to do so they have set up a number of groups and financial assistance. The main ones are: The Arts Council which spent £100 million (€127) between 1999 and 2001 encouraging theatre groups, artists and musicians to develop their work for the benefit of the people. The Cultural Development Incentives Scheme has helped provide money to open new theatres and arts centres in Portlaoise, Letterkenny, Macroom, and Cork. They have also helped other theatres with renovations and extensions. Schemes have been set up to develop community projects, the music industry, and the setting up of an Academy of Performing Arts.

2. Cultural institutions: The Department provides funding and operational policies and helps these institutions to develop services for the public. The National

Cultural Institutions Act 1997 controls the way these institutions operate. The main aim now is to expand the buildings in order to increase public viewing areas. Taxation laws were also changed so that anyone who donated objects of heritage to the State was able to get tax relief; this has resulted in objects being donated to the Irish Museum of Modern Art (IMMA) and the Hunt Museum. The Department has eight cultural institutions, mostly located in Dublin, under its control.

- The National Archive houses many ancient documents including census information.
- The National Concert Hall, Dublin consists of the main Hall, and the John Field Room, and is available for all types of concerts, recitals etc.
- The National Gallery of Ireland, displays the work of Ireland's most important artists.
- The National Library houses the national collection of newspapers, books and documents. This will be extended so that there will be more room for Library facilities, and visitor services.
- The National Museum at Collins Barracks has been extended to allow new exhibits to be put on view for the public; before this they were all in storage. The museum has silverware, costumes and a range of other treasures on display. The National Museum in Kildare Street continues to display many of our most famous treasures, e.g the Ardagh Chalice.
- Museum of Country Life, Turlough Park House, Castlebar is the new museum for the Folklife Collection.
- The Irish Museum of Modern Art (IMMA) at the Royal Hospital Kilmainham houses modern art. There will be new space to house a permanent collection of modern art.
- The Chester Beatty Library displays the collection of art and literature collected by the industrialist Chester Beatty from all over the world. This has been moved from Ballsbridge to the Clock Tower building in Dublin Castle, and the numbers visiting it have increased greatly.

The Department has also been encouraging the establishment of local museums by County Councils. These display objects that are of interest to the local area.

3. **Heritage**: The aim of the Department in this area is to 'protect, maintain, conserve, manage and present the built and natural heritage'. In order to do this it has developed a National Heritage Plan, which deals with the built heritage, sets out the main priorities of the Department, and outlines its strategies to achieve these aims. Its policy is to protect the architectural heritage of the country, and this involves carrying out conservation work on buildings. Money came from the European Regional Development Fund until 1999, and this was spent on such famous buildings as Trim and Maynooth Castles, Ardfert Cathedral, and Scattery Island. Money has also been spent setting up a new visitor centre at Dún Aonghasa in the Aran Islands,

and an archaeological trail at Newmarket-on-Fergus in Co. Clare. Other sites that have been improved include Charles Fort in Kinsale, Kilkenny Castle, a new visitor centre at the Botanic Gardens, Dublin, and restoration work has been undertaken at Fota Arboretum in Cork. The Heritage Council is an independent statutory body that advises the Government on its policy.

The Department is also concerned with the natural heritage, which is protected by such laws as the Flora Protection Order 1999, and the Wildlife Bill which looks to protect the habitat of animals. The Department enforces such international agreements as CITES (International Trade in Endangered Species of Flora and Fauna), and AEWA (Agreement on African Eurasian Migratory Water birds) which prohibit trade in endangered species and water birds.

Dúchas was set up to look after Ireland's heritage; this was formerly the Office of Public Works (OPW). It looks after six National Parks, and seventy-seven Nature Reserves, Special Areas of Conservation (SACs) and Special Protection Areas (SPAs). Examples of SACs include the Burren and the Nore River Valley. SPAs are mainly concerned with the natural habitats of birds, for example Bull Island and the Saltee

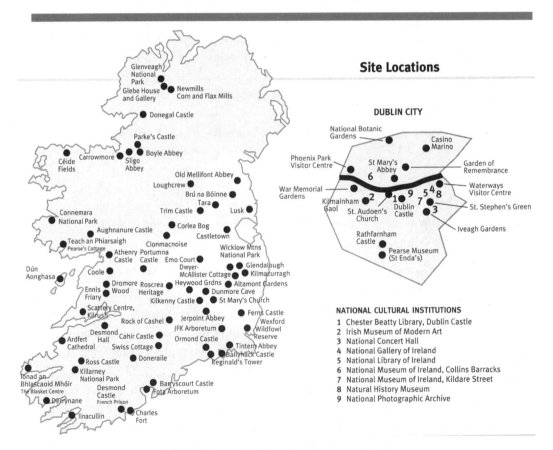

Fig. 3.1: Map of Dúchas sites Courtesy of Dúchas

Islands. Proposed National Heritage Areas include areas of the Grand Canal. Bogs, river sites, coastal shingles, etc. are all included in these areas of conservation and protection. Dúchas carries out research on the birds, fish and animals found in Ireland, many of which now live in Special Protection Areas etc. Dúchas are also involved in the Protection of the Archaeological Heritage. This means that they grant about 1,200 licences for carrying out archaeological excavations. They allow work to take place in bogs, in the sea on shipwrecks, and they have carried out an archaeological survey of Ireland. They look after 750 national monuments and nineteen historic houses and gardens.

The Waterways have been conserved and enhanced by the Department, to develop them as a recreation resource for cruisers, boating, fishing, walking, swimming etc. The 900km of waters in Ireland, north and south, are now looked after by the new cross-border body, Waterways Ireland, which has its headquarters in Enniskillen. The European Regional Development Fund has financed many of the improvements on the waterways; these include dredging of the Barrow Navigation and River Suck, the building of jetties and moorings on the Shannon Navigation, and on the Royal and Grand Canals. There are over 3,500 boats registered on the Shannon Navigation, and only 500 or 14 per cent are for rental by tourists.

Education and visitor service: Dúchas was set up to help the public understand and appreciate our heritage, whether natural or manmade. The number of tourists visiting Dúchas sites has risen steadily, with 2,309,000 visitors in 1999. The most popular sites were Brú na Bóinne, the Rock of Cashel, Muckross House in Killarney, Kilkenny Castle and Clonmacnoise. Dúchas operate sixty-six fee-paying sites, and employ 300 guides to take tourists around these sites explaining their history. They produce literature to promote the sites, and to help tourists understand them. Dúchas also attend workshops run by the Incoming Operators Association and Bord Fáilte. They also are present at overseas consumer and trade promotions. Apart from booklets, information panels are also produced for national monuments and nature reserves. Heritage cards have been developed to encourage people to visit the sites all year around. During Heritage Week in September a number of events all over the country attract about 200,000 people.

4. Irish Language and the Gaeltacht; this section of the Department is mainly concerned with the lives of people living in Gaeltacht areas, and to a lesser extent with the tourist industry. There are schemes and grants that encourage large numbers of people to visit the Gaeltacht areas of Donegal, Connemara, Kerry/Cork, Ring in Waterford, and Ráth Cairn in Meath, to learn Irish. In 1999, over 25,000 students and 1,146 adults attended Irish-language summer schools.

5. Offshore Islands are a major attraction for large numbers of tourists; this is because of their wildlife, their isolation etc. The Department is involved in improving access to these islands; this includes building quays, airfields, bridges, and in the

Fig. 3.2: Map of Gaeltacht areas

case of Inishbiggle in Co. Mayo a cable car. Ferry services to these islands have also been improved. Better access will not only help tourists to reach the islands, but also improve life there for the permanent inhabitants.

THE DEPARTMENT OF PUBLIC ENTERPRISE

The Department of Public Enterprise is concerned with the growth of the Irish tourism industry because it is so heavily involved with airfares that give access to tourists to Ireland. This means cheap airfares and ferry fares, which are essential to the growth of the tourist industry. The programme for tourism development in 1987 looked for a reduction of fares by 20 per cent in order to increase the numbers of tourists visiting Ireland.

Some transport in Ireland is under the control of the Minister for Public Enterprise. There are four semi-state bodies under the Department with interests in transport:

1. Aer Lingus which has three companies within it: Aer Lingus London and Europe, Aer Lingus Ireland and USA, and Aer Lingus Commuter which serves the domestic and regional airports in the UK
2. Aer Rianta which has two parts, Aer Rianta, and the Great Southern Hotel Group

3. The Irish Aviation Authority
4. Córas Iompar Éireann which includes Dublin Bus, Iarnród Éireann, and Bus Éireann.

The Department of Public Enterprise devises Irish aviation policy. Its aim is to improve the competitiveness of air transport in Ireland, in order to create jobs and wealth in Irish airlines and the aviation industry. It has to ensure that there is at least one substantial, domestically based and financially viable airline that provides services all year round to Ireland and its export markets. The Department is also involved in promoting air traffic to the regional airports so that there is balanced economic growth in the country. It is responsible for providing the necessary facilities at the airports and making sure that these airports are competitive with similar airports elsewhere. The air policy has included the development of liberalisation for the air transport industry, strategic alliances for Aer Lingus, and bi-lateral agreements with states outside the EU. The USA which is Ireland's second biggest market is regulated by the Ireland–US Air Transport Agreement, under which the US nominate the US airlines that fly into Ireland, and designate the cities (five) that Irish airlines serve. There are no restrictions on pricing or capacity. The Irish Government have designated Aer Lingus as the Irish company to serve the USA (see Chapter 7).

THE IRISH AVIATION AUTHORITY

This authority works under the Irish Aviation Authority Act 1993 and provides the following:

- Air traffic manage over 100,000 square miles of airspace, which covers the area 5° 31′ W to 15° W (about 240 miles across the Atlantic). Nearly 79 per cent of all traffic crossing the North Atlantic flies through Irish airspace
- Ensuring the safety aspects of aircraft, including airworthiness checks on 600 Irish registered aircraft
- Ensuring that all airline companies in Ireland operate according to European and International safety standards
- Ensuring the competence of Irish-licensed flight crew and aircraft maintenance engineers.

Airlines that provide a service to or from this country can only do so if they are authorised under the Air Navigation and Transport Act 1965. Companies must also hold an operating licence and an Air Operators Certificate. This allows the airline company to carry passengers, cargo or mail. The Irish Aviation Authority must confirm that the company has the professional ability and organisational resources to run a safe aircraft operation.

TOURISM IRELAND LIMITED

This is the new all-Ireland tourism body, formed as a result of the Good Friday Agreement, and the North–South Ministerial Council meeting in October 2000. Its task will include:

- Marketing Ireland overseas as an all-Ireland destination
- Taking over from Bord Fáilte and the Northern Ireland Tourist Board (NITB) in promoting the regions (RTAs) and products abroad.
- Using the Bord Fáilte and NITB offices to promote Ireland in overseas markets.
- Managing Tourism Brand Ireland.

This has changed the role of Bord Fáilte. The aim of joining the industries North and South is to send a signal to the world that peace reigns here. All sections of the industry, for example IHF and ITIC, have welcomed the move. It will also create a synergy in the industry, and encourage more tourists to come to Ireland. The headquarters for the new body is in Dublin, with an office also in Coleraine, Co. Derry. The members of the board of Tourism Ireland Limited include the chairman of the NITB, CEO of Bord Fáilte, and representatives from Irish Ferries, P&O, and Microsoft Ireland.

BORD FÁILTE

Bord Fáilte was set up in 1952 to develop the tourism (product) industry, while Fógra Fáilte was developed to promote (market) the tourism industry. In 1955 these were joined to form Bord Fáilte Éireann.

Product development was an important area of work for Bord Fáilte. As Bord Fáilte was successful in its marketing it was soon realised that the Irish hotel product was not up to the quality that was required. This led to the introduction of incentives to encourage the upgrading of hotel accommodation, and the attracting of international companies to Ireland to build new hotels. Loan schemes, tax write-offs and grants were all used to encourage the building of new hotels. As a result Trusthouse Forte, Ryans, and the Intercontinental Group all built new hotels in Ireland. Bord Fáilte classified and graded hotels and other types of accommodation.

Marketing abroad was Bord Fáilte's other major task. Novel techniques were used by staff to get to their markets; this included concentrating their advertising in the USA in areas where there were large numbers of Irish Americans. They brought over media people and guidebook writers to sample Irish hospitality; these in turn wrote favourable articles about Ireland. Bord Fáilte attended the American Society of Travel Agents' convention and tempted them with Irish coffees, golf competitions and Ireland's tourist attractions.

Bord Fáilte ran tidy towns competitions, to improve the overall look of Irish towns.

In 1994, after the Arthur D. Little Report, Bord Fáilte was restructured. The Report recommended that Bord Fáilte should concentrate on three areas:

- Promoting and selling Ireland overseas. This involves organising advertising, promotions and PR activities in these main markets. Local overseas offices provide Bord Fáilte with expertise about the local markets.
- Helping Ireland's tourism industry to develop products and marketing. Where product gaps appear Bord Fáilte helps entrepreneurs to develop new products and then helps them to market these overseas. Bord Fáilte is involved in the Independent Management Board for Product Development, which approves grants for EU funding.
- Supplying market information to the tourist industry, which will help it to plan for the future. The Marketing Information Partnership was set up, which has representatives from the industry, the Department of Tourism, Sport and Recreation and Bord Fáilte.

At the same time many of what were considered 'non-core areas' were removed from Bord Fáilte.

- The registration, grading and approval of hotels and guesthouses was sub-contracted to Tourism Quality Services (Ireland) Ltd. Bord Fáilte continues to set the standards that are required for the industry, to monitor their approvals, and deal with any appeals.
- The approval of B&B accommodation and granting of the Shamrock was given to the Town & County Homes Association, Irish Farmhouse Holiday Association etc., who self-regulate their members. Bord Fáilte sets all standards.
- Bord Fáilte's role in the domestic market was also reduced, with the production of magazines, for example *Ireland of the Welcomes*, being sub-contracted.
- The approval of grants was handed over to a commercial body.
- The Tidy Towns Competition was transferred to the Department of the Environment.
- The Gulliver System was handed over to Fexco.

The result of these changes meant an increase in international marketing, with a corresponding increase in the numbers working abroad. Bord Fáilte is now involved in a range of marketing activities. These include:

1. Marketing Tourism Brand Ireland. This was developed in November 1996 as part of an all-Ireland initiative between Bord Fáilte and the Northern Ireland Tourist Board. It was agreed to market Ireland as one destination, and emphasise the friendliness and warm welcome we have for strangers, our green environment and the range of sporting and cultural activities available to tourists at a relaxed pace. Since the formation of the Marketing Tourism Brand Ireland, a number of

Fig. 3.3: Logo

logos have used by Bord Fáilte. All have incorporated a shamrock in one form or another.

2. Attending, with tourism producers, over 150 Trade and Consumer Promotions. Bord Fáilte staff organise a two-day workshop in May which over 350 tour operators from twenty-nine countries attend to meet 750 Irish tourism operators. They bring over 1,000 journalists and more than a hundred TV crews to Ireland to experience the tourism product so that they can return home and write and produce programmes about Ireland. Conference and incentive planners also attend promotions.

3. Using modern technology to develop the industry. E-commerce, the internet and digital TV are all in the process of changing the way people organise their holidays. Bord Fáilte uses its web page to provide information about Ireland; it also uses it to target its markets in a more cost-effective way. Bord Fáilte operates a web site especially for those in the travel trade.

4. Sponsoring an extensive advertising campaign on TV, radio, in newspapers, magazines, and in cinemas (in the Netherlands). This is done in conjunction with tourist operators, on a public–private partnership basis, for example Aer Lingus, Irish Ferries, hotel groups.

The bulk of Bord Fáilte's budget is spent on marketing (73.5 per cent); the remainder is spent on administration (10.6 per cent), pensions (7.8 per cent), Regional Tourism Authorities, or RTAs (6.4 per cent), and development (2 per cent).

In 2002 the role of Bord Fáilte will change because of the establishment of Tourism Ireland Limited. The new role will include:

- Being responsible for promoting the development of regions and tourism products in all markets
- Marketing tourism in the domestic market
- Being responsible for developing new tourism products, and administering £100 (€127) million under the National Development Plan
- Providing marketing information to tourism providers so that they can improve their performance
- Identifying infrastructure and environmental limitations that will affect tourism development in Ireland.

Talks are taking place to merge Bord Fáilte and CERT as of February 2002 and this will mean that a new body will be dealing with the training and marketing for the tourism industry.

REGIONAL TOURISM AUTHORITIES

There are six Regional Tourism Authorities in Ireland:

- Dublin – city and county
- Midlands East – Louth, Meath, Longford, Westmeath, Kildare, Wicklow, Laois, and North Offaly
- South East – Wexford, Kilkenny, Carlow, and South Tipperary
- South West – Cork, and South Kerry
- West – Galway, Mayo and Roscommon
- North West – Donegal, Leitrim, Sligo, Cavan and Monaghan.

They were set up in 1964, and were originally called Regional Tourism Organisations (RTOs). The name was changed in 1996 to Regional Tourism Authorities. In 1989–90 the RTOs were restructured, so that geographically they corresponded with EU regional planning areas. This in particular changed the Midlands, and the Dublin East area, which became Midlands East, and Dublin. A two-tier system was set up that consisted of a Regional Council and a Management Committee. Local tourism interests in the areas are members of the RTAs, along with corporation and county council members, county tourism committee chairpersons and a Bord Fáilte representative. The RTAs have four areas of responsibility:

1. To provide Tourist Information Offices and an accommodation reservation service
2. To encourage awareness of the environment and to monitor planning so that the highest standards are maintained
3. To monitor and promote development in the tourism industry and invest in tourism services and products, such as visitor attractions
4. To work with local interests in marketing their area abroad.

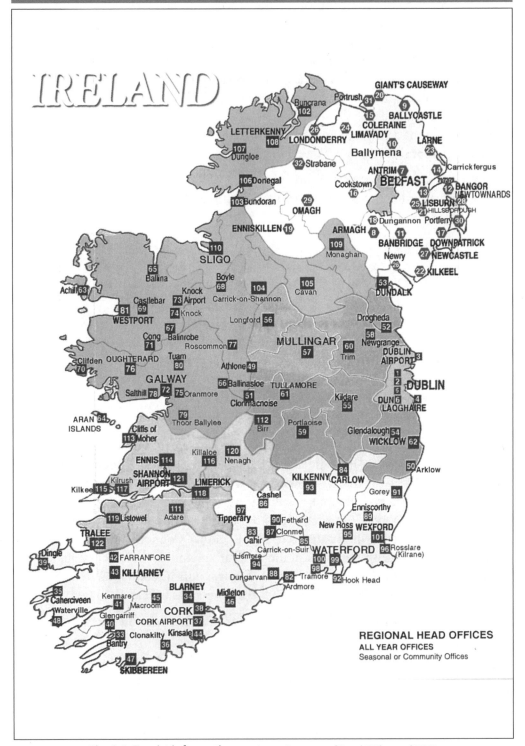

Fig. 3.4: Tourist information centres Courtesy of Bord Fáilte and NITB

There have been improvements in the facilities that are provided by the RTAs.

- Computerisation has been introduced into their Tourist Information Offices, resulting in every year more tourists using them. In 1999 4 million tourists called into their offices, and they made reservations for accommodation worth £9 (€11.25) million.
- RTAs attend promotions both in Ireland and overseas. In 1999, they attended 250 trade and consumer promotions. At these they distribute brochures and give advice about holidaying in their areas. RTAs produce brochures for their regions, promoting a wide range of tourist activities. The Department of Tourism, Sport and Recreation allocates marketing funds for this activity. RTAs work with Bord Fáilte to offer journalists and travel agents familiarisation trips in their regions.

Fig. 3.5: Map of Regional Tourism Authority areas

- They are also involved in the 'People and Places' programme of the Irish Travel Industry Confederation (ITIC), and they organised a marketing seminar for 10,000 ITIC members in 1999.
- RTAs are involved in helping their regions improve their tourism products. They work in partnership with many different agencies to advise them on future development. These include the County Enterprise Boards, Tidy Towns Competitions etc. Some RTAs have developed their own tourism products, like Dublin Tourism Enterprises who operate Malahide Castle, Dublin Writers Museum and five other attractions.
- RTAs carry out Bord Fáilte policy on a regional basis. While Bord Fáilte is concerned with bringing tourists to Ireland, it is the work of each Regional Tourism Authority to make sure that those tourists come to their area in order to create wealth and employment.

The role of the Regional Tourism Authorities were reviewed by Bord Fáilte in 1999, so their functions will change again.

SHANNON DEVELOPMENT AUTHORITY

Shannon Development was set up in 1959 to develop Shannon Airport. At the time the airport only dealt with transit passengers; now it deals with a large variety of passengers. The company was originally involved in

1. Setting up the first duty-free shop
2. Developing tourist attractions in the area like Bunratty Folk Park, and Medieval Banquets
3. Developing the Rent an Irish Cottage Scheme
4. Bringing factories to Shannon, developing the airport free zone for industries, and the airfreight business.

In 1968 Shannon Development was given the job of developing industry in the area of Limerick and Clare. In 1988 its work was extended again, and it was given the task of developing tourism in the old Regional Tourism Organisation of the Mid West. This area now includes the counties of Limerick, Clare, North Tipperary, north Kerry, and south Offaly.

Shannon Development has been successful in developing a number of new tourism products in the area. These are operated by the subsidiary Shannon Castle Banquet and Heritage Company. This company runs five evening entertainment venues and eight visitor attractions, which include:

- King John's Castle and Castle Lane Project with its eighteenth-century public house
- Bunratty Folk Park, and Medieval Banquets at Bunratty, Knappogue and Dunguaire Castles

Fig. 3.6: Brochure of Shannon Development

- Craggaunowen, Killaloe Heritage Centre Co. Clare and Lough Gur Heritage Centre.

In 1997 Shannon Estuary Development, another subsidiary of Shannon Development, was set up to develop the Shannon Estuary. This included the development of the Kilrush Marina in Co. Clare.

Shannon Development also oversaw the distribution of European Regional Development Funds amounting to £2.86 (€3.6) million in 1998. These grants were given to a range of projects including:

- The Limerick City Navigation Project, which will allow cruisers to travel to Limerick City
- The restoration of the Vandeleur Gardens in Kilrush (the Vandeleurs were the local landlords)
- Birr Castle Science Centre, where the largest nineteenth-century telescope can be seen
- Kilkee Waterworld, and Sea Life Centres in Fenit, Co. Kerry and Lahinch, Co. Clare
- Forest Holiday Village in Ballyhoura, Co. Limerick.

Shannon Development works together with local tourism interests to promote activity holidays in the region. Such marketing groups include Slieve Bloom Development Ltd., Ballybunion Marketing Group etc. They help in the production of promotional brochures, attend consumer and trade fairs abroad, and in Ireland hold promotions, for example in shopping centres.

Shannon Development also operates twelve Tourist Information Offices. In 1998 over 500,000 visitors were dealt with in these offices, and many used the accommodation booking services. It is also concerned with planning tourism for the future, and carried out the tourism survey called Shannon Pulse Tourism. This looked at the present trends among 140 tourism businesses in the region, and from this Shannon Development hopes to be able to develop future marketing plans and influence future investments for the industry. Its survey found that the smaller businesses were less successful than larger tourism businesses, and that many were busy only at weekends, and had yet to reach their full potential.

Assignment

Students should get the most recent annual report and brochure from their own Regional Tourism Authority, and research its operations. This should be done under the headings of:

- Visitor services – Tourist Information Offices
- Promotion – literature, trade fairs, familiarisation trips etc
- Product development in the region
- Future developments.

CERT

CERT is the state tourism-training agency. It was set up in 1963 to provide education, training and recruitment for the tourism industry. It provides a wide range of courses; these include short ten-week basic courses, two-year trade courses like those in professional cookery or tourism skills, part-time courses in tour guiding etc. For those who have successfully completed CERT courses, there is also the opportunity to do supervisory courses.

CERT courses are Government financed, and from the 1970s European funded. Since 1999 funding was cut back in this area, because financing under European Social Funding only applies to early school leavers, and to women returning to work. The EU believes that the training of staff for the industry should be financed by the tourism industry itself, because they are the ones that directly benefit from trained staff.

CERT has a number of responsibilities for improving standards in the industry. It has worked both with those in the industry and those in education. Its main services include:

- Education, training and career development
- Development of curriculum at third level, PLC and second level (Tourism Awareness)
- Work placements to provide experience for those in training
- Support services for those in the industry
- Research in manpower and training
- Materials for training
- Accreditation and certification of courses
- Career development overseas.

Training is provided by CERT in its Headquarters in Dublin, in centres in Limerick and Cork, and in hotels that it leases during the low season. Courses are also provided in a range of colleges and schools in the country. Training is provided in the Institutes of Technology, the Dublin Institute of Technology (DIT), and through FETAC in Colleges of Further Education.

A wide range of skilled jobs are found in the tourism industry. These include: hotel receptionist, chefs, waitress/waiters, housekeeping, tourism information office assistants, travel agency consultants, hotel managers, tour guides. CERT provides courses for those who want to become professionals in the tourist industry.

Assignment

Students should select a career mentioned above and get all the information about training, courses, job opportunities etc. from CERT, or their career guidance teacher, and write a short report on their chosen career.

NORTHERN IRELAND TOURIST BOARD (NITB)

The NITB is an agency of the Department of Economic Development (DED) in Northern Ireland. It was set up in 1992 by the Tourism (Northern Ireland) Order. Under this it has a range of responsibilities.

- It develops tourism in Northern Ireland and advises the Department on its tourism policy.

- It promotes Northern Ireland as a tourist destination through advertising, public relations activities, establishing offices abroad etc.
- It carries out research into the tourism industry, producing statistics and a profile of tourists that visit Northern Ireland. This information is provided to those in the tourism industry to help them improve their performance.
- It works in close co-operation with other DED agencies, i.e. the Industrial Development Board, The Training and Employment Agency and the Local Enterprise Development Unit.
- It also works closely with the English Tourist Board, Scottish Tourist Board and Bord Fáilte.
- It operates twenty-five networked Tourist Information Centres (TIC). These centres provide information about the local area, attractions etc., an accommodation booking service, bureau de change and a shop that sells books, maps, souvenirs etc. The TICs are located at airports and major tourist attractions, for example Causeway Visitor Centre.

The board of the NITB is made up of business people from the tourism industry in the North of Ireland.

PRIVATE GROUPS INVOLVED IN THE TOURIST INDUSTRY

The Irish Tourist Industry Confederation (ITIC)

This is made up of all the tourism interests in the country, including Government interests like Bord Fáilte, CERT, RTAs, County Tourist Boards, and also businesses and their organisations, for example the Irish Hotel Confederation (IHF), Irish Farmhouse Holidays, Heritage Towns of Ireland, Avis car hire, GHS, Fitzpatrick Hotels, Stena etc. The aim of the ITIC is to lobby the Government on tourism interests.

The ITIC has also developed 'People and Places' programmes. It is currently involved in promoting this programme throughout the industry. This is to make the industry more aware of the core values of tourism in Ireland, which are the friendliness of the people, and the beautiful unspoilt countryside. The programme encourages everyone working in the industry to be aware of these values, and to make sure that they are preserved.

An Taisce

This is Ireland's National Trust. Its beginnings were in Dublin in 1946 when a number of groups such as the Royal Irish Academy, An Óige, and the Royal Society of Antiquaries of Ireland met with the aim of setting up a group to help preserve historic buildings and areas of great natural beauty, and to allow the public to view these sites. The first meeting of An Taisce took place in 1948 and it had just 250 members, most of whom were concerned with conserving the countryside. An Taisce is a voluntary body and receives no funding from the Irish Government. It has to be notified of all new developments that occur close to historical or geographical sites, or which affect people's access to these sites. Since 1963 An Taisce has to be notified of all new developments that occur close to historical or geographical sites, or which affected people's access to these sites. Unfortunately, An Taisce still does not get Government funding and has to depend on voluntary subscriptions to carry out the extra work.

By 1999 An Taisce had over 5,000 members, many of them elderly. Its headquarters is located at the restored Tailors' Hall in Dublin. Members are involved in organising a number of projects nationwide, for example the National Spring Clean Campaign, and Blue Flag Beaches. They constantly lobby the Government on environmental issues, and advise them on conservation law. They also own some properties, which they consider to be of major national interest, such as land near Mullaghmore in the Burren, Kanturk Castle Co. Cork, Booterstown Marsh in Dublin. They encourage owners of old historic buildings to restore them 'sensitively'. They also publish policy reports, such as 'New partnership for sustainable development in the regions' and 'Living Heritage'.

The National Trust

Tha National Trust was founded in 1895 to conserve historical sites and places of natural beauty in England, Wales and Northern Ireland. It operates independently of the Government. It is a charity and depends on donations and membership subscriptions. There are over 2.7 million members in the National Trust. It owns 248,000 hectares of land, much of it coastline, and 200 historic houses and gardens. Most of these are open to the public. It spends much of its income on maintaining and protecting its properties, which are all of outstanding interest and importance. The National Trust properties in Northern Ireland are important because of their wildlife interest; they include Strangford Lough Wildlife Centre, Slieve Donard in the Mourne Mountains, Co. Down, the Giant's Causeway, the Carrick-a-rede rope bridge in Co. Antrim and Florence Court in Co. Fermanagh.

The Irish Hotel Federation

This is the organisation that was formed by hotel and guesthouse owners to promote their interests. They are involved in lobbying the Government to have their interests recognised in Tourism Policy. They produce their brochure 'Be Our Guest', which advertises hotels and guesthouses in Ireland.

Other private bodies involved in the tourism industry include the Town and Country Association, the Irish Farmhouse Holidays Association, Independent Holiday Hostels of Ireland, the Caravan and Camping Council. The members of these groups all provide accommodation in these areas. They look after the interests of their members on the ITIC and with Government Bodies, and publicise their facilities both in Ireland and abroad.

REVISION EXERCISES

1. Who is the current Minister for Tourism, Sport and Recreation?
2. List the main functions of the Department of Tourism, Sport and Recreation
3. Name the ways the Department of Arts, Culture, Gaeltacht and the Islands has helped the development of Arts in Ireland over the last few years.
4. Name the main cultural institutions in Ireland, and briefly explain what each exhibits.
5. Explain the work of Dúchas.
6. Name the main Gaeltacht areas in Ireland, and the types of tourists who go there.
7. Describe the work of the Department of Public Enterprise
8. Name the semi-state bodies that operate under the Department of Public Enterprise.
9. Describe the work of the Irish Aviation Authority.
10. Outline the main operations of Bord Fáilte.
11. How does Bord Fáilte market Ireland abroad?
12. Where are the six RTAs in Ireland?
13. What are the RTAs' four areas of responsibility?
14. Describe the role of Shannon Development.
15. Explain the work of CERT.
16. How does the operation of the NITB differ from that of Bord Fáilte?
17. Name four private bodies that are involved in the tourism industry.
18. Describe the role of the ITIC.
19. Explain the difference between An Taisce and the National Trust.

References and further reading

Annual Report from the Department of Tourism, Sport and Recreation 1999. Government of Ireland, 1999.

Department of Tourism, Sport and Recreation Statement of Strategy 1998–2001. Government of Ireland, 1998.

Annual Report from the Department of Arts, Heritage, Gaeltacht and the Islands 1999. Government of Ireland, 1999.

Department of Arts, Heritage, Gaeltacht and the Islands Statement of Strategy 1998–2001. Government of Ireland, 1998.

Annual Report from the Department of Public Enterprise 1998. Government of Ireland, 1998.

CERT Review of Year 1999. www.cert.ie.

Annual Report Shannon Development 1998. www.shannondevelopment.ie.

Bord Failte Report and Accounts 1996, 1997, 1998, 2000.

Bord Failte Annual Review and Outlook 1998, 2000.

People and Places Newsletter ITIC 2000.

Duchas The Heritage Centre, A Guide. Department of Arts, Heritage, Gaeltacht and the Islands, 1998.

CHAPTER 4

Marketing the Irish Tourism Product

INTRODUCTION TO MARKETING

The British Institute of Marketing defines marketing as 'the management process responsible for identifying, anticipating, and satisfying customer requirements profitably'. In order to do this a company must undertake market research. It must then develop a product that satisfies the needs of the customers, at a price that they can afford, at a location that is accessible, and promote the product where they can see it (this is the marketing mix). In doing all of this the company must also make a profit from the sale of its product; otherwise the business will fail. The aim of marketing is to find customers who are happy with their products, who return again and again to buy them and recommend them to others. This applies to all marketing-orientated businesses, including tourism.

Each business must develop a **marketing plan**. It must look at the business environment in which it operates. The business environment includes a range of factors that will affect businesses; these include the Government, banks, competitors, customers, shareholders, suppliers, opinion leaders, media people, distributors, climate and population changes. The following have influenced the business environment for tourism industries:

1. The Government since 1988 has been helpful to the tourist industry, investing large amounts of money in projects.
2. Bank interest rates are low; this influences the amount of money that is borrowed for investment in the tourism industry.
3. All businesses need to know as much about their competitors as they do about their own business. Small companies cannot compete with established businesses head on, so they need to make their own business unique and therefore attractive to customers.
4. Ireland is a popular destination at the moment and customers like our products, but this could change and producers must be aware of this. Holiday programmes influence the popularity of certain destinations.
5. The climate in Ireland is unpredictable; to counteract this there has been major investment in all-weather tourism activities.
6. The performance of the economy, at domestic and global levels, influences

tourism. This includes the value of the euro, inflation, etc. and this influences whether people have the money to spend on holidays in Ireland. When the Irish economy is strong many Irish people have the money to enjoy weekend breaks and short holidays during the year. When recessions occur there is less demand for tourism products. During 2001 the value of the punt and the euro was low compared with sterling and the US dollar, and this meant that both UK and US tourists found that their money went a long way. A decrease in the value of sterling and the dollar makes Ireland more expensive as a destination.

7. Businesses must be aware of standards imposed by the industry. Consumer groups, environmental groups, etc. are all involved in lobbying for laws to be introduced. They must be aware of legislation that will affect them.

8. Other problems that can affect the tourism industry include, for instance, the outbreak of foot-and-mouth disease in the UK, which came to Ireland and forced the Government to impose restrictions on the movement of people and animals. This posed a serious threat to all tourism activities located in the countryside. War and terrorist activities all deter tourists from travelling.

All of these factors must be taken into account when the company is developing its marketing plan.

A **SWOT analysis** must be undertaken of the environment in which the business will be operating. SWOT stands for Strengths, Weaknesses, Opportunities and Threats. The strengths of the business are looked at from the point of view of the customer vis-à-vis Ireland as a holiday destination. The following is an example of a SWOT analysis:

Table 4.1: SWOT analysis	
Strengths Good reputation with customers Value for money Good location	**Weaknesses** Close to noisy road Poor parking facilities Difficulty in getting experienced staff
Threats Strong competition Loss of best manager Poor road access	**Opportunities** New tourist attraction next door Regional airport to open shortly

It is important that all the aspects of the business are looked at under the SWOT analysis, so that a true picture is seen.

When the Company knows its position, it then needs to develop its strategy. Three choices are available:

1. Try to win customers over on price, by undercutting your competitors. Only very large, strong companies usually do this.
2. Make your product different from your competitors' and emphasise your differences in promotions, for example Ireland as a niche market.
3. Concentrate on a small section of the market and become a 'big fish in a small pond'. In this way you can become very good at meeting the needs of your particular customers and therefore become successful. Many small Irish tourism businesses aim for this type of niche marketing.

MARKET RESEARCH

This is carried out in two principal ways: primary research and secondary research. It is normal to carry out secondary research first because it is less costly.

1. Secondary research is also called desk research. It involves getting printed material that is related to your business and reading up on these to find out all you can about the numbers of tourists that use your product.

- Bord Fáilte carries out a lot of research on the Irish tourism industry and copies of recent research can be purchased from Bord Fáilte's Market Research and Planning Department. Bord Fáilte carries out a survey of overseas travellers and the Central Statistics Office carries out a country of residence survey.
- Annual reports from Bord Fáilte, the Regional Tourism Authorities, Aer Rianta, Aer Lingus, Ryan Air, Stena and Irish Ferries are available for research and will give you information on the trends in Irish tourism.
- Subscribe to market research companies who carry out surveys and get reports from them related to the tourism industry.
- Trade associations such as the Irish Hotel Federation also produce reports.
- Specialist magazines, newspaper articles, etc. provide information on the business.

2. Primary research involves actually carrying out the research oneself and not just reading up reports. There are three main ways of doing this, not all of them suitable to the tourism industry.

(a) Observation: This involves watching people to see how they behave in a particular situation. It can be achieved by visiting a tourist attraction and making note of how information is displayed, how customers are dealt with, what facilities are available, and finding out as much as possible about the way the tourists are treated.
(b) Experimentation: This means carrying out an experiment in a controlled environment and then analysing the results. It could be used in a restaurant, by putting a new dish on the menu and then recording its success over a period.
(c) Survey: this is the most expensive way to collect information. It involves the construction of a survey and the way this is done depends on the information that you

want to collect. Questions can be of many different types, calling for Yes/No, multiple choice, open-ended answers etc. Each will provide different amounts of information. Then a decision has to be made on the sampling technique that is to be used and on how the surveys will be carried out. They can be done by post, telephone or face-to-face. Postal surveys are the cheapest to carry out but get the poorest return per hundred, while face-to-face give the best return but are the most expensive. The answers then need to be quantified and reports written up. Using an expert, like a market-research company, is the best way to carry out these types of surveys.

Whatever method you decide to use to do the research, the most important aspect of marketing is carrying out the market research and then using the results to make your business decisions.

The tourist market refers to all the customers who buy tourism products. Tourists are all very different. In order to understand what their needs and wants are, the producers must understand their consumers. People have a range of needs and once their basic needs like food, drink, sleep, and a place to live are satisfied, then their needs change. As each need is satisfied, we look for a higher level of motivation.

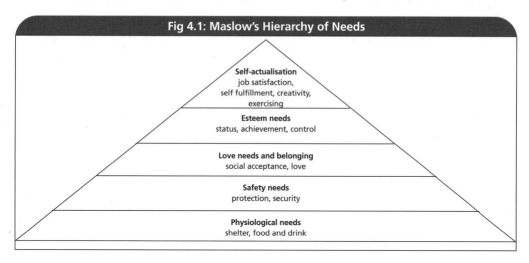

Fig 4.1: Maslow's Hierarchy of Needs

The influences on these needs, and therefore the demand for any type of product, and tourism products in particular, are demographic and psychological variables. Demographic variables include age, gender and family cycle. Psychological variables include the culture of the people, ethnic groups within countries and social class. The influence of peer groups such as fellow students, workers, or family, can all play a major role in helping one decide where one chooses to go on holidays, how to get there and what needs are satisfied on arrival.

The tourism market can be segmented or divided in a number of different ways:

- Decide on the basis of the location where the tourists live; this involves advertising only in that area, promoting on the local radio and in the local press, getting local travel agents to sell your product and organising flights from there to Ireland.
- Specialise on the basis of age, like Saga who provide package holidays for the over fifty-fives, or Ryan Hotels who have their Golden Years holidays.
- Sell on the basis of specific lifestyles. Tourists who have outgoing personalities want to explore new places and do new things; adventure and activity holidays are offered to them. Tourists who are inhibited and nervous will prefer organised package holidays at sun destinations, where everything is organised for them.
- Sell on the basis of product benefits. Often hotels have both holidaymakers and businessmen/women using them, but the services they provide are different for both groupings. Hotels in cities like Dublin have business people midweek, while holidaymakers use the hotels for weekend breaks. The needs of businesswomen differ from those of businessmen; they are more security conscious and hotels must take this into account.

Three particular types of holidays exist. The first, **domestic long holidays,** were the two weeks at a seaside resort but also include package holidays for groups, activity holidays, and independent travel. The second type is **domestic short breaks** (four days) and includes special-interest holidays, events and attractions, package holidays for groups and independent travel. The third type is the holiday for **overseas tourists**. These come on package tours for groups or individuals, and as independent travellers. This profile of holidays in fact gives a range of possible markets for selling our tourism product.

THE MARKETING MIX

The marketing mix is made up of the four Ps, that is product, price, place and promotion. The aim of the marketing mix is to develop each of these so that they interact, satisfy the needs of the customers, and maximise sales. It is important that each element of the marketing mix is correct. If any of it is wrong then the company will more than likely lose money.

Product

It is important to get the product correct, right from the beginning. Product development should be based on market research. Products that satisfy the needs of the customers ensure repeat business in the future and satisfied customers will recommend to friends. Products have two aspects:

(a) The features, that is the physical characteristic of the product, for example the size of the hotel room, the exhibits in the museum, the flowers that are seen in the garden

(b) The benefits that the customer gets from them, for example a comfortable night's sleep in the hotel room, an educational day out in the museum, and ideas for the customer's own garden.

The tourism product can provide a range of satisfactions. These can be: physiological (a full stomach after a meal), economic (good value for money), social (good service), psychological (status, because the five-star hotel is a fashionable place to stay).

Companies selling similar products need to make them different from those of their competitors. This can be done by:

(a) Emphasising the USP, or Unique Selling Proposition; this comprises the extra benefits the company has, like free parking, leisure and conference facilities, etc.

(b) Branding; many fast-food restaurants trade on their brand names, e.g McDonald's; hotels also use branding, e.g. Ryans and the Jury's Hotel Group. A brand name reflects the characteristics of the product and value for money. When a brand name is used it should be on all company uniforms, stationery, literature, etc. This ensures that the company gets the maximum impact from the branding. Bord Fáilte developed its Tourism Brand Ireland, following consumer research in 1995, and this is now used in its marketing campaign abroad.

Companies often sell more than one product, and this is referred to as a product mix. Some of these products may be aimed at different target markets. For example Budget Travel has summer sun holidays, long-haul destinations, winter sun holidays.

All products have a **life-cycle**. At each stage of a product's cycle the company will operate differently.

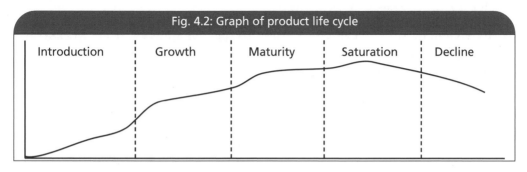

Fig. 4.2: Graph of product life cycle

| Introduction | Growth | Maturity | Saturation | Decline |

1. At the Launch stage, the company advertises to tell people about the new product. Sales are slow; this is partly because there is a very small distribution network. There are no profits.

2. During the Growth stage, sales are growing, there is less advertising, and so costs are falling. More companies are distributing the product, perhaps tour operators are using the hotel, and this means that profits are beginning to be made.

3. In the Maturity stage the sales continue to grow but more slowly. The product is popular and fashionable; repeat purchases take place from satisfied customers. Profits are also rising. Brand advertising takes place to remind the customers of their product.

4. At the Saturation stage the sales peak. Competition from other companies is intense, as they look for market share. Profits begin to drop.

5. The product goes into Decline as sales and profits fall. Irish seaside resorts are in the declining stage, as they fail to compete with tourist resorts abroad.

An example of the life-cycle can be seen in the case study of Bray, Co. Wicklow (see chapter 2).

All marketing managers must know the stage that their product is at so that they can plan their marketing campaign. Some products in the saturation stage try to revitalise themselves, before they go into decline. For example many one-star and two-star hotels have revitalised themselves by providing bedrooms with bathroom ensuite and improving the hotel's general facilities, so that they are now three-star hotels.

Launching a **new product** into the market is a very risky business, with large numbers of products failing within a short time of being launched. Most new products are modified versions or improvements of products already on the market; this is very true of the tourism industry. These products will fail if they are either poor copies of other products, or where competition is too great. New products should look for gaps in the market; they must be priced correctly, and promoted so that the consumers are aware of them. It is possible to prevent products from failing by screening them at each stage of their development. Products that fail at any stage are discarded. The stages are as follows:

1. Idea Generation – ideas come from a range of sources, from workers, or managers who have seen a similar product elsewhere, sometimes abroad, or they may come from trade magazines.

2. Idea Evaluation – involves carrying out a SWOT analysis, deciding on the target market, listing the benefits of the new product and comparing these with other similar products.

3. A Business Analysis – this looks at the sales potential, costs for setting up the business, the profit potential etc. Market research will look at the customer's reaction to the new product. A feasibility study will take place where the project is large; this will particularly need to be done if the company is hoping to receive grants to develop the new product.

4. Product Development – can be as small as developing new menus for the restaurant or as large as putting together designs for a new hotel.
5. Test Marketing – may be introduced to find out the success of the product. A product may be offered to a limited group of consumers to see their reaction, to test out the pricing policy etc.
6. Commercialisation – this involves the launching of the product on the market. Many Irish tourism products go straight from stage three, the business analysis, to the launching of the product and a system of trial and error is used.

Even by using this screening process there is no guarantee that the product will be a success. The restaurant business is an area which is notorious for industry failure, with many restaurants opening and closing each year. In 1989 over £4 (€5) million was invested in the tourist attraction Celtworld in Tramore. Its early performance was very good, but within three years it had failed to meet its sales and profit targets and it went into liquidation, with the property being sold.

Pricing

Most customers look for value for money when they buy a product, but sometimes if a product is unique and is considered luxurious, such as a five-star hotel, high prices can be charged. If similar products are for sale in the market place companies must keep in mind what the competition is charging. When demand is low or high the price of product can be reduced or increased; this can be seen in the price charged for package holidays and hotels during the high and low seasons. Some customers (holidaymakers) are affected by price, while others, such as business people, are less so. The company must look at all of these influences as they decide what their pricing policy will be.

In deciding the price that will be charged for any product the company must look at the target market and decide whether they will compete on low prices, or look for a niche market which will have few competitors and choose a market segment and aim for that. Cost will influence the price that can be charged, as costs must be covered if the product is to make a profit. During the low season hotels may have special offers in order to recover some of the costs. Some tourism companies cross-subsidise products; this was done by many of the ferry companies before the abolition of duty free, where duty-free sales cross-subsidised the cost of tickets on the ferry.

There are many types of pricing policies:

1. Return on investment. The company decides on the percentage of profit it would like to make; this is usually a few percentage points above inflation.
2. Pricing for market share: In this case the product is introduced into the new market at a low price, so that it can establish market share. Later when the

product is well known and sales go up the company will begin to make profits by charging higher prices. Financially strong companies, with products that have long life-cycles, pursue this type of policy; otherwise the company could run into cash flow problems.

3. Increasing turnover: Profits increase as sales increase. This is achieved by getting new customers to buy the products and old customers to repurchase more often, by increasing the price of the product, and introducing new events or lines to be sold by the business. These could be done by having conferences in the hotels, or getting regular summer holidaymakers to return on a weekend break during the low season.

4. Short-term profit maximisation: This involves charging a high price in order to maximise profits when the product is first launched; then as sales increase the price drops. New tourism attractions or museums that are unusual might expect people to pay a high price for the newness of the product. Hotels use this policy when major events are taking place, like the Olympic games, when they know the demand will be very high.

5. Premium pricing: This is where the quality and status of the product is high, and therefore the price charged is high. Holidays that involve the use of castles for holiday accommodation can charge higher prices than those that use hotels.

6. Price leadership: The going rate is charged and price is based on what the competitors are charging. Small hotels and guesthouses in seaside resorts use this policy.

7. Cost plus pricing: The company works out its costs and then adds a percentage of profit to make up the selling price. Marginal costs for hotel rooms are usually small, so customers arriving late at night can often negotiate prices.

Once the price is decided, it must be remembered that it will not remain the same over the year. Sometimes products will be sold at a discount with 'special offers' occurring during the low season. Tour operators who buy in bulk will negotiate better prices by guaranteeing sales. Early cash payments may also mean reductions in the normal price, for example APEX tickets for airlines.

Distribution or place

The aim of distribution is to get information about the product to the target market, so that it can influence the public to buy the product. Selling directly, by phone, internet, mail or face-to-face, can do this. No commissions need to be paid on these types of distribution. Intermediaries can also be used if an indirect distribution system is chosen; this involves using travel agents, tour operators, incentive and conference travel companies and tourist information offices.

The type of distribution system that is chosen depends on:

- The target market: When a company is selling to international tourists then it is best to use intermediaries. Bord Fáilte brings tour operators to Ireland for work shops in order to buy from Irish tourism service providers. Some markets make more use of travel agents than others. Bord Fáilte has information on all markets and this is available to producers.
- Budgets: It is expensive to have a wide distribution network, because all of them have to be supplied with brochures and commissions have to be paid. Small businesses make use of Tourist Information Offices, the internet and perhaps tour operators, while large businesses use a range of distributors.
- Competitors: Instead of small companies competing on the international market many now join together in consortiums or alliances and produce brochures and market abroad together. This reduces marketing costs. Examples are: Heritage Towns of Ireland, Best Western Hotels.

The main intermediaries are:

1. Travel agents: Using global distribution systems like Galileo and Amadeus they can access information and make bookings for a range of tourism products. They sell 90 per cent of airline tickets, 25 per cent of hotel accommodation and 50 per cent of car hire. They charge commission on each sale.
2. Tour operators: They put together package holidays and must buy transport, and accommodation. Conference and incentive organisers put together packages for business travellers. These organisers are buying top-of-the-range products for their business clients and are an important part of the tourist market because they are organising for such large numbers.
3. Computer reservation systems (CRS): These can operate within hotel groups, within consortiums, or by using commercial companies like Utell Reservation System or Gulliver.
4. Tourism information offices: These are located around the country and are operated by the Regional Tourism Authorities. Bord Fáilte has tourist offices in many countries around the world. These provide information on tourism products in Ireland, along with brochures in which tourism companies can advertise. Booking services are also available, and 10 per cent commission is charged.

A study of the distribution channels used by visitors when booking accommodation in Dublin in 1999/2000 by G. Dunne and Dr S. Flanagan of DIT found the following results:

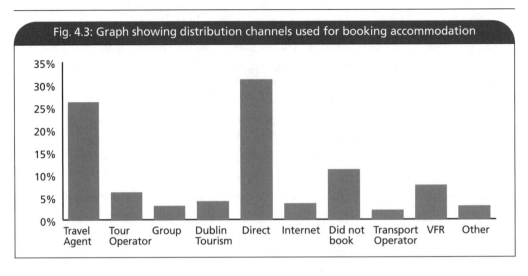

Fig. 4.3: Graph showing distribution channels used for booking accommodation

The major change in distribution systems is the growth of the internet. In 1999 400,000 Irish people used the internet and this number is growing all the time. In the USA 80 per cent of homes are linked to the internet and many companies in the area of travel and tourism are increasing their use of it. More tourists are booking on the internet. While airline companies have increased sales on the internet, hotels have been slower to adopt the new technology. Ryanair in particular made use of the internet to cut down on costs, and this in turn lowered their prices. A range of other marketing activities can take place on the internet including making reservations, marketing of destinations by national tourist boards, advice and information, package holiday bookings and guidebooks.

Promotions or communications

This is the way the company gets its message to its consumers, employees, the Department of Tourism, banks, tour operators. The communication mix involves advertising, sales promotions, direct marketing, merchandising, personal selling and public relations. While each of these can be used individually, they make a greater impact if they operate together.

The communication process involves the company deciding what message they want to deliver. They may be delivering different messages to their different markets. For example airline companies may be emphasising their 'on-time record' to the business market, and lower prices to their leisure market. Having decided on their message, they then must decide how this information will be delivered to the customer. Printed material in newspapers and magazines can display large quantities of information like flight times and dates, while radio and television require short snappy messages. The message should be clear and easily understood. Then the company must decide on the category of media, whether newspapers, consumer magazines, trade magazines, newsletters.

The method of promotion to use will depend on:

1. The product being sold. For example, package holidays are best sold by personal selling by travel consultants who can explain what is on offer in different countries.
2. The target market. If the promotion is aimed at the trade, then sales promotions and direct selling can be used. If the promotion is aimed at the consumer then advertising is best.
3. The stage the product is at in its life-cycle. New products use advertising, while older products use sales promotions.
4. The place of the company in the market place. This will depend on how well-known the product is within the country or region where it is being promoted.

Budget will determine the type of promotion that can be used. Many of the companies in the tourism industry are small and have very small budgets for promotions, usually 1 per cent to 6 per cent.

1. Advertising

The AIDA principle is often used in advertising. This involves: attracting Attention, creating Interest, fostering Desire, and inspiring Action. Advertising agencies are used to develop an advertising campaign. They are the experts in designing adverts and they purchase advertising space cheaper in newspapers and on television because of bulk buying. The effectiveness of any advertising campaign depends on:

1. The idea chosen. The message from the company should be emphasising the uniqueness of product (USP), the extra benefits of products on offer, the lower selling price, special offers.
2. The medium used in the promotion – radio, magazines newspapers. The target market must read the newspaper. For example, expensive hotels advertise in quality newspapers.
3. The reach and frequency of the campaign. This means the number of people who will see the advertisement and the number of times it will be shown. It is important that the advert is repeated over and over, so that potential customers will remember the advert and the product.
4. Competition. Other advertising campaigns will take away from the impact that the advertisement will have, so this needs to be avoided.
5. The timing of the campaign. For example, package holidays are advertised after Christmas as people begin to plan their summer vacation.

The most popular places for advertising tourism products include women's magazines, specialist magazines, weekend supplements in Sunday papers, radio and television guides, national tourist board (Bord Fáilte) publications, guide books, outdoor billboards, the internet, radio, or television. All of these have advantages and

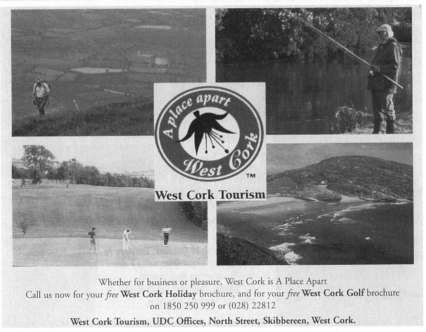

Whether for business or pleasure, West Cork is A Place Apart
Call us now for your *free* **West Cork Holiday** brochure, and for your *free* **West Cork Golf** brochure
on 1850 250 999 or (028) 22812
West Cork Tourism, UDC Offices, North Street, Skibbereen, West Cork.

Fig. 4.4: Advertisement for west Cork

disadvantages. The most expensive form of advertising is television, especially at peak time. Sometimes companies advertise on television around the time a specialised programme is shown, e.g. advertising gardening holidays at the time gardening programmes are being shown.

2. Direct mail

Satisfied customers can become repeat customers, if they are approached in the proper way. Tour operators, hotel owners, travel agents, leisure and conference centres can all contact their previous guests because they have their names and addresses on file. This involves sending out letters to these customers, along with the most recent brochure or special offer that will attract them back for another visit. With the development of computers the production of such mail is very easy and inexpensive. Lists of names can also be purchased from PMI – Precision Marketing Information – and it is possible to contact people from these lists who have particular hobbies and who perhaps would like to go on a special interest holiday. For example, hotels that offer golfing holidays can contact golfers using direct mail. Direct mail has grown by over 50 per cent since 1995.

Door-to-door distribution of leaflets is less expensive than direct mail, but it is often perceived as junk mail and may not in fact be read. This is a useful method for local restaurants to reach their target market in their area. Sometimes these leaflets may include vouchers that can be used in local museums or restaurants and these get a better response rate.

3. Sales promotions

This is sometimes referred to as below the line promotion and includes a range of ways of promoting products. The aim of sales promotions is to get the attention of the public, and then to turn this into a sale. Sales promotions often have short-term objectives and can be aimed at

1. Company staff – who receive incentives and bonuses for meeting targets.
2. Dealers and retailers – for them there are contests, trade exhibitions, brochure launches including receptions, giveaways like pens and diaries, direct mail and joint promotion schemes.
3. Consumers – they are offered point-of-sale material including brochures, post cards, window displays, competitions, low interest financing, 'twofers', money-off vouchers, joint promotions like Tesco stamps and Aer Lingus flights, direct mail.

Merchandising is a form of sales promotion and is sometimes known as 'in-house selling'. The aim of merchandising is to increase the expenditure of the customers. This includes encouraging hotel guests to use the minibar and video channels provided in their rooms, to eat in the hotel restaurant. Theme parks expect their customers will buy food in their restaurants, souvenirs from their shops.

Merchandising works by:

1. Having the products easily accessible to the customers. For example, the tourism attraction places its craft shop at the end of the tour to encourage impulse buying.
2. Using four senses to attract customers to the products: Sight – attractive posters, signs and displays are put at eye level. Hearing – public address systems announce events taking place. Smell and touch – aromatic coffee or the smell of fresh bread appeal to most people, and dessert trolleys and salad bars are all used to remind customers that they are hungry. After customers have had their senses aroused, they are then motivated to buy.

4. Exhibitions and travel workshops

These are important to the tourism and travel industry. There are three types of **Exhibitions:** 1. Those aimed at consumers. 2. Those aimed at the trade. 3. Those that are by invitation only.

Among the most important are the World Travel Market in London and the

International Tourism Exchange in Berlin. These are organised so that on set days they are open to the trade only and open to the general public at other times. A wide range of tourist interests attend these exhibitions, including those involved in inbound and outbound tourism and domestic tourism, i.e. tour operators, travel agents, national and local tourist offices. The emphasis is on destinations and, more recently, special-interest holidays like fishing or golfing. Entertainments such as folk dancing, videos, films, food, and wine-tasting are provided. Brochures and written material are handed out. Holiday booking also takes place. The main tourism consumer exhibition in Ireland is the Holiday World eXperience held in Dublin, Belfast, Cork and Galway. These have been held at the end of January and beginning of February each year since 1989. Special promotions for consumers can also take place at events, e.g. at major golf competitions where golfing holidays are promoted.

Travel workshops are organised by Bord Fáilte to bring together both trade buyers, like ground handling agents, tour operators, conference organisers and Irish tourism industry interests, such as hotel owners or airline companies, who are selling their products. These workshops occur over several days and tour operators can put together package holidays for the next season, while Irish producers can make thousands of pounds worth of bookings. This is an important way of promoting Ireland.

To introduce new products to their customers, the tourism and travel trade uses **presentations**. These are by invitation only and a reception usually precedes the talk. They often take place in the local hotel. Sales staffs are available to sell the holidays. Many such presentations are joint promotions between tour operators and travel agents or National Tourist Board and National carriers. These presentations are very successful in creating tourism business.

5. Public relations (PR)

PR is used to create and maintain favourable relations between the company and its customers, shareholders, distributors, suppliers and trade unions. PR helps to support a company's image. The image is presented in an unbiased way; it is therefore more objective than advertising and for this reason can influence sales. PR is best used for long-term planning. It can be used to create favourable publicity and to counteract unfavourable publicity. PR Campaigns can involve:

1. Bringing in journalists and travel writers to visit a destination and part take in tourism facilities; the articles that follow will usually generate good publicity for the tourism industries that have been visited. This is used by Bord Fáilte to generate good publicity in the foreign press.
2. Filming on location. County Wicklow in particular has benefited from this with Kilcoole being better known as Glenroe, and Avoca as Ballykissangel. Both of these are now on the tourism trail.

3. Education study trips for travel agents and tour operators, to improve their knowledge of the destination; in this way they will be able to sell the product better. Often staff who work in the travel industry consider such trips a major perk. This encourages staff to push the product in the market place.
4. Sponsorship. This can take many forms, for example providing prizes for competitions, providing financial support for festivals, providing academic scholarships for students who want to train in the industry. Good will can be created by companies when they support local events, such as charities.

6. Personal selling

The tourism industry is very much a people business. Most of these are involved in personal selling. Travel consultants, sales and marketing managers and hotel representatives spend most of their time selling their company's products. There are others, like receptionists, banqueting, front office and food and beverage managers in hotels, waiting staff, tour guides and visitor-centre staff, also involved in selling. In personal selling, salespersons must:

1. Match the needs of the customer with the products that they are selling
2. Listen carefully to what customers are saying about their needs
3. Present and explain to customers the benefits of the product. This requires good product knowledge.
4. Reassure customers, if they raise objections to a particular product, that the product best suits their needs.
5. Close the sale.

Customers must never be pushed into decisions because this will only cause resentment and prevent future sales. Customers must always be happy with what they purchased, so that they recommend the company to their friends and return at some stage in the future.

Case study: Bord Fáilte's marketing campaign in Britain in 1999

This campaign involved not only Bord Fáilte but also the Northern Ireland Tourist Board, air and sea carriers and many other private tourism businesses in Ireland. Both Bord Fáilte and the Overseas Tourism Marketing Initiative (OTMI) financed it.
The aim of the marketing campaign was to

1. Attract high-spending UK tourists to Ireland
2. Have the tourists visit regional attractions
3. Bring the tourists to Ireland during the low season.

The economic outlook was good in the UK; the economy was strong, with low inflation and unemployment. The £ sterling was strong against the Irish £ which was linked to the weaker Euro. This meant Ireland was an attractive destination, and many people could afford to take holidays.

The marketing campaign consisted of:

1. **Advertising**. This began in late 1998 with brochures being sent out. The television advertisement campaign ran from January to May, at the same time there was also advertising in the newspapers, in the *Sunday Times*, the *Telegraph* and in magazines like the *Radio Times*. The 'Ireland's Hidden Treasure' campaign, which was a joint Bord Fáilte and NITB advertising campaign, was aimed at the Scottish and Northern England markets and took place on TV. There was also a special angling and golfing colour advertising campaign in the press. A banner advertising campaign took place on the internet.

2. **Promotions**. This included the Celtic Flame on Tour. This traditional music show was held in five of the UK's main cities, and 12,000 holiday information packs were handed out to the audiences. Bord Fáilte and the NITB visited eighty trade and consumer shows including the Holiday Shows at Glasgow, Manchester and London. They also attended special-interest shows like the Open Golf Championship in Scotland to promote golfing holidays, and Hampton Court Flower Show to promote gardening holidays in Ireland. Large trade shows like Confex (Conference Exhibition) at Earls Court, London and the British Travel Trade Fair in Birmingham were attended. At these shows contacts were made between Irish companies and 77,000 tour operators and travel agents in Britain.

3. **Publicity**. Two-hundred-and-fifty media and press journalists were brought to Ireland. They produced 400 articles on holidays in Ireland for newspapers and magazines. Ireland was on a total of twenty-five different travel shows on television. Articles in the press included 'Angling Memories' in *The Times*, 'Partying in Temple Bar' in the *Mirror*, 'Lismore Castle for your House Party' was recommended in *Harpers & Queen*, while the *Sun* had articles on Ashford Castle and Dromoland Castle, and gardening holidays were highlighted in *Woman's Weekly*. Ireland was also seen in UK television programmes like *The Antiques Inspectors*, *Country Tracks* and the very popular *Ballykissangel*. The St Patrick's Day festival received major coverage on television and radio.

4. **Other promotions**. These included the Expo Ireland festival in the Olympia in London which celebrated Irish food, travel and fashion, and attracted over 17,000 people. A season of Beckett plays took place in the Barbican Centre in London; this was used to launch Ireland as a centre for cultural holidays. Irish sports stars, for example racing-car driver Eddie Irvine and champion jockey Adrian Maguire, were used in advertising and promoting Ireland for holidays. Fifty top conference organisers were brought to Dublin to take part in a workshop in order to develop Ireland as an important centre for conferences. Nearly 500,000 'The Ireland' brochures were given out at consumer shows. Seven hundred travel agents were trained to sell Ireland as a tourism destination.

The budget for the campaign came from Bord Fáilte and the OTMI. It broke down as follows:

Table 4.2: Budget for Bord Fáilte's marketing campaign in Britain in 1999 Courtesy of Bord Fáilte	
Advertising	£2,709,000/€3,409,00
Promotions & Publicity	£3,095,000/€3,895,000
Total	£5,804,000/€7,254,000

This promotion campaign, and improved accessibility from Britain to Ireland due to increased capacity on Irish Ferries' fast ferry service and new air routes linking Ireland and Britain, encouraged more British tourists to come to Ireland. In 2000 3.49 million British tourists came to Ireland spending over €1,115 million, an increase on the previous year of 2 per cent and 10 per cent respectively.

REVISION EXERCISES

1. Give five influences that may operate in the business environment.
2. What does SWOT stand for? Carry out a SWOT analysis of your local area.
3. Explain the difference between primary and secondary research.
4. Describe four ways in which the tourist market can be segmented.
5. Explain two ways in which products can be differentiated from each other.
6. What are the five stages of the product life-cycle? Explain sales during each stage.
7. Explain five types of pricing policies.
8. Explain with examples the difference between a direct and an indirect distribution policy.
9. Explain five different ways of promoting tourism products.
10. From reading the case study of Bord Fáilte's marketing plan in Britain in 1999, explain the most innovative ways of marketing Ireland in the British market.

Assignments

1. Look at the different ways in which your local area is promoted as a tourist destination. Collect local brochures, advertisements for local hotels in newspapers, magazines, on the internet, and look at sales promotions, PR etc used by the tourism industry.
2. Prepare a critical essay on the strengths and weaknesses of the marketing strategies employed by any tourism business with which you have been associated.

References and further reading

Bord Failte, *Marketing Ireland to the World*. Bord Failte 1998, 1999, 2000.
Bord Failte, 'Tourism Watch' Magazine. Bord Failte.
F. Buttle, *Hotel and Food Tourism Service Marketing*. Cassell, 1986.
Gibson and Neilson, *Marketing Ireland to the World*. Gill & Macmillan, 2000.
J.C. Holloway and R.V. Plant, *Marketing for Tourism*. Pitman, 1988.
R. Stefanou, *Success in Marketing*. John Murray, 1993.

CHAPTER 5

The Impact of Tourism on the Economy

INTERNATIONAL AND NATIONAL TOURISM NUMBERS AND REVENUE

Internationally tourism is the world's most important industry. It is an industry which has been growing steadily since the 1950s.

Table 5.1: Tourism growth Figures courtesy of World Tourism Organisation		
Year	1950	1995
Numbers of trips	25 million	563 million
Revenue earned	US$2.1 million	US$401 billion
Employment created		127 million

Along with an increase in tourism numbers, there has also been an increase in tourist spending, and in the amount of employment created by the tourism industry. The most important tourism-generating regions are Europe, North America, and Japan, the world's most industrialised regions. In 1995 the world's most important tourism generating countries were: Germany ($50m), USA ($45.9m), Japan ($36.8m), the UK ($24.7m) and France ($16.3m). The amount of money that is spent by tourists is more important than the actual number of tourists that visit a country. Among those countries that spend the most money per capita on holidays are the Nordic countries. The world's largest potential market for tourism is the Japanese market; this is because they are big spenders when on holidays, and at present only 9 per cent of Japanese travel abroad. Australians, Americans and tourists from South East Asia also spend a lot on holidays. Some countries, for example India, put restrictions on the purchase of foreign currency; this encourages domestic tourism.

The value of tourism is that it creates many jobs directly within the industry. This is currently heading towards 200 million jobs. Jobs can be created both in the generating and the destination areas. Jobs that are created in the generating area include travel agents, tour operators and airlines, while jobs created in the destination area include hotel managers, chefs, guides and receptionists. In some countries, for example Caribbean islands, tourism employment accounts for up to 25 per cent of the workforce.

The Irish tourism industry grew during the 1990s because:

1. There was a growth in short-break holidays, especially from the UK.
2. The open skies policy meant that more people travelled by air, as the cost of getting to Ireland reduced.
3. New carriers (Ryanair, City Jet) and greater capacity on flights brought more tourists.
4. Dublin is a fashionable destination for city breaks, especially the Temple Bar area.
5. Increased marketing, by Bord Fáilte, Aer Lingus, hotels, has attracted more tourists.
6. The success of the Irish economy means that more Irish people have money to eat out, go on short-break holidays.
7. Business tourism grew and now stands at 21 per cent.

As a result, the numbers of tourists coming to Ireland have increased, revenue has increased, and this has resulted in more employment in the industry, and more taxes for the Government.

The **Irish tourism industry** did not begin to grow significantly until the Irish Government began to take an active role in promoting it in 1987. The numbers of tourists have grown rapidly since then.

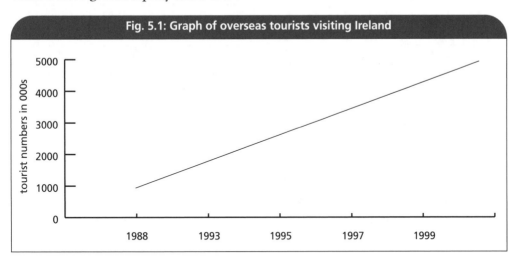

Fig. 5.1: Graph of overseas tourists visiting Ireland

The main sources of tourists in Ireland are Britain, Europe (Germany, France, Italy, Netherlands, the Nordic countries and Switzerland), North America, and other areas which include Australia, New Zealand and Japan, Northern Ireland and, largest of all, domestic tourists. Since 1995 there has been growth in most of these markets, both in the numbers of tourists and in the amount that they spend.

This shows overall growth in all markets, except in the Northern Ireland market. Within the European market the Nordic countries of Norway, Sweden, Finland,

Table 5.2: Major Irish markets Figures courtesy of Bord Fáilte tourist numbers in (000s)					
Country	1995	1996	1997	1998	1999
Britain	2,285	2,590	2,850	3,199	3,340
Europe	1,101	1,177	1,168	1,255	1,321
N America	641	729	777	858	950
Other Overseas	204	186	213	221	243
Northern Ireland	587	607	580	530	460
Domestic Trips	6,924	6,170	6,850	6,934	7,285

Denmark and Iceland (20 per cent), and Italy (31 per cent) all rose, while France and Switzerland only increased marginally, and the German market declined slightly (-2 per cent).

The earnings from these tourists during the period 1995 to 1999 have generally risen dramatically.

Table 5.3: Tourism revenue Figures courtesy of Bord Fáilte (Revenue in £ /euros millions)					
Country	1995	1996	1997	1998	1999
Britain	£501.2/€613	£574.0/€716.	£683.0/€854.	£757.4/€947	£796.9/€996
Europe	£413.7/€520	£466.6/€583	£457.7/€607	£467.2/€587	£496.6/€626
N America	£275.0/€345	£316.6/€396	£348.2/€435	£384.4/€480	£437.2/€547
Other Overseas	£96.5/€122	£93.8/€117	£99.7/€126	£103.0/€131	£114.3/€142
Northern Ireland	£82.6/€103	£85.0/€107	£101.9/€129	£96.3/€122	£89.4/€112
Domestic Trips	£610.9/€764	£578.8/€734	£670.8/€840	£751.0/€945	£879.3/€1100
Transport Carriers	£302.0/€382	£345.0/€430	£400.0/€508	£470.0/€590	£560.0/€705

Over the five-year period the value of tourism revenue has gone up by just under 50 per cent. This revenue has had a major impact on the Irish economy. Tourist Revenue impacts on the economy in four ways: 1. Income earned from the industry. 2. Employment created by the industry. 3. Balance of Payments. 4. Investment in the industry.

INCOME

Income can be generated in a number of different ways: from the wages of those employed in the industry, from rents received from tourism businesses, from profits made in tourism businesses, and from interest paid by tourism businesses. The tourist industry is very labour intensive, with most of the costs being labour costs. Most of this income is earned by those employed directly and indirectly in the tourism industry in the form of wages. Those directly employed include hotel managers, waiting staff, chefs and guides. Their incomes in turn create demand for goods and services in the areas where they live. Other indirect incomes include the butchers and farmers who provide steaks for the restaurants and hotels in an area, the fishermen who sell the fresh fish to fish restaurants, the printers who make the many brochures available in the tourist information centers. In areas of the country where there are large tourist numbers, there is also a lot of revenue earned from tourists.

Regional tourism earnings in 1999
1. South west   £588.1/€735 million
2. Shannon   £321.3/€425 million
3. West   £408.9/€511 million
4. North west   £226.6/€283 million
5. Midlands east   £284.4/€356 million
6. Dublin   £707.5/€878 million
7. South east   £276.9/€346 million

Some of these areas are more dependent on tourists than others, because there are fewer other industries to create wealth there, for example south-west and west regions.

Rental income can also be earned from tourism activities. This includes the renting out of mobile homes in coastal areas or the renting out of shop premises to sell crafts. Interest is repaid on loans that are taken out, for instance, to expand hotels or build swimming pools. The financial sector has also benefited from the success of the tourism industry over the last ten years or more. Most of these hotels are making good profits, and this is another source of income for the tourism businesses.

The tourism income multiplier allows us to work out the value of tourists' money to a region. This is accepted as double the amount of revenue that tourists spend. The reason for this is that those who earn money within the industry then spend their wages on services locally; they buy food and other products required for the industry locally. Approximately 50 per cent of tourist spending remains within the local area, being spent on wages and local goods; while the other 50 per cent is sent out of the area on tax, savings and imported goods. Local industries and services supported by the tourist industry will in turn spend their wages within the locality, creating further demand and making money for other services. The actual money spent by tourists in 1999 amounted to £3,386.3 (€4,231) million, but as a result of the tourism income multiplier, that tourism was worth £6,772.6 (€8,462) million to the country.

In some countries leakages occur; this is where money is lost to a region, and this happens when:

• Hotels are owned by outsiders, and profits are sent home to the company headquarters

- Much of the food and wine is imported
- Foreign tourist workers send part of their wages home.

In western Europe the leakage is only about 10 per cent, while in some countries it can be much higher.

Taxation is another source of income; numerous types of taxes are imposed on tourists including:

1. VAT is earned on the sale of all goods and services. It can range from 0 per cent to 21 per cent. Tourists who are bringing gifts home with them to areas outside the EU can reclaim the VAT.
2. Departure taxes are imposed on tourists leaving a country.
3. Excise duty accounts for a large percentage of the price of tobacco, spirits, wines and petrol.
4. Some countries have levies imposed on tourists; in Austria this is known as the Kurtaxe. There have been suggestions that such levies be imposed on Irish tourists by Dublin Corporation and on tourists going to the Aran Islands. So far tourism interests have managed to prevent these being imposed; they view them as being very short sighted.
5. Those who work in the industry have to pay income tax and PRSI on their earnings.
6. Large hotels, restaurants, etc. have to pay corporation tax on their profits.

The total value of taxation earned from the tourism industry amounts to 57 per cent of tourism spending. The value of tourism in the form of taxation to the Irish Government amounts to well over £1 (€1.25) billion.

EMPLOYMENT

Between 1996 and 1999 there was a 22 per cent increase in the number of jobs available in the tourism industry. These were in a number of areas, but were especially high in the area of self-catering accommodation and restaurant work. In 1999 there were 246,843 people employed in the industry.

Table 5.4: Tourism employment growth Figures courtesy of CERT				
Sector	1992	1996	1999	%Change
Hotels	30,693	38,915	53,906	+76%
Guesthouses	2,768	2,963	3,115	+13%
Self catering accommodation	1,154	2,558	4,580	+297%
Restaurants	19,893	26,026	40,283	+102%
Licensed Premises	72,957	76,239	78,300	+7%
Fast Food Outlets	7,222	14,605	15,221	+111%
Tourist Services and Attractions	20,362	25,161	33,910	+67%

Most of this employment growth is in new businesses. Shortages of skilled staff have arisen; this is particularly acute in the pub trade where there are 3,800 vacancies, while there are also vacancies in hotels (1,800) and in restaurants (1,500). Staff from other EU countries and from the ranks of the long-term unemployed, for whom training was provided by CERT, have helped to cope with these shortages.

One of the difficulties facing those employed in the industry is the seasonal nature of the work. There have been many attempts by the industry to increase the length of the season, by offering special breaks and by the provision of leisure and conference facilities. This has resulted in many hotels staying open all year around. Unfortunately there are many tourist attractions that still only operate between March and October. Until these are able to operate all year round, then the industry will only attract those who want to work on a seasonal basis. Some employers have high expectations of their staff who often work long hours and receive insufficient pay. This means that the industry is threatened by a lack of trained staff, or by a high turnover of staff. Many in the industry treat their staff well, by providing training, good salaries, and good time off; unfortunately those who do not look after their staff give the industry as a whole a bad name.

Developments in technology affect all businesses. The overall effect on the tourism industry has been minimal because so many of the jobs require personal service. The use of computers has been mainly in the reservations area. This has meant that fewer staff are required by airlines, travel agents. Fortunately this has occurred at a time when there has been growth in these businesses, and the overall effect has been that few jobs have actually been lost. Tourists require the service of people. Technology has not been able to provide these services, so employment has been growing.

Employment operates similarly to the TIM (Tourism Income Multiplier). Extra jobs created in the tourism industry in turn create jobs in other services. When jobs are created in the tourism industry, new hotels are opening, or there is a new tourist attraction in the area, and indirectly more new jobs will be created. This is especially important in the regional areas.

BALANCE OF PAYMENTS

International tourists bring money into the Irish economy. This could be in the form of US dollars, £ sterling, euro, etc. Those who travel on Irish airlines or ferries also earn foreign currency for the Irish economy. All of these earnings are known as invisible exports, and they help the Irish Government to pay its import bill. When Irish people travel abroad, for instance to Spain or France, they are spending Irish money abroad, in the same way as they would if they purchased a car made in Japan or wine made in France. This money goes out of the country. The Irish Government has to balance its imports and exports. In the late 1990s the Irish economy was buoyant, with a surplus of exports between January and August 2000 of €17 billion.

In other countries where more tourists leave the country than enter, a tourism deficit occurs. This has applied to English tourism since 1986, because more English go abroad than foreign tourists visit England. Many countries do not like this type of situation to operate because the economy is losing money. When this happens they have a number of alternatives available to them:

- They can limit the amount of foreign currency that their citizens take abroad.
- They can prevent the movement of their citizens abroad; some countries require people to have exit visas in order to leave the country.
- They can encourage their citizens to take their holidays at home, by advertising and other promotions. Bord Fáilte does this with their 'Discover Ireland' Brochures.
- They can encourage foreign tourists to come to their country. In Ireland Bord Fáilte encourages this by having advertising campaigns, special promotions, etc. in its major markets.

Some countries can afford to let their people travel abroad because their manufactured goods provide a surplus balance of payments. These countries include Germany and Japan. They do not need to worry about tourism creating a balance of payment deficit. Other countries like Spain and Italy have large tourism surpluses because such large numbers of tourists visit their country each year. In these countries tourism also creates many jobs, and provides billions of dollars in revenue.

INVESTMENT IN THE INDUSTRY

There has been major investment in the tourism industry in Ireland since 1989 with over £1 (€1.25) billion being invested. This investment has been in a whole range of tourism facilities, for example new hotels, conference and leisure facilities, self-catering accommodation, tourist attractions. These new amenities were built with a mixture of private and public funding. The public funding included the following:

- European Regional and Development Funding (ERDF). This came to Ireland as part of the Operational Programmes for Tourism 1989-1999. These grants applied to buildings, marketing and training. In 1999 ERDF grants paid out £83 (€104) million on large regional visitor attractions, tourist information offices, heritage attractions, garden restoration.
- Capital Development Fund. This is Government finance that is provided for visitor facilities, and amounted to £4.5 (€5.65) million in 1999.
- InterReg and Maritime InterReg. This is EU funding that applies to border areas. It applies between Ireland and Wales and to the counties bordering the North of Ireland. In 1999 nearly £300,000 (€375,000) was paid out with 90 per cent applied to the border counties. The aim of this finance is to encourage cross-border co-operation and stimulate economic activity in these areas.

- The International Fund for Ireland. This was a fund that was developed during the peace process and applied to the border counties of Donegal, Leitrim, Sligo, Cavan, Monaghan, and Louth.
- Peace and Reconciliation Programme. This is funding that Bord Fáilte and the Northern Ireland Tourist Board receive, which is applied to special projects in the border counties.
- Funding from the RTAs and Shannon Development for agri-tourism projects. This amounted to £8 (€10.5) million between 1994 and 1999. Many of these tourism projects are small businesses that provide accommodation, leisure facilities, small cultural or heritage centres. Many of the businesses that applied for this funding are located in Irish Country Holiday areas.
- BES scheme (Business Expansion Scheme). This allows a company to raise money and gives tax benefits to the investors over five years. Thirty tourism projects were approved for BES schemes in 1999, and this raised £7.5 (€9.8) million for investing in hostels.

Many of the grants above are given on a pro rata basis, with the businesses providing 25 per cent to 75 per cent of the investment, and the remainder given in a grant for approved businesses. All of this investment ensures that many jobs are created in the construction industry and among those who provide services for this industry. The impact that all of this has had on the economy has been enormous. During the 1990s the Irish economy was transformed from one of high unemployment to one where there are now major shortages of staff in a range of industries. The £1(€1.25) billion investment in the tourism industry has helped create this transformation.

Regional case study: Ireland West

Ireland West includes the counties of Galway, Mayo and Roscommon. Access to the region is via Shannon and Knock airports, and the smaller Galway airport. It is quite a distance from the ferry ports. Access is poor for short break holidays during the shoulder and off peak season. Direct air services need to be improved if the west is going to benefit from growth in these types of holidays.

Tourism is important to the region with 1.2 million overseas tourists visiting in 1999, and many more domestic tourists. The numbers increased by 14 per cent since 1998. Revenue from tourism has grown steadily since 1987.

Ireland West is the third most important region in Ireland for tourism, and it has maintained this position since 1987. Spending by tourists in Ireland West has been broken down as follows:

Table 5.5: Tourism revenue earned in Ireland West Figures courtesy of Ireland West Tourism			
1987	1990	1995	1999
£117	£217.4	£286	£408.9
€146 million	€272 million	€358 million	€510 million

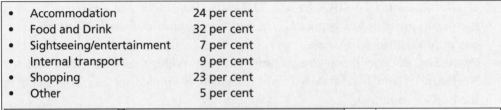

- Accommodation   24 per cent
- Food and Drink   32 per cent
- Sightseeing/entertainment 7 per cent
- Internal transport   9 per cent
- Shopping   23 per cent
- Other   5 per cent

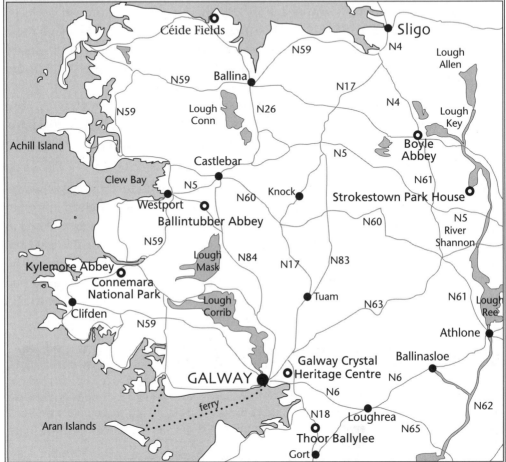

Fig. 5.2: Map of Ireland West

Investment during the period 1994-99 went to Co. Galway £23.6 (€29.6m); Co. Mayo £19.1 (€24.1m) and Co. Roscommon £8.5 (€10.7m). This money came from two sources. The European Regional Development Fund provided money for: improving hotels with leisure and conference centres, for sign posting at Gort Heritage Town, marketing support for the Galway Oyster Festival, the Suck Walking Route, new aircraft for Aer Árann, restoration of gardens, a ferry service to Clare Island, new tourist information offices in Westport, Clifden and Boyle.

The Agri-tourism schemes gave smaller amounts of money: Galway £567,315 (€717,315), Mayo £695,931 (€875,900), and Roscommon £275,076 (€345,076). This money was invested in smaller businesses like riding centres, self-catering accommodation, small heritage centres and angling facilities. There has been rapid growth of accommodation in coastal resorts in Co. Mayo and Co. Galway especially in the self-catering area. Much of this has been part-financed by the urban renewal schemes that have operated in seaside resorts. More accommodation has meant greater competition for some providers.

Ireland West has twenty tourist information offices, many of which only operate during the high season. Financing for Ireland West comes from four sources. The Bord Fáilte grant provides 15.6 per cent; local authorities provide 9.1 per cent; membership fees 9.1 per cent and commercial sales 66.2 per cent. Tourism is more important in Galway and Mayo than in Roscommon. There are 1,842 members of Ireland West; they are the owners of hotels, guesthouses, camping and caravan parks, tourist attractions, restaurants, language schools, craft shops and others who are involved in the tourism industry. The tourist information offices generate business worth €2.5 million in the sale of brochures, crafts and accommodation bookings. Ireland West is involved with local tourism interests in promoting the region as an attractive tourist destination for both domestic and overseas tourists. These initiatives are with product marketing groups for activities such as coarse and game angling or walking holidays, and with large groups like Shannon Development, Aer Rianta Shannon, Mayo Naturally, and Galway Tourism 2000. There has been an increase in the number of tour operators distributing Ireland West holidays.

REVISION EXERCISES

1. What nationalities spend the most money on holidays?
2. Give five reasons why the Irish tourism industry grew in the 1990s.
3. Where do most of Ireland's tourists come from?
4. Which is Ireland's largest market?
5. Who spends the most money when they are on holidays in Ireland?
6. How is income generated within the industry?
7. Which are the top three tourism regions in Ireland?
8. What is the tourism income multiplier?
9. What kind of taxes do tourists pay in Ireland, and how much is such tax worth?
10. How many people are employed in the industry, and which are the most important sectors?
11. What employment problems exist in the tourism industry?
12. How does the tourism industry influence the balance of payments?
13. What are the main sources of money for investment in the tourism industry?
14. How valuable is the tourism industry to Ireland West?

Assignment

1. Discuss the proposition that tourism is not a cost-effective industry from the point of view of Government investment.
2. Prepare a case study on the economic impact of a tourism incentive scheme in your area.

References and further reading

Bord Failte, Annual Report 1996, 1997, 1998, 1999, 2000. www.ireland.ie.

Bord Failte, Fact Sheet for the Regions 1998.

Central Statistics Office, Statistics on Tourism in Ireland.

Ireland West Annual Report 1999, 2000. www.westireland.travel.ie.

North West Tourism Annual Report 1999, 2000. www.northwestireland. travel.ie.

Dublin Tourism Annual Report 1999, 2000. www.visitdublin.com.

Midlands East Tourism Annual Report 1998, 2000. www.midlandseastireland. travel.ie.

South East Tourism Annual Report 1998, 2000. www.southeastireland.ie.

Shannon Development Annual Report 1999, 2000. www.shannon-dev.ie/tourism.

South West Tourism Annual Report 1998, 2000. www.cork-kerry.travel.ie.

Part 2
The Tourism
Industry

CHAPTER 6

The Hospitality Industry

In 1999 overseas tourists spent £2.5 (€3.2) billion in Ireland. Of this 24 per cent or £600 (€750) million was spent on accommodation and food, and a further 32 per cent or £800 (€1,000) million was spent on food and drink in non-residential outlets. This accounts for 56 per cent of the tourists spending in Ireland, and is therefore the most important sector of the tourism industry. Domestic tourists also contribute to these sectors of the tourism industry, as do locals using restaurants and bars.

ACCOMMODATION

The range of accommodation available to tourists is very wide, and includes:

- Commercial facilities: hotels, guesthouses, B&Bs, self-catering apartments and cottages, hostels, caravan parks
- Non-commercial facilities: house swaps, staying with friends and relatives, second homes, own mobiles or caravans.

Those who contribute most to the tourist industry use commercial accommodation facilities.

Accommodation is categorised into serviced and non-serviced accommodation:

- Serviced accommodation: hotels, guesthouses, B&Bs, farmhouses, some hostels
- Non-serviced accommodation: self-catering cottages and apartments, caravan and campsites, horse-drawn caravans and motor homes, mobile homes.

In 1998 overseas tourists stayed in a range of accommodation:

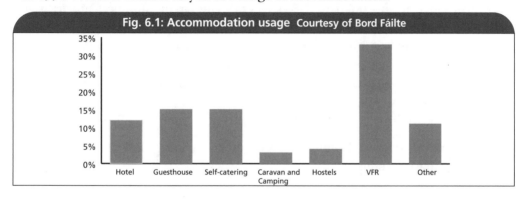

Fig. 6.1: Accommodation usage Courtesy of Bord Fáilte

The serviced sector of the business accounts for 35 per cent of tourist accommodation, the non-serviced sector 20 per cent, but the most popular accommodation is staying with friends and relations.

Accommodation is classified into the type provided, for example hotels, guesthouses. This was originally done in the 1940s on the basis of comfortable beds, hygiene standards, and good food, but now it also includes the facilities provided by the various establishments and the levels of service. There has been an increase in the capacity (rooms) in all categories in Dublin. Hotel rooms doubled between 1991 and 1998, from 4,500 to 9,000. Guesthouses and B&Bs increased from 1,300 to 2,450. Self-catering rooms increased from 260 in 1991, to 1,350 in 1997.

Hotels

All hotels in Ireland must be registered with Bord Fáilte, and are inspected and graded. This provision was introduced under the Tourist Traffic Act 1939. From an early date the inspectors were concerned with the levels of hygiene in hotels. Quality Services Ireland Ltd now carries this out for Bord Fáilte.

Hotels in Ireland are mainly owned by Irish people, and are mostly family run, but this is changing. Many international and Irish companies have recently opened large hotels. This expansion has taken place as a result of either buying or building new hotels, or franchising. Such companies are building new hotels, e.g. the Hilton Group built the Conrad Hotel and bought over the Stakis Hotel on the Grand Canal. Franchising is another way in which hotels are being developed; this involves the hotel owner paying royalties to the parent company in return for using the brand name and expertise. Hotels that have developed under franchises include Holiday Inns, and Quality Hotels. The merging of Jury's Hotels and the Doyle Hotel Group in 1998 created Ireland's largest hotel group, with a range of thirty hotels and inns in Ireland, the UK, and the USA. Many of the smaller family-run hotels still dominate rural Ireland, especially at seaside resorts and in smaller towns. The top Irish hotel groups are Jury's Doyle Group, which has over 2,500 bedrooms, Great Southern Hotels, Ryan Hotels and the Regency Hotel Group.

The typical tourist who stays in Irish hotels is on business (50 per cent), while a smaller number are on holidays (35 per cent). The largest numbers are Irish, followed by British and Americans. While British tourists have shorter stays in hotels (less than eight nights), American tourists stay longer (between six and fourteen nights). Hotel guests are usually adults, with few families staying. Most are from the managerial and professional classes (60 per cent), and there is a high percentage of repeat business, about 50 per cent.

There have been many changes in the hotel business since the late 1980s:

- The building of new hotels has resulted from increased demand and the growing tourism industry.

- Investment from the operational programmes allowed hotels to upgrade, for example increasing the number of bedrooms, adding leisure and conference facilities.
- There has been an inward movement of international hotel companies into Ireland; these include Granada who own the Forte hotels; Hilton Hotels, Holiday Inns, Choice Hotels Accor who own Ibis Hotels and the Four Seasons.
- Irish hotel companies have also been growing, both in Ireland and abroad, for example Ryan Hotels, GHS Hotels, Jury Doyle Group.
- Smaller independent hotels have tried to make themselves more competitive by joining consortia, so that they can compete on an equal footing, for example Best Western Hotels.
- In Dublin there was a major rise in the number of hotels between 1988 and 2000. The major area of growth was in three-star hotels and of the forty-three hotels in this grade in 2000 only fifteen existed in 1988. The number of four-star hotels doubled to twelve, while two-star hotels rose from seven to nineteen. Growth was smaller in the five stars (four new hotels) and there was a single one-star hotel. A number of hotels (twenty) opted out of grading for one reason or another, while some are still waiting to register or be graded. Other parts of the country have also seen a change in the number of hotels, but perhaps not as dramatic as Dublin.
- There has been growth in the number of economy hotels. These are medium in size, about 150 bedrooms. They charge a flat rate per room, rather than per person. Some are located on the edge of the city, such as the Ibis Hotel on the Naas Road. Others are close to the city but away from the main tourist areas, for example Jury's Custom House Inn or the Mespil Hotel on the Grand Canal. It is believed that this sector of the hotel industry will continue to expand until 2003.

The number of people using hotels has been rising, up 14.4 per cent between 1997 and 1998. At the same time the number of bedrooms have been rising too, from nearly 27,000 in 1997 to nearly 30,500 in 1998. This has meant that room-occupancy levels have been falling, from 65 per cent to 63 per cent. This could be a sign that hotel investment in the future will slow down as supply begins to outstrip demand. Hotels will now need to be more careful with their marketing.

Grading of hotels was introduced in the 1940s. The Irish Hotels Federation (IHF) and Bord Fáilte developed the present system of grading, and a star system was adopted. There are five grades:

1. ***** Five-star hotels. These are the most luxurious hotels in Ireland. Their standards are of the highest. They are located in many different types of buildings, from modern city hotels to elegant castles, and include many country

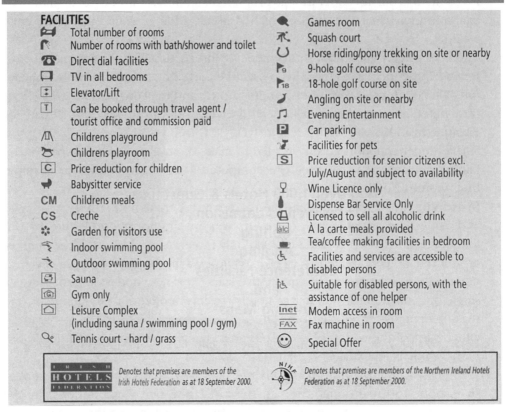

FACILITIES

⋈	Total number of rooms
↖	Number of rooms with bath/shower and toilet
☎	Direct dial facilities
▢	TV in all bedrooms
⬍	Elevator/Lift
T	Can be booked through travel agent / tourist office and commission paid
⌂	Childrens playground
⌣	Childrens playroom
C	Price reduction for children
↩	Babysitter service
CM	Childrens meals
CS	Creche
✿	Garden for visitors use
⤳	Indoor swimming pool
⤳	Outdoor swimming pool
S	Sauna
🏋	Gym only
⌂	Leisure Complex (including sauna / swimming pool / gym)
℺	Tennis court - hard / grass
⛳	Games room
⚔	Squash court
∪	Horse riding/pony trekking on site or nearby
⛳9	9-hole golf course on site
⛳18	18-hole golf course on site
♪	Angling on site or nearby
♫	Evening Entertainment
P	Car parking
🐾	Facilities for pets
S	Price reduction for senior citizens excl. July/August and subject to availability
⚲	Wine Licence only
♦	Dispense Bar Service Only
⚐	Licensed to sell all alcoholic drink
alc	À la carte meals provided
▬	Tea/coffee making facilities in bedroom
♿	Facilities and services are accessible to disabled persons
♿	Suitable for disabled persons, with the assistance of one helper
Inet	Modem access in room
FAX	Fax machine in room
☺	Special Offer

HOTELS Denotes that premises are members of the Irish Hotels Federation as at 18 September 2000.

NIHF Denotes that premises are members of the Northern Ireland Hotels Federation as at 18 September 2000.

Fig. 6.2: Facilities in Irish hotels Courtesy IHF *Be Our Guest*

clubs. Both holiday-makers and business people stay in these internationally renowned hotels. They have excellent restaurants offering a range of à la carte or table d'hôte menus for both dinner and lunch. They provide a warm, friendly welcome and personalised service. Most have a range of leisure facilities, golf clubs and golf courses to entertain their clients. Examples of five-star hotels are: Ashford Castle, Cong, Co. Mayo; Kildare Hotel and Country Club, Straffan, Co. Kildare; Jury's Berkeley Court Hotel; the newly-opened Four Seasons in Ballsbridge, Dublin; and Park Hotel, Kenmare, Co. Kerry.

2. **** Four-star hotels. These include both period houses that exude charm and modern hotels furnished to a very high standard of comfort. They provide a range of bedrooms and suites for their guests and excellent restaurants, with both à la carte and table d'hôte menus available for lunch and dinner. Leisure and conference facilities are normally available for their clients. Examples of four-star hotels include: Slieve Russell Hotel, Golf and Country Club, Ballyconnell, Co. Cavan; Mount Juliet Estate, Thomastown, Co. Kilkenny; Dingle Skellig Hotel, Dingle, Co. Kerry; Killarney Great Southern Hotel, Killarney, Co. Kerry; Gresham Hotel, O'Connell Street, and Moran's Red Cow Hotel, Naas Road, Dublin.

3.   *** Three-star hotels. These include a wide range, from large modern hotels to smaller, independently-run family hotels. Guests are offered ensuite bathrooms with their comfortable bedrooms. The restaurants provide excellent surroundings and offer a range of good quality food on both à la carte and table d'hôte menus. These hotels provide a wide range of services. They appeal to tourists who want comfort but are looking for value for money. Examples of these hotels are widespread throughout Ireland, but some of the more well known include Jury's Inns, Gleneagles Hotel in Killarney, Co. Kerry, and theLimerick Ryan Hotel.

4.   ** Two-star hotels. These are smaller hotels that are often family run; they offer facilities that are comfortable. Most of their bedrooms have bathrooms ensuite. They provide full dining facilities, with good quality food at excellent value. These are located throughout the country, often in seaside resorts and in county towns.

5.   * One-star hotels. These again are small hotels, where the emphasis is on a warm welcome, coupled with all the services that are mandatory for a hotel to provide. Facilities are simple and to a satisfactory standard, with some bedrooms having ensuite facilities. These hotels provide the opportunity to have a relaxing,enjoyable stay in comfortable surroundings. The numbers of these hotels are declining, as hotels invest and refurbish their properties in order to upgrade them.

The distribution of these hotels varies from county to county. The following table shows a comparison of hotels at different grades in Galway and Dublin.

Table 6.1: Graded Hotels in Galway and Dublin Figures courtesy of Bord Fáilte					
	*****	****	***	**	*
Galway	1	11	26	17	1
Dublin	7	12	43	19	6

Hotels are also graded by private organisations like the AA (Automobile Association) and the RAC (Royal Automobile Club); they use the five-star system of grading. Often Irish hotels use this system along with the Bord Fáilte grading, and display both at their entrances.

Case study: Jury's Doyle Hotel Group

This group began as two separate hotel companies. Jury's Hotel was first located in Dame Street, in Dublin, in the nineteenth century, to accommodate business people. This hotel was finally closed in 1973, and Jury's bought out the interests of the Intercontinental Hotel in Ballsbridge Dublin, in Cork and in Limerick. The Doyle Hotel Group was founded in the 1960s, with the provision of modern hotels aimed at the middle market. Their hotels were first located on the main routes into Dublin. Later the hotels became larger and more upmarket. In 1990 the Doyle Group was twice the size of Jury's Hotels, but since then there has been little growth in the Group. At the same time Jury's Hotels grew, due to its becoming a publicly quoted company on the stock exchange. The extra funding allowed Jury's to expand. By 1998 Jury's had seventeen hotels and inns while Doyle's only had ten hotels. Much of the expansion by Jury's was in the budget end of the market, with the development of Jury's Inns in cities both in Ireland and Britain. The Doyle Group was offered for sale on the market, and other hotel companies apart from Jury's were looking at it.

It was possible for Jury's to purchase Doyle's without running into monopoly problems, because the 1990s was a period of expansion in the hotel industry, especially in Dublin. The purchase of Doyle's Hotels increased the number of hotels under Jury's control to twenty-nine by the end of 1998. Only twenty of these hotels are in Ireland. The Jury's Doyle Hotels range in quality, from the five-star Berkley Court and The Towers, right through all the grades to the three-star Jury's Inns. Their hotels are located in Ireland's major cities, the major UK cities and Washington DC in the USA.

The Jury's Doyle Group offer a range of packages to tourists, including weekend and midweek breaks, Golden Year getaway breaks, summer sensations in Jury's Inns, and Jury's Irish Cabaret breaks in Ballsbridge Dublin. Their hotels appeal to different markets; business people and celebrities stay in the five-star hotels, while tourists on package holidays, and independent travellers on budgets, stay in three-star hotels. Business people are catered for in their extensive conference facilities. Leisure facilities including gyms and swimming pools are provided at some of the hotels. Jury's Cabaret, which has been running since 1962, offers tourists the best of Irish traditional and contemporary comedy, music, and song and dance. This in particular appeals to American tourists.

The Jury's Doyle Group run a central reservation system for their customers, along with online booking on the internet. The size of the Group means that they are more competitive in the areas of marketing, bulk purchases, provision of training. None the less, the increased size of the Group has not meant that they have lost their personal attention to their guests.

Guesthouses and B&Bs

There have been major changes in the guesthouse and B&B sector since the 1980s. There has been a growth in the number of purpose-built guesthouses. These now provide many of the bedroom facilities that in the past were only associated with hotels. These guesthouses are more professionally run on a year-round basis, rather than being used to supplement an income during the summer months. Most of these new guesthouses have Bord Fáilte approval. They also market their guesthouses in the Bord Fáilte *Discover Ireland* brochure, and in the Irish Hotel Federation's guide *Be Our Guest*. B&Bs advertise in their association's guides.

The main attractions of guesthouses are their warm welcome, high standards, value for money, quality of home cooking, time to talk to guests, personal attention, friendliness, and advice on what to see and do in the local area. This appeals to many tourists who want to get to know the real Irish people as opposed to just those working in the tourism industry. One guesthouse owner in Co. Donegal is prepared to collect guests from Derry, help plan their visits around the area by offering advice on the best things to see and offer them drinks on their arrival. The owner's personal involvement in their holiday makes it special, and they in turn tell their friends about her guesthouse. Satisfied guests stay longer and return.

The larger guesthouses are professionally run as businesses, many providing similar facilities to hotels on their premises. While these larger guesthouses offer better quality accommodation in many cases, they may be lacking in the homely touch that many tourists are looking for. These guesthouses often provide tea-making facilities in the bedroom and a television; this may reduce the interaction between the guests and owners. It is important for owners of guesthouses to get this balance right. When they lose the personal touch, then they become more like hotels, and they lose the main advantage that guesthouses and B&Bs have over other types of accommodation.

Guesthouses are facing competition on price from budget hotels which offer all-in prices for rooms, and at the other end of the market from hostels which offer family rooms and single rooms. The main facility lacking in guesthouses is the provision of evening meals. This particularly affects those located in rural areas. To solve this problem B&Bs are being encouraged and trained to provide these facilities. One farmhouse B&B in West Cork provides both a high standard of accommodation and quality food. So successful has this B&B been that it is now recommended in *Bridgestone's 100 Best Places to Stay in Ireland*. Quality breakfasts and evening meals are provided for all the guests. A country house in Blarney, Co. Cork which provides accommodation to the American market, also offers evening meals in their attached restaurant so the guests now spend their evenings enjoying good food and drink. Most B&Bs lack bar facilities which many tourists demand; these tourists are now opting for cheaper hotels to fill their needs.

The types of tourists who stay in B&Bs are predominantly independent travellers. They stay in guesthouses because it brings them closer to the Irish people. They enjoy talking to their host to find out about the best things to see and do in the area. They enjoy the relaxed pace of life. Between 1994 and 1998 there was growth in the number of approved B&Bs and guesthouses in Ireland by 16 per cent to 4,689. There are many unapproved B&Bs around the country, particularly in scenic areas and in towns. B&Bs are most popular in the west of Ireland and the Cork–Kerry region. The numbers using guesthouses and B&Bs rose from over one million in 1994 to nearly one-and-a-half million in 1996; since then the numbers have fallen back slightly. The largest market is the UK, and this has been consistently rising, while the other markets have fallen.

Unapproved guesthouses are those that have not been inspected by any tourist body, either by Bord Fáilte in the past, the B&B Associations, and Quality Approved B&B. This means that standards can vary, although many which have been running for a long time provide a very good standard of service. Many which are not approved may not have ensuite bathrooms or extra toilets, and may not be able to afford to install these extra facilities, but they offer clean accommodation, good quality food and a friendly welcome. Some operate during the summer months only, so their short season makes providing extra facilities too expensive. The disadvantage of not being approved is that they are not included in any guides, and many tourists only stay in approved accommodation. Some of these unapproved B&Bs depend on local hotels recommending them, or on guests returning on repeat business. The Town and Country Homes Association has for many years lobbied the Department of Tourism to register, license and inspect all premises that offer accommodation, as in the North of Ireland, but this has not happened by February 2002.

Guesthouses are graded into four categories:

1. **** Four-star guesthouses. These are the best guesthouses in the country. Their bedrooms all have ensuite bathrooms, and they also supply some half suites. They provide room service. Full breakfast and dinner is available with the usual range of table d'hôte and à la carte menus. They also provide extra facilities like car-parking, baby-sitting services and newspapers.

2. *** Three-star guesthouses. All of these guesthouses offer ensuite bathroom facilities with their bedrooms. Some have restaurant facilities for dinner at night. They also have a television lounge for their guests to relax in. They will accept payment by credit cards or traveller's cheque, which is a great help to foreign tourists.

3. ** Two-star guesthouses. Only 50 per cent of their bedrooms have ensuite bathroom facilities. They provide a lounge for their guests to relax in, and some provide restaurant facilities.

4. * One-star guesthouses. These provide simple accommodation to a satisfactory level.

Guesthouses are usually in larger premises, either in Georgian, Victorian or modern buildings.

B&B accommodation is not graded but it is categorised into three areas:

1. Farmhouse accommodation. This is located in both old-style and modern farmhouses. These are working farms, with access being provided to guests to enjoy the life on Irish farms, to learn about Irish traditions of farming, and the slower pace of life that visitors find so attractive. Being in the Irish countryside allows the tourist the opportunity to relate to nature. Farmhouse accomm-

Fig. 6.3

BUNRATTY WOODS COUNTRY HOUSE

LOW ROAD, BUNRATTY,
CO. CLARE
TEL: 061-369689 FAX: 061-369454
EMAIL: bunratty@iol.ie

GUESTHOUSE ★★★ MAP 6 G 7

Bunratty Woods is a 3*** luxurious guesthouse situated in the old grounds of Bunratty Castle (2 mins drive) to Bunratty Castle and Folk Park and the renowned Durty Nellies pub. All rooms are en suite with DD phone, TV, tea/coffee making facilities and hair dryer. Magnificent mountain views. Bunratty Woods is furnished with style and taste of a bygone era - featuring items such as a settle bed and a famine pot and many, many other items from yesteryear.

WEB: www.iol.ie/~bunratty/

B&B from £22.50 to £25.00
€28.57 to €31.74

MAUREEN & PADDY O'DONOVAN
Owners

Diners

Mastercard

Visa

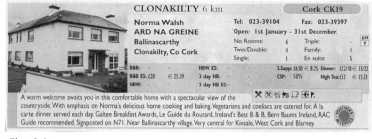

Fig. 6.4

Fig. 6.3: Extract from Town and Country House Association Courtesy IHF *Be Our Guest*
Fig. 6.4: Extract from the Irish Farmhouse Association

odation offers good wholesome food. The Irish Farmhouse Holidays Association inspects its members to ensure that the standard of accommodation is of the highest and they also produce their own brochure.

2. Town and country homes. These include a range of accommodation in the Irish countryside and in towns. Some of these are modern bungalows, while others are older period houses. They all provide a friendly atmosphere that is a home away from home. Dinner is often provided in these B&Bs. The Town and Country Homes Association inspect their members, and provide them with the Bord Fáilte Green Shamrock approval. They also advertise their premises in the Town and Country Homes brochure that promises the personal touch.

3. Specialist accommodation. Includes accommodation in activity centres, in local homes (for example for language students), and in pubs.

In 1999 a marketing initiative was set up to help with the promotion of B&Bs in Ireland. It was to operate at three levels.

1. To help individual B&Bs to promote their business. The emphasis here was, firstly, to provide their present guests with a very comfortable stay, and in this way encourage these guests to return to the B&B in the future. Secondly, the owner could later send the guest a reminder of the B&B (such as a Christmas card or calendar) so they perhaps would book for the following year. Thirdly, to encourage B&Bs to link up with other local tourism providers, and to develop the tourism industry in the area.
2. To help the B&B representative associations, like the Town and Country Homes Association and the Irish Farmhouse Holidays Association, to market more effectively both at home and abroad. This involved producing brochures, being on the internet, attending trade fairs and workshops.
3. To make the travel trade more aware of the B&B accommodation market. This was done by developing a marketing plan, which involved:
- promoting low-season holidays on the UK and French market
- setting up a direct-mail campaign to the Italian, American and Australian markets
- increasing publicity for B&Bs by bringing over trade and travel writers
- increasing sponsorship by providing prizes for travel agents' education programmes
- carrying out market research on B&Bs among both consumers and the trade, so that the product can be improved for future needs.

There is an example of how this operates in Cashel, Co. Tipperary. Here a group of B&B providers (two farmhouses and two town and country homes) decided to come together, instead of competing against each other in a small market. They decided to work together to increase the market's size. They did this by producing their own brochure, and highlighting local facilities. They organised walking activities and set-dancing evenings. Brendan Tours, the US tour operator, decided to use these B&Bs as part of their 'Tour with a difference' which provides accommodation in farmhouses and country homes. The tourists enjoy Irish home cooking, their Irish evening of song and dance, and they feel that they experience the real Ireland. This small campaign has been so successful that many of the tourists return again and again.

Self-catering accommodation

Self-catering accommodation comes in many types in Ireland. It includes modern purpose-built cottages (first begun by Shannon Development), older thatched cottages, and apartments. Some of these provide accommodation all year round for tourists, while others, like student accommodation at the universities, are only available during the summer months, for example UCD Village in Dublin. Some of the newer cottage complexes have facilities like swimming pools and games rooms attached to provide entertainment for wet days, for example Quilty Cottages in Clare.

Many tourists opt for self-catering accommodation because it provides them with flexibility and good value for money. There has been major development in the provision of this type of accommodation since 1987. Between 1994 and 1998 there was a 22 per cent increase in its provision. Growth in usage of self-catering accommodation rose steadily, with over eight million nights stayed in self-catering accommodation. European and British tourists are the most frequent users of this kind of accommodation. The market is very seasonal, with holiday-makers mostly using it during the high season (63 per cent), and very low occupancy between October and March (8 per cent). Tourists who use this type of accommodation often have use of a car while holidaying in Ireland.

The Irish Cottage Holiday Homes Association represents thirty-eight self-catering providers. These are located all around Ireland, from inland locations on Lough Derg, to seaside resorts like Rosslare. They produce a brochure to market their members' accommodation, and also operate a central reservation office, and web site. The organisation was set up in 1984.

All self-catering accommodation is rated in four grades:

1. **** Four stars. These premises have a very high standard of comfort and fittings; two bathrooms are included and all beds are located in bedrooms, not sharing in the living room.
2. ***Three stars. These premises also provide a high standard of fittings and comfort in well-landscaped areas. Laundry facilities are provided locally.
3. **Two stars. These premises are comfortable, have well-equipped kitchens, and a good standard of fittings and furnishings.
4. *One star. These provide the minimum standard of facilities that Bord Fáilte requires for self-catering accommodation.

Hostels

Hostel accommodation is provided by two organisations in Ireland.

*   **An Óige** dates from 1931. It was set up to encourage walking holidays, and many of the hostels are located in Ireland's most scenic areas like Wicklow and Kerry. An Óige has thirty-four hostels located both in the major cities and in many isolated parts of the country. The hostels vary in size, from twenty-two beds in Ballinskellig's house to 200 in Killarney's. These hostels offer accommodation to groups, families and individuals. The facilities include family bedrooms, twin rooms with ensuite bathrooms and larger dormitories, self-catering kitchens and dining rooms. An Óige hostels are for the use of members, but membership is inexpensive (from €5), and allows members to access over 5,000 hostels worldwide. Strict regulations exist.

- **Independent Holiday Hostels of Ireland** is a more recent organisation. It was founded in the 1980s, and started to brand its hostels in 1993. It consists of 145 hostels located all over Ireland, and each is independently and often family run. Many of these developed to fill a gap in the market during the 1980s and 1990s, when there was little budget accommodation available. They are located in a range of buildings from monasteries to railway stations. They offer good value, hospitality and individuality. The facilities range from single ensuite rooms to dormitories. They cater for individuals, families and groups. They provide self-catering kitchens, or food in restaurants. There is no membership required, and from their beginning no curfews were imposed. They are located all over the country, with many in Dublin, Galway, Killarney and Cork; others are located throughout the countryside especially in the south west and west.

CO. CLARE		PHONE	FAX	OPEN	HIGH SEASON IR£	LOW SEASON IR£	No OF BEDS	No OF PRIVATE ROOMS	HIGH SEASON IR£	LOW SEASON IR£	NOTES
64 KILKEE HOSTEL O'CURRY ST, KILKEE	T	(065)56209		1/2-30/11 G	6.00	5.50	42				ceg
65 ABBEY TOURIST HOSTEL HARMONY ROW, ENNIS	T	(065)22620 (065)28974	21423	ALL YEAR	5.50	5.00	80	3	6.50	6.00	bcef
66 COROFIN VILLAGE HOSTEL MAIN ST, COROFIN	V	(065)37683	37239	ALL YEAR	6.00	6.00	30	3	7.50	7.50	bcdeghi
67 LAHINCH HOSTEL CHURCH ST, LAHINCH	V	(065)81040	81704	ALL YEAR	6.00	6.00	48	3	8.00	7.00	ce
68 LISCANNOR VILLAGE HOSTEL LISCANNOR	V	(065)81385	81417	ALL YEAR	5.50	5.50	76	4	7.00	7.00	cdg

Fig. 6.5: Independent hostels in Co. Clare

There has been a growth in the number of hostels in Ireland in the 1990s. In 1998 nearly 300,000 overseas tourists stayed in hostels. Europeans are the biggest market; they make up more than 50 per cent of the market. Usage of the hostels is all year round, with August being the busiest month. Hostels appeal mostly to those on budgets, and the young. Most of the tourists who use this type of accommodation are between 15 and 35 years of age, white-collar workers, and adults travelling alone or in groups (78 per cent). It is believed that many who use hostels today will develop into high-spending tourists in the future, for many of these young people are students. The most popular destinations are Dublin, the south west and west. Hostels tend to be used for long holidays rather than short breaks; most tourists spend at least a week on holidays in Ireland. Bord Fáilte or the NITB approve all hostels, but there is no grading system in place, so standards vary greatly. Some of the hostels are of a very high quality offering bedrooms with ensuite facilities, while some still offer dormitories and communal showers. Over time no doubt all of these standards will be improved.

Caravan and camping parks

There are over 110 caravan and camping parks located in Ireland, open to tourists who bring their own caravans and tents, or who wish to hire mobile homes. They range in size from small family-run sites, to large ones that offer a range of amenities which may include restaurants and shops on site. The Irish Caravan and Camping Council market these parks both at home and abroad through their brochure and internet site. There has been an increase in the number of caravan and camping parks in Ireland since 1990; this occurred in areas of the country that were not being served by this type of accommodation product. It is only since the opening of the Camac Valley Park in Clondalkin that a caravan and camping park adequately services Dublin.

Fig. 6.6: Lahinch Camping and Caravan Park Courtesy Caravan and Camping Parks

All caravan parks must be registered and graded by Bord Fáilte. The grading is as follows:

1. **** Four stars. These parks offer a wide range of facilities, and have high management standards, for example Lough Derg, Killaloe, Co. Clare.
2. *** Three stars. This is a well-managed site with a wide range of facilities, for example Barna, Galway.

3. ** Two stars. These parks have a limited range of facilities, for example Clonakilty, Co. Cork
4. * One star. These parks provide the minimum facilities acceptable for registration, for example Downings, Co. Donegal.

Caravan and camping holidays appeal to those on budgets. Ireland is a popular destination for British caravaners, and also appeals to European campers, including families. Irish weather is not always kind to campers and this can be a deterrent to overseas tourists.

There are also many mobile-home sites situated around the country. These provide a range of services for their residents, for example Jack's Hole, Brittas Bay, Co. Wicklow; Rosscarbery, Co. Cork.

Holiday centres, camps and villages

These have been popular both in the UK and on the Continent, with such companies as Butlins, Pontins, Centre Parcs and Club Med providing such holidays. In Ireland there is only one main centre and this caters predominantly for the domestic market. Holiday camps were very much aimed at the working classes in both the UK and Ireland, with the camps offering weekly holidays from Saturday to Saturday. Since 1980 the image of the holiday camp has altered to appeal to a wider audience; this included the name change from camp to centre. Accommodation was changed from chalets to self-catering apartments. Food was no longer provided in canteens, but self-catering restaurants offering a wide variety of food were set up. Money was also spent on upgrading swimming pools, leisure facilities and entertainment.

The main holiday centre is Trabolgan, Co. Cork. The Mosney holiday centre was the oldest in Ireland; it provided all-in entertainment at a low price in chalet accommodation but it is now closed to provide accommodation for refugees. Trabolgan on the other hand was originally set up by a Dutch pensions scheme, but is now run by Pontins. The Holiday Village is located in a 140-acre estate, and its main attraction is its indoor sub-tropical swimming pool, which makes waves and has a large waterslide. The bar offers entertainment at night. Customers have the option of self-catering or restaurant facilities. Other facilities include tennis courts, a golf course and an indoor sports complex for a variety of games. Accommodation is in modern bungalows or houses, or it is possible to bring touring caravans. All the facilities are available to guests who pay on a self-catering basis. The season is from March to November.

Other types of accommodation include adventure holiday centres, sailing schools, hire of cruisers on the inland waterways, health farms.

CATERING

The catering industry is divided into different sectors. Some of these are very important to the tourist industry, while others are not.

Hotels and restaurants. A wide range of hotels and restaurants provide food for their clients. **Five-star hotels and top-class restaurants** provide top quality food, with good service, in a suitable ambience. These restaurants are among the most expensive in the country. They are located throughout the country, and are often frequented by business clients. The best of these restaurants have been recognised by the Michelin Guide, and Egon Ronay. Patrick Guilbaud's in Dublin is one of the holders of a Michelin 1*, among the best restaurants in the world. There are many middle of the road restaurants, where prices are more modest, and yet the food is of good quality. Gallagher's Boxty Restaurant is one of the middle-range restaurants found in the Temple Bar area of Dublin. Some smaller hotels and restaurants offer good value table d'hôte menus or carvery during lunchtime; this is popular among tourists.

Ethnic restaurants offer food from a particular country, for example Indian, Chinese, Italian. As Ireland has become cosmopolitan these are increasingly found in larger towns and cities. **Speciality restaurants** serve one main type of food like fish or steak. Seafood is very popular with European tourists, many of whom find it both difficult and expensive to buy fish at home. All these restaurants serve lunches and dinners in the evening. The quality of service and food is usually very good. Some provide special tourist menus at a lower price than usual. **Self-service restaurants** are often located in large department stores, for example Clery's restaurant in Dublin, and provide snacks and lunches during the daytime. These are a cheap way for tourists to have a satisfying meal during the day. **Cafés** operate during the day, providing snacks and lunches. These are cheaper than restaurants, but then the quality of service is not the same. Bewley's are the most famous cafés in Dublin, and stay open until late in the night. **Fast-food restaurants** provide food quickly for the customer, and the emphasis is on serving the clients quickly and having a quick turnover of customers. Many fast-food outlets operate under franchise, where the franchiser looks after training staff, buying in bulk, advertising, etc., while the franchisee pays a royalty on each burger sold. The cost in these outlets is less than in restaurants, but many clients find that this type of food is not as satisfying as other kinds. The most well known are McDonald's and Supermacs. **Take-away**s provide cheap food but no place to eat on the premises. Some take-aways are also fast-food outlets or specialise in ethnic foods.

Transport catering. This is the provision of food by different types of transport. Food on some **airlines** is included in the airline ticket. The food is prepared at the airport, and is then stored in the aircraft, which has special ovens on board to heat it, but cold salads are often served to avoid this. First-class passengers are offered a menu with a selection of food, while economy travellers are given no choice. **Railways** provide snacks, and often long-distance trains also have dining cars. The food is prepared in kitchens attached to the dining cars. Food is usually expensive, often because it has a captive market. **Ships** provide a range of restaurants on board to serve different tastes and price ranges, from self-service restaurants to waiter-service restaurants of high quality. On ferry services passengers pay for food, while on cruises it is included in the ticket. All the food is prepared freshly in kitchens on the ships. **Motorways** often have service areas, which provide a range of restaurant facilities. These can include self-service restaurants, fast-food restaurants. Again, food tends to be more expensive at these restaurants than in nearby towns because competition is limited.

Others include **pubs, and outdoor catering**. There has been a major improvement in the provision of food in Irish **public houses** since the 1970s. There are three main types of foods served in public houses. The first is finger food, and this includes sandwiches; most pubs in Ireland serve these during the day. Second, proper meals that are served in the lounge during lunchtime, which can include salads, steak and chips etc. Some public houses operate a carvery during lunchtime. This requires a chef and a proper kitchen for the preparation of the food, but is an important part of many public houses' business. This is often a cheaper alternative to restaurants. The third, and best, area are restaurants attached to public houses. These are open during the day and in the evening, and they have both table d'hôte and à la carte menus. **Outdoor catering** means the provision of food at various types of events such as horse races, the national ploughing championship, concerts. The providers of this type of catering usually prepare the food and then bring it to the event. Food may also be prepared *in situ* if the facilities are available. These types of events usually attract large numbers of people, so there is much demand for food which must be provided quickly, but prices paid are often higher than in other locations.

Irish food does not have the same reputation worldwide as perhaps French cuisine, but the **quality of Irish food**, and in particular Irish seafood, is gaining recognition by travel writers and food experts. This is because of the increase in the standards of excellence of the ingredients used in Irish cooking. This quality can be experienced in the top restaurants and food festivals that exist around the country, for example Kinsale, Co. Cork.

Food attractions for tourists. A number of these have been developed. The first was the Bunratty Medieval Banquet, which was started by Shannon Development to attract American tourists to the Shannon region. These banquets provide food, drink and entertainment for an all-in price. The entertainment includes traditional Irish music. Banquets also take place at Knappogue and Dunguaire Castles. Jury's Hotel developed their Irish Cabaret over thirty years ago. This provides a first class dinner, with Irish entertainment provided by many of Ireland's top singers, dancers and comedians. This type of cabaret has been so successful that a number of venues around the country provide it. There are also a number of festivals based on Irish food; these include the Clarinbridge and the Galway Oyster Festivals, the Limerick Food Festival and the Gourmet Festival in Kinsale. These all occur during the shoulder season and emphasise the quality of Irish food.

Fig. 6.7: Medieval Banquet entertainers, Knappogue Castle

REVISION EXERCISES

1. Explain the difference between serviced and non-serviced accommodation.
2. Explain the terms categorisation and grading.
3. What changes have occurred since 1990 in the hotel industry in Ireland?
4. What type of overseas tourists stay in hotels?
5. Explain what a consortium is, and give an example of one that operates in Ireland.
6. Who grades hotels?
7. What are the main differences between five-star and three-star hotels?
8. Why do tourists prefer guesthouse and B&B accommodation to other types of accommodation?
9. What are the associations involved in the guesthouse B&B sectors? Explain the work of one of them.
10. Explain the difference between approved and unapproved guesthouses.

11. Describe the steps being used to promote the guesthouse and B&B sector to tourists.
12. Explain the grading system used for guesthouse accommodation.
13. What type of tourists like self-catering accommodation?
14. Why do tourists choose self-catering accommodation?
15. In what type of building is self-catering accommodation found?
16. Name two organisations providing hostel accommodation.
17. What type of tourists stay in hostel accommodation?
18. What is the attraction of caravan and camping holidays?
19. What is the difference between four-star and two-star caravan and camping parks?
20. Explain the different types of catering facilities available for tourists in Ireland.
21. Name tourist attractions in Ireland that are linked to food.

Assignment

1. Carry out a complete audit of the accommodation found in your area. Each category and grade should be investigated. Collect brochures from as many of these establishments as possible.
2. Visit hotels in your local area, so that you fully understand how grading systems work, i.e. facilities and standards for each grade.
3. Carry out research on the availability of catering facilities in your local area. This should be done under the following headings:

• Category of catering establishment
• Type and price range of food
• General market that the restaurant/catering business is aimed at.

4. Prepare a case study on either a food festival or a top-class restaurant in your region.

References and further reading

F. Corr, *Hotels in Ireland*. Jemma.
Irish Hotel Federation, Be Our Guest 2000, 2001.
Bord Failte, Spring and Summer 2000, 2001 Holiday Breaks.
Bord Failte, Guesthouses and B&B, Self-catering, Hotels, Hostels Fact Cards 1998.
Bord Failte, 'Link' Magazine.
Kinton, Ceserani and Foskett, *The Theory of Catering*. Hodder & Stoughton 1993.
www.irelandyha.org.

CHAPTER 7

Access Transport to Ireland

The development of the tourism industry has been tightly linked to the development of transport. This will be examined as we look at the various types of transport that are available to tourists travelling to Ireland.

Tourists can use transport in three different ways:

1. They may use it to travel to their destination. As Ireland is an island this means that they must use either air or sea transport to get here.

Figures for entry to Ireland by overseas tourists for 1998 indicate the methods of transport used:

Table 7.1: Transport used by overseas tourists 1998 Figures courtesy of Bord Fáilte	
Air Transport	67%
Sea Transport	29%
Road Transport via Northern Ireland	4%

2. Tourists may use transport to travel around a destination. A wide variety of transport can be used for this, but it normally includes rail transport, coaches, local buses, taxis, cars (including car hire) and bicycle hire. These are all available to tourists visiting Ireland.

3. Tourists may use transport as the central part of their holiday, for example going on a cruise or hiring a cabin cruiser on the Shannon. This type of holiday not only involves transport to travel to see places, but the transport will also provide accommodation, catering and entertainment. This includes holidays on cruise ships or the hiring of cabin cruisers on Ireland's inland waterways.

AIR TRANSPORT

Air transport has grown to become the most important form of travel for international tourism. This is because it offers fast, reliable service. With the development of large-capacity planes since 1970 and deregulation of the air transport industry, the real cost of air travel has been reduced and as a result air transport has grown to its present dominant position. Air transport will be looked at under the following headings: (a) The different types of air services. (b) Changes that have occurred in the airline business since 1970. (c) Ireland's air transport industry. (d) Irish airports and Aer Rianta.

Air Services

There are three types of air services available in Ireland:

1. Scheduled Services

These are usually offered by national flag carriers, like Aer Lingus or British Airways, private companies like Ryanair or Virgin, and small companies like Aer Árann Express. Scheduled flights run to published timetables and on particular routes. The Department of Public Enterprise awards licences for these routes. They run regardless of the numbers of passengers that are actually on the flight; because of this the airline company tries to recoup its costs by charging prices that can be higher than those on unscheduled flights. The break-even point is a load factor of 60 per cent approximately.

Airlines that provide these services also sell them directly to their customers, which involves them having company offices, to market and advertise. Many also sell their tickets through travel agents and some sell on the internet. Competition from unscheduled services forced these airlines to introduce Advance Purchase Excursion (APEX) tickets, which allows the consumer to buy cheaper, or specially-priced tickets in advance of the flight; but all these tickets have conditions attached. This type of regular scheduled service is very important to business people who require a reliable service regardless of cost.

2. Unscheduled Services

These are also known as chartered flights. They are offered by subsidiaries of large national airline companies, for example Condor, which is owned by Lufthansa, and by companies that operate only in the charter business like Air 2000. Chartered flights do not operate to any published timetables, so a flight can be organised or cancelled at will. They are often organised by tour operators, who hire or charter a plane to bring a group of tourists to a particular destination on an organised package tour. If they are unable to fill the plane, then it will be cancelled, and instead passengers are put on a different flight. Charter flights usually work on a passenger load factor of over 90 per cent. Such a high load factor means that charter seats can be offered at a cheaper rate than most scheduled flights. Charter flights occur mainly in the summer high season and often during the night. The introduction of APEX tickets by scheduled operators and the liberalisation of air services in Europe in the last ten years means that many charter companies have come under financial pressure. Charter companies do not sell to the public; instead they sell to tour operators who do all the advertising and marketing, and they do not own public offices in city centres; all of this ensures that their overheads are kept to a minimum. Charter companies often charter their planes to other airlines during busy times of the year; when this occurs, the planes appear to represent the company that is doing the hiring, same colours, logos. The uncertainty of flights means that many chartered flights only appeal to holiday-makers who will take a charter flight in order to save money.

3. Air taxis

These are privately chartered aircraft and helicopters. The size of the aircraft can vary from holding four to eighteen passengers. These planes are usually small and they can be used to get to small airfields that are perhaps close to a business. The range of these aeroplanes is usually 300 to 900 miles, which means that they are ideal for short hops. The hirer will decide on the destination, timing of flights, etc. The companies that provide such a service include WestAir Aviation and European Corporate Air. Irish Helicopters and Celtic Helicopters also provide a similar service. Business people, film industry and racehorse people use such a service when they want to get to a destination quickly, which perhaps is not close to a large international airport. This is an expensive way of travelling but it is an area of the market that expands in a booming economy.

Case study: European Corporate Air

European Corporate Air is a newly-established company (1998) that provides private jets for business people for £2,500 (€3,150) per hour. The aircraft carries up to eight passengers. The benefits of such a service are privacy, flexibility and speed. The jet will get a passenger from Dublin to a small airfield close to London in forty-five minutes and a car can then take the person from the aircraft straight to a meeting, cutting out the many delays that occur when using a scheduled flight. It is also very useful for getting business people to destinations on the Continent that would perhaps involve two connecting flights, for example Dublin to Bordeaux. The company's business is growing and it is expecting to become profitable by 2001.

Changes in the airline industry 1970-2000

1. Regulation of the airline industry

International air transport was heavily controlled from its early development. Regulation of the industry was when Governments decided on the following:

1. Who would receive the licences for scheduled routes
2. The fares that were charged on these routes

3. Whether routes would exist between countries and which cities flights would go to.

The International Air Transport Association (IATA) was also involved in the regulation of the airline industry. IATA was set up in Cuba in 1945. Its aim was to promote safe, regular and economical air transport. It held traffic conferences at which fares for passengers and cargo rates were decided. The first conference took place in Rio de Janeiro in 1947. Apart from fares, it also decided on baggage allowance, ticket design and rules for multi-sector trips. This led to 300 airlines accepting each others' tickets and debt settlement between airline companies was made through the IATA clearing house. In 1947 seventeen airlines used the clearing house to move US$26 million; in 1994 that figure had risen to US$22.8 billion. IATA is concerned with seven broad areas; these include safety, the environment, security, medical issues, legal issues, finance and accounting, and the standardisation of fares and documents.

Improvements in the standards of aeroplanes between 1945 and 1970, including the introduction of jet engines and wide-bodied planes such as the Jumbo, made air transport more attractive to tourists. They could now get to their destination faster and cheaper. Competition began in the 1960s between chartered flights and scheduled flights. The US Government first allowed charter services to operate in 1962 and by 1974 one third of all air traffic from the USA to Europe was on chartered flights. Airfares in the US and the allocation of routes were all the responsibility of the Civil Aeronautics Board. Their job was to give Americans access to airlines at a fair price. They also controlled the airlines, so that carriers could not enter new routes or leave old ones quickly; they also could not expand too quickly. During these years the US Government exempted IATA traffic conferences and airline companies from the Anti Trust Law, but this ended in 1978.

2. Deregulation of the industry

This ending of control of the airline industry came about when the US Government introduced the Airline Deregulation Act 1978. This act only applied to USA flights, both domestic and international, but because of the important role of the American airline business it impacted around the world. Under the Deregulation Act, between 1978 and 1983 airlines were able to decide on their fares within a 'zone of reasonableness'; after 1983 they could set any fare they wished; there was no control other than market forces. The airline industry in the US was characterised by increased competition that led to a fall in the price of airfares. This boosted demand for air travel. New airlines came into the business, but many were economically unsound, tried to expand too quickly and soon collapsed. Even older airlines like Pan American Airways failed to compete in the new market's environment. As prices fell, profits fell and costs had to be reduced which led to confrontations with unions. In many cases job specifications and pay were changed. Companies used new marketing ploys such as 'frequent flyers' to keep old trusted customers from moving to the opposition. Only the fittest companies survived and within ten years of deregulation being introduced, the airline industry changed completely. New airline companies dominated the American market, and they developed a system of flying called hub and spoke.

This is when smaller planes fly from regional airports to a large airport. The regional airports are called the spokes. At the large airport, the hub, bigger planes are used for international, transatlantic, or intercontinental flights. The aim of such a system is to cut down on costly flights between cities; but while it does this, it also creates problems of co-ordinating flights and congestion at airports. US airlines that use this system include Delta, which flies into Atlanta, and Continental, which flies to Newark and Houston. Many European airports are also hubs, for example Schipol airport in Amsterdam for KLM and Copenhagen airport for SAS.

After deregulation in the USA, European consumer groups and the EC commission wanted deregulation introduced into Europe. This was opposed by the airline business. Liberalisation was introduced in stages.

1. The **first Directive** was introduced in **1983** allowing access to routes between regional airports of member states for small aircraft.

2. The **second Directive** was introduced in **1988**. It allowed airlines to set their own fares without consulting anyone else. Market access was allowed to any airline on any route up to 60 per cent and it was easy to set up new routes. Even fifth-freedom rights were allowed, and Ireland was able to go above the 30 per cent level because of its position on the edge of Europe. The **fifth** freedom is the right to fly into the territory of the grantor state and take on or set down traffic to or from a third state. This right had been passed at the IATA Chicago Conference 1944. It allowed, for example, Aer Lingus to fly to Manchester, pick up passengers there and then fly on to Zurich; the same could be done on the return route.

Some of the European countries wanted to go further than this, particularly the UK, Belgium, Netherlands and Ireland. Bi-lateral agreements were signed in 1986, which allowed open route schedules between the UK and Ireland. Any number of airlines could fly on these routes and fares were not controlled (within reason: predatory pricing was not allowed). Fifth-freedom rights were allowed to Irish airlines and Concorde. Aer Lingus set up flights to Zurich via Manchester, and Concorde used Shannon on its way to the Caribbean.

3. In January **1993** a **third Directive** came into force. This opened up access to EU air routes, fares could be set at any level and fifth-freedom rights were granted to EU airlines. This was very similar to the rights that had been agreed between Ireland and the UK in 1988.

4. In April **1997 cabotage rights** were given to all EU members. Cabotage is the carriage on routes within the territory of a country; after this the EU was seen as one country. Liberalisation was completed in Europe.

The effect of this was that airfares dropped, leading to an increase in passenger numbers. New companies were formed to provide these new services, but many did not last very long. Liberalisation caused congestion at European airports This forced some of the new airline companies to use secondary airports, for example Ryanair use Beauvais for Paris-bound passengers. The new operators, mainly low-cost airlines, increased their market share and it has meant that the national carriers lost out; most now have fewer than 70 per cent on EU routes. The national carriers face little competition on long-haul routes. European skies are still overcrowded, particularly those at London, Frankfurt and Düsseldorf. Many airports force aeroplanes to stack above them, increasing costs for fuel; there are also departure delays at airports, forcing some airlines to use alternative airports. Larger aircraft may solve some of these problems. The development of the Channel Tunnel and fast trains may reduce demand for short-haul flights, particularly in areas close to Paris, Brussels, and Cologne.

After deregulation IATA divided into a two-tier system:

1. A trade association, which looked after technical, legal, financial, traffic services and agency matters
2. Tariff co-ordination, which still deals with fares, cargo rates and agents' commission.

Only countries that have opted for deregulation are now members of the trade association.

3. The growth of strategic alliances

The 1990s was a period of recession for the airline industry; this was caused by lower profits from intense competition in the 1980s. Rising oil prices also affected economies and recession in the UK and USA caused a down-turn in demand. The long-term answers to these problems were the development of alliances between different airline companies.

The two main strategic alliances formed since 1999 are: the Star Alliance and the Oneworld Alliance. The membership of both of these alliances includes important European and American airlines.

The benefits of strategic alliances are as follows: (a) They can achieve economies of scale. As their costs are reduced they can then compete better in the international market. (b) Members are linked so that it is easier to transfer from the flight of one member to that of another. Passengers can transfer easily from short-haul to long-haul flights. Companies will also share member airlines' lounges and operational costs at airports. (c) Customers will be able to earn frequent-flyer points on one company and redeem it on another. (d) Finance for investing in the airline company is also possible either through access to private capital for development purposes, or through part privatisation of national airlines. Airlines were hoping that

Table 7.2: Air alliances Source: Irish Times 22 Sept 1998		
	ONE WORLD	**STAR ALLIANCE**
Total revenue	$42.3 billion	$45.7 billion
Annual passengers	174 million	184 million
Number of employees	215,000	230,000
Daily departures	6,200	6,692
Number of destinations	632	642
Countries served	138	108
Fleet	1,524	1,446
Cargo tonne per year	2.6 million	2.6 million
Year formed	Early 1999	1997
Members	American Airlines, British Airways, Canadian Airlines, Cathay Pacific, Qantas, Finnair, Iberia, LanChile and Aer Lingus	Lufthansa United Airlines, Thai, SAS, Air Canada and Varig (Brazil)

these alliances would bring security to their businesses in the years ahead.

Unfortunately recession in the USA in 2001, and a slow-down in economies worldwide, followed by the terrorist attack on the World Trade Centre in New York in September 2001 destroyed confidence in air travel. This caused a massive down-turn in numbers travelling, which resulted in companies taking drastic measures in order to remain in business. Strict new security measures were introduced for all air travel, resulting in higher costs for airlines, and increased check-in periods.

4. Low-cost airlines

There are a number of 'no frills low cost, point to point operations'. These include Ryanair and Virgin Express. They have developed both in North America and in Europe. The main thrust of these airlines is to provide cheap services between city-destinations. There are many differences between these and regular airline companies.

Low-cost airlines:

- Offer low fares on most of their seats
- Operate mainly out of secondary airports, which have excess capacity, so that there is less congestion, and this allows for a quick turn-round; airport charges are low, and this keeps costs down
- Run a standardised fleet which lowers maintenance costs and training
- Concentrate on leisure passengers and VFRs (visiting friends and relations)

- Pay lower travel-agent fees and encourage direct booking via the internet and telephone
- Are not members of alliances and do not operate frequent-flyer programmes.

National carriers on the other hand:

- Have a complex fares system, with business fares, economy fares and APEX fares on each flight
- Use the main airports, for example Heathrow, as passengers want to go to the main cities and business centres. Using hubs and integrated scheduling makes it easier for passengers to connect with other flights
- Operate a range of aircraft for different types of routes, although this is changing and most use airbus fleets
- Concentrate on high-yielding business-class passengers
- Use travel agents as an important distribution point for the sale of tickets. However national carriers are also developing direct sales
- Focus on alliances, code sharing. The airlines also operate a frequent-flyer programme, in order to keep the loyalty of business passengers. They also differentiate their product by assigning seats, providing meals and drinks. It is this that makes them different from other airlines.

As can be seen, the airline industry has gone through a number of major changes since 1970, and no doubt it will face further challenges in the future.

Irish airline companies

Ireland has two main airline companies: Aer Lingus and Ryanair. There are also a number of smaller companies such as Aer Árann. Both Aer Lingus and Ryanair serve the international market while Áer Arann serves the domestic market.

Case study: Aer Lingus

Aer Lingus was founded in April 1936 and was originally called Aer Loingeas meaning 'air fleet', but this was soon changed to Aer Lingus. Its first flight was to Bristol in May 1936 on the *Iolar* a de Havilland Dragon DH-84. During the Second World War Aer Lingus operated flights between Dublin and the UK. After the war flights were expanded to Paris, Amsterdam and Lourdes. In 1947 plans were made to open a transatlantic service and five Constellations were bought to provide this service. A change of Government led to a change of policy and the planes were sold to BOAC. Ten years later (April 1958) transatlantic flights began to New York and Boston, using Lockheed Super Constellations that were leased. Boeing jets were introduced into Aer Lingus in 1960. During the 1960s and 1970s Aer Lingus expanded its services throughout Britain, Europe and the USA. The transatlantic route always caused financial losses for Aer Lingus. Liberalisation of air travel increased competition for Aer Lingus and in order to compete successfully routes were reduced and aircraft were changed to those that would prove more cost-effective, for example the move from Boeing 747s, or 'Jumbos', to Airbus A330s on its transatlantic routes. They also use BAC 146-300 'Whisperjets' to domestic and UK regional airports.

The company faced major financial problems in the early 1990s. The air transport reported losses of £100 (€127) million over the three years 1989–92. These losses were reported on all routes. The Atlantic route had only 40 per cent of American tourists using direct flights to Ireland, while 60 per cent came to Ireland via UK airports. The introduction by Ryanair of a £58 (€73) fare between Dublin and Stansted in 1986 forced Aer Lingus to reduce its fares to remain competitive but it lost 10 per cent of market share and millions in revenue. Many of the aircraft needed replacing and this cost the company nearly £300 (€380) million. Borrowings were high which resulted in very high interest payments. At the same time as the core air transport was losing money, the ancillary businesses like CARA computers and the Copthorne hotel chain were in profit, and keeping the company afloat. In 1993 Aer Lingus was faced with options to save the company, these involved

- Winding down the air transport business with the loss of 4000 jobs
- The closure of the Atlantic business with the loss of 950 jobs
- The consolidation of the air transport business on both the Atlantic and European routes with the loss of 450 jobs.

The third option was accepted along with the disposal of the ancillary businesses including TEAM Aer Lingus. This became known as the Cahill Rescue Plan. The return to the core air transport business resulted in a return to profit by the end of 1994, but TEAM was still a problem. Along with the restructuring plan, the Government gave Aer Lingus £125 (€157) million; this reduced the company's debts. TEAM was eventually sold to the Danish company FLS Aerospace.

Since then the company has moved to being more competitive and providing a quality service for its passengers. In December 1999 Aer Lingus joined American Airlines, British Airways and six other airlines to become a member of the Oneworld Alliance. It has offered the benefits of membership of this alliance to its customers since 2000. Aer Lingus are hoping that such a 'massive global audience will reap benefits for Ireland beyond the normal tourism and commercial business markets'. It should also provide Aer Lingus with the opportunity for developing new customer bases around the world and boost tourist traffic into Ireland. Another change that Aer Lingus will be involved with is the privatisation of the company. Management in Aer Lingus feel that the flotation of the company will raise new capital for fleet investment and this will allow the company to develop and grow.

The 2001 season was not good for Aer Lingus; the poor performance of the US economy led to a decline in air traffic on the Atlantic routes. Industrial action, which included strike days, cost the company millions of pounds, and increased the wages bill by £20 (€25) million per annum. Foot-and-mouth disease caused the closure of many tourist attractions for three months, and resulted in a 20 per cent fall in bookings on the American market. The terrorist attacks in the USA in September resulted in cancellations, and a fall in future bookings. Faced with all these problems, and a fall in profits from £60 (€76) to £15 (€19) million, the company introduced major changes. These included a cut-back in operations by 25 per cent, closure of routes, for example Dublin to Washington, Newark, and Stockholm; and other routes have reduced numbers of flights. Seven aircraft were taken out of the fleet, and over 2,000 jobs were cut, costing €51 million in redundancy payments. The company also had to introduce improved security, which increased costs. The company also looked for the Irish Government and EU to help them to survive this period of uncertainty.

The following table shows the changes of fortune for Aer Lingus

Table 7.3: Aer Lingus Source: Business and Finance		
	Turnover	**Profit**	**Number of Employees**
1994	£1,480.50/€1,855m	£128.8/€161m	11,370
1995	£795.00/€1,005m	£17.80/€24m	10,102
1996	£765.00/€990m	£40.90/€51.20m	5,617
1997	£802.30/€1,002m	£48.00/€60.00m	5,090
1998	£901.00/€1,131m	£52.40/€64.00m	5,000

Aer Lingus has a range of aircraft including the Airbus A330-300, (315 passengers), and the Airbus A330-200 (275 passengers) which are used on the transatlantic routes. Smaller Boeing 737-400 and the Airbus A321 are used on UK and European routes.

Aer Lingus was a company that was successful during the 1990s after the Cahill plan was instigated. This can be seen in the above table. But events in September 2001 have forced the company to make many changes in its operations.

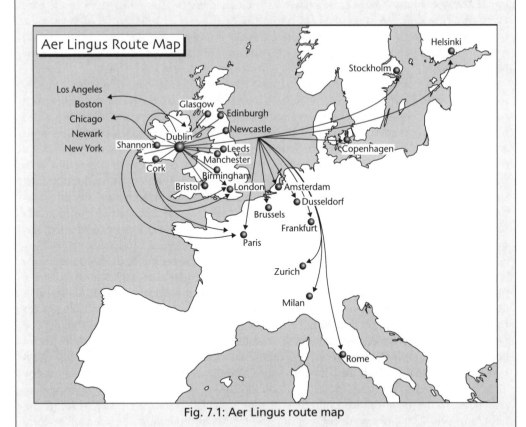

Fig. 7.1: Aer Lingus route map

Case study: Ryanair

Ryanair, which was a privately-owned Irish airline, started providing a scheduled air service in June 1985 in a fifteen-seater plane between Ireland and the UK. Within a year it was using a forty-four-seater on flights between Dublin and Luton; this flight offered an unrestricted fare of £94.99 (€116). All other fares were double this. Such competition was supported by the then Minister for Transport who wanted to increase competition between the airlines. Europe in the 1980s had very high airfares and liberalisation was only in its infancy. In 1987 Ryanair set up services from Knock and Cork to London. By 1990 it was providing services between Dublin, Cork and Knock to all major airports in the UK. The many Irish emigrants and their families who lived in the UK were using its services to the West of Ireland.

The advent of liberalisation in Europe allowed Ryanair to compete successfully first on the UK market and later to provide services within the UK. Ryanair offered fares on its UK routes that were half the price of their competitors. This encouraged the numbers flying on these routes to increase from 1.8 million in 1985 to 5.76 million in 1995. Many of these passengers were new to flying; lower airfares had tapped into a completely new market. In 1991 Ryanair started providing services to the newly-opened Stansted airport. It continued to provide more routes. In 1995 it started its first domestic UK service from London Stansted to Glasgow Prestwick. The numbers of passengers continued to grow. Ryanair increased its fleet by buying more B737s. In 1997 the company started to provide flights to the Continent from Ireland and the UK; Ryanair has made full use of its rights under the cabotage introduced in April 1997. Ryanair Direct was established in 1997 to allow potential customers to buy direct from the company, thereby cutting out the travel agents.

Ryanair has employed 200 people at its call centre and a further 1,100 staff work in the airline. In 1997 Ryanair was floated on the Stock Exchange and has now become a successful public company. The company adopted direct booking by means of the internet. In 1998 Ryanair launched six European routes from Stansted and these were further expanded in 1999. The company decided to operate from England because of landing charges at Dublin airport. The use of Stansted airport has increased the market potential of Ryanair for its flights. The success of the company has been due to its no-frills, low-cost policy. It also provides flights to smaller airports, for example Beauvais for Paris.

Table 7.4: Summary table of Ryanair results Source: Ryanair			
Year	Mar 31, 1998	Mar 31, 1999	% Increase
Passengers	3.9 million	4.9 million	24%
Operating Revenues	IR£182.6/€228 million	IR£232.9/€289million	28%
Adjusted Profits after tax	IR£ 37.7/€47million	IR£ 45.3/€56.8 million	20%
Basic EPS	23.55p	27.47p	17%

Ryanair has been very successful since 1998. It has developed 14 new European routes. It has taken delivery of 25 new aircraft and carried almost 5 million passengers on 27 international routes. It has increased its profits by 20 per cent. By 2000 it was the most profitable airline company in the world. Ryanair has been very successful finding its niche in the market place. Its expectation is that this growth will continue.

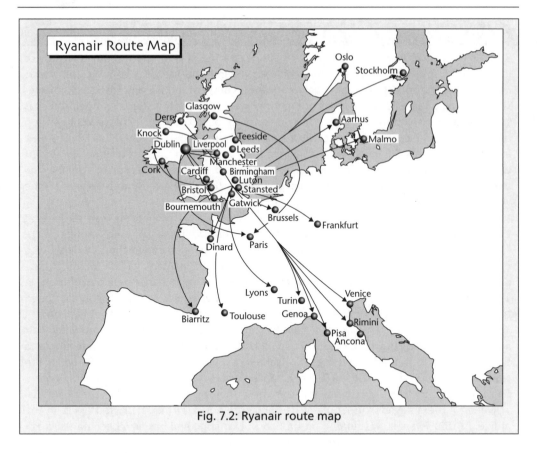

Fig. 7.2: Ryanair route map

Irish airports and Aer Rianta

Ireland has nine airports that provide scheduled services. The airports include the large international airports of Dublin, Shannon, Cork, and the smaller regional airports of Knock, Carrigfinn in Donegal, Kerry, Sligo, Galway, Waterford. Áer Arann uses the airfield at Connemara. The regional airports are privately owned, while the international airports are state owned through Aer Rianta. These airports have been helped with EU funding to allow balanced economic regional development in the country. Traffic through regional airports began in 1987 with 99,000 passengers and this rose due to liberalisation. Numbers have increased since then but growth has been uneven. Kerry and Knock are the most popular with over 200,000 passengers each; the remainder have less than 80,000.

The Government currently provides a large amount of funding for these airports in the form of:

- Capital grants for development work
- £300,000 (€375,000) per airport for marketing the airport
- £3 (€3.75) million to airlines to subsidise routes that are not viable; this is paid under the 'Public Service Obligation'.

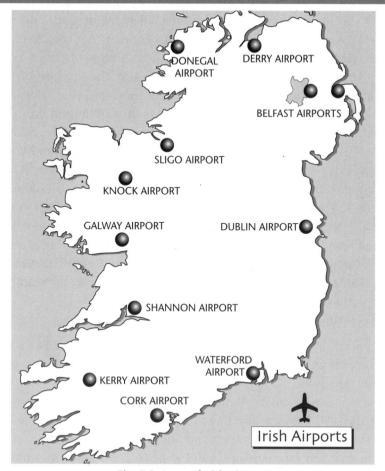

Fig. 7.3: Map of Irish airports

Both Galway and Kerry airports have development plans for their airports, with both expecting to spend about £5 (€6.25) million on upgrading their facilities. Some of the airports suffer from the problem of being situated very close to each other; for example Sligo is thirty-five miles from Knock, Galway is one hour away from Shannon and Donegal is very close to Derry City airport. The Government is encouraging the development of inward package holidays using the regional airports along with local accommodation and activities to provide short-break activity holidays.

Aer Rianta

Aer Rianta is a state company which first began operations in 1937. Its original task was to 'operate lines of aerial conveyances directly or by means of Aer Lingus Teoranta.' It was also charged with the development of aviation in general. In 1940 Aer Rianta, as part of Aer Lingus, took responsibility for the management of Dublin airport. The Air Companies Act 1966 separated Aer Lingus and Aer Rianta. In 1968, Aer Rianta took on responsibility for the management of Cork and Shannon airports. The 1998 Air Navigation and Transport Amendment Act transferred ownership of the three airports to Aer Rianta, which today owns, operates and develops Ireland's major airports at Dublin, Shannon and Cork. The company has been very forward-looking in its approach to business. The first duty-free shop in the world opened at Shannon in 1947 and Aer Rianta is now the fifth largest duty-free provider in the world. Its shops are located in Europe, North America, the Middle East and Asia as well as in Ireland. In the face of the abolition of duty free to EU destinations, Aer Rianta has now devised 'travel value' alongside its duty-free shops. In this way it hopes to minimise the effect of the loss of duty-free sales by continuing the sale of luxury goods VAT free. Aer Rianta has always been prepared to move with the times, investing in new infrastructure, developing new business and new markets. It took over the management of the Great Southern Hotels from CIÉ when they were facing a crisis and has successfully turned them around and expanded the group. Overall Aer Rianta has been a very successful company, being constantly in surplus, unlike many semi-state companies.

Today it faces new challenges:

- Developments in the airline industry, e.g. liberalisation, means that airlines are more competitive and therefore want to keep their costs down including airport costs. Air traffic has grown.
- The development of alliances means that airports are looking to become hubs because this will increase airport traffic; but this is a two-edged sword, because it also means increased congestion and the problems that brings.
- Emergence of low-fare carriers, who want to keep all costs down, including airport charges.
- There are pricing issues that need to be considered in the light of the abolition of intra-European duty free. Duty-free sales accounted for a large amount of Aer Rianta's revenue, £105 (€126.5) million in 1998, and 85 per cent of Irish passengers are on EU flights. At the same time airport charges have not been increased since 1987 and only account for 16 per cent of revenue. The Government has decided to establish a regulator to set airport charges for the future, a move strongly welcomed by Aer Rianta.
- Airport capacity and traffic growth means that there must be major investment in the airports to ensure that they are safe and secure for the travelling public.
- Privatisation of airports is now taking place on a worldwide scale and while only 5 per cent are now in private hands, it is expected that by 2010 most international airports will be privately owned. Aer Rianta believes in privatisation and has bought into two such airports at Birmingham and Düsseldorf. It also recommended to Government that there be partial flotation of the company on the equity market. Aer Rianta carries out a wide range of duties at the airport, these

include: (a) airport management, (b) airport security, (c) maintenance, (d) car parking, (e) catering.

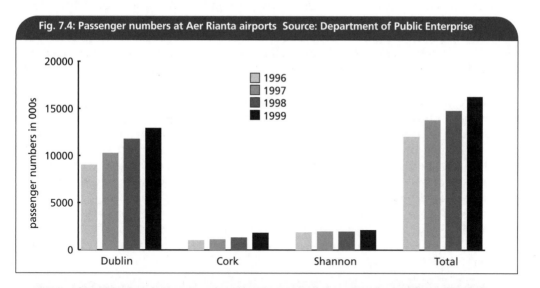

Fig. 7.4: Passenger numbers at Aer Rianta airports Source: Department of Public Enterprise

Case study: Dublin Airport

This is Ireland's most important airport, providing access to business and tourists from a wide range of countries on scheduled flights. During the summer these flights are supplemented by chartered flights.

Table 7.5: European airlines serving Dublin Source: Aer Rianta

European Scheduled Flights			
Cities	**Airline Company**	**Cities**	**Airline Company**
Amsterdam	Aer Lingus	Barcelona	Iberian Airways
Brussels/Charelroi	Ryanair	Brussels	Aer Lingus
Bucharest	Taarom	Budapest	Malev
Copenhagen	SAS/Aer Lingus	Dusseldorf	Aer Lingus
Frankfurt	Aer Lingus, Lufthansa	Geneva	KLM Alps
Helsinki	Finnair	Luxembourg	Luxair/CityFlyer
London City	City Jet, Jersey, Aer Lingus	London Gatwick	CityFlyer, Ryanair, Aer Lingus
London Heathrow	Aer Lingus, British Midlands	London Luton	Ryan Air
London Stansted	Ryanair	Madrid	Iberian Airways
Malaga	CityJet	Malta	Air Malta
Milan	Aer Lingus, Alitalia	Moscow	Aeroflot
Nice	BA	Paris/ Charles de Gaulle	Air France
Paris/Beauvais	Ryanair	Prague	Czech Airlines
Rome	Aer Lingus	Stockholm	Finnair / Aer Lingus
Vienna	Tyrolean Airways	Zurich	Aer lingus

Apart from these cities, a large number of UK provincial cities are also served. Aer Lingus, Delta, and Continental service six US cities. The result of all these available routes has been an increase in the number of passengers by 10 per cent to 13.8 million in 2000. The effect of this has been to make Dublin airport one of the fastest growing airports in the world. The Dublin-London route is the busiest international route in Europe. Increased access has led to the development of Dublin as a major centre for tourist activity. Within Europe Dublin airport is considered a secondary hub, on a par with such airports as Manchester or Athens.

The graph below shows the breakdown of passenger sources for Dublin airport. It also shows that each passenger type has grown consistently since 1997.

Dublin airport plays a major role in generating wealth nationally and in the region, particularly employment. Over 100 companies are located at the airport and the airport employs 60,000 people; that equates to 10 per cent of the jobs in Dublin city. The success of the airport has not happened by mere chance. It has evolved due to good planning, going back over forty years. The construction that is currently taking place in the airport was planned in the 1960s. Aer Rianta was planning Dublin airport for forty million passengers when it only had one million; this vision is one of the reasons why by 2001 it had 13.8 million passengers and the numbers were growing. Between 1998 and 2001 £275 (€350) million was invested in Dublin airport.

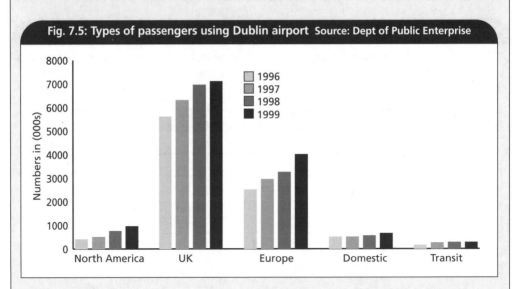

Fig. 7.5: Types of passengers using Dublin airport Source: Dept of Public Enterprise

The development of the airport is in four areas:
1. **The airfield**. At present this consists of three runways. The main runway is 10/28 (1989) and is on the southern edge of the airport. It is used by 85 per cent of the traffic. There are two smaller runways, a cross runway 18/34 which is used by smaller aircraft, and a small runway used by light aircraft. There are plans to build a runway parallel to 10/28 on the northern edge of the airport by 2010. In the 1990s there was large investment in the building of apron (aircraft parking space) and taxiways (these are to the airfield side of the terminal buildings). There is also land to the south and west, subject to the planning process, for future development as the need arises.

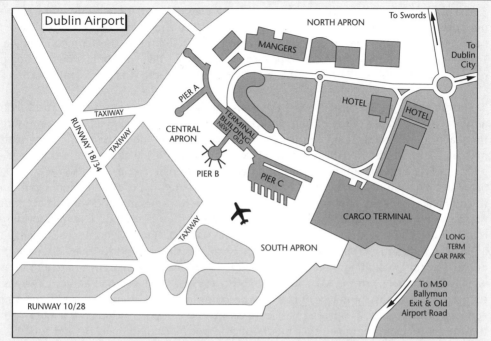

Fig. 7.6: Map of Dublin airport and its facilities

2. **Landside and terminal building.** The present terminal building was built in 1972 and, along with boarding area capacity, it is currently presently being doubled in size. In the arrivals hall passengers can get hire cars from five different car-hire firms and chauffeur-driven cars. There is also a tourist information office. The departure hall on the first floor has check-in areas for the various airline companies that provide services from Ireland, for example Aer Lingus, Ryanair, British Airways, Delta. Tour operators also have representatives at the airport to provide a service for their many package holiday-makers. There is also a bureau de change and a range of shops in this area. Beyond the departure gates are the duty-free and travel-save shops. The top floor of the airport is dedicated to a range of restaurants and bars. The extension to the terminal building will provide extra space for arriving and departing passengers, therefore easing the congestion that occurs at peak time in the airport. The terminal building will be able to cope with up to 40 million passengers annually. Three piers provide access to the aircraft, through air bridges, or just by walking to the planes. Pier A was built in 1962; this provides access to the 'no frills', low-cost airlines like Ryanair and Aer Lingus Commuter. This boarding-area zone accounted for just under half of the airport's departing-passenger business in 2000. Pier B was built in 1964; passengers who are flying out on full-service airlines such as Aer Lingus or Lufthansa use this boarding area and also Pier C. This accounted for the balance of the airport's passenger business in 2000. Pier C was built in 1998 to the south east of the Terminal. All of these can be extended as passenger numbers grow. Pier D has been approved for building as a boarding area for low cost flights; it will be completed during 2003. Other areas that face on to the airfield include the hangers at the north apron, and the cargo area near the south apron.

3. **The planned transport inter-modal centre**. This is planned for the site opposite the terminal building which are now the mult-storey and surface short-term car parks. The coach park is located at the rear of this area. Taxis and buses are outside the terminal building. The range of bus services has been improved greatly since 1999, with Dublin Bus providing direct links to many Dublin suburbs, Dart stations and mainline rail stations.

4. **Surface access to the airport**. Over the years this has been a major problem for Dublin airport. This is because of the mixing of airport and M1 Traffic at the main airport entrance roundabout. It is exacerbated by the fact that over the years there was such an emphasis on road transport and in particular private cars. This is due to the absence of a fully developed public transport system in the Dublin area. It is hoped that by 2003 some of these problems will have been alleviated, particularly by the extension of the M1 from Cloghran to Lissenhall east of the airport. This will greatly reduce the amount of non-airport M1 traffic now using the main airport entrance. The relevant authorities responsible for providing road infrastructure, Fingal County Council and the National Road Authority, have plans to improve significantly road access in the vicinity of the airport. This includes dispersal of demand by fully exploiting the existing three exits from the M50 adjacent to the airport as well as enhancement to the M1 and M50 motorways and the local road network. As passengers rise to almost 14 million it has now become viable and essential that the relevant agencies provide greatly improved public transport to the airport, including a rail link with the city centre connecting to other modes of transport, including mainline and suburban rail. There are also plans to connect light rail to the airport, as part of the proposed Metro and LUAS network in the city. In other airports in the UK and EU, conventional heavy rail (mainline/suburban) and light rail (Metro/LUAS) are seen as complementary services serving different markets.

The vision for Dublin airport in the future is to have an airport of world-class standards comparable to any international airport. Primarily due to the vision shown over forty years ago it has enormous potential to meet forecast growth. Given the major improvements now nearing completion and the longer-term plans in place, it will have excellent access and its infrastructure and facilities will be able to deal with 40 million passengers. This will ensure that Ireland and the Dublin region benefit from the significant social and economic benefits this will bring.

REVISION EXERCISES

1. List the main differences between scheduled and chartered flights.
2. What are the advantages and disadvantages of air taxis over other services?
3. Explain what regulation of the airline industry meant.
4. Why did the Americans introduce deregulation?
5. List the effects of deregulation in the USA.
6. Explain the steps in introducing liberalisation to Europe.
7. What were the effects of introducing liberalisation into Europe?
8. What major problem did liberalisation cause in Europe? How will this problem be overcome?
9. Why were strategic alliances developed?

10. What benefits does the alliance have for members?
11. Name the Irish airline companies that operate from Ireland.
12. List the markets from which Aer Lingus provides access to Ireland.
13. List the main challenges that have faced Aer Lingus since its foundation.
14. Explain the success of Ryanair.
15. Compare Aer Lingus and Ryanair under the headings of passengers carried, routes, and percentage growth, quality of service, airports used, and ownership.
16. Name the international and regional airports in Ireland.
17. Explain the types of services that Dublin airport provides.
18. Name the countries in Europe that still do not have direct access to Dublin.
19. Explain the duties of Aer Rianta.

ASSIGNMENT

1. Using the Internet, newspaper articles and Aer Lingus Company Reports, research the following on Aer Lingus: the company's turnover, profit, numbers of employees and routes serviced.
2. Using the Internet, source information on Ryanair and research the changes that have occurred in the company in the areas of turnover, profits, number of employees and routes serviced.

SEA TRANSPORT

There are three main types of sea transport.

1. Ocean liners. Until the 1950s these were important for travelling long distances, but after this they went into decline as air transport became more competitive. Shipping lines, including Cunard, P&O Ferries and Union Castle, all visited Cobh, Co. Cork. Today some of these ships, such as the *Queen Elizabeth II*, provide summer services between Southampton and New York and they call into Cóbh. The remainder of the year they operate as cruise ships.

2. Cruising offers tourists the ultimate in luxury holidays, with their every need looked after by caring crews. Cruises offer excellent food all day; facilities include pools, shops, casinos, bars and entertainment on an all-inclusive basis. A high proportion of those who go on cruises are repeat customers, who enjoy the luxury. Most customers are over forty-five. No cruises commence in Ireland, but some of Royal Caribbean's and Cunard's originate in the UK. Many cruise ships call into Cóbh, Dublin, Dun Laoghaire and Bangor, Co. Down. During 1999 twenty cruise ships called to Cóbh bringing over 20,000 high-spending tourists to the port. Dublin port is also a destination for cruise ships, with thirty-eight vessels visiting the port in 1998. It is of course an ideal stopping-off point for those who want to see one of the most popular city destinations in Europe. While larger cruise ships need to berth in the port itself, smaller cruise vessels can navigate to within five minutes' walk of Dublin's city centre.

3. Ferries. Sea transport is of great importance to the many tourists who wish to bring cars, caravans and camper-vans on holidays. It is also of importance to those passengers who may be making use of coach or rail transport. Both of these services are provided at all the ports. Ireland is well served by ports along the east coast. These link Ireland with Scotland, Wales, England and France. Travellers from further afield must first travel to ports before they can visit Ireland; for many tourists this may be a deterrent to visiting the country, for example Italians have to drive to northern France. The cost of travel to Ireland from the Continent, whether directly or indirectly (via England), is an expensive venture. A large range of ferry companies serve Ireland. Services have increased greatly since 1996 (as can be seen in the case studies of Irish Ferries).

The Republic of Ireland has four main ports: Dublin, Dun Laoghaire, Rosslare and Cork. Northern Ireland has two major ports: Larne and Belfast.

Rosslare was established in 1856 to provide services to Wales; this is often referred to as the southern corridor. Rosslare is a very busy port; 34 per cent of all ferry passengers coming to Ireland arrive in Rosslare, which is also used by 50 per cent of all car passengers; it also accounts for 15 per cent of all RoRo (Roll on, Roll

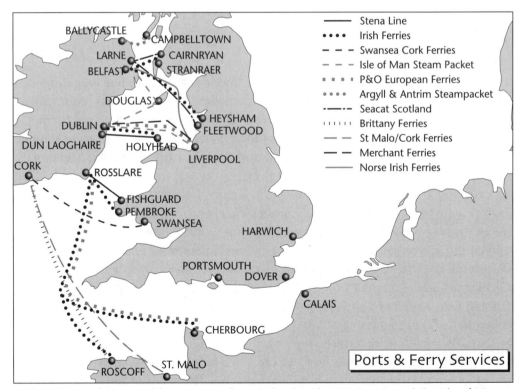

Fig.7.7 Map of ports and ferry services from Ireland to the UK, France and the Isle of Man

Table 7.6: Ferry companies providing services out of Rosslare Source: ferry companies			
Ferry Company	**Destination**	**Ships**	**Frequency**
Stena Line	Fishguard	Superferry *Konigin Beatrix* *Stena Lynx III*	2 daily 2 daily in winter 4 daily in summer
Irish Ferries	Pembroke	Cruise Ferry *Isle of Innisfree*	2 daily
Irish Ferries	Cherbourg Roscoff	Cruise Ferry *Normandy* Cruise Ferry *Normandy*	3 days a week None in low season 3 days a week instead of Cherbourg
P&O Ferries	Cherbourg	Ferry for freight and passengers summer	3 days a week

off) freight arrivals. In 1998 these translated into 1,469,000 passengers, 436,008 tourist cars, 5,993 coaches and 92,125 freight movements. The port has many advantages:

- It is the shortest route to the Continent.
- It offers congestion-free access, and is linked to national primary roads.
- Iarnród Éireann (which is the port authority) has made major investments.

All of this has resulted in the most modern port in these islands.

Dublin is the country's largest port and 40 per cent of Ireland's cargo passes through it. Six companies offer a range of services to the UK from here. The port is divided into three areas on the North Quay, with the Coastline container terminal, the Dublin Ferry Port terminal and the Marine terminal; the LoLo terminal is on the South Quay.

Dublin port faces a number of problems, the most important being traffic congestion. It is hoped that the development of the Port Tunnel will alleviate this. Another ongoing problem that the port faces is the silting which occurs on the main approach channel. This is caused by the deterioration of the two breakwaters – the North and South Walls. These are being refurbished with the aid of EU Interreg Funding; £60 (€75) million has been invested in the port in recent years and this has improved the facilities for its customers.

Table 7.6: Ferry companies providing services out of Dublin Source: ferry companies

Ferry Company	Destination	Ships	Frequency
Stena Line	Holyhead	Superferry *Challenger*	2 daily
Irish Ferries	Holyhead	Cruise Ferry *Isle of Inishmore* *Jonathan Swift*	2 daily 4 daily in summer
Merchant Ferries	Liverpool	*Dawn Merchant* *Brave Merchant*	2 daily 1 overnight
P&O	Liverpool	Ferry	6 days per week
Isle of Man Steam Packet	Douglas	Seacat	2 days a week winter
	Liverpool	Supercat	3 days a week summer Daily

Case study: Irish Ferries

Irish Ferries is one of the most modern ferry-company fleets in Europe. For the last three years it has been voted the Best Ferry Company by Irish travel agents. Its routes are on the Irish Sea to the UK and across to France. In 1968 a direct ferry commenced to France when Normandy Ferries provided a weekly service between Rosslare and Le Havre. Normandy Ferries stopped providing the service in 1971 and the Irish Government wanted to continue the service to the Continent. Irish Shipping joined forces with Swedish and Norwegian partners to re-open the Ireland-France service. In 1973 the *St Patrick II* was launched to service the Rosslare-Le Havre route and the Irish Continental Line was formed into a company. They started off with three return sailings weekly. They formed a subsidiary, called Freighters, to provide 'all-inclusive holidays'. In 1977 Irish Shipping bought out the Swedish and Norwegian interests and the service was increased by the purchase of a second ship, the *MV St Killian II*. Increased demand during the following year led to the operation of a daily service between April and October, and the commencement of a second route between Rosslare and Cherbourg.

A new company was formed in 1981 called Oceanbank Developments Ltd.; this was owned by both Irish Shipping (75 per cent) and AIB (25 per cent). They set up a subsidiary, Belfast Car Ferries, to operate a daily service between Belfast and Liverpool. In 1983 another route was opened during the peak summer months, linking Cork to Le Havre. In 1984 Irish Shipping was put into liquidation and out of the ashes of this receivership grew the Irish Continental Group (ICG), with Belfast Ferries providing the Belfast-Liverpool service and Irish Ferries the Ireland-France service. In 1989 they recorded a profit of £1.5 (€1,875) million, up 31 per cent. They also refurbished the two ships *St Patrick* and *St Killian*. In 1991 ICG bought B&I from the Irish Government. This made them Ireland's main passenger ferry company, providing services to the UK, France, Belgium and Holland. The larger ICG was divided into three divisions: Ferry Services; European Container Services; Dublin Ferryport

Terminals. A superferry, the *Isle of Innisfree,* serviced the Rosslare-Pembroke route. Later in 1994 it was put on the Dublin-Holyhead route reducing the crossing time to three-and-a-half hours, while the *Isle of Inishmore* operated the southern route.

In 1995 Irish Ferries introduced a new route, Rosslare-Roscoff, which takes fifteen hours. New superferries replaced the older ferries on the Irish Sea routes. While Irish Ferries were successful on the UK routes, they were less so on the French routes, and they decided to close them down during the winter months and to provide summer services only. This service was now provided every second day to France. In 1998 the *MV Normandy* was introduced on the Ireland-France route; the larger ship provided economies of scale. They now provided services to Cherbourg and Roscoff from Rosslare. In 1998 the high-speed ferry the *Jonathan Swift* commenced its service between Dublin and Holyhead.

Irish Ferries is a company that has been showing continuous growth in spite of competition from low-cost airlines, and from increased capacity by Stena Line and new ferry companies operating similar routes. Ireland's growing economy and tourism industry have created demand for this increased capacity. The company's accounts show the following:

Table 7.8: Growth of Irish Ferries Figures from Irish Ferries			
Year	Passengers carried	Car Capacity on Irish Sea	Car Capacity on French routes
1992	1,337,802	310	380
1996	1,383,839	850	380
1999	1,700,000	1,455	580

Irish Ferries is indeed a success story:
1. Passenger numbers using Irish Ferries have increased.
2. Turnover has grown annually by 18 per cent since 1995.
3. The fleet has grown. They now own the *Jonathan Swift*, the *Isle of Inishmore, Isle of Innisfree, Normandy*, the *Pride of Bilbao* and *Egnatia II*; the last two are chartered to other ferry companies.
4. Larger ferries allow increased capacity for freight, cars and passengers, and they offer economies of scale.
5. Profits have risen each year by £5 (€6.25) million, from £16 (€20) million in 1995 to £36 (€45) million in 1999.
6. Irish Ferries employed 1,372 in 1999, a rise of 271 on the previous year, nearly two-thirds of whom work at sea on ferry vessels.
7. Irish Ferries source most of their traffic on the Irish Sea routes from Ireland, while on the Continental route Irish people account for only 50 per cent of the passengers; the remainder are German (20 per cent), French (20 per cent), and Italians (10 per cent). Irish Ferries need to increase their share of the British market; they have tried to do this by offering special rates to groups like the UK Caravan Club.
8. The ending of duty free in 1999 posed problems for Irish Ferries, like others involved in the transport business. In 1998 £5 (€7.5) million profit was earned from duty-free sales; they now have to find some other way to increase their profits.
9. The Ferries division of ICG contributes 78 per cent to their profits and is a very important part of the company.

REVISION EXERCISES

1. Explain the main differences between ocean liners, cruises and ferries.
2. Name Ireland's four ports and the ferry companies that provide services to them.
3. How important are ferries to Ireland's tourism industry?
4. Explain why Irish Ferries is important to the Irish tourism industry.

Assignments

1. Visit either your local airport or port and discover the following: (a) Facilities available for customers. (b) Flights and airline companies or sailings and ferry companies that provide services. (c) What changes have they undergone in the last 5 years? (d) What are the benefits of this facility to tourism in your area?
2. Collect ferry brochures, look up the following information and write a report on: (a) Sailing times from your local port. (b) Tariffs charged by the various companies. (c) The facilities provided on the ship serving your port. (d) Why it is important to support Irish ferry companies.
3. Using the internet, source information on Aer Lingus and Ryanair and research the changes that have occurred to both of these companies, in the area of turnover, new routes, employment, profits.
4. Prepare a case study on either a charter airline company or Stena Line.

References and further reading:

Annual Report Aer Rianta 1998, 1999, 2000. www.aer-rianta.com.
www.dublin-airport.com.
Aer Rianta Future Strategic Direction 1998–2002.
Annual Report Aer Lingus 1998, 2000. www.aerlingus.com.
Annual Report and Accounts, Irish Continental Group plc 1999.
www.irishferries.ie.
www.ryanair.com.
Annual Report Stena Line AB 1998.

CHAPTER 8

Internal Transport in Ireland

When tourists arrive in Ireland, most want to travel beyond the city or port they have entered, so therefore make use of one of the types of transport that exist within Ireland. They have the option of using rail, coach, or road transport. Most tourists who come to Ireland make use of at least one of these. In 1999 internal transport accounted for 9 per cent of spending on holidays. (The spending by all markets is approximately the same, with only the UK market spending slightly less than any others.) This amounted to approximately £211 (€265) million in Ireland.

RAIL TRANSPORT

Rail transport first developed in Ireland in 1834 when the Dublin-Kingstown (Dun Laoghaire) line was built. The building of railway lines all over the country followed, until in 1921 there were 3,300 miles of track. This was the high point of the railways. By 1924 the twenty-six railway companies that operated in Ireland were running into financial difficulties. A Railway Act was introduced which joined all the small railway companies into one company, the Great Southern Railways Company (GSR). By 1944 GSR had still not made a profit; this prompted the formation of CIÉ (Córas Iompair Éireann), the nationalised railway system in Ireland. Financial problems persisted in the new CIÉ and branch lines were closed; at the same time the company invested in new diesel engines and carriages. These changes did not make any difference to the profitability of CIÉ. A further report in 1957 led to the closure of many railway lines, including some that could have aided tourism development, for example Waterford to Tramore, and the Hill of Howth tramway. These closures eventually led to CIÉ reaching a break-even point in 1962. In 1972 another report was carried out on CIÉ and management decided to invest in new tracks, signalling, etc. These improvements began in the 1970s. In 1984 the Dublin Area Rapid Transit (DART) was set up. This proved to be very important in providing public transport in Dublin, with over 80,000 people using it each day.

In 1987 CIÉ was divided into three sections: Iarnród Éireann, Bus Éireann, and Dublin Bus.

Iarnród Éireann is in charge of all trains in Ireland. It operates 1,900 km of railway for both passengers and freight. In 1999 earnings from passengers came to £83 (€104) million, and freight £20 (€25) million. It operates a number of passenger services; these include Inter-City services between Dublin and the following: Belfast, Rosslare Europort, Waterford, Cork, Tralee, Ennis, Limerick, Galway, Westport, Ballina, and Sligo. The main stations in Dublin are Heuston (for trains to the south and west) and Connolly (for trains along the east coast, and to the north west). There are also services from Rosslare to Limerick, Cork to Tralee, and Cork to Limerick. Trains have two classes, standard and super-standard, on these routes. The Dublin-Belfast route provides the 'Enterprise' service which is jointly run by Northern Ireland Railways and Iarnród Éireann, offering a fast service in luxury carriages. The track on this line has been upgraded, and the signalling improved. This train has been able to improve the numbers of passengers travelling on the route by 20 per cent. The CityGold service operates between Dublin and Cork, and is especially aimed at business people. The cost of travelling on the Inter-City services varies between £22 (€27.5) for a monthly return to Westport and £42 (€52.5) for a monthly return to Galway. There are special day-return tickets, student rates, family and rambler tickets.

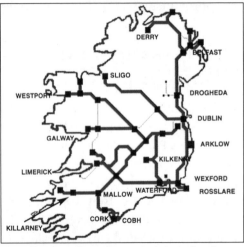

Fig. 8.1: The rail network in Ireland

Iarnród Éireann also provides other services such as 'Railbreaks', which are package holidays in Ireland that make use of trains and hotels. It is also possible to hire an executive train to hold a conference, or for a special occasion. Iarnród Éireann has a catering company which provides food on the trains, for its Restaurant na Mara in Dun Laoghaire (which has a very good reputation as a fish restaurant), and for a contract catering service.

Suburban rail services are very important to Iarnród Éireann because this is a growing market. The DART has recently been extended to Malahide and Greystones. There are also suburban services to Louth, Wicklow, Westmeath and Kildare. In 1999 20 million passenger journeys were made on the DART and suburban railways, and this is likely to continue to grow in the future.

During the 1980s there was little investment in the railways. Finally, in the late 1990s, it was realised that the railways were environmentally friendly, eased congestion, and were good for tourism, so, after years of neglect, money is now being invested in Iarnród Éireann. The programme known as Track2000 is investing £1 (€1.27) billion in the railways. This is being spent on:

- New locomotives, which are faster and reduce journey times
- New carriages, both for Dart and Inter-City trains
- Continuous welded rail tracks on some of the lines, and this will apply to all tracks by 2004
- The installation of a new centralised traffic computerised control system; this system will improve safety
- Extending DART and suburban trains to provide commuter services, and therefore ease the congestion on the roads in the greater Dublin area
- Investment in updating the Rosslare Europort.

Train transport in Europe has improved greatly since 1980. In France the TGV has transformed French travel, reducing travelling time between Paris and Lyon, and making it competitive with airlines. The Channel Tunnel, which was opened in 1994, has improved communication between France and Britain. It now takes only thirty minutes between Calais and Folkestone. The numbers using the Tunnel have increased annually, and this has caused major competition for the ferries serving the English Channel. Upgrading of the UK rail system will eventually lead to cities all over the UK being linked to European capitals via the Channel Tunnel. These cities include Glasgow, Manchester, and Swansea. SNCF (the French national railway company) expect that 90 per cent of travellers making two-hour journeys will travel by train, and that this will fall to 75 per cent for those making three-hour journeys. This is because of the comfort of travelling by the TGV and people will use the train instead of short-distance flights. Other countries have also improved their railway systems, for example Germany, Italy and Japan. Both Japan and Germany have developed magnetic levitation (MAGLEV) trains. This is the future of rail transport.

Old steam trains are popular with tourists. While there are over forty such trains in operation in the UK, only a few operate in Ireland, for example Shane's Castle, Co. Antrim, and the Tralee Blennerville line in Tralee. The latter was restored as a tourist attraction and it is about two miles in length. Stradbally, Co. Laois holds a festival each year to commemorate steam transport. Luxury trains, like the Orient Express, which provide luxurious travel reminiscent of the 1920s and 1930s, are very popular with tourists. Other luxurious trains operate in England, Scotland, and southern Spain. These appeal to the luxury end of the tourist market. There is a campaign to develop the old railway line between Ballina and Limerick, and to use it for transporting tourists through some of the most scenic areas of the west of Ireland.

COACH AND BUS TRANSPORT

Coaches are used by a variety of people, from students to the elderly. Coach companies provide four main types of services:

1. Expressway services between the main cities and towns within Ireland and internationally. This is usually the cheapest form of transport, and is an alternative to air or rail. The main providers of this service are Bus Éireann, and private companies, for example City Link, Kavanaghs.
2. Private hire by clubs, schools etc. for tours or transport to special events. Dublin Bus and many small bus companies provide this service. Some provide a regular school bus service, and during the summer months they will provide services to tourists.
3. Package tours by coach around Ireland or abroad. This is most popular among the over fifty-five age-group because of the cost, the door-to-door service between hotels which reduces the problems of baggage, and the tour guides to interpret foreign languages and deal with documentation. The major companies offering these kinds of tours in Ireland include CIÉ, PAB Travel, and the Paddywaggon, which specialises in tours for backpackers. Tour operators from abroad also bring large numbers of tourists to Ireland on these types of package tours. Some bring their own coaches, for example Wallace Arnold, while others use Irish coach companies to bring their groups around the country, for example Trafalgar. Coach companies that provide such a service include Cronin's, and Éirebus. The season for coach tours runs between March and October.
4. Transfers between airports and hotels for package tours. A large number of tourists come to Ireland on package tours. Aircoach has provided this service between the airport and hotels around Dublin since November 1999.

The coach business is highly regulated. The 1932 Transport Act controls who can provide bus services within Ireland. Licences must be obtained before services can be provided; the Department of Public Enterprise, Transport section, grants these. Coach companies must also have a transport operator's licence; for this they must have a qualified employee who holds a certificate of professional competence. They must abide by EU directives, such as 543/69, which limits the hours that a driver can drive. These are recorded on tachographs, which were introduced in order to improve safety standards and to reduce the number of accidents involving coaches, particularly on the continent. The safety record in Ireland for coaches is one of the best in Europe.

In the 1980s deregulation was introduced into the coach business in the UK. Deregulation increased demand for coach transport, but it also resulted in more coaches operating on the roads. This increased competition led to lower load factors, and lower profit margins. It resulted in three companies dominating long-distance travel: National Express, Stagecoach, and First Group. Wallace Arnold and Shearings dominate the package coaching business. It had been hoped that when the industry was deregulated there would be many small companies competing, but in fact the opposite occurred. Now instead of state-operated bus companies dominating the business, a small number of private companies do. Ireland is now in the process of deregulating its coach transport business. It must ensure that the best routes are not cherry-picked and that unprofitable routes are not under-serviced.

Irish coach companies have been advocating the introduction of deregulation in the coach business since the 1980s, but the Government, Bus Éireann and Dublin Bus have opposed this. It is only since November 1999 that the Government has been holding discussions on radically changing public transport in Ireland. Mindful of what occurred in Britain, they have been studying Scandinavian operations. In Scandinavia licences are granted to companies who must provide a certain level of service; where they fail to do so, they lose the licence. Both state and private companies receive subsidies for unprofitable routes. A regulatory body will be established in order to oversee the competition between private and public companies. So far deregulation of coach transport only applies to Dublin. In December 2000 it was decided to ask coach companies to provide bus services in the greater Dublin area. These services include feeder services to the DART, QBCs (quality bus corridors) and suburban train stations; dedicated services to business parks, park-and-ride sites, and Dublin airport; orbital routes around Dublin city and links from commuter towns to Dublin. Deregulation of regional transport is not now as advanced as in Dublin and perhaps will copy the Scandinavian model.

Over the years there have been many different organisations providing a national bus service in the country. In 1926 it was called the Irish Omnibus Company, in 1945 the Road Passengers Division of CIÉ, and in 1987 it split into Bus Éireann and Dublin Bus. In September 2000 these became two separate companies.

Bus Éireann provides a coach and bus service throughout the country. These services include:

- Expressway coach services that link all of Ireland's large towns and cities. They operate fifty routes, and work with Ulster Bus in Northern Ireland
- A coach service to the UK in conjunction with Eurolines/National Express
- Half-day and full-day coach tours from the main cities for tourists; for example, from Dublin to such destinations as Newgrange and Glendalough
- Short holiday breaks around Ireland
- City bus services in Cork, Galway, Waterford and Limerick
- Local bus services in the countryside
- Coach hire for groups, such as schools, clubs and societies
- The school transport scheme for the Department of Education.

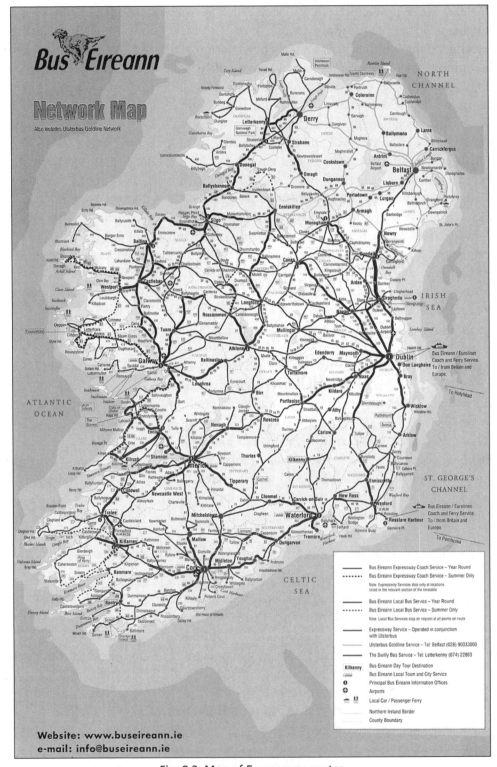

Fig. 8.2: Map of Expressway routes

Dublin Bus provides bus services in Dublin city and the surrounding areas. It operates 120 scheduled routes. There are a number of different types of bus services, for example: City Imp which is a minibus service; City Swift buses which operate on QBCs; Xpresso services which operate at peak time directly between the outer suburbs and the city centre; ordinary double- and single-decker buses; Nitelink services which operate between midnight and 4.30 a.m. on weekend nights on twenty routes that radiate from the city centre; Airlink routes which link the Airport with Bus Áras and the railway stations; private hire of buses for special outings – weddings, for instance; City Tours operating in open-top double-decker buses where the tourists get a guided tour through the city; and RaiLink which joins Heuston Station with Connolly Station and Tara Street Station.

Dublin Bus numbers have increased as a result of these new services. At the same time Government subsidies have fallen. Revenue has increased from £6,705,000 (€8,405,000) in 1987, to £10,253,000 (€12,753,000) in 1997. Ongoing improvements included the introduction of prepaid tickets, the development of QBCs and the purchase of new buses.

The Coach Tourism and Transport Council is the largest organisation of coach operators in Ireland with forty-four members. It represents their views to Bord Fáilte, the Department of Public Enterprise on issues affecting their members.

Case study: Cronin's Coaches

This company began in Cork in 1954 as a taxi service. In the 1960s it progressed to a minibus and provided transport for show bands, school runs, bingo, etc. It has now grown into one of the largest coach companies in Ireland, which it has achieved by developing services and moving into many different areas of the coach business:

- Between 1975 and 1995 it provided coaches for Funtrek Holidays. These holidays were aimed at the eighteen to thirty-five age-groups, and involved travelling by coach between cities and staying in tents. It was a very successful form of holiday. Eventually the life-cycle of this product ended, and the tour operator, Crossan Travel, decided to end them.
- A daily bus service was organised between Cork and Dublin during the 1980s. This service was provided under a permit from the Department of Transport and customers had to pre-purchase tickets.
- Today the coach company rents its buses to large travel companies like Trafalgar and Colette Tours and other tour operators. Trafalgar organise seven- and ten-day holidays around Ireland for English speaking tourists from New Zealand, Australia, Canada and the USA. The company provides the coach and the driver, with the coach in the colours of the tour company. The tour companies have their own representative who meets the tourists at their point of entry into the country. An average of ten coach tours operate each week between March and November.
- During the year Cronin's also provide coaches for clubs, school trips, associations, etc.

The drivers who work for Cronin's on organised coach holidays around Ireland may be seasonal drivers from March to November. After the tourist season is over the level of work usually drops dramatically, with only occasional day trips taking place. Many of the drivers find this work very demanding, and usually only do it for a couple of seasons.

The costs that face coach companies like Cronin's include: rising fuel costs, rising wages, the cost of leasing or buying coaches – new coaches cost approximately €310,500; insurance costs, as coaches must have unlimited indemnity insurance; buses must be of excellent quality and roadworthy, they have to pass a NCT test; drivers' hours are strictly controlled for safety reasons so that there must be two drivers if very long hours journeys are involved. These costs must be covered in the short season that the coach tour business operates (March–November). By leasing out coaches through their Dublin, Cork and New York offices to a variety of businesses, the company has continued to grow and be successful.

Fig. 8.3: Cronin's Coaches

CAR HIRE, AND OTHER FORMS OF ROAD TRANSPORT

There has been an increase in the use of motorcars since the 1950s and especially since the mid 1990s. Cars are popular because they offer great flexibility and freedom of movement. To meet the increase in the use of cars the tourist industry has provided new services; these include motorway restaurants, motels, car ferries, self-drive car package holidays that include a variety of accommodation, for example Eurocamps, and fly-drive holidays. On the Continent car owners can make use of the motor rail service, which allows them to travel hundreds of miles with their cars overnight on SNCF (the French railway).

Car numbers in Europe have been rising annually. Sales in Ireland have risen by 20 per cent per annum since 1994, with over 150,000 being sold in 1998. The increase in the number of cars on the road has caused congestion, particularly in the greater Dublin area. This has prompted the development of park-and-ride schemes in Dublin, to encourage more people to use public transport and to park their cars on the outskirts of the city. In Britain the number of cars in 2000 was approximately 25 millions. There are fewer cars on Irish roads than other countries, and this makes many Irish roads quieter and more relaxing to drive on. The quality of Irish roads is not the same as many European roads, with only a few motorways in the country. Good ferry services to Ireland encourage many tourists (22 per cent) to bring their own cars with them. Many of these tourists also bring their own caravans or tents, encouraged by the special deals on ferries.

Many tourists (20 per cent) hire cars when on holidays in Ireland; the greatest percentage of these come from America. In Ireland there are twenty-seven car-hire companies that are approved by the Car Rental Council of Ireland, and Bord Fáilte. The numbers of hired cars have risen steadily since 1994 when there were only 14,000 available. This has been due to the removal of Vehicle Registration Tax (VRT), which has considerably reduced the cost of replacing hired cars each season. In 1998 there were 20,000 cars available, and in 2000 there were 24,000. There are two types of car-rental companies:

1. Large international companies or franchise operations. These usually have a large fleet, and a large choice of cars and locations where cars can be picked up and dropped off. This is flexible and convenient for the business travellers who use these companies. The cost of hiring cars from them is usually higher than the smaller companies, but many companies offer business people a discount. These include Avis, which is the largest company in Ireland, with a fleet of 4,000 cars. Cars can be picked up at twelve locations around Ireland, eight of which are airports. Ireland's top six car-hire companies have 17,000 rental cars between them; they are Avis, Budget, Hertz, Europcar, National and Sixt.
2. Small, locally-based, independent car-rental companies. The number of cars they rent out ranges from 1,750 down to thirty, so the choice of car can be quite limited. These companies offer their cars at a lower price, but they do not offer the same convenience. These appeal to holiday-makers who will be arriving by air and will pick up and drop off the car at the same airport. Holiday-makers are more conscious of cost than business people, and many use these companies.

Car-hire costs depend on a number of factors including the time of year, size of car, duration of rental. Small local companies on average charge €265 for a medium-sized car per week, this rises to €312 plus 12.5 per cent tax from a large international company for the same type of car. This cost includes third party insurance and collision damage waiver (CDW). The tourist must pay for all petrol. Most car-rental firms will deliver the car as part of the regular service.

Car-rental companies operate in a very competitive market, and they promote their business in a variety of ways:

1. They use desk space at airports; there are five desks at Dublin airport.
2. The companies have links with hotels and airlines; this may involve desk space, or paying hotel receptionists commission for selling.
3. Travel agents also sell car rentals, for which they receive approximately 15 per cent commission. This is an important way of selling cars in the USA.

4. Computer Reservations Systems and Global Distribution Systems like Sabre and Galileo are an important way of selling for larger rental companies.
5. Internet booking.

For tourists who are visiting Ireland and who want to hire a car, often the best option is to organise a fly-drive holiday. This includes both the airline ticket and the hire of the car. Ireland is very suitable for a driving holiday. A motor home provides the renter with accommodation as well as transport. There are three operators who provide this service, Cara Rent a Car/Motorhomes in Limerick, Lisduff Campers in Tullamore and Motorhome Ireland in Northern Ireland. Chauffeur-driven cars are also available to tourists who want the luxury of letting someone else do the driving.

Tourists also use taxis. In late December 2000, the Irish taxi industry was deregulated. Demand for taxis had grown during the 1990s, and the Government felt that there was a need for extra taxis in Dublin. This resulted in over 2,000 new taxi plates being issued by the Carriage Office in Dublin Castle. The taxi drivers opposed the deregulation of their industry. Demand for taxis by tourists and locals has remained high and it seems that deregulation has been accepted by all.

Bicycle hire is available at many different locations around the country. This appeals to the young and fit. In 1999 approximately 130,000 came on cycling holidays to Ireland. Some of these were on organised cycling holidays with bicycles provided, and some brought their own bicycles to Ireland, with the remainder hiring them from the many outlets that are found around the country.

INLAND WATERWAYS AND FERRIES

Ireland's inland waterways are only used by leisure craft, unlike the main canals and rivers in Britain and Europe, which are used by commercial traffic. A number of companies offer barges and cruisers for rent on the River Barrow, Grand Canal and River Shannon.

This type of holiday offers tranquillity and is very popular with continental tourists. The cruisers operate over a short season, April to the end of September. Cruisers, which sleep up to eight people, range from £500 (€625) to £800 (€1001) per week. Among the companies who rent cruisers are Derg Marina and Emerald Star. A popular destination for many boats is Carrick-on-Shannon in Leitrim where many boats are moored. These include Carrick Marine, Emerald Star Line and Crown Blue Line.

Ireland has many small islands off its coast, and they are linked to the mainland by ferries.

- Cape Clear and Sherkin Islands off the Cork coast are linked by ferry to Baltimore and Schull.
- Aran Islands are linked to Ros a'Mhil, Galway city and Doolin, Co. Clare by ferries.

- Inishbofin off west Galway is reached by ferry from Cleggan.
- Clare Island off the Mayo coast is reached by ferry from Westport.

The most popular ferry crossing in Ireland is the Killimer (Clare) to Tarbet (Kerry) ferry, which crosses the Shannon Estuary. Another ferry joins Passage East in Waterford to Ballyhack in Co. Kilkenny across the River Suir.

Ireland has a wide range of transport that is available to tourists so that they can visit every part of the country. Many of these forms of transport are undergoing major changes and the current ranges of services are likely to expand in the future.

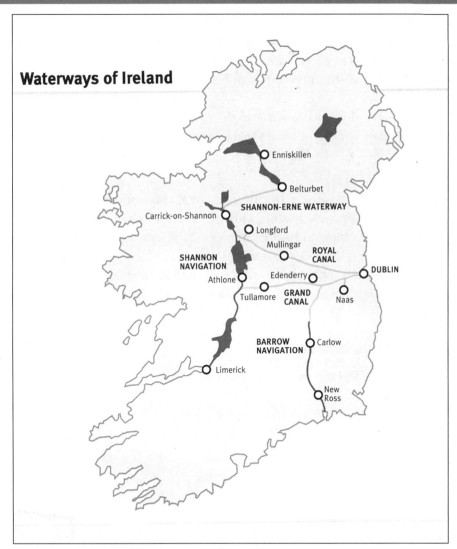

Fig. 8.4: Waterways of Ireland Courtesy of Dúchas

REVISION EXERCISES

1. Name the main Inter-city services provided by Iarnród Éireann.
2. What other services do Iarnród Éireann provide?
3. What is Track 2000?
4. What is the future of railways in Europe and could Ireland follow the same route?
5. Name the main types of bus services.
6. What was the effect of deregulation on the coach business in England?
7. What are the plans for deregulation of the bus business in Dublin?
8. List Bus Éireann services.
9. Name the services that Dublin Bus provides.
10. What advantages are there for tourists who use cars while holidaying in Ireland?
11. What services have been created to serve holiday-makers using cars?
12. What are the distinguishing features of the two categories of car-hire companies?
13. What effect has deregulation had on the taxi business?
14. Name the most important ferries that operate within Ireland.

Assignment

1. Research internal transport in the local area. This should be done under the headings of: rail, coach (public and private services), car hire, internal air transport, bicycle hire, and water transport. The research should compare and contrast the different modes of transport.
2. Using the table opposite, plan a week-long coach or self-drive holiday, visiting a number of important scenic areas around Ireland, but not travelling more than 80 miles or 130 km per day.

Reference and further reading

Annual Report CIE 1999. www.cietours.ie, www.buseireann.ie, www.irishrail.ie.

M. Yallop, ed, *Bus Coach and Tour Book*. Marketing Access Ltd, 1988.

J.C. Holloway, *The Business of Tourism*. Longman, 1998.

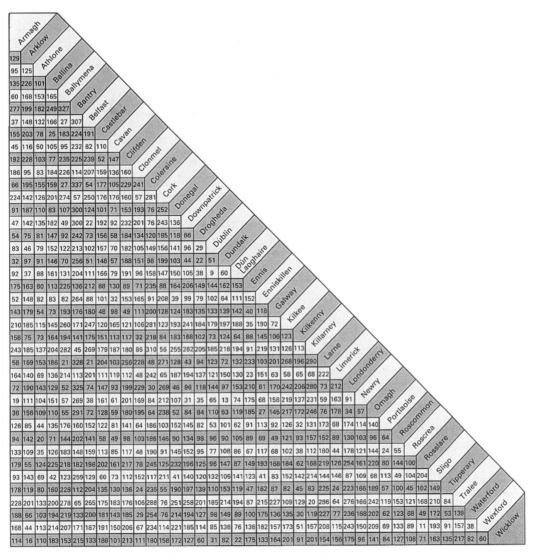

Fig. 8.5: Distances between Irish towns

CHAPTER 9

Business Tourism

Business tourism accounted for over 16 per cent of tourism in 1999 in Ireland. This makes it therefore an important sector within the tourism industry. There are four main areas of business tourism:

1. General business travel. This includes journalists or sales reps who travel as part of their work, and stay overnight while on business. They make use of accommodation and other facilities.
2. Meetings. These can involve just small groups of people, and may last only a few hours while contracts are discussed or signed. Or they can involve large numbers of people at a major conference and last for a week. These people make use of hotel, transport and other tourism products.
3. Trade fairs and exhibitions. These attract both the exhibitors and those who attend the fairs. All of those who attend such fairs make use of a range of tourism products.
4. Incentive travel. This is when employees are repaid for their hard work by a special prize of an all-in expenses-paid holiday for them and, in many cases, for their partners too.

It is possible that sometimes two of these events can take place at the same time, for example a medical conference and pharmaceutical exhibitions.

Business tourism is of particular importance to airline companies, four- and five-star hotels and car-hire companies, because business people generally make use of these more expensive tourism products. Larger profits are made from business tourism than from leisure tourism because companies are prepared to pay higher costs for the best quality products. Business tourism takes place all year around, with conferences and exhibitions occurring mainly in the shoulder seasons. Business tourists are usually well behaved, they often spend the day indoors attending conferences, and evening events are organised, so there is little adverse impact on the local environment. Often, a businessman or woman who has been impressed with an area visited as a conference delegate, will return in the future as a tourist.

The differences between business tourism and leisure tourism are many:

*   Employers are paying the cost of the trip.

152

- Trips occur during the mid-week, and throughout the year. There is no seasonality.
- Many trips are organised at the last minute, so airline tickets are at full price.
- Destinations are decided by those organising the conference or event, not by those travelling.
- The person who travels is going there to work, not for enjoyment.
- Many destinations are city locations, and in industrialised countries.

Business tourism can be very lucrative, and it is for this reason that Bord Fáilte, and the Convention Bureau of Ireland are there to help in the organisation and promotion of this type of tourism.

CONFERENCE TOURISM

Conferences are large meetings of people who are members of the same company, profession, trade union, religion, or other group and come together to discuss items of mutual interest. The corporate sector hold a range of meetings; these include sales meetings, product launches, and training sessions. Conferences can also be known by other names, for example: summits, conventions, congresses. Conferences can be held in a number of venues. These include:

- Hotels, like the Burlington Hotel in Dublin, the Slieve Russell in Co. Cavan
- Civic halls, for example City Hall, Cork
- Museums, for example Royal Hospital Kilmainham, Dublin
- Castles, for example Dublin Castle
- Universities, for example University of Limerick, UCD Dublin
- Purpose-built conference centres, for example the National Events Centre in Killarney, and the planned ICC.

The type of venue chosen depends on the number of delegates who are attending the conference. Smaller meetings and conferences are often located in small hotels, while larger conferences are located in purpose-built conference centres or universities. About 70 per cent of the market involves conferences of up to 50 people, while less than 7 per cent involves over 200 delegates. These larger conferences bring the most economic benefit to an area, and this is why large, purpose-built conference centres have been built in Ireland and the UK since 1980. The conference centres themselves do not make big profits, but they bring in large numbers of business tourists who spend money in hotels, restaurants and shops, and this benefits the areas where these centres are located.

Conference seating can be organised in a number of different ways. The style used influences the number of delegates that can be accommodated at each venue. There are usually five layouts used in Irish hotels. These are: (1) theatre style, (2) class-room style, (3) boardroom style, (4) banquet style, (5) cocktail style.

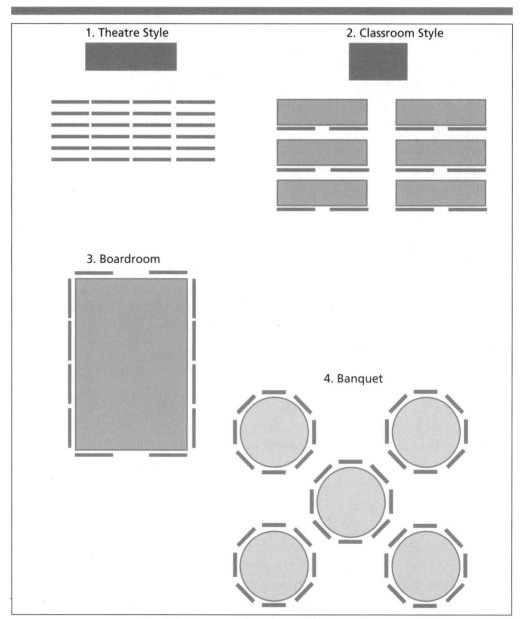

Fig. 9.1: Diagram of conference layout styles

Conference centres or hotels have a range of audio-visual equipment available for conference use, including sound systems, 35mm projectors, overhead projectors, laptop connections for projectors using PowerPoint, video equipment, screens, lecterns, stages, teleconferencing facilities and technical help. Some of the venues also have interpreting equipment available for international conferences. Often conference centres are part of the facilities provided by a hotel, but where they are not, there are usually a range of quality four- and five-star hotels in the area that can provide accommodation. These hotels provide restaurants, bars and leisure facilities where visitors can relax. Most conference centres have rooms that cater for different sizes of conferences. These rooms can be joined for a large conference, or a number of small conferences take place simultaneously.

Conferences are usually organised by professional conference organisers. They work together with a liaison person from the company or organiser in charge of the conference. The main buyers of conferences are companies, and professional and voluntary associations. Professional conferences are at international, national, regional and local levels. International meetings take place less often, but involve much greater planning and travel. There are twenty-five conference and corporate-meeting organisers operating in Ireland at the present time. Most of these are located in Dublin (twenty of the twenty-five). Some are part of a large group that deal with both leisure and business tourists, while others are small companies that concentrate on just one sector of the business. Many deal with both conference and incentive travel. Most are members of at least one of the groupings that govern the operations of this area of business. These groups are:

- AIPCO, The Association of Professional Conference Organisers. This was established in 1999 for Irish organisers. It ensures that its members know what the customer expects from the industry in terms of high standards and quality. It works together with many organisations around the world bringing conference business to Ireland. There are six members only; Abbey Tours and Conference Partners Ltd. are two of them.
- ITOA, The Irish Incoming Tour Operators Association (see chapter 19)
- SITE, The Society of Incentive and Travel Executives. This was founded in 1979, and is an international organisation that operates in eighty-seven countries, and has over 2000 members. The Irish chapter was founded in 1998, and has sixty active members. The members of SITE work with Bord Fáilte in order to make Ireland an important incentive travel destination. Members of SITE in Ireland include hoteliers, incentive houses, DMCs (destination management companies), conference centres and caterers.

Conference organisers use a variety of tourism products, for example accommodation, banquets, coach transport, air transport, entertainment. Each conference has its own requirements.

Often the first task is to find a suitable venue for the conference organiser, and this depends on the needs of the customer. These needs include, for example, closeness to an international airport, city or motorway, and easy access to the venue. The numbers of delegates influence the type of venue. About 25 per cent of delegates at conferences make use of leisure facilities. If delegates are bringing partners, a range of interesting activities will be organised for them, such as tours to areas of scenic interest, historic buildings, gardens. Once the organiser knows the needs of the customer, they then send the relevant brochures, advising the client so that the client can choose the best venue.

The next step is to plan the event. This means booking conference rooms, hotel accommodation, airline seats, catering facilities, coaches to bring delegates to the hotel, excursions, entertainment and so on. Deposits then have to be paid where bookings are made. All of this information must be passed on to the company and the delegates.

Details of the conference must be organised, for example, the various audio-visual needs, or interpretation equipment. The company liaison official knows the company's requirements, which are then passed on to the professional organiser, who in turn passes these on to the conference manager. The aim of all of this is to ensure that the conference runs smoothly.

The Convention Bureau of Ireland, part of Bord Fáilte, provides advice for conference organisers. This includes information and publicity material from hotels with conference rooms, and from conference centres, so that this information is then passed on to their customers. Ireland is divided into four regions for the promoting of conference business;

1. Northern – Sligo, Leitrim, Donegal, Cavan, Monaghan and Louth. The largest conference centres in this region are in the Great Northern Hotel in Co. Donegal, which can accommodate 1,100 delegates, and the Slieve Russell in Co. Cavan, which accommodates 800 delegates.
2. South – Cork and Kerry. The largest venues in this region are both in Killarney; the Gleneagle Hotel, and the National Events Centre that accommodate 2,000 delegates. There are two other hotels in Killarney that can cater for 1,000 delegates, and one in Cork City.
3. East – Dublin, Meath, Longford, Westmeath, Offaly, Laois, Kildare, Carlow, Wicklow, Wexford, Kilkenny and Waterford. Dublin has the largest venues, with the Irish International Convention and Exhibition Centre in the RDS accommodating up to 6,500 delegates. Other large conference centres in Dublin include the Doyle Burlington Hotel, City West Conference and Leisure Centre, and UCD; all cater for over 1,000 delegates.
4. West – Galway, Mayo, Roscommon, Clare and Limerick. There are only four conference centres in this region that can deal with over 1,000 delegates. These are the Hodson Bay Hotel near Athlone, the University of Limerick; Fitzpatrick Bunratty Hotel and West County Conference and Leisure Hotel both in Co. Clare.

All of these regions have many other hotels that cater for smaller conferences and meetings.

Bord Fáilte wanted the International Conference Centre built in Dublin under the Operational Programme for Tourism 1994–1999. It was to consist of three halls that could accommodate over 3,000 delegates and two large hotels. The main international conferences go to the USA, France and the UK. Bord Fáilte is trying to increase Ireland's role in this area of tourism by organising workshops for conference and incentive travel organisers. These bring together the managers of conference venues organisers to inform them about Ireland's conference facilities.

Ireland has a number of advantages for this business:

- Ireland is an English-speaking nation, and English is the language of most international business.
- Dublin is very accessible with links to international airports in Europe and the USA.
- The country is small and easy to travel around.
- Eight hundred hotels offer 70,000 rooms. This accommodation ranges from five-star hotels to campus accommodation and is located in major cities like Dublin, Cork, and Limerick, or in areas of natural beauty like Killarney.
- Quality Irish cuisine is available.
- Ireland provides unspoilt countryside to relax in, interesting historic buildings and gardens, golf courses.
- Ireland offers quality entertainment, including theatre, music and themed evenings.

In 1999 the conference market accounted for 93,000 tourists coming to Ireland, approximately 16 per cent of the total number of tourists. The main markets were the British (39,000), followed by Europeans (33,000). Most of these tourists arrived by air, but 33 per cent of those who came from Europe arrived via London. The shoulder season is the most popular time for conferences. The most popular location

Fig. 9.2: Ashling Hotel conference room

for conferences in Ireland is Dublin (78 per cent), with the south west (Cork and Kerry), and the Shannon area being other regions used by overseas conference organisers. Most UK conferences take place over a short period, three nights or less, while European conferences split evenly between one to three nights and four to eight nights. Most conference delegates stay in hotels and while UK delegates found Ireland good value for money, Europeans, who generally stay longer, found that it was only fair value. European delegates generally did more than just attend the conference; they also visited historical and cultural attractions while they were here.

The conference market will change in the future, for a number of reasons. Asia, with its new purpose-built conference centres, will now challenge the old conference destinations. Future conferences will be more environmentally friendly, with the use of recyclable paper, CDs instead of paper brochures, greater use of coaches. Disabled delegates will have to be catered for. This will mean designing hotels for use by wheelchairs and devices for people with hearing and sight problems. To cater for more businesswomen there will have to be increased security and healthier food in restaurants. Other changes will include the market becoming more segmented, especially in the areas of budget and size of conferences. During economic down-turns conferences will be smaller, or the length of time spent at conferences will be reduced; these will both have a major effect on the incomes earned from conferences.

MEETINGS

These are catered for in a number of venues around Ireland. Meetings vary in size from ten people to 340, and there are twenty-nine hotels around Ireland providing these facilities. Many of these are located in Dublin. The Temple Bar Hotel in Dublin has five different meeting rooms which can be laid out in a variety of ways and cater for different numbers.

The hotel is wheelchair-accessible and provides the usual audio-visual facilities. It has bars, restaurants, and 129 bedrooms, so it can provide for all the needs of business meetings. The types of meetings that take place in this hotel include sales meetings, training sessions and union meetings.

EXHIBITIONS AND TRADE FAIRS

Exhibitions and trade fairs are used by industry to sell products to the trade and to the general consumer. They are attended by two groups of people: the exhibitors, who have goods or services on display and for sale, and the visitors or buyers who attend in order to see new products. Both groups, exhibitors and visitors, buy a range of tourism products, transport, accommodation, catering. Overseas exhibitors spend more at a trade fair than locals do. The earliest trade fairs in the UK were organised in the late eighteenth century in London, and there have been many famous buildings associated with fairs, for example, the Crystal Palace in London, and the Eiffel Tower in Paris.

There are three main types of trade fairs:

1. Agricultural shows. These often take place in the open air, using marquees. Ireland's most famous agricultural shows include the Horse Show in the RDS in Dublin, and the Ploughing Championships. Agricultural shows earn money from exhibitors, who pay to show their livestock, craft workers with crafts, and farm machinery companies which pay to display farm equipment. They also earn money from those who attend the show, from entrance fees, catalogues, parking, and concession sales – of drinks, chocolates and ice cream, etc. These shows take place usually over a period of one to five days, and have attendances of up to 20,000 people.

2. Consumer shows which are aimed at the public alone. These include such shows as the Holiday World eXperience, which is held at the RDS in January. Other shows include the Ideal Homes Exhibition, the Boat Show, and the Garden Show. The main venues for such events in Dublin are the RDS and the Point. These shows are advertised through the newspapers, on the radio and on television, with many different promotions such as competitions and free tickets on offer.

3. Specialised trade shows and exhibitions. These are very specialised shows and are aimed at those within a trade or industry. They are usually organised for the shoulder seasons, March to June, and September to November. Some of these shows are held each year, for example The National Catering Exhibition, or the Irish Hardware, House Wares and Garden Trade Exhibition.

There are a number of types of exhibitions. These are art, culture and sport; industrial; services; information technology; home and lifestyle; transport and marine; catering; agriculture; clothing; and medical. Large-scale exhibitions often only occur in one venue in Ireland, that is Dublin. Popular consumer fairs take place at a number of locations around the country, in Cork, Galway and Belfast.

About 20 per cent of exhibitions are held at the same time as conferences. Workshops demonstrate the use of these products, which is of practical benefit to those attending, and it helps to reduce costs, for example medical conferences and pharmaceutical exhibitions run in tandem.

The benefit of exhibitions to exhibitors is that they attract a specific target market. The National Catering Exhibition attracts only those who are involved in catering either in hotels, restaurants, and institutions or in training. Most of those who attend are looking for new products and have the authority to make purchases. The benefits to the visitors and buyers are that they meet the personnel of the sales company and can build up a relationship with them. The products are often demonstrated for them, so they know how they work before they purchase them.

There is a range of manufacturers in close proximity so it is possible to compare products easily. Companies have found that attending trade fairs is the best method of developing quality sales leads, and that they are good for launching new products and for PR purposes.

Exhibitions are held in a number of types of venues, but purpose-built exhibition centres, like the RDS, attract the largest number of big exhibitions in Dublin. Others are organised in hotels, large halls. The suppliers of halls allow transport access for deliveries, and provide receptions for visitors, parking facilities, catering, cleaning, security. Exhibition organisers who operate in Ireland are often from the UK, because they travel around with a particular show to venues both in the UK and Ireland. They do the research on the venues and exhibitors, and promote the event, which is aimed at a specific target audience, through advertising and PR. They sell stands or space to the exhibitors. Brochures are produced for potential exhibitors, who will want to know the costs of attending (which can be very high), dates of the exhibition, the numbers that are expected to attend, and references from those who have been involved in previous exhibitions co-ordinated by the organiser.

The next step, having bought a space at the exhibition, is to hire a stand, fittings and lighting. The exhibitor can provide these; or they can be hired from the hall or the exhibition organiser. Stands need to be safe and to comply with all safety regulations that are stipulated by the fire officer and local authorities. The company then has to work out a budget, staffing must be provided for the exhibition, brochures have to be printed or samples prepared for display, some promotion needs to be organised. Promotions often involve competitions, attendance of celebrities at the stand.

Like other areas of the tourism industry, the exhibition and trade fairs are affected by the economy. When the economy slowed down in the 1980s in Ireland, the numbers of exhibitors fell. When the economy improved, companies took large stands, and more exhibitors attended.

INCENTIVE TOURISM

Incentive tourism is when an employer pays for a holiday, because the employee has reached production or sales targets. The employer pays all the expenses for the holiday, and may even absorb the taxation incurred by such holidays. Many companies have become involved in incentive tourism because they want to:

1. Reach business targets, either in production or sales
2. Improve morale within the company; happy workers work harder
3. Improve loyalty to the company
4. Improve social interaction and communication among staff.

Staff are often rewarded in different ways, and a survey of such rewards was carried out in 1993 by the Society of Incentive Travel Executives in the UK, who found that the most popular way of rewarding staff was through travel; next came cash payments, merchandise, vouchers.

Incentive travel encourages workers to work harder, because it is luxurious, and often the workers could not afford these types of holidays. When the workers return after such trips they often tell their friends about them, and this encourages other workers. The result is a more industrious workforce. Often such trips involve spouses being brought on the holiday, which happens on about 70 per cent of European incentive trips, while in the US it happens only on about 30 per cent. Incentive travel was first developed in the USA in 1906, and it is much bigger there than anywhere else. It was only in the 1960s that Europeans developed incentive travel, principally in Germany and the UK. It is most popular in the pharmaceutical, computer, financial services and car industries. Increasingly, large companies are now applying their incentive trips to other groups such as administrative workers. Fifty per cent of European trips are domestic, while in North America this rises to about 80 per cent. Destinations are often influenced by the budget for these trips.

Trips are organised by Incentive Travel Organisers, Incoming Tour Operators, and members of SITE. They put together these special holidays, which involve transport, accommodation, attractions and guides. Each trip should be unique and often it is exotic. The quality of the holiday is of the highest standard. Areas that offer these kinds of holidays must be accessible, offer high standards of accommodation with leisure and conference facilities, attractions that are varied, and give an image of being exclusive. These can involve:

*   A weekend in the exclusive Mount Juliet in Thomastown, Co. Kilkenny, which offers four-star accommodation, with a range of leisure activities such as horse riding, golfing, or fishing
*   A week in Dublin in a top hotel, with tickets for some special sporting or other events, for example concerts
*   A trip to Miami followed by a week's cruise of the Caribbean
*   A trip to a South African safari park.

The organising of such trips is divided into three areas: accommodation, flights, and activities, with all being of equal importance. The type of trip must be suitable for those who will be awarded such holidays. Often those who cannot afford long-haul holidays love the opportunity for such travel, while those managers who travel for their work, prefer a unique event closer to home. Where the budget is less than €980, then the trip tends to be domestic, for a short time; for example, a weekend at a hotel or country house. As the budget rises, further destinations can be considered; between €980 and €1,875 European destinations, for example Cyprus for a week in the sun, can be considered. Over €1,875 will allow destinations in the US like Florida, and Caribbean cruises, while amounts above this will allow long-haul destinations like South Africa or the Far East. US companies considering Ireland as a destination should have a budget of over €2,500. Built into the cost of the trip is spending-money for the duration of the stay.

Incentive tourism is very much at the upper end of the tourism market, and for this reason Bord Fáilte is involved in promoting this type of tourism. It is also an area of the market that is growing, and Ireland wants to be involved in this expanding market. Many of the large five-star hotels that have been developed of late are accommodating these tourists. They work together with the airlines and Bord Fáilte to attract incentive tourists here. They produce brochures, and attend incentive-tourism meetings and exhibitions, which Bord Fáilte arrange for organisers and buyers of this tourism product.

A new development in this area is the design of pre-packaged incentive trips; these are similar to normal package holidays, with the companies buying an already organised trip. As they are ready-, rather than custom-made, they are cheaper for the company. Other ways of reducing costs include the development of incentives meetings, which are a merging of incentive tourism and meetings; this is done in order to write off the cost of the trip against taxation. Other companies have reduced the length of these trips, and therefore the costs involved. Short-haul trips are now often only three to four days, while long-haul trips only last about eight days. Sometimes the size of the group has been reduced, again to cut back on costs. Ireland is now facing competition in the incentive market from Eastern Europe, which, very much like us, offers a rich heritage and cultural tradition, but the infrastructure is not as well developed. Ireland is also facing competition in this sector of the tourism business from long-haul destinations, for example Brazil and the Far East. There has been a move away from resort hotels to more eco-tourism and outdoor leisure activities; this should be of benefit to Ireland as a destination for incentive tourism. A return to recession will result in a cutback in this type of tourism, as companies economise.

REVISION EXERCISES

1. Name the four types of business tourism.
2. Name five differences between business and leisure tourists.
3. Where can conferences be held? Give examples.
4. Describe five ways that a conference can be seated, and explain how this affects the numbers attending.
5. Who organises conferences in Ireland?
6. Why is Ireland a popular destination for conferences?
7. Why does Ireland need a National Conference Centre?
8. What changes have come about in the conference business that organisers have to be aware of?

9. What is the difference between a meeting and a conference?
10. What are the different types of exhibitions?
11. Why do people attend trade fairs? There are a number of types of exhibition, give examples of five.
12. What are the benefits of exhibitions and trade fairs to the tourism industry?
13. Why do employers provide incentive travel? Who goes on incentive holidays, and where?
14. Who organises incentive holidays? Who promotes incentive tourism in Ireland?
15. Recommend a venue that is suitable for incentive tourism in your area.

Assignments

1. Visit the Holiday World eXperience or similar holiday exhibition. Make a note of the following:
   - The numbers of overseas exhibitors and foreign tourist boards.
   - The different types of promotions that are offered by different stands.
   - The numbers of Irish regional tourism authorities, and county tourism boards. Collect brochures from each of the regional tourism authorities.
2. Prepare a case study on a conference centre, or a special event or exhibition.

References and further reading

R. Davidson, *Business Travel.* Longman, 1994.
Bord Failte, Ireland Conference and Meetings Guide 1999.
www.incentive-ireland.ie.
www.conference-ireland.ie.

Part 3
Geographical
Tourism

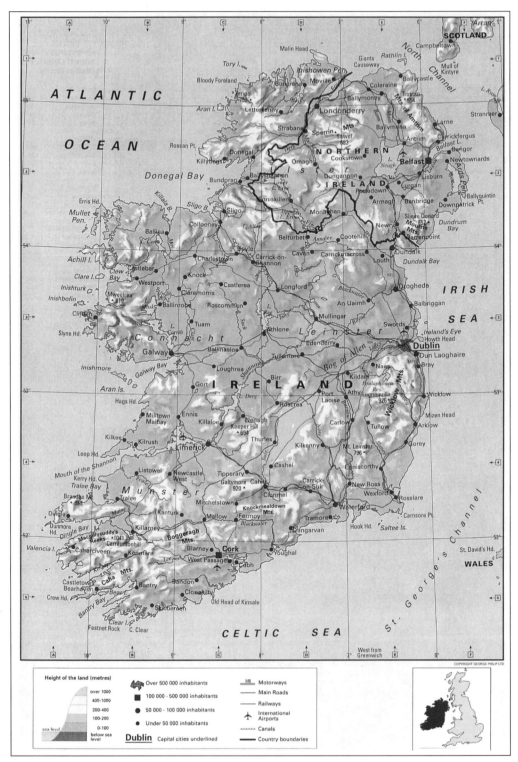

Fig. 10.1: Physical map of Ireland

CHAPTER 10

Ireland's Natural Beauty

Ireland's beautiful scenery has been the major attraction for tourists since the eighteenth century. Today 29 per cent of overseas visitors come to Ireland because of the quality of our scenery. They come to see our varied landscape. This landscape has resulted from millions of years of geological formations, climatic change and the influence of humans. The formation of its rocks and the folding of its mountains during the Caledonian and Armorican periods have influenced Ireland's physical landscape or natural features. Weathering and the action of rivers have worn down the mountains so that now only 25 per cent of the country is above 150 metres in height. Ireland has also been affected by glaciation and by the action of the sea. Ireland's landscape has man-made features, for example castles, canals. The combination of natural features and man-made buildings has resulted in a very beautiful and complex landscape.

IMPORTANT NATURAL LANDSCAPES IN IRELAND

Giant's Causeway, Co. Antrim: This is a World Heritage Site. It consists of thousands of hexagonal basalt columns, which were formed by lava flowing upwards to create a basalt plateau; the sea has now attacked these. The columns form cliffs over 170 metres high. Legend has it that Fionn mac Cumhaill built the causeway to join Antrim to Scotland. Today the Giant's Causeway is a very popular destination for tourists and an information centre provides an explanation of the area.

Fig. 10.2: The Giant's Causeway Courtesy of NITB

The Burren, Co. Clare: This is made up of Carboniferous limestone that was later affected by glacial erosion resulting in an apparently barren landscape that has very little surface water. Instead the rivers flow down swallow holes along the joints and when they hit other rock types, they cut out caves along the bedding planes. Aillwee Cave is the best known of the caves in the area. Above ground, grey limestone dominates the area, with its miles of bare pavements. The pavement has been eroded into clints and grykes and within these are often found calcium-loving plants, for example blue spring gentians. Slieve Elva, in the north west, is the highest mountain in the area at 350 metres. There are also depressions, like the Carran Depression, which resulted from the collapse of caves. These fill up after heavy rain and form lakes. Two interpretive centres, at Kilfenora and Ballyvaughan, explain the formation of the Burren, its flora and fauna and history.

Fig. 10.3: The Burren, Co. Clare. Limestone pavement with clints and grykes

Killarney, Co. Kerry: This is Ireland's most famous destination since the eighteenth century. It is the combination of hard, resistant sandstone mountains meeting the limestone plain that helps make it spectacular. Glaciers affected this area in the past and this resulted in the formation of corries such as the one at the Devil's Punch Bowl on the side of Mangerton Mountain. It also created the Gap of Dunloe that divides the MacGillycuddy's Reeks from the Purple Mountain (so called because of the colour of the rock). From Ladies' View on the Kenmare Road one can look down on Killarney and its lakes. There are four lakes: the Upper Lake, Lough Leane, Muckross Lake and Lough Guitane. The Upper Lake is a narrow glacial trough; Lough Leane is a soloution lake formed on the limestone rock; Innisfallen, the largest island is in Lough Leane and is reputed to have been where Brian Bórú received his early schooling; and Muckross Lake, also a soloution lake, has the Colleen Bawn caves close by. Lough Guitane is to the east of the other three lakes. Killarney is not only famous for its mountains and lakes but also for its vegetation. Around the Upper Lake two-hundred-year-old native oak trees are found. These are among the oldest remaining native woods. The mild climate also allows the Mediterranean strawberry trees to flourish.

Fig. 10.4: The Lakes of
Killarney, Co. Kerry.

Glendalough, Co. Wicklow: This means the valley of the two lakes. The glaciated valley was formed as ice moved through it, deepening and widening it. Along the high sides, hanging valleys were hollowed out, as the glacier cut off the lower parts of their valleys. A large lake was formed in the valley floor. Later, deposits from the Pallanass stream built up an alluvial fan which now forms the land that has divided the lakes into the Lower and Upper Lakes. Glendalough became the home of St

Fig. 10.5: Glendalough, Co. Wicklow

Kevin's monastery and it is now one of Ireland's most popular tourist destinations. A Dúchas information centre explains the area to tourists.

Clew Bay, Co. Mayo: The underlying rock in Clew Bay is limestone, which is covered by glacial drift. Clew Bay consists of a large number of islands which are in fact drumlins. Several thousand drumlins are found in the general area. They were laid down by the melting glaciers, and are made up of boulder clay. This clay is exposed on some of the islands as cliffs where the sea has eroded them. The drumlins extend inland and block Westport off from the sea. On the south side of the bay is Croagh Patrick, which is composed of quartzite. It is a place of pilgrimage. For those who climb Croagh Patrick, there is a wonderful view of Clew Bay.

Bantry Bay, Co. Cork: This is a ria. These are very common in the south west of Ireland. Glengarriff is at the head of Bantry Bay; it has a south-facing valley and is surrounded by mountains that are made of old red sandstone and grits. Thick woodlands cover these mountains and these are one of the major attractions of the area. Sugar Loaf Mountain behind Glengarriff, at 500m, offers a fantastic view of this ria coastline. The Italian gardens on Garinish Island can be reached by boat from Glengarriff.

Cliffs of Moher Co. Clare: These rise to 200 metres and extend for five miles. They are dramatic, because they appear abruptly where the land ends and the sea begins. The cliffs are made up of layers of black shale at the base of the cliff, then flagstone and finally near the top of the cliff yellow sandstone. These layers are easily visible from the viewing points. Westerly gales blow onto the Cliffs during winter, making them spectacular. Many varieties of seabirds nest along the cliffs. The Cliffs of Moher are a very popular destination for tourists throughout the year.

Fig. 10.6: Cliffs of Moher, Co. Clare

Dunmore Caves, Co. Kilkenny: These have formed in a limestone area. The entrance became obvious when the roof of the cave collapsed; before this there were rumours that a cave system existed. There are numerous calcite formations to be seen here, straws, stalagmites, stalactites, and columns. The caves are known to have been inhabited during the ninth and tenth centuries because remains have been found; it is thought that these people were fleeing from Viking raiders. In 1999 a deposit of Viking coins was found in the caves. These caves, like four other limestone caves, are open to the public.

Fig. 10.7: Dunmore Caves, Co. Kilkenny, showing columns, stalactites and stalagmites

The River Shannon: The Shannon starts its journey to the sea in a pool known as the Shannon Pot in the Cuilcagh Mountains in Co. Cavan. It then meanders slowly southwards, joined by many small rivers as it moves through the Central Plain. It flows through three solution lakes en route, Lough Allen, Lough Ree, and Lough Derg. The river at this time has a wide plain and flows slowly. After Lough Derg the river cuts between the Arra Mountains in Tipperary and Slieve Bernagh in Clare. Once a waterfall existed between Killaloe and Limerick, but the river now has a

Fig. 10.8: The River Shannon Flood Plain south of Athlone

hydroelectric station there, Ardnacrusha. This section of the river is known as a superimposed river. Below Limerick the Shannon widens out into a fine estuary.

Errigal: This is Donegal's highest mountain at 749m and it rises from the lowland bog of Gweedore. It has a bare, jagged summit and its lower slopes are covered with weathered, shattered rock called scree. From the top of Errigal there is a beautiful view of the Atlantic to the west; this shows the indented coastline south of Bloody Foreland and the quartzite island of Aranmore in the distance.

Fig. 10.9: Mount Errigal

The Skellig Islands: These are nine miles off the coast of south-west Kerry. They rise 200m out of the Atlantic and are formed from grits and slates. They have been heavily weathered into spectacular spires and pinnacles. This bare rock was once home to a monastic settlement. At Portmagee the Skellig Heritage Centre explains the wildlife on the islands and the monastic life on Skellig Michael in the first millennium.

Fig. 10.10: Skellig Islands

Connemara: This is the area that stretches west of Galway city. It consists of lakes, bog, and mountains that have been affected by glaciers. This is the wettest and windiest part of the country, which means that there are few trees to be seen, but much bog. Most of the people live along the coast. The Twelve Pins are formed from quartzite and the valleys from schists, gneiss and the famous Connemara marble. This is one of Ireland's wildest and most beautiful areas. There is a National Park at Letterfrack and a visitor centre provides information about the formation of the area, the wildlife and fauna.

All of the above scenic areas of Ireland are examples of natural attractions.

Fig. 10.11: Connemara

IRELAND'S CLIMATE AND ITS INFLUENCE ON TOURISM

Ireland has a cool, temperate, oceanic climate. This is influenced by our location north of the equator (51° to 55° approximately), which puts us in the cool temperate zone. Ireland is also affected by the Atlantic Ocean, which brings many rain-bearing clouds on westerly winds. The ocean ensures that our annual temperature-range is low: we do not have very cold winters or very warm summers. See Figure 10.12 for the type of weather experienced in the west of Ireland.

Temperatures in Dublin are usually one degree lower in winter and one degree higher in summer than shown in Figure 10.12. Rainfall is usually 20 to 30 mm less each month, giving it a drier climate.

It is obvious from Figure 10.12 that our weather is not suitable for all types of holidays. Tourists who want warm, dry weather that will allow them to spend their days at the beach do not come to Ireland on holidays; instead they go to sunnier climes. Those who want activity holidays like golfing, sailing and fishing do not have to worry about the weather being a bit wet and temperatures being low. For most of the summer months the weather changes constantly, from rain showers to sunny days, with really wet days only occurring during the winter. It is often said of the weather in Ireland, 'if you don't like it, just wait fifteen minutes.' Most tourists come prepared for our weather. Only 6 per cent of tourists in 1999 cited bad weather as the reason that their holiday in Ireland did not meet their expectations. Investment

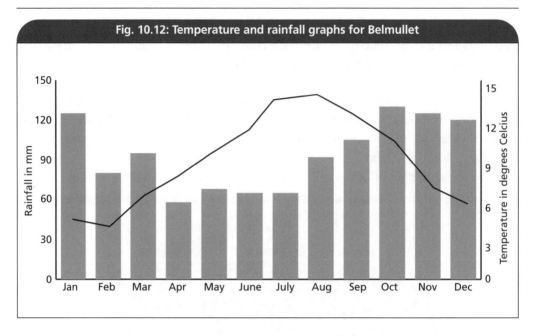

Fig. 10.12: Temperature and rainfall graphs for Belmullet

in tourist facilities since 1992 has tried to provide activities for tourists when the weather is inclement. There has been major investment in indoor facilities. These include:

- Leisure facilities in hotels, swimming pools, exercise equipment etc
- Historical houses, heritage centres, churches
- Sporting facilities including swimming pools that are open to the public, for example Aquadome Tralee
- Factory visits, for example Waterford Glass, Belleek Pottery, Bushmills Distillery.

Most areas of the country now have something to offer the tourist on a wet day. But of course we have to remember that all this rain is the reason for Ireland's 'Forty shades of green', which is what attracts so many foreign tourists to visit the 'Emerald Isle'.

IRISH FLORA (PLANTS), PARKS AND GARDENS

Ireland's climate has influenced our natural vegetation. This consists of deciduous broadleaf woods of oak and elm, with alder being found close to rivers and ash and yew growing on rocky outcrops. These forests covered Ireland undisturbed for an estimated 20,000 years. Then early farmers started to clear the forests in order to grow their crops. They planted crops for a few years until the soil lost its fertility, so they then moved on and the fields were taken over by hazel, and later were re-colonised by the woodland trees such as oak. This situation continued until the sixteenth century, when these trees were systematically cut down for:

(a) shipbuilding and houses

(b) charcoal that was used to smelt iron

(c) barrel making.

Within a hundred years most of Ireland's oak forests had disappeared and the only remaining woodlands were in areas too steep for farming or protected behind the walls of demesnes. Today, native oak woods occur in only four areas, Wicklow, Kerry, Donegal and Connemara.

Case study: the Killarney oak woods

The natural oak woods of Killarney stretch from the famous lakes up the mountain slopes to the south. They were originally preserved because they were part of an estate; today they are preserved because they are within the National Park. The wood is made up of sessile oak and native yew. The damp mild weather also allows the arbutus (strawberry tree) to flourish here. Below the leaves of the oaks are found mosses and liverworts and sometimes holly, but under the holly there is not enough light for any other plants to grow. On the branches of the oaks lichens and ferns grow abundantly. These woods are rich in bird life, with wrens, robins, tits, and chaffinches.

The introduction of foreign plants such as rhododendron, from the formal gardens in the area, has affected the development of the oak wood. This is because under rhododendrons, small oaks do not get enough light on the floor of the wood to grow into full-size trees. The National Parks administration is trying to control and remove rhododendron from the surrounding areas. Another threat to these woods is sika deer. These were introduced from Japan, for similar reasons as the rhododendron. The deer eat the young saplings or trees and this prevents the wood regenerating itself.

Modern forests

Coillte has planted most modern forests. The trees planted are usually coniferous, like sitka spruce, lodge-pole pine and Norway spruce. These were planted on moorlands and took no account of changes in soil types. Conifers were grown because they produce softwood timbers, a commodity that Ireland imported in large quantities. These forests usually have little undergrowth, and few animals or birds.

The future looks good for broadleaf woodlands because:

• National Parks and nature reserves are protecting them

• Conservation measures like the removal of rhododendron will allow the oak woods to grow

• The ending of CAP (common agricultural policy) means that marginal land will no longer be used for farming and instead the land will go back to scrub and woodland

• Forestry grants encourage the planting of broadleaved woodlands by farmers and other investors

• Government bodies and councils are planting more broadleaf trees in parks, and along roads.

Ireland still has less woodland than the rest of Europe, 9 per cent as compared with 20 per cent, but woodland wildlife still survives in the hedges.

Tourists visit our forests and woodlands because there are many forest walks, for example, the Wicklow Way. Such walks offer lots of fresh air and tranquillity, as well as allowing the walker to get closer to nature and wildlife. In the Glencree valley and on Djouce Mountain, in the vicinity of Dublin, wild deer herds are readily visible to walkers.

There are other types of natural habitats to be seen in Ireland. Each is distinctive in its plant and animal life:

- Grassland and meadow are found in the Shannon Callows. The typical flora is grasses, cowslips, white dog daisy; fauna includes blue butterflies, stoats, and the corncrake.
- Limestone hillsides of the Burren have many unusual flowers, including spring gentian, mountain avens, and maidenhair fern, which feed moths and butterflies such as the red admiral.
- Turloughs found at Coole Park and Rahansane, Co. Galway have a variety of flora including blackish mosses, hawthorn, blackthorn and violets. They have fauna such as white-fronted geese, whooper swans, widgeon and freshwater shrimp.
- Machair is found along the Mullet Peninsula in Mayo. The sandy plain is home to sedge, purple marsh orchids and bird's foot trefoil. The rare red-necked phala-rope, lapwings and dunlins are all found there.
- Sand dunes like those at Lady Island Lake in Wexford, and Inch in Co. Kerry, have marram grass and sea holly plants, and cottonweed is found in Wexford. A number of moths feed on this vegetation, along with meadow pipits and, in Kerry, the natterjack toad.
- Mountain streams have few plants but are rich in mayfly, freshwater pearls and mussels.
- Hedgerows that divide many fields in Munster and Leinster are rich in hawthorn, ash, gorse, holly, and honeysuckle and in mild areas fuschia. Many birds and other animals live in these hedges, such as thrushes, redwings, butter-flies, wrens, robins, sparrow hawks, and hedgehogs.

Irish peatlands

Peat is a soil that formed from the remains of dead plants that have accumulated over many years. It consists of sphagnum moss together with roots, seeds, leaves. There are three types of bog:

1. Blanket bog is found above 200m all over the upland areas of the country (mountain blanket bog) and along the western counties below 200m (lowland blanket bog). These cover a large area of land and look like a carpet.

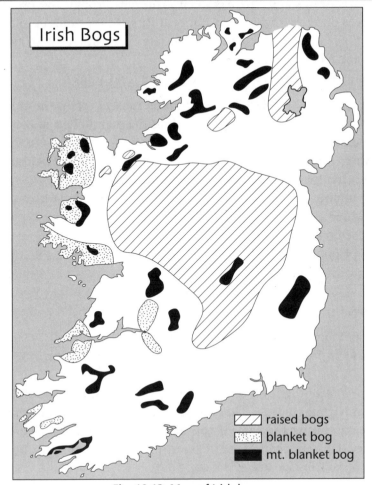

Fig. 10.13: Map of Irish bogs

2. Raised bogs are found in the Midlands; they are dome-shaped bogs that formed themselves in old lake basins.
3. Fens are found around the edge of land and waterlogged areas.

Bogs are usually formed because of (a) high rainfall (175 days) and (b) poor drainage due to the underlying boulder clay; the hollows form lakes and these were gradually filled in with fen and peat. The mosses that formed the peat absorbed rain like a sponge and stopped further drainage.

Bogs have been declining all over Europe and in Ireland too. Peatland once covered 17 per cent of Ireland. We have lost 92 per cent of raised bogs and 82 per cent of blanket bog. So today only a total of 220,902 hectares is still in bog, more than half of it blanket bog. Nineteen per cent of Ireland's bogs are in good condition and worth conserving. The Irish Peatland Conservation Council was formed in 1982, and its aim is to ensure the preservation of Ireland's bogs. The Irish Government wants to preserve Irish bogs and this has been achieved through the establishment of nature reserves or being included in National Parks. The setting up of Special Areas of Conservation (SACs) under Dúchas is an effort to protect 200,000 hectares of blanket bog and 8,000 hectares of raised bogs.

Bogs are important habitats for a range of plants and animals:

- Bog cotton and a variety of sphagnum mosses grow in the pools. The hummocks, which are drained, have ling heather, lichen and bog rosemary growing on them.
- Frogs, water beetles and water spiders are found in the pools. On the drier parts butterflies, moths, and dragonflies feed on the plants.
- A large number of birds – curlew, meadow pipit, skylarks and Greenland white-fronted geese – live on the bogs. Birds of prey like kestrels and hen harriers feed on the smaller birds.
- Sundew plants that trap flying insects and bladderwort which traps aquatic animals are found in the bogs.

Other reasons:

- Bogs are of international scientific importance.
- Bogs preserve historical artefacts, wood and pollen remains from 4,000 years ago.
- The bogs control the level of water in rivers. During the winter the rain soaks into the sphagnum moss, while in summer the bogs are a source of water.
- Bogs are an important part of the habitats that form the mosaic of raised bog, lake, river and woodland. A good example of this can be seen at the Clonmacnoise Heritage Zone.

Bogs are important to tourism, because of their uniqueness, for example in Connemara. The **Pollardstown Fen** is an internationally-renowned site. Its waters feed the canals and the Fen itself is fed by a series of streams in its centre. The Fen is rich in such plants as reeds, black bog-rush, meadow thistle and saw sedge. These attract orange-tip butterflies and many insects, which in turn feed warblers, swallows and martins.

Some of the new tourism activities that have been developed in the 1990s include:

- The Bog Train, from close to Shannonbridge; this brings tourists on a Bord na Móna train through the Bog of Allen and explains about the bog landscape, its distinctive flora and fauna
- A Day in the Bog, between Listowel and Tralee, Co. Kerry
- Lough Ree Environmental Summer School, Lanesborough, Co. Longford.

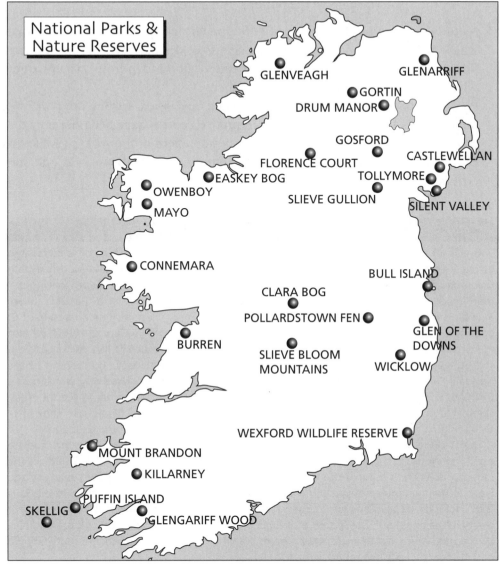

Fig. 10.14: Map of National Parks and nature reserves

National Parks

There are currently six National Parks in the Republic of Ireland; they are managed by Dúchas. They are: Killarney National Park, Co. Kerry; the Burren, Co. Clare; Connemara, Co. Galway; Glenveagh National Park, Co. Donegal; Wicklow National Park; Mayo National Park. Northern Ireland has twelve Forest Parks throughout the six counties. These include Tollymore in the Mourne Mountains and Glenarriff in the Antrim Glens. These are the eqivalent of the Republic's National Parks.

In 1996 nearly 750,000 tourists visited the Republic's National Parks. The land is owned by the State. The aims of the National Parks are:

- Nature conservation. They prevent development taking place within the parks, which would take away from the uniqueness of the park. Wildlife is protected. Broadleaf trees are encouraged and planted. Rhododendrons are cut down where they are threatening the native timbers.
- Public use and appreciation. Walks have been developed, starting off at many of the car parks located in the parks. Interpretive centres have been developed to provide visitors with information on the development of the parks, wildlife that can be seen. The interpretive centre at Letterfrack in Connemara is one such centre.

Case study: Wicklow Mountains National Park

This was set up in 1991 and is managed by Dúchas. It consists of 20,000 ha of land, located in Glendalough, the Glenealo valley and the Liffey Head bog. The Wicklow Mountains are made up of granite and there were many examples of minerals found there, leaving disused mines, like the one at the upper end of Glendalough valley. Most of Ireland's native animals are found in the Wicklow Mountains National Park. These include a large herd of deer, foxes, hares, badgers, which can be seen by the watchful observer. There are also many birds of prey, like peregrine falcon and hen harriers. Gamebirds like red grouse can still be seen in some areas. Many of the rivers have trout, stickleback. The benefit of the National Park is that there are many forest walks, including the Wicklow Way which passes through it. These offer the best way for tourists to get a feel for the area, to see the trees, climb through the open moorland and relax in the peace and quiet. There are many spectacular sights to behold, like the Glenmacnass Waterfall, Glendalough and Luggala.

The Wicklow Mountains are very popular with tourists and Dubliners alike; this leads to traffic congestion in the summer months. But this congestion is not to be found on the mountains. There is a Park Information Office in Glendalough at the Upper Lake car park. Plans to build an interpretive centre for the Park in the 1990s at Luggala, close to the Sally Gap, met with opposition from conservationists and the plan was eventually shelved after a very bitter dispute. It was feared that the interpretive centre would attract large numbers of coaches, which would mean that crowds walking in the area around the centre would destroy the fragile bog habitat.

City parks

A number of towns and cities in Ireland provide parks for the pleasure of the local people and tourists. These provide a range of facilities, including ponds for wildfowl, wooded areas growing both native and exotic trees, formal flower beds, seats for the weary, playgrounds for younger children and sports facilities for tennis, football and other games. Local government funds all of these parks. They often provide a haven of peace and tranquillity away from the hustle and bustle of city life.

Case study: Phoenix Park, Dublin

This is Ireland's most famous city park, covering over 700 hectares, making it one of the largest enclosed parks in the world. The Duke of Ormond set it up as a Royal Deer Park in 1662. Sixty-five years later Lord Chesterfield opened it to the public as a park. In 1831 the Zoo was opened; it is one of the oldest in the world. The management of the park was transferred to the Commissioner of Public Works, and later to the Office of Public Works (OPW), who manage it today with Duchás.

The Phoenix Park has a number of important buildings located there, including Áras an Uachtaráin where the President of Ireland lives, the American Ambassador's residence, the Ordnance Survey, the Zoological Gardens, St Mary's Hospital and Ashtown Castle. Ornamental trees are grown close to these buildings.

The Park is divided into different zones:

- The natural zone to the west end of the park includes the Furry Glen. Here wild birds including sparrow hawks, owls and jays can be seen. The area is frequented by birdwatchers. At Knockmaroon Gate visitors can find out about the park's wildlife and a nature trail brings them from there, through the Furry Glen, to the Fifteen Acres. Around the Fifteen Acres and Oldtown Wood fallow deer can be seen; there are over 500 of them. Nearly one third of the Park is planted with trees. These are mainly broadleaf, like oak, ash, lime, beech, sycamore and horse chestnut. Different types of wild plants are associated with different habitats in the Park.
- The main avenue runs straight through the park from Parkgate Street to Castleknock Gate, and this is planted with limes, beech and horse chestnut. Off this road can be seen the Wellington Monument, People's Flower Garden, Zoo, polo grounds, cricket grounds and the Papal Cross.
- The Sports Fields provide a range of pitches for many sports such as hurling, football and soccer. The Park is also used for charity walks, cycle races and other events. The OPW who manage the park are involved in a programme of tree conservation. They have planted 10,000 broadleaf trees and plan to plant more. This is all part of their woodland restoration programme.

The Park offers a range of facilities for the tourist. Ashtown Castle, which is a tower house dating from the early seventeenth century, can be viewed by tourists. It was only discovered in 1986, when work was being done on the former Papal Nuncio's House and there beneath the Georgian facade was the tower house. A new, purpose-built visitor centre is close by and an explanation of the development of the park and its facilities is provided. Áras an Uachtaráin is open to tourists on Saturdays.

Irish gardens

Gardens are very popular with tourists. There has been a general growth in interest in the area of gardening, as can be seen in the number of magazines, television and radio programmes on the subject. Interest in gardens is particularly high in the UK, our largest tourism market. A large number of gardens are open to the public there. Since 1990 Bord Fáilte has encouraged the opening up of gardens to the public. This has been very successful and in 1996 nearly 600,000 tourists visited Irish gardens. Ireland's mild, moist weather allows a large variety of plants to be grown here and this makes Irish gardens popular with tourists. Irish gardens are generally unspoilt and there are few problems of overcrowding.

Forty Gardens Open to Tourists in Ireland

Co. Down
5. Mount Stewart, Newtownards
6. Castle WArd, Strangford
7. Rowallane, Strangford
8. Castlewellan National Arboretum

Co. Wicklow
17. Killruddery, Bray
18. Avondale, Rathdrum
19. Powerscourt, Enniskerry
20. Mount Usher, Ashford
21. National Garden Exhibitions, Kilquade
22. Kilmecurra, Rathnew

Co. Kerry
35. Muckross, Killarney

Co. Meath
9. Butterstream, TRim

Co. Laois
25. Emo Court

Co. Leitrim
39. Louth Rynn, Mohill

Co. Kilkenny
27. Kilfane, Thomastown

Co. Westmeath
11. Belvedere House, Mullingar
10. Tyllynally Castle, Castlepollard

Co. Dublin
14. Talbot Gardens, Malahide
15. War Memorial Gardens, Islandbridge
16. National Botanic Gardens, Glasnevin
13. Ardgilla, Balbriggan

Co. Derry
1. Downhill Castle

Co. Antrim
4. Antrim Castle Gardens

Co. Waterford
30. Lismore Castle

Co. Galway
37. Kylemore Abbey

Co. Roscommon
38. Strokestown Park

Co. Donegal
40. Glenveagh, Churchill

Co. Roscommon
38. Strokestown Park

Co. Wexford
28. Johnstown Castle, Murrintown
29. John F. Kennedy Arboretum, New Ross

Co. Fermanagh
2. Tully Castle, Church Hill
3. Florence Court, Enniskillen

Co. Limerick
36. Glin Castle Gardens

Co. Kildare
23. Japanese Gardens, Tully

Co. Offaly
24. Birr Castle Demesne, Birr

Co. Carlow
26. Altamont, Tullow

Co. Cork
31. Fota Arboretum, Fota Island
32. Anne's Grove, Castletownroche
33. Ilnacullin, Garnish Island, Glengarrif
34. Bantry House, Bantry

Fig. 10.15: Irish gardens Source: The Hidden Gardens of Ireland

Case study: Powerscourt Gardens, Co. Wicklow

Wicklow is known as the Garden of Ireland, and this is not only because of its beauty, but also because of the number of gardens open to the public. The best known of these is Powerscourt, which is situated on the outskirts of Enniskerry. Richard Cassels built Powerscourt House in 1743 in the Palladian style. The gardens are best known for their terraces, fountain and views of the Sugar Loaf. In the nineteenth century Daniel Robertson updated the garden using Italian designs. Classical urns, mosaic steps, winged horses guarding the pool were all added to the garden, giving it a look of grandeur, along with rare statues, plants and trees. The garden covers 10.7 hectares and this includes not only the formal garden and the ornamental lake, but also walled gardens, and rambling walks in woodland. Powerscourt Garden is very popular with day-trippers from Dublin, and also foreign tourists. Powerscourt is a popular destination of coach trips visiting Co. Wicklow.

Fig. 10.16: Powerscourt Gardens

Fig. 10.17: Irish birds

FAUNA (ANIMALS)

Some of Ireland's bird and animal species are of international importance and many tourists come to see them. They fall into seven categories:

- Japanese sika deer, the herd that is found in Killarney, contains some of the purest sika deer in the world, and these are of interest to Japanese tourists.
- Irish red deer are also found in Killarney, and this is the largest group in the world of this species. These deer are also found in Glenveigh.
- Nearly 50 per cent of the world's Greenland white-fronted geese spend their winters on the Wexford Slobs.
- Ireland is important internationally as a centre for waterfowl. These birds, ducks and geese come here either to breed or for the winter. There are 50 sites in Ireland, where these birds can be seen, including Bull Island, on the north side of Dublin city.
- The corncrake, which is extinct in most of Europe, still breeds in the Shannon Callows and in parts of Donegal. Corncrakes nest in the centre of meadows and

Case study: North Bull Island Nature Reserve, Dublin

The 1930 Game Preservation Act, the 1976 Wildlife Act, and the Open Space Act, protect the North Bull Island and in 1981 it was made a designated biosphere reserve by UNESCO. The reason for all this is because the island, 5 kilometres long and 800 metres wide, has unique characteristics:

- A wide range of natural habitats is found there, including mudflats, salt and fresh-water marshes, dunes and beach.
- The island is visited by 27,000 birds including brent-geese, curlew, and bar-tailed godwit.
- The freshwater marsh has important wild flowers like orchids.
- The plants from salt marsh to dune vegetation have remained undisturbed.
- The interpretive centre, which was set up with EU Environment Funding in 1985, allows the public to be educated; it provides conservation and recreational functions.

Bull Island developed after the North Bull wall was built in 1825 to prevent silting in the port. The sand built up outside the wall instead, and formed the island, which continues to grow. Marram grass stabilised the sand and salt-marsh plants grew on the mudflats behind the sand. Behind the dunes, other plants like red fescue grow, forming mossy dune grass-land. A wide variety of insects feed on the plants and flowers. The largest animals found on the island are rabbits, Irish hares and foxes.

The birds are the most important attraction on the island. They arrive between autumn and spring. They include long-legged waders like the redshank, curlew and oystercatcher; wildfowl like shelduck, teal, brent-geese and gulls. These two groups of birds feed on the mudflats, some on the plants, some on the surface of the mudflats and some on the animal life in the mud. These birds come in large numbers over the winter, 30,000 waders, 5,000 duck and 3,000 geese. The brent-geese come all the way from Arctic Canada. It is impor-tant that the island be preserved because it has become one of the most important wetlands of north-west Europe. This is a paradise for bird-watching tourists.

with the introduction of mechanised hay cutting, the birds and their young usually cannot escape fast enough and are killed, reducing the population.

- The west coast and our islands in particular are the home to twenty-two species of breeding sea birds. Great Saltee, Co. Wexford has 220,000 auks, i.e. guillemots, razorbills and puffins, along with 224,000 other pairs of birds (for example, fulmars, storm petrels, choughs) nesting and breeding there in summer. Most of these birds feed on the waste from fishing trawlers in the Irish Sea. The Skellig Islands have the largest gannet colony in Europe.

- Our location on the edge of the continental shelf, with the waters of the Gulf Stream passing close by, provides waters rich in plankton. This attracts many whales, porpoises, dolphins, and basking sharks, along with visitors from tropical waters like turtles and sunfish. Seals are found in large numbers along the west coast, waiting on the arrival of the salmon each year.

Case study: Dolphin watching, Dingle and the Shannon estuary

The Irish Government has introduced a series of acts to protect whales, dolphins and porpoises.

- The 1976 Wild Life Act protects all wilful interference, i.e. damage to habitats and breeding places, to wild animals including dolphins and whales.
- The Whale Fisheries Act 1982 banned the hunting of whales, dolphins and porpoises.
- In 1991, the Government declared that all Irish waters were a whale and dolphin sanctuary.

This means that Irish waters are now important breeding and feeding grounds for dolphins, porpoises and smaller whales. Twenty-three species have been recorded in Irish waters. During the summer months, there are usually 20,000 harbour porpoises off the south-west coast. Bottle-nosed dolphins, risso dolphins, and long-finned pilot whales are also found in Irish waters.

In 1983 Fungie, a bottle-nosed dolphin arrived at the mouth of Dingle Harbour in Co. Kerry. The dolphin has remained there and boats are now hired from the Harbour to see Fungie, and tourists can even swim with him. The development of Fungie-watching in Dingle Harbour was rather haphazard, with no regulations in place. The Shannon Estuary is home to 133 bottle-nosed dolphins, forty of them living there permanently. It is now possible to go dolphin-watching from Kilrush and Carrigaholt in Co. Clare, and from Ballylongford and Ballybunion in North Kerry. There are nine boats operating from these four locations according to accreditation given by the Minister of Arts, Heritage, Gaeltacht and the Islands. It is only possible for three boats to be with the dolphins at any one time. The boats are tightly controlled, they can only travel at a maximum of seven knots, they cannot surround the dolphins or chase them, and they can only stay thirty minutes viewing the dolphins. The Shannon Estuary is a Special Area of Conservation under the EU Habitats Directive, and this is why dolphin-watching is being strictly controlled. The dolphins are one of only six groups in Europe. In 1999 4,000 tourists went dolphin-watching in the Shannon Estuary; it is planned that this number will rise to 25,000 per year earning €1.25 million for the tourism industry. This type of sustainable eco-tourism is popular with many tourists.

REVISION EXERCISES

1. Draw an outline map of Ireland. Locate on the map the scenic areas named above.
2. Locate on the map the following scenic areas:
    (a) River Blackwater, Co. Cork
    (b) Mitchelstown Cave, Co. Tipperary
    (c) Lough Erne, Co. Fermanagh
    (d) Ben Bulben, Co. Sligo
    (e) Glenmalure, Co. Wicklow
    (f) Rosslare Strand, Co. Wexford
    (g) Slieve League, Co. Donegal
    (h) Galtymore, Co. Tipperary
    (i) Aran Islands, Co. Galway
    (j) Killary Harbour, Co. Mayo
    (k) Powerscourt Waterfall, Co. Wicklow
3. Name similar landforms that are found worldwide which are major tourist attractions.
4. Explain briefly the following geographical terms: glaciated valley, solution lake, karst area, ria, meanders, drumlins, basalt plateau, alluvial fan.
5. Explain the main differences between (a) National Parks, (b) city parks, (c) gardens.
6. Give five reasons why animal lovers would come to Ireland on holidays.
7. (a) Name the main destination for bird watchers to visit on holidays to Ireland.
    (b) What can they see at each of these places, and what time of the year would you recommend?

Assignments

1. Choose a park close to where you live and find out who manages it, what area it covers, and what facilities are provided within it.
2. Visit an area of natural beauty located close to where you live. Explain what it has to offer to tourists today. Suggest ways of improving the presentation.
3. To tourists interested in flora and fauna, suggest a weekend tour of the more famous destinations in your area.
4. Visit or write to your Regional Tourism Authority and get brochures on the following in your area: National Parks, nature reserves, gardens, Special Areas of Conservation. Write a report detailing their tourist potential for the future.

Reference and further reading

F. H. Aalen, M. Stout and K. Whelan, eds, *Atlas of the Irish Rural Landscape*. Cork University Press, 1997.

G. Cunningham, *Exploring the Burren*. Dublin Town House & Country House, 1998.

E. de Buitlear, ed, *Wild Ireland*. Amach Faoin Aer, 1984.

E. de Buitlear, *Ireland's Wild Countryside*. Boxtree, 1993.

J.B. Whittow, *Geology and Scenery in Ireland*. Pelican, 1974.

CHAPTER 11

Sustainable Tourism

The future of tourism in Ireland will involve the expansion of tourism to the countryside. This will mean growth in rural tourism and more activity holidays, with the minimum of impact on the environment. Expansion of sustainable tourism involves the whole community, not just those in the industry. This ensures that tourists will continue to be welcome as the industry grows. It encourages tourism to take place all year round. In this way growth can continue, without causing overcrowding. Current government policy is to create opportunities for Irish tourism that can be continued into the future and which will not have a negative effect on the environment; this is contained in their Strategy for Tourism Development 2000–2006.

Tourism in the countryside has developed over many years and has three distinct stages.

1. The first was the development of agri-tourism. This involved the provision of farmhouse accommodation and, later, farm visits.
2. The second was the expansion into rural tourism. This included agri-tourism businesses, also leisure, and cultural activities that are found in the rural area.
3. The most recent development has been sustainable tourism. This tries to bring together the three main elements of the tourist industry: the community of tourism destinations, the tourism businesses, and the visitor; and it develops to form a balanced type of tourism that is of long-term benefit to all three groups. This form of tourism protects the environment for future generations to enjoy, and also allows the economic development of the area. Most rural tourism businesses fit into this form of sustainable tourism.

RURAL TOURISM

Rural tourism developed in Ireland and elsewhere because rural areas were facing a crisis, caused by the following factors:

- Jobs were lost and fewer jobs were created in rural areas, due to mechanisation on farms and in the forestry industry.
- Farm incomes dropped because of changes in the common agricultural policy.
- Young people moved to cities for education and jobs because many saw no

future in farming: this left older people on the farms and the population declined.

- The drop in population led to a reduction in the services being provided in towns and villages, with closures of, for example, schools, post offices and banks.

The aim of rural tourism was to reverse these trends, and to bring vitality to these communities.

Rural tourism is a growing category of the tourism industry. Increased levels of education have resulted in a greater interest in the environment, local historical sites, and outdoor recreation. People have more disposable income and more leisure time so they are taking short-break holidays more often, many of them in the countryside. Improved transport ensures that the countryside is easier to reach. People are more health conscious, so they are participating in leisure activities, for example walking. The countryside also offers peace and tranquillity; this allows people to switch off from their busy lives. Tourism businesses in rural areas are often small, family-run concerns, so they provide the personal touch that is often lacking in larger tourism ventures. The World Tourism Organisation has watched the rural tourism market grow from 3 per cent in 1985 to 15 per cent in 1989 in the USA and it has continued to grow through into the twenty-first century. In European countries it is a popular option for holidays.

Ireland is ideally suited for the development of rural tourism. Our countryside has low population densities, and open space. We have many small villages and towns, which have the potential for the development of a range of intimate tourist facilities. Our rural pace of life is slow and relaxed. The Irish people have a reputation for being friendly. The land is used mainly for farming and, to a lesser extent, forestry. There are many open areas of bog and mountain, which are rich in a variety of flora and fauna. There has been little industrialisation and as a result little pollution. The natural landscape is ideal for many leisure activities, such as walking, fishing, horse riding.

This type of lifestyle appeals to many urban dwellers, who are in stressful jobs, located in polluted cities, and who want to get away from it all and relax. This is a growing market.

Areas that are most suitable for rural tourism should have the following:

- Scenery, such as mountains, woods, lakes, rivers, coastal areas, islands
- The presence of wildlife, flora and fauna
- Historic buildings, quaint towns and villages
- Sporting facilities, for example, fishing, walking, swimming, boating
- Good transport, which allows ease of access from cities
- Good marketing, management and business skills. Where these are not initially available, they can be developed through education and training.

Much of the development of rural tourism in Ireland came from the development of the **Leader Programme** in 1988, (Leader stands for Liaison Entre Action de Développement de l'Economie Rurale and this translates into English as the links between actions for the development of the rural economy). This was an EU initiative, which provides funding on the basis that 50 per cent came from the local areas and of the remainder two-thirds from EU funding and one-third from national Government. The ideas for developing tourism came from the communities themselves; they provided a business plan for the area. The funding was for a range of rural community development activities, of which rural tourism was just one of six. In the past tourism in rural areas had consisted of the provision of accommodation and visitor attractions. Under Leader it had to include local transport, craft production, cultural activities, and the co-ordinating and marketing of these new products.

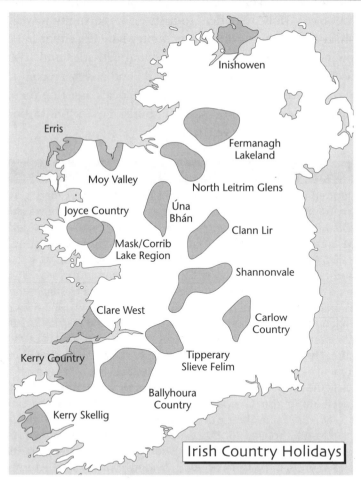

Fig. 11.1: Locations of the Rural Community Tourism
Co-operative Society/Irish Country Holidays

The purpose of these developments was to revitalise communities. Leader opens new opportunities for rural areas, provides training for those who want to develop new enterprises, improves telecommunications to help them market their products, and provides funding for marketing.

The Rural Community Tourism Co-operative Society brings together groups from all over the country that are involved in rural tourism. All of these groups have looked at their local resources and used them to develop tourism in their areas. The members are not only tourism businesses but also community groups and public bodies. They provide training and education for their members. The products provided by these groups are of the highest standard, and include a range of accommodation and attractions. They must also provide extra services to the visitors, like tourism information packs on local facilities. The Rural Community Tourism Co-operative Society provides centralised marketing, produces brochures, contacts tour operators and travel agents, and organises reservations over the internet. Its product, Irish Country Holidays, offers tourists an opportunity to visit and become part of rural Ireland, through staying with country families, either in B&Bs or in self-catering accommodation and taking part in rural activities and Irish culture. The society promises a unique experience, lots to do and a very relaxed pace of life. Its members also offer a very personal service; with locals assisting them and offering advice on what activities would best suit the tourist. Leader funds the Society. There are sixteen members located all over Ireland.

Case study: Ballyhoura Country

Ballyhoura is located in the fertile valleys and rolling hills of east Limerick, south Tipperary and north Cork. Traditionally it was not a tourist area, although there was some accommodation available and a few tourist attractions. Small farms that provided low incomes dominated the area. It was suffering from rural population decline and its villages were being left derelict. In 1986 the Ballyhoura Fáilte Society was set up as a tourism co-op by local bodies, such as FÁS and the country councils operating in the area, and a few tourist providers. The Co-op offered holidays to students who wanted to stay in the area in order to experience rural life, and were on agricultural study tours. In 1988 the Co-op prepared an integrated plan for the development of the area. With the help of FÁS they appointed a full-time manager, and Limerick VEC provided them with an office at the Kilfinane Education Centre. They carried out a resource audit of the area; in other words, they found out what natural attractions, amenities and activities Ballyhoura had to offer tourists. This led to a pilot scheme offering Irish Country Holidays to the German market. Shortly after this the National Rural Tourism Co-operative was formed to market Irish Country Holidays.

In 1991 the Ballyhoura Fáilte Society prepared an integrated plan for the development of the area and successfully applied for EU Leader funding which gave them £1.5 (€1.9) million. Funding for the Society came from four sources: shareholders; grants; commission; advertising and sponsorship. The Society provided training and education for those involved. This included training in hospitality skills, languages, business, and back-to-work courses. A range of Government agencies provided these courses, including Teagasc, CERT,

Limerick VEC, and FÁS. The result of this was to develop new tourism products such as the O'Sullivan Beara Way (long-distance walk), Ballyhoura Mountain Park, Golden Vale Cycle Route, Ballyhoura Drive, signposting to historical and archaeological sites and a promotion brochure for the area. Two main types of holidays were now offered:

- Irish country holidays, which provided tourists with the experience of rural life in Ireland: they stayed locally, could visit farms, and take part in local games, sports and entertainment.
- Special-interest holidays which were organised for groups and included agricultural study tours, activity holidays at the Kilfinane Centre, language learning, walking and horse-riding holidays.

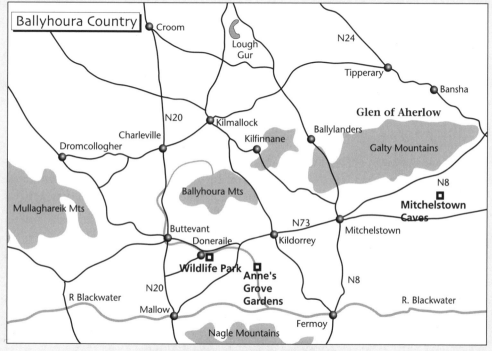

Fig. 11.2: Map of Ballyhoura Country

Major investment went into the area which resulted in earnings over £1 (€1.27) million by 1993, £2.6 (€3.25) million in 1995 and by 1998 this had grown to nearly £5 (€6.25) million.

This growth rate was 88 per cent between 1995 and 1998 much higher than the national average of 21 per cent.

This increase was due to the following factors:

- A good central marketing organisation provided proper advertising.
- Tourism development in the area was well-organised and provided good training and marketing links.
- They had the support of tourism organisations in the area, e.g. Cork Kerry Tourism and Shannon Development.

- They had financial support for development from Leader, the Operational Programme for Tourism and the Operational Programme for Rural Development (1994-9).
- There was growth in the provision of accommodation, visitor attractions and restaurants.

Apart from increases in revenue, there have also been increases in the numbers employed in tourism. In 1998 there were 270 employed in rural tourism, and these numbers are growing all the time.

Most of the tourists who visit Ballyhoura are overseas tourists (67 per cent). Today it offers the following:

- Five different types of accommodation, including hotels, B&Bs, self-catering, home stays and hostels. In 1998 this area generated nearly £2 (€2.5) million for its many accommodation providers.
- There are fifty-five food outlets in the area, and these earned over £2 (€2.5) million.
- There are ten open farms for tourists to visit; these include a deer farm, dairy farms, and farms available for agricultural studies which deal with dairy and organic farming.
- The Ballyhoura Walking Festival, which takes place over the May Bank Holiday, provides package holidays for the serious walker, through the Ballyhoura and Galty mountains.
- There is a range of sporting facilities available including golf clubs, bike trails, fishing, and equestrian centres.
- For less energetic tourists there is a range of historical sites to visit like the famous Robinsonians' Anne's Grove Gardens, the De Valera Museum at Buree, the Irish Dresden Workshops at Drumcollogher, the Lough Gur Heritage Centre, and the medieval Heritage Town of Killmallock. There are also scenic sites like the Ballyhoura Mountain Park, Ballylanders Wildlife Bog and Mitchellstown Cave.

Ballyhoura offers overseas tourists the opportunity to savour life in the slow lane, away from the hustle and bustle of popular tourist destinations along the south and west coasts of Ireland. There is good quality accommodation and plenty to do while they are there. Rural tourism has revitalised the area, kept many of the young at home, providing work for them, and kept services available in the local towns. Many of the towns and villages have restored vacant houses for tourism accommodation and for their growing population. Ballyhoura Fáilte has been successful in developing rural tourism.

THE ENVIRONMENT UNDER THREAT

The environment is Ireland's most important tourist asset. Many visitors come to Ireland because of our scenery, so it is essential that we maintain our environment in an unpolluted state. Our environment is continually under threat from economic development. The main threats come from the following:

1. Ribbon development and visual pollution: European tourists are amazed at the ribbon development on the approach to Irish towns. The Irish countryside is covered with urban houses. Some of these are bungalows, others Spanish haciendas, but rarely do you see the traditional thatched cottage. One of the worst areas of this type of development is on the Connemara coast from Barna westwards; the building of such houses on the seaward side of the road has destroyed the view for the thousands of tourists who come to see our unspoilt countryside. This problem is replicated all over the country, where houses destroy beautiful views. The cause of this apparently unplanned building is the use of 'Section 4'; this allows a county council to overturn any refusal of planning permission from their planning department. The reason for the refusal may have been that the planners wanted to protect high-amenity areas, or prevent the pollution of ground water from septic tanks. Between 1987 and 1997 50,000 such houses were built in rural Ireland.

This problem does not exist in Northern Ireland, where a policy of central planning operates, and where all urban dwellings occur within towns. In the Republic, the movement of people from towns to the countryside has meant that in many cases houses in towns have become derelict. The Government's Sustainable Development Strategy is opposed to this type of development, but will they succeed in stamping it out?

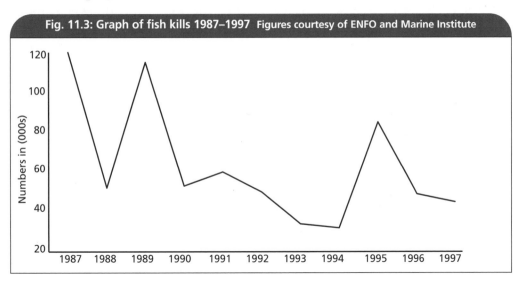

Fig. 11.3: Graph of fish kills 1987–1997 Figures courtesy of ENFO and Marine Institute

2. Water pollution: This is a major crisis facing Ireland's rivers and lakes. Clean water is essential for tourism because so many tourist activities depend on rivers and lakes, such as fishing, cruising and swimming.

The main causes of water pollution are: (a) silage leakage, (b) enrichment from fertilisers, and slurry discharges, (c) industrial effluents, (d) partially-treated sewage.

Where phosphates, nitrates, slurry or sewage enter a river, eutrophication occurs. The plant life in the lakes and rivers is encouraged to grow (the algae blooms), which blocks channels in the rivers and as it does this the oxygen in the water is reduced. The water becomes unpalatable to drink, and fish die because there is not enough oxygen in it. Water pollution is most likely to occur during the summer months of June to August, when water levels are low. This pollution has been very prevalent in recent years and is the most serious threat to our environment. In July

1998 the Owenacurra River near Midleton was polluted and 5,000 fish were killed. A chlorine-based product was the source of the pollution and it came from a factory which was located close to the river.

Pig slurry in Co. Cavan badly affected the famous trout lake of Lough Sheelin. Loughs Mask and Corrib are now under threat from intensive farming. Once pollution occurs in a river or lake, it is first cleaned. On the Mulkear River, for example, in Co. Limerick, where farm effluent wiped out eight miles of river, the cost to clean up the river was £10,000 (€12,500). It takes a minimum of three years for the pollution to clear. This is too long for tourism interests who depend on angling tourists. Both Loughs Derg and Ree suffer from pollution and local authorities have advised the public not to swim in them because of the dangers of illness.

3. Marine pollution: This occurs in a number of ways. Ships can cause it at sea, by dumping their waste which is then swept ashore, and is left along the tide line on the beach. This sight is particularly seen during the winter months when storms bring a variety of articles ashore. In November 1997 an oil leak occurred as a ship was unloading oil at the Whitegate refinery in Cork. Twenty-five tonnes of oil was spilt, and this spread through the water, washing up on beaches, and into inlets, and killing 1,300 birds. Such oil leaks are regular occurrences.

Pollution can also be caused along the coast by pumping untreated and partly treated sewage into the sea. The sewage soon finds its way back to the beach because of the movements of tides. Swimming in these kinds of waters can lead to a range of illnesses, including diarrhoea, and, more seriously, hepatitis A. For many years Dublin Bay was affected by this kind of pollution, because the sewage plant in Ringsend was not able to cope with the demands being made on it. The upgrading of the plant to deal with tertiary treatment has resulted in cleaner beaches around Dublin Bay, and the granting of blue flags to some of these beaches.

4. Litter: Over the years one of the most disappointing aspects of holidaying in Ireland has been the litter. On average Bord Fáilte gets 5,000 letters a year from tourists complaining about Ireland's litter. It is especially a problem in our towns, cities and beaches, but it is also found in the countryside. So bad is it that a group called Irish Business Against Litter put up signs saying 'Welcome to Dublin. Excuse the litter.' They also offered a reward of £100,000 (€125,000) to Clare if they cleaned up their litter. It not only spoils the countryside, but can also be a health hazard, attracting vermin and causing salmonella outbreaks. Litter, especially plastic bags, can cause the death of birds and animals. The disposal of litter costs at least £13 (€16.25) million each year. When Irish people travel abroad they find European cities clean. Our European tourists expect the same when holidaying here.

5. Congestion: This can be both physical and psychological. Physical congestion includes the following:

- Dublin suffers from severe traffic congestion. This has meant that coaches cannot park close to tourist sites like Trinity College for longer than thirty minutes. It also causes delays when travelling to hotels, tourist attractions, the airport etc., and this cuts down on the number of sites that tourists can visit.
- Many tourism resorts like Killarney, the Ring of Kerry, the Dingle Peninsula and Galway suffer from too many tourists. Many tourists want to meet the Irish people, not just other tourists. For them the success of Irish tourism since the 1990s is in fact an off-putting factor. Some now come during the low season to avoid other tourists. Others could be encouraged to go to rural tourism areas, where tourist numbers are much lower and the service more intimate.
- Too many tour buses and visitors to historic buildings can result in queues for guided tours. During the summer season tour buses pre-book tours, and they must be there on time, otherwise they have to miss that site. This occurs in all the popular sites, for instance Newgrange, Kilkenny Castle.

Congestion can be psychological, and this relates to the number of people we can accept in a place before we feel that it is overcrowded.

- A study of Brittas Bay Beach in the 1970s discovered that people needed ten square metres each before they felt the beach to be overcrowded. Brittas Bay still attracts large numbers of day trippers from Dublin on hot sunny weekends, and during these times the beaches become overcrowded, especially the areas close to the lifeguards; elsewhere down the beach numbers thin out.
- Wilderness areas in the mountains will not take more than four or five people per square kilometre. Access to mountainous areas by car increases the numbers of visitors to the areas. Close to car parks, the numbers of visitors are high, while four kilometres away the numbers have reduced drastically. People who like isolation walk these distances to find peace and quiet. A study of walkers in Ireland found that over 70 per cent visited Irish mountains for peace and tranquillity. By restricting the access of cars to areas, the numbers of tourists can be kept down. Ireland's mountains generally have very low densities of tourists, especially during mid week and outside Wicklow. This makes them very attractive to tourists.

6. Erosion: A fragile environment is under threat from too many tourists. For example, walkers on bogland trample the vegetation and encourage erosion when it rains, resulting in the path becoming a quagmire. Sand dunes can be destroyed by the use of dune buggies, or the building of golf clubs or caravan parks. There are a number of cases where golf clubs have caused damage; for instance, to sand dunes at Castlegregory in Co. Kerry, and to machair dunes at Magheraclogher Co. Donegal.

The Boyne Valley visitor centre was built in order to protect the passage graves at Newgrange, Knowth and Dowth. Until 1997 Newgrange had 200,000 visitors a year, and these numbers were expected to rise to 300,000 within a few years. This causes problems for Newgrange, which is narrow, and as visitors squeeze through they must be careful of bags and cameras in case of damage to the passage. The visitor centre contains a replica of the Newgrange burial chamber, and after a visit to the centre, visitors have the option of visiting one of the sites. At other historic sites, for instance the stone circle at Stonehenge in England, and the stone alignments at Carnac in Brittany, too many tourists caused damage and now tourists view from afar. If too many tourists damage Newgrange then it may be closed to the public like other ancient monuments.

Souvenir hunters who collected limestone from the Burren greatly reduced the area of its unusual natural sculptures of stone. Visitors who take wild flowers also affect natural habitats; the Burren in particular could be ruined by such activity. Similar problems exist in other parts of the world. These fragile environments are threatened by thoughtless, selfish tourists.

The actions of our sheep farmers have ruined many of the upland areas of the west of Ireland. Headage payments by the EU led to a massive increase in the number of sheep; many grazed on the open mountains with devastating consequences. Once the heather and grasses were removed, there was nothing to protect the soil, and when our Atlantic weather reached the mountains, the rain washed away large parts of the covering soil.

7. Air pollution: In Ireland this is mainly caused by emissions from motor cars. Most smog develops in large urban areas during the winter, when high pressure lies over Ireland. High pressure brings very cold weather, with little wind movement, and a temperature inversion occurs (this is when cool air near the surface is trapped by warm air above). This traps the discharges from cars and smog develops. When this happens in Dublin the line of smog is easily visible from Three Rock Mountain to the south of the city. The area around Trinity College and College Street in Dublin is one of the worst areas for high levels of nitrogen oxide.

Bituminous coal caused major smog problems in Dublin in the 1980s, but legislation in 1990 banned the use of this coal, and introduced smokeless coal, which led to a marked reduction in air pollution. With increased numbers of tourists coming in off-peak periods, especially to Dublin, action needs to be taken on the problem of air pollution. For Irish citizens it is important that air pollution does not exist because it has a detrimental effect on people who suffer from bronchial diseases, and it can even cause deaths.

8. Noise pollution: This is the noise from bars, discos and restaurants. The Temple Bar in Dublin is one area where noise pollution is a problem. Other causes of noise pollution include concerts, especially at open-air venues, such as the RDS, or Slane Castle. Residents close to these venues opposed these noisy concerts. Aircraft traffic also causes noise pollution. This is especially true of 'stage 2' aircraft that have not been fitted with 'Hush kits' which reduce the noise. Jet skis and motorboats are a source of noise on lakes and along the coast, while scrambler bikes and racing cars are noisy on land, disturbing the peace and tranquillity.

SOLUTIONS TO ENVIRONMENTAL PROBLEMS

Where houses or hotels have been built disrupting a beautiful view, **visual pollution** cannot be restored, unless of course they are removed. So the task facing planners is to enforce the planning laws strictly, for example, make the 'Section 4' loophole illegal, and prevent people building wherever they want. The revelations of corruption in planning during the tribunal investigations of the late 1990s and early 2000s may result in planning being taken out of the remit of local councils altogether, and becoming centralised, as it is in Northern Ireland. Housing needs to be confined to town boundaries as it is in Northern Ireland; this makes sense as local services are within walking distance and this reduces the need for private transport. Local materials and traditional designs ought to be used in new buildings, so that it is more authentic to the region. The renovation of older buildings should also be actively encouraged with more grants being available for these, rather than new housing.

The solutions to **water pollution** include a variety of strategies, some to encourage farmers and industrialists to minimise the risk of pollution, and where these do not work then the imposition of penalties should ensue. The strategies include:

1. Enforcement of EU and national standards and the Water Pollution Acts
2. Policing of discharges with large fines being imposed on polluters
3. Forcing polluters to pay for the damage they cause and for the clean up of the pollution
4. The provision of grants to help farmers reduce pollution, and upgrade slurry and manure storage.
5. A ban on the use of phosphorous detergents and fertilizers
6. The development of waste-water treatment plants for inland towns, which will treat urban waste, water, sewage. This will remove phosphorous before the water is discharged into the inland waterways.
7. The provision of facilities at moorings and marinas for the pumping out of effluent from leisure boats. All boats using the waterways should be equipped with holding tanks.

Marine pollution is a more difficult problem to police, because it is more difficult to locate the offenders, but when they are found, high penalties need to be imposed on them. Dumping of waste should not be allowed at sea by any company, and those who fail to comply should have to pay large fines, and be disgraced in the eyes of the public who are, after all, their customers. Again here the polluters must pay for the clean-up of any pollution that they cause.

The EU also uses the carrot approach, by encouraging local authorities and National Governments to award **blue flags** to **unpolluted beaches**. This award is given to both marinas and beaches, which must excel in four areas. These are:

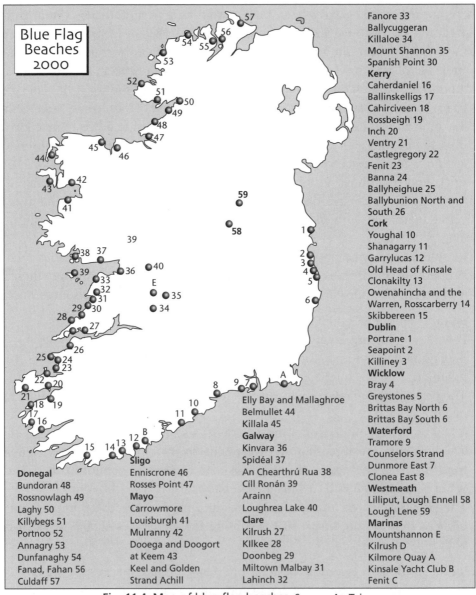

Blue Flag Beaches 2000

Fanore 33
Ballycuggeran
Killaloe 34
Mount Shannon 35
Spanish Point 30
Kerry
Caherdaniel 16
Ballinskelligs 17
Cahirciveen 18
Rossbeigh 19
Inch 20
Ventry 21
Castlegregory 22
Fenit 23
Banna 24
Ballyheighue 25
Ballybunion North and South 26
Cork
Youghal 10
Shanagarry 11
Garrylucas 12
Old Head of Kinsale
Clonakilty 13
Owenahincha and the Warren, Rosscarbery 14
Skibbereen 15
Dublin
Portrane 1
Seapoint 2
Killiney 3
Wicklow
Bray 4
Greystones 5
Brittas Bay North 6
Brittas Bay South 6
Waterford
Tramore 9
Counselors Strand
Dunmore East 7
Clonea East 8
Westmeath
Lilliput, Lough Ennell 58
Lough Lene 59
Marinas
Mountshannon E
Kilrush D
Kilmore Quay A
Kinsale Yacht Club B
Fenit C

Elly Bay and Mallaghroe
Belmullet 44
Killala 45
Galway
Kinvara 36
Spidéal 37
An Chearthrú Rua 38
Cíll Rónán 39
Arainn
Loughrea Lake 40
Clare
Kilrush 27
Kilkee 28
Doonbeg 29
Miltown Malbay 31
Lahinch 32

Sligo
Enniscrone 46
Rosses Point 47
Mayo
Carrowmore
Louisburgh 41
Mulranny 42
Dooega and Doogort at Keem 43
Keel and Golden Strand Achill

Donegal
Bundoran 48
Rossnowlagh 49
Laghy 50
Killybegs 51
Portnoo 52
Annagry 53
Dunfanaghy 54
Fanad, Fahan 56
Culdaff 57

Fig. 11.4: Map of blue flag beaches Source: An Taisce

1. Areas of clean water and land. For this, water samples are taken every two weeks, to check that there are no faecal coliforms or faecal streptococci in the water. There must also be no litter or oil. There must be no sewage or industrial discharge close by.
2. Environmental management and services. This includes the availability of refuse and hazardous-waste collection (this is for marinas and includes paints and anti-fouling used by boat owners). Litter bins and toilets must be available. The beach must be cleaned daily.
3. Safety, which includes the availability of lifeguards, and keeping cars off beaches unless this is specifically allowed, as it is on some beaches. First aid must also be available.
4. Access to environmental information. It includes information about local habitats, educational activities, laws on beach conduct, and the posting up of information on water samples.

In 1995, blue flags were given to 1,870 beaches and 407 marinas in eighteen countries. Ireland received sixty-six blue flags for beaches (three of them at inland locations), and two for marinas. In 2000, seventy beaches and seven marinas were awarded blue flags; this was seven down on the previous year. Tourists prefer to swim in areas where blue flags have been awarded. Ireland has a high number of blue flag beaches, and this fits in with our image of having an unspoilt environment.

Litter problems can be solved by a four-pronged approach:

1. Education: People must learn to put their litter, including cigarettes, in bins, and if there are none to bring it home with them.
2. Local communities are encouraged to tidy up their towns, villages and local areas, by such competitions as the Tidy Town Competition. By cleaning up their houses, using litter bins, tidying up open spaces and planting flowers, the improvements are pleasing to the tourist's eye, but also develop a sense of pride for the local people.
3. Implementation of the Litter Pollution Bill, 1996. This puts an onus on occupiers of houses, and the areas around them, to keep them clean. Organisers of outdoor events and fast-food owners must keep the areas around them clean. Dog owners must clean up after their dogs. Failure to keep this law can result in a £1,500 (€1,875) fine. Pedestrians who litter can face an on-the-spot fine of £50 (€62.5).
4. Local authorities have to play their part too, ensuring that they empty bins, sweep up and wash streets, and collect rubbish on a regular basis. This will ensure that there is no accumulation of waste on the streets, which in itself poses a litter problem. County councils are currently developing new waste management plans.

Simply reducing the numbers of cars on the roads can solve **air pollution**. This can be done by a massive investment in the public transport system. At present plans are going ahead in Dublin to build LUAS and an underground rail system. There is need to put more buses on the street. People need to be encouraged to leave their cars at home and take a bus or train; if this were done then one of the main causes of air pollution would be solved.

The ways that **congestion** can be reduced include the following:

1. The use of park-and-ride systems to get in and out of towns, with car parks located on the edge of towns, is an effective method. This is very poorly developed in Ireland, with a number close to rail and DART stations, but plans for bus park-and-ride schemes are only in the development stages. A similar system could be used for narrow roads, substituting minibuses for coaches. This idea was discussed for the Dingle area.

2. Off-peak and shoulder season tourism should be encouraged more. The twin benefits of such a policy are: less congestion at resorts during the high season, and more work for the hotels all year round. Tourist attractions should be open all year round. This would benefit the workers by providing permanent employment in the tourism industry.

3. Charges may discourage tourists from visiting resorts; so may insistence on advance ticket purchases. Special cheaper tickets can be offered in the off-season.

Noise pollution can be reduced by introducing and enforcing strict laws which limit the amount of noise during certain hours. Such legislation exists in other European countries, notably Switzerland, where no one can make noise after 9.30 p.m.

ACTIVITY HOLIDAYS

Ireland is ideal for activity holidays, the climate is suitable, the countryside is not heavily populated and it is generally unspoilt. There is a wide range of activity holidays in which holiday-makers can take part. The numbers of tourists involving themselves in activity holidays have increased because people want:

1. A healthier lifestyle that involves taking regular exercise, and being in the clean open air

2. A move away from hotter climates that could cause health problems like skin cancers.

Outdoor events take place all year round due to improved outdoor clothing. Additionally people have more leisure time and are wealthier so they are taking more short breaks during the year.

Irish tourism has increased enormously over the last 10 years and activity holidays have grown likewise. The most popular activity holidays are shown below:

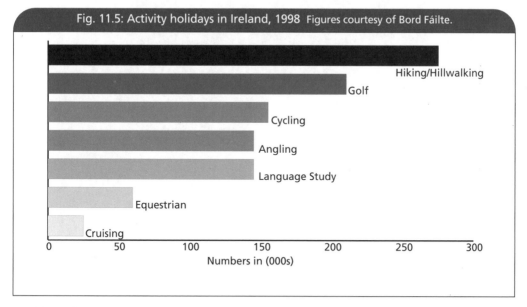

Fig. 11.5: Activity holidays in Ireland, 1998 Figures courtesy of Bord Fáilte.

Walking holidays in Ireland

These really only began in 1982 when the Wicklow Way, which stretches from Marlay Park in Dublin across the Wicklow Mountains to Clonegal in Co. Carlow, was marked out. Now there are thirty-one walks throughout the country. The walks are found on towpaths along the canals, and across mountains. They were developed with reasonably fit people in mind, and while distances reach 200 kilometres, all the walks are broken into stages with the longest walks being usually fifteen to twenty-five kilometres a day. Accommodation and evening meals are available at the end of each stage. This type of holiday has great potential. In Germany there are twenty-nine million hill walkers who go on regular walking holidays and in Britain 3.2 million (1995). These are two of Ireland's major markets and Irish walking holidays can be marketed there. Our walking areas are uncrowded. The most popular walking destinations are the south west, and the west, which include areas like the Macgillycuddy Reeks and Connemara. The most popular months for walking holidays are July and August. A number of companies offer package holidays for walkers, for example, Connemara Safari offer island-hopping trips, which involve not just visiting Clifden and Killary Harbour, but also Inisbofin, Inish Shark, Inish Turk and Clare Island. Accommodation is provided in hotels or B&Bs, meals and transport are included, so all the visitors have to do is walk and enjoy the scenery and camaraderie. There is also a series of walking festivals offered in Ireland during the spring and autumn.

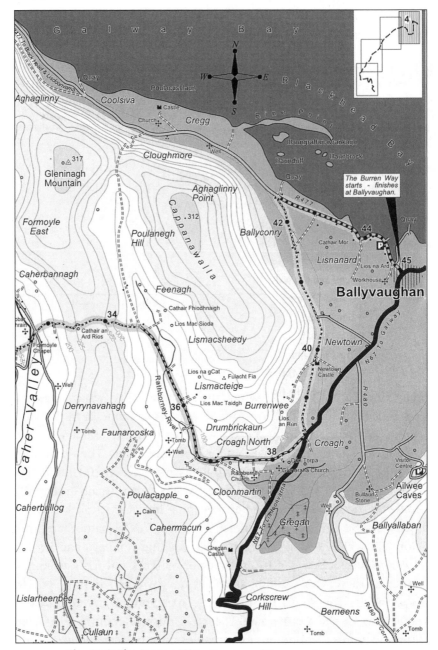

Fig. 11.6: The Burren Way Courtesy of Shannon Development

Golfing holidays

Since 1987 there has been major growth in the number of golf clubs in Ireland (from 191 to 386 in 1999). Some tourists play a few games of golf during their holidays, while others come on a golfing holiday just to play golf. Golf Partnership Ireland is a body which promotes Ireland as a destination abroad. Ireland hosts important golf competitions like the Murphy's Irish Open, Junior Open Ryder Cup, which is good publicity for Irish golf. In 1998 overseas tourists spent nearly £100 (€127) million on golfing holidays in Ireland. British and American tourists dominate this type of holiday. There is major potential for marketing these to the Japanese market, because large numbers of Japanese play golf on holidays in Hawaii and Scotland. It is expected that by 2010 one million golfing tourists will be coming to Ireland. Many of our top hotels have top-class golf courses attached to them, for instance, the K Club in Sallins, Co. Kildare, Mount Juliet in Thomastown, Co. Kilkenny, Ashford Castle in Cong, Co. Mayo. The south west, Shannon, and west are the most popular golfing destinations; 55 per cent of golf tourists come on package holidays.

Cycling holidays

Ireland is only beginning to develop cycle paths that are for the sole use of cyclists, but many of our minor roads are suitable for this type of holiday. In 2000 there were nine cycle routes in Ireland, similar to the walking ways, for example the Táin Trail and Cycling Route from Roscommon to Co. Louth. There are a number of package holidays on offer, which provide accommodation, food, and transfer of luggage each night and of course the bicycle with maps, information and sometimes guides. These are offered, for example, by Celtic Cycling, situated in Carlow, Cycle Ireland and Go Ireland, which are both in Kerry. The most popular destinations for cyclists are the south west and west, some of which have the busiest roads in the country, along with some of the best scenery. Since 1994 there has been a decline in the numbers of tourists taking cycling holidays, especially among Europeans. Cycle paths bearing a crown symbol are being developed in Kerry for tourists. They already exist on the Ring of Kerry and will be introduced into other areas soon.

Angling holidays

Ireland has thousands of lakes, 14,000 kilometres of fishing rivers, and a long coast-line. Our weather is suitable to anglers both in summer and winter. We have a variety of fishing on offer:

1. Game angling. This involves fishing for salmon and trout, both of which are native fish to Ireland. The habitat of both species is very fragile, and the rivers must be very clean as any pollution may lead to fish kills. Sea-trout can be fished for in the Moy Estuary, and in Lough Carrowmore in Mayo, as well as in other rivers. In order to fish for salmon and sea-trout fishermen must have permits and licences. On lakes it is possible to hire boats, and gillies or guides who know the lakes and can show the tourist the best places to fish. This costs about £45 (€56) per day. The salmon and trout season runs from March to September. There are game angling festivals held on Lough Corrib, Lough Mask and Lough Conn.

Fig. 11.7: Coarse fishing festival Courtesy of NITB

2. Coarse angling. These fish were brought into Ireland over the centuries and include pike, rudd and carp. Their ecosystem is not as fragile as that of game fish and they can survive in water where trout cannot. Fishing takes place all year round and no licence is required. Most of the coarse fisheries are in the Midlands, from the Erne to the Blackwater. Normally these fish are fed before being caught, and then kept alive in a net, before being released back into the water. Most coarse anglers are more concerned with the fun of catching the fish than eating them, except for pike. Legislation had to be introduced in order to preserve stocks of pike. Anglers are only allowed to have one in their possession. Pike are found on the Rivers Shannon, Suck and Barrow, and on lakes in Cavan. Coarse angling festivals are organised from April to October, in Fermanagh, Cork, Offaly, Kildare, Monaghan and elsewhere.

3. Sea angling. Ireland has 4,830 kilometres of coastline; this includes a multiplicity of beaches and quiet estuaries. A wide variety of fish is caught in Irish waters. Charter boats are available along the south and west coasts. It is also possible to fish from the shore. Much of the shore fishing occurs along the east coast. Plaice, mullet, cod and tope are all found along the eastern seaboard. Shark fishing occurs between June and October along the south coast. Shark fishing is popular in the deeper water. Wreck fishing is also popular, with anglers wanting to catch conger eels and turbot. The Atlantic waters of the west coast offer the best fishing. Sea-angling competitions take place each year from February to November.

Language study

Ireland attracts large numbers of visitors who choose to learn or improve their English. The Irish have a long tradition of producing writers who have played an important role in English literature, so it is only natural that we help students who want to learn our spoken language. There are many schools located all over the country, with staff qualified to teach English as a foreign language (TEFL). Courses are run all year round at some of the schools while others only operate during the summer months. A range of accommodation is available to students, home stay, residential accommodation in a school, or in a hotel or guesthouse. During the summer months, thousands of students visit Dublin and other centres. They not only earn money for the language schools, but also for many host families who are part of Ireland's tourism industry. In 1998 nearly 185,000 visitors came to Ireland to learn English. This earned £230 (€287.5) million for the tourism industry.

Irish is Ireland's first language, although it is usually spoken in the Gaeltacht areas only. Thousands of Irish students visit Irish Colleges in Gaeltacht areas to attend classes and to become completely immersed in the Irish language. Students live with host families, and this brings revenue into these Gaeltacht areas.

Equestrian holidays

Ireland with its rich green grass, open spaces and well-known love of horses is ideal for equestrian holidays. A wide range of equestrian holidays exists:

1. Trail riding allows participants to go on well-organised trail rides, for periods from a weekend to a fortnight. The trails travel across Ireland's best countryside, on beaches, or through forests.
2. Equestrian centres are approved horse-riding centres that can be found all over Ireland. They offer the beginner lessons in horse riding, and for the experienced riders, dressage, cross-country and show jumping. Short trekking can also take place from these centres.
3. Many famous show jumping events take place in Ireland, for instance the Kerrygold Horse Show at the RDS in Dublin, Millstreet Show in Co. Cork and the Connemara Pony Show in Clifden, Co. Galway. Throughout the country gymkhanas take place during the year, and give a real flavour of rural Ireland; some of these are attached to country shows or agricultural festivals.
4. Ireland is famous for its horse racing especially the Budweiser Irish Derby at the Curragh, Co. Kildare, and the Irish Grand National at Fairyhouse, Co. Meath. Ireland has twenty-seven racecourses, which offer either national hunt or flat racing. Racing is an all-year-round activity, especially at the weekend. Racing festivals include Galway Race Week and the Punchestown Festival in Co. Kildare. Both of these attract large numbers of tourists. The most unusual horse racing takes place at Laytown, Co. Meath. Here the racing occurs once a year on the

Fig. 11.8: Equestrian holiday Courtesy of NITB

strand, the only such race in Europe. Point-to-point races take place in the spring.

5. Hunting occurs all over Ireland between October and March. Tourists can hire horses for the day's hunting, but they must be experienced riders. While some hunts are only drag hunts, others hunt hares, foxes and stags. There has been much controversy in the past few years between hunts people and animal rights groups about the hunting of live animals, and the future of hunting is uncertain.

6. Horse-drawn caravans offer a unique type of self-catering holiday. Tourists stay in the horse-drawn caravan, and travel about fifteen kilometres a day through the countryside. It allows people the time to enjoy the countryside and the slow pace of life, and to meet the country people. It also provides horse and animal lovers with the opportunity to look after a horse for a week, feeding, grooming, and harnessing it. These types of holidays are available in Kerry, Galway, Mayo, Laois, and Wicklow.

Cruising holidays

The main areas of cruise holidays are the Shannon basin, the canals and the Fermanagh lakes. Since the development of the Shannon–Erne waterway, it is now possible for tourists to move between the Erne Lakes and the Shannon system. Cruising only accounts for a small proportion of the tourism industry (3 per cent); it appeals only to a small market, mainly because this type of holiday is expensive. Tourists on the waterways are of two types, those who own their own boats and use them for day sails and holidays, and those who hire cruisers from commercial companies like Emerald Star Line, or Derg Line Cruisers. Ireland's waterways are not used for commercial vehicles, and the density of boat use is low. This compares well

Fig. 11.9: Cruising on the Shannon
Courtesy of Emerald Star Line

with similar holidays in Britain where boats queue to get through locks. The fresh air, the slow pace of life, and the scenery make these holidays attractive. Tourists on the Shannon can visit historical sites like Clonmacnoise, or they can watch birds, or fish from the boats. Most of the cruisers are hired between June and September. There have been major improvements on Ireland's waterways, such as the provision of better mooring facilities, and solving the problems of vandalism. Private service-providers have been encouraged to provide restaurants, entertainment, etc. for tourists.

Water sports holidays

These are very popular with tourists; a range of water sports is available, some through specialist providers and some at adventure centres. They appeal mainly to the young. Many who go on these holidays are already involved in similar clubs at home; others take it up just for their holidays.

1. Canoeing occurs in Ireland, around the coast, on rivers and lakes. It is an all-year-round activity. There are a number of canoe centres located all over the country that have been approved by AFAS, the Association for Adventure Sports.
2. Windsurfing is well suited to Ireland; we have lots of water, and steady winds. Windsurfing centres offer classes for beginners in calm sheltered waters such as Oysterhaven near Kinsale in Co. Cork. The west coast of Ireland offers more challenging windsurfing for the experienced windsurfer. There are a number of approved (Irish Windsurfing Association) windsurfing centres around Ireland, with three located in Dublin.
3. Surfing is very popular along the west coast of Ireland, with resorts like Strandhill, Co. Sligo, offering surfing which is some of the best in the world. A number of centres offer surfing along the west coast.

4. Sub acqua diving is popular along the Atlantic coast, which offers beginners sheltered harbours, and rocky cliffs for the more experienced divers. The sea floor is interesting with a wide variety of sea life including shoals of fish like mackerel and pollack, and large fronds of kelp, which wave from the seabed. The water is very clear, and underwater photography is very possible in these waters. There are a number of centres around the coast (for example the Baltimore Diving and Watersports Centre) where tourists can dive from, but these holidays are only for experienced divers.

5. Outdoor pursuits centres offer a range of activities including water sports, hill walking, rock climbing, abseiling, archery, orienteering, horse riding. A number of these centres are located around Ireland, offering package holidays which include accommodation, food and a range of activities. Outdoor pursuits centres are open all year round providing activities for all ages. Such centres are located, for example, at Cappanelea Co. Kerry, and Kilfinane Co. Limerick.

REVISION EXERCISES

1. Explain the essential elements of sustainable tourism.
2. Why is rural tourism becoming more popular with tourists?
3. Why is Ireland suitable for developing rural tourism?
4. What are the characteristics of tourists interested in having a rural tourism holiday?
5. Name five areas where local rural tourism operates.
6. In the case of Ballyhoura Country: (a) Why was rural tourism developed there? (b) How successful has it been? (c) Why was it so successful? (d) Name some of the facilities offered by Ballyhoura Country.
7. Describe five environmental problems that Ireland is facing.
8. Explain the causes of eutrophication, and how it affects Irish tourism.
9. Why is it important that we clean up our environment?
10. Suggest two soloutions for the environmental problems described in question 7.
11. Explain the value of blue flag beaches to tourism.
12. How can each individual help solve Ireland's litter problem?
13. Why are more people taking activity holidays?
14. Name three marked Walk Ways close to where you live.
15. What are the characteristics of golfing tourists?
16. Describe briefly the three types of angling
17. List two advantages and two disadvantages of language-study tourists.
18. Name three different types of equestrian attractions that are promoted for overseas tourists.
19. Name four areas where cruising holidays take place.

20. Describe three different types of water sports that tourists participate in while on holiday in Ireland.

Assignments

Students should:

1. Using the internet, and collecting brochures from their Regional Tourism Organisation, develop their own case studies for activity holidays.
2. Carry out a tourism resource audit of their local area, including accommodation, activities, transport etc. From this they should develop a brochure for the promotion of their local area as a centre for sustainable tourism, especially rural tourism or leisure activities.
3. Plan a weekend in their local area, with the emphasis being on geographical and ecological tourism.
4. Write an essay on 'The impact of foot-and-mouth disease on the Irish tourist industry in 2001'.

References and further reading

L. Aronsson, *The Development of Sustainable Tourism*. Continuum, 2000.

J. Feehan, ed, *Tourism on the Farm*. UCD Environmental Institute, 1992.

K. Hewel, *The Concept of Sustainability in EU and Irish Regional Policy with Special Regard to Visitors Centres in Ireland*. Trinity College Dublin, 1994.

Irish Country Holidays Brochure 2000. www.irishcountryholidays.com.

J. Lynham, *Best Irish Walks*. Gill & Macmillan, 1994.

P. Sommerville-Large, *Ireland's Islands, Landscape, Life and Legends*. Gill & Macmillan, 1999.

Tourism Policy on International Tourism in OECD. OECD, 1994.

English Tourist Board/Countryside Commission, Tourism in National Parks.

J. Meldon and C. Skehan, *Tourism in the Landscape*. Bord Failte and An Taisce, 1996.

Bord Failte, Fact Cards on Activity Holidays 1998.

ENFO Briefing Sheets on 'Sustainable Tourism', 'Fish Kills', 'Air Pollution', 'Water Pollution', 'Farming and Wildlife', 'Keep it Clean'.

www.ballyhouracountry.ie.

Part 4
Historical
Tourism

CHAPTER 12

Historical Attractions

Ireland's history and tourism are intertwined. Most tourists visiting Ireland visit at least one historical building or museum. They may be deeply interested in history and want to discover our historical past, or they may have visited these buildings because they are good wet day options. None the less, historical buildings are a very important product in the Irish tourist industry.

Groups such as Duchás, Heritage Island, Houses Castles and Gardens of Ireland, and Heritage Towns of Ireland market these historical buildings abroad. In 1998 Europeans were the biggest market visiting historical buildings, followed by the British and North Americans. Most coach tours visit a range of historical buildings in the country. The most popular areas are the south west (26 per cent), Dublin (20 per cent) and then Shannon and west (16 per cent). There are about 350 fee-paying tourist attractions and many others, like the National Museum, which are free. A wide variety of historical buildings can be visited which span Ireland's 8,000 years of history. Some are historical buildings that have been restored while others are reconstructions of older buildings. Some of the restored buildings are now museums while others may be hotels or entertainment centres.

Table 12.1: The most popular Duchás heritage centres in 1999	
Rock of Cashel, Co Tipperary	246,490
Muckross House, Co Kerry	237,895
Brú na Bóinne, Co Meath	219,186
Kilkenny Castle, Co Kilkenny	179,940
Dublin Castle	160,000
Clonmacnoise, Co Offaly	144,595
Glendalough, Co Wicklow	110,680
Kilmainham Jail, Dublin	107,836
Dun Aonghasa, Aran Islands, Co Galway	72,858
Cahir Castle, Co Tipperary	68,575
Figures from Dúchas, Dept of Art, Heritage, Gaeltacht and the Islands	

PRESERVATION AND CONSERVATION

To qualify as historical, buildings must be at least 100 years old. They symbolise our culture because of their historical, political, religious or archaeological significance. All over the country there are numerous such buildings. Many have fallen into disrepair, and need to be conserved and preserved for future generations to enjoy.

There are many causes for the deterioration of buildings. Man may have contributed, and their decay may be due to neglect, fire and vandalism. During the Reformation in the sixteenth century, abbeys were closed and neglected; during the seventeenth century tower houses and castles were abandoned as people moved into houses; during the War of Independence and Civil War in the twentieth century the burning down of landlords' houses led to their destruction and neglect. Weather – rain, wind and sunshine – can also cause houses to deteriorate. Rain causes damp which can destroy the plasterwork and timberwork of the house, eventually leading to its total destruction. Natural disasters such as flooding can also destroy towns and buildings costing many millions of pounds. Whatever the reason for these historical buildings, falling into disrepair, it is necessary for them to be repaired and restored to their former glory.

Many groups have been involved in restoring these buildings, including the OPW (now Duchás), An Taisce, local authorities, communities, and private individuals. Funding for much of this restoration has come from the European Regional Development Fund. FÁS is also usually involved in providing trainees to carry out the work. There has been a major increase in the restoration of buildings since 1989, because of EU funding. Before this, work was much slower because there was a shortage of money for the restoration of castles, etc. Work has also been done on archaeological sites, allowing us to discover how our ancestors lived.

Conservation prevents decay. It is done in order to keep the building in a habitable condition. When conservation is taking place it involves the minimum amount of work, and it should be possible to reverse the work at some time in the future if the need arises. The new work must blend in with the original building, but it should also be possible to pick out the new from the old. Depending on the state of the building and the amount of work that needs to be carried out, there are various levels of conservation:

1. **Indirect conservation prevents buildings from deterioration**. The main problem at this stage is neglect and poor maintenance. Good housekeeping, and keeping vandals out, will protect the building from deteriorating even further.
2. **Preservation** keeps the building in its present condition, and means carrying out repairs to prevent decay, particularly that caused by water and damp.
3. **Direct conservation** strengthens the fabric of the building to maintain it. As far as possible traditional materials and skills should be used in this work.

4. **Restoration** replaces decayed or missing parts of buildings. The part that is replaced should be clearly identifiable and distinguishable from the original. Another type of restoration involves cleaning buildings of pollution. The aim of the restoration is to preserve the historic value of the building, to respect the original material. The unique form of the building should be maintained and nothing should take away from its original appearance.

5. **Rehabilitation** keeps buildings in use or returns them to use. This is often the best way of preserving them. Frequently the new function is in keeping with the building's original purpose, for example, a museum.

6. **Reproduction** copies an artefact, such as a stone cross or a statue. This is often done so that the original can be removed to a museum and the copy is put in its place, for example the South Cross at Clonmacnoise, Co. Offaly.

7. **Reconstruction** is the rebuilding of a historic house or cottage, which uses historical information to create an imitation of the original. Buildings of this type are of less value than their originals. Reconstruction is used at many of Ireland's heritage and folk parks.

Every time a building is interfered with its value is reduced, so it is most important to keep the level of conservation to a minimum. The most valuable buildings are those that have indirect conservation done to them and the least valuable are those that are reconstructed. The procedures for conservation include:

- Duchás carrying out work on a National Inventory of Architectural Heritage in Ireland. These are buildings of international, national, regional and local significance.
- Important buildings being inspected every five years so as to ensure that they are kept in good condition. This will minimise the level of conservation they require.
- Records being kept on all work that is undertaken. This information is for future conservationists hundreds of years from now.

Conservation requires the skills of a range of professionals including conservation architects, landscape architects, specialist craftsmen like stonemasons, plasterers and stucco-workers, cabinet-makers, antiquarians, and art historians. These work as a team under the guidance of an expert and experienced co-ordinator. Records are taken before and after the work, and these and the materials and processes used are recorded in an archive for future reference.

A report in the *Irish Times* on 20 August 1998 by Frank McDonald, entitled 'Destroying the heritage that tourists come for', cited examples of buildings being destroyed rather than preserved. His first example was of the house where J. M. Synge stayed on Inishmaan when he visited there in 1898, where instead of the minimum being done to prevent the building from deterioration, a major reconstruction job was done. The whole house was gutted, its original earth floors were replaced with concrete and its original timbers were replaced with new ones. There was apparently no attempt to blend the new work with the old building. This attempted restoration in fact destroyed the authenticity of the cottage. In Clonmany, Co. Donegal, a market house that was supposed to be restored was in fact knocked down and a replica put in its place. There are other examples in Kilkenny, Maynooth, Rathfarnham, and Enniskerry where new developments are destroying our heritage, and threatening our historical buildings.

HISTORICAL AND CULTURAL PERIODS IN IRELAND'S PAST

1. Mesolithic Period, 8000 B.C.

This refers to the earliest people who came to Ireland. They were Stone Age hunters and gatherers, who lived in Ireland's forests feeding off wild berries, deer and boar. There are few remains of these primitive people. A flint factory was discovered in Co. Antrim, and an example of their settlement was found at Boora Bog in Co. Offaly. A reconstruction of their primitive houses can be seen at the Ferrycarrig Heritage Park in Wexford.

2. Neolithic Period, 2500–1750 B.C.

These were the earliest Stone Age farmers who came to Ireland, cutting down forests with stone axes in order to grow their crops and graze their animals. There are many sites associated with this period. Most of them are burial tombs. Neolithic man built four types of burial tomb: court cairns, dolmens, passage tombs, and wedge tombs. These are all called megalithic tombs because of their use of large or great stones.

The earliest type of megalithic tomb was the **court cairn**. The tomb consisted of a long chamber that was divided into a number of areas where burials took place. The front of the tomb was semi-circular in shape and was flanked by standing stones. It is thought that the funeral rite took place here. These types of tombs are found at Creevykeel and Moytirra in east Sligo.

Passage graves are the best known of Irish megalithic tombs. These were round earthen mounds; a passage led from the edge of the tomb and near the centre the passage turned into a cruciform shape. It was there that the burials took place, usually in large stone basins. The passages consisted of large stones, and the roofs were constructed with a technique known as corbelling. The stones in these graves were highly decorated with spirals, diamonds and other designs. Visitors can visit passage graves in the Boyne Valley at Newgrange and Knowth, at Carrowkeel in Co. Sligo, and at Lough Crew in Co. Meath. Some of these graves are aligned to the movement of the sun; Newgrange's chamber is lit up at the winter solstice when the rising sun fills up the passage on 21 December. Knowth was built so that the passages are filled with light during the March and September equinox, the east passage getting the rising sun, and the west passage getting the setting sun. Many of the large passage graves also had smaller satellite graves.

Fig. 12.1: Newgrange, Co. Meath

Portal dolmens are stone tables, often thought to be Druid altars. They usually consist of three or four standing stones covered by one large capstone. Dolmens are found all over the country, but the most famous are at Poulnabrona in Co. Clare and Browneshill in Co. Carlow.

Fig. 12.2: Poulnabrona dolmen, Co. Clare

Wedge-shaped gallery graves are the latest of the megalithic tombs dating from 2,000 B.C. They are called wedge-shaped because the passage is wider at one end than the other. Similar to the passage graves, the large stones which formed the passage were covered by a mound. Wedge tombs can be seen at Lough Gur, Co. Limerick and Ballyedmond, Co. Dublin.

The **Céide Fields** in Co. Mayo is a site where Stone-Age farmers lived. The area was preserved because changes in the weather formed bog land, and the peat covered up the old stone-walled fields used by these ancient farmers. Local people discovered the fields perhaps fifty years ago and, later, archaeological digs took place. Today visitors can visit the Dúchas interpretive centre and discover how the Stone-Age farmers lived, their types of fields, the houses they built and the crops they grew.

3. The Bronze Age 1750–500 B.C.

The Bronze Age developed when people started using bronze implements instead of stone axes and weapons. The new metals were originally developed in the Middle East and spread throughout Europe as a result of trade and migration. Many examples of Bronze-Age artefacts can be seen in museums in Ireland, but there are few buildings dating from this period. It is believed that this is because megalithic tombs continued to be used by the Bronze-Age people for burials. **Stone circles** are the principal monuments from the Bronze Age. These are basically circles made of large stones and, like Newgrange, they are aligned with the rising or setting sun at the summer and winter solstices. It is thought that they were of religious significance. The largest example in Ireland is Grange Stone Circle at Lough Gur, Co. Limerick; other examples are at Drombeg, Co. Cork and Beltany, Co. Donegal.

4. Iron Age (Celts) 500 B.C.–500 A.D.

When the Celts came to Ireland from Central Europe they brought iron implements and weapons with them. They were farmers and introduced a number of different types of farmhouses, which they built to protect themselves and their animals. These included hill-forts, ring-forts, promontory forts and crannógs. Until the 1980s there were still thousands of forts in the Irish countryside because people were superstitious about the remains, which were known as fairy forts. **Hill-forts** were situated on hilltops, and consisted of a large stone wall with ditches, either inside or outside, providing extra protection. The location of the hill-forts protected the inhabitants, for they could see for miles around, for example, Tara in Co. Meath and Dun Allininne in Co. Kildare. **Ring-forts** were smaller than hill-forts and were surrounded by a stone or earth wall. It is thought that they were more like farmhouses, protecting the family and their animals. Inside the wall was found the house also made of stone and the fulachta fiadh or cooking pits. The *fulachta fiadh* were stone-lined pits that were filled with water; stones were heated in a fire and put into the water to bring it to the boil. Meat was cooked in the water; cooking it in this way takes about the same time as roasting it. Animals were brought into the ring-fort at night. Some of the forts also had underground stone-built passages known as souterrains that were used for storage and for escaping from the fort. Ring-forts can be seen at Rathcroghan in Co. Roscommon, the inauguration site of the kings of Connacht. **Stone forts** are military fortifications, and consist of strong stone walls with platforms inside that allow the defenders to use weapons against attackers. The Grianán of Aileach in Co. Donegal and Staigue Fort in Co. Kerry are examples of these. The walls of Staigue Fort are three metres high and two metres thick, and the Fort is thirty metres in diameter. A bank or ditch surrounds it. **Promontory forts** were located along the coast, protected to seaward by steep cliffs and on the landward side by walls and ditches. Dunbeg on the Dingle Peninsula, Co. Kerry and Dún Aonghasa on Inishmore, Co. Galway are examples of forts located along cliffs.

Fig. 12.3: An Grianán Aileach, Co. Donegal

Crannógs were artificially-constructed islands in lakes; palisades or fences made of wood defended them. Inside the crannóg were buildings for both animals and inhabitants. Crannógs can be seen at Lough Gur, Co. Limerick, and Cragaunowen, Co. Clare. Other remains from the Iron Age include ogham stones that date from 300 A.D. These were large stones on which Ireland's earliest writings are found. Letters are represented by a series of horizontal lines positioned on either side of a central line, usually the corner of the stone. The words begin at the bottom, and usually consist of the name of the person commemorated by the stone. Examples are to be found at Dunloe, Co. Kerry and Drumlohan, Co. Waterford. The Celts also produced La Tène art; a famous stone decorated in this style can be seen at Turoe, Co. Galway.

5. Early Christian Ireland 500–1200

St Patrick brought Christianity to Ireland; this led to the decline of the power of the Druids (Celtic priests). St Patrick organised his church on an Episcopal basis but this soon went into decline as a large number of monasteries were founded all over the country in the sixth and seventh centuries. It is these **monasteries** that we most associate with the period of Early Christian Ireland. Many of the monasteries were set up in isolated areas of the country like Skellig Michael, Co. Kerry and Glendalough, Co. Wicklow. This was to allow the monks to lead lives of rigorous hardship and penance. These monasteries soon became centres of culture, as the monks produced beautiful manuscripts, silver and gold chalices, stone crosses, etc.

From their isolated monasteries many monks travelled to Europe and founded new monastic settlements in Germany, Italy and Austria. This is the period when Ireland is often referred to as the Island of Saints and Scholars, for it coincided with the period in Europe called the Dark Ages, when barbaric hordes invaded from the east. Irish monks reintroduced Christianity and learning to Europe. Life in the monasteries was disrupted by the arrival of the Vikings, who attacked the monasteries because of their reputation for great wealth.

Skellig Michael, Co. Kerry, off the south-west coast of Ireland, is an example of an early monastic settlement. It was built out of local rock. The monks carved stone steps and built beehive huts out of stones. There was little soil for them to grow crops and much of their cereals and vegetables had to be brought from the mainland. The islands were rich in birds for eggs and meat, and the surrounding seas provided fish, but life was very austere. At this location the monks spent many hours praying. Tourists can discover what life was like for the monks by visiting the Skellig Experience, and going out to the islands by boat. Other monastic settlements include Clonmacnoise in Co. Offaly, Monasterboice in Co. Louth, and Clondalkin in Co. Dublin.

Round towers are Ireland's only indigenous buildings. They are slender and tall, with the door about three metres above ground, and three or four windows. Their exact use is not known, but it has been suggested that they were used as a bell tower to call the monks to mass, or as a means of storing their treasures, and as a refuge for the monks when they were being attacked. Round towers were built until the 1200s. They can be found at many monastic sites, including Glendalough, Clonmacnoise, and Monasterboice.

High crosses are recognised by the ring which surrounds the cross form and are decorated with scenes from the Bible. It is thought that they developed from the merging of the Christian crucifix and Celtic worship of the sun. The crosses are highly decorated with scenes from both the Old and New Testaments and were used to explain the story of Christianity to an illiterate population. The earliest crosses date from the seventh century and were simple standing stones that were carved

Fig. 12.4: St Kevin's Monastery, Glendalough
Courtesy of Dúchas

with crosses; these can be found in north Donegal. The more intricate high crosses date from the ninth century onwards and include those that can be seen at Kells in Co. Meath, Clonmacnoise in Co. Offaly and Monasterboice in Co. Louth.

The earliest stone churches date from the ninth century. They replace the older wooden churches, which were vulnerable to Viking attacks. The earliest churches consisted mainly of stone, including stone roofs. Gallarus in Dingle, Co. Kerry looks like an upturned boat, and a corbelling technique was used for its roof. St Kevin's Church in Glendalough and Cormac's Chapel in Cashel both have stone roofs. Later, churches were built using the Romanesque style of architecture. Instead of being rectangular in shape, they were widened to incorporate naves and chancels. Reform in the Irish church led to an increased number of churches being built. Romanesque architecture is characterised by round doorways, chancel archways, and windows. Many of these features were decorated with geometric designs, human masks and animals. Churches that have such designs include Cormac's Chapel in Cashel, Glendalough, Clonmacnoise and Clonfert.

Fig. 12.5: Romanesque architecture; the 'whispering' arch at Clonmacnoise

6. The Vikings 800–1100

The Vikings first arrived in Ireland in 795. They attacked the rich monastic settlements along the coast, and then using the rivers attacked the monasteries along the Shannon. They came from Norway at a time when the population there was too large for the land available. So they took to the sea in their long ships, in search of land and riches. They travelled far and wide, from Newfoundland in Canada to the Black Sea in the Ukraine. Riches from Irish monasteries are still to be seen in the museum in Trondheim in Norway. Later the Vikings came as traders, and they set up towns along the Irish coast. Before their arrival there were few towns in Ireland, as most Irish people lived in the countryside. The Vikings set up the towns of Dublin, Wexford, Waterford, Cork and Limerick. These towns traded with other Viking towns like York in England, and the Isle of Man. While no buildings remain in Ireland from the Viking period, we have a rich treasure trove of Viking artefacts. Archaeologists uncovered these during the 1970s and 1980s at Wood Quay in Dublin, and in Waterford. These artefacts can be seen in the National Museum in Dublin, and the Granary Museum in Waterford. The Vikings lived in the new towns at the same time as monasteries continued to develop in the countryside.

7. Norman Ireland, 1169–1600

Diarmait Mac Murchada was king of Leinster, and was involved in a dispute with the king of Bréifne. Mac Murchada went to the Norman King Henry II to get help to restore his lands. He got support from Norman lords in Wales, and the first Norman soldiers landed in Baginbun, Co. Wexford in 1169. The Normans soon conquered Wexford, Waterford and Dublin. Within two years Henry II came to Ireland and the Normans and the Irish kings submitted to his rule. The Normans' arrival in any area was followed by the construction of a motte and bailey, and later of castles and abbeys.

Fig. 12.6: King John's Castle, Limerick

A **motte and bailey** consisted of a flat-topped mound of earth, on which was built a wooden bailey. The soldiers lived in these protected towers. The wooden towers no longer exist but there are still examples of mottes around the country, close to Clonard in Co. Meath, and at St Mullins in Co. Carlow.

The Normans built **stone castles** in the thirteenth century when they had conquered half of the country. Hugh de Lacy's castle at Trim in Co. Meath was one of the finest in the country; it consisted of a strong outer wall with towers and was surrounded by a moat. Access was by a drawbridge, which had a portcullis gate. Within the walls there was a bawn in which animals and soldiers lived. The castle, or keep, was built within the walls, and consisted of four towers and the castle building itself. Trim Castle is currently being restored by Dúchas (it will take years to complete). Cahir Castle in Co. Tipperary is another example of a restored Norman castle.

Tower houses, which were square in shape, were built from the fifteenth century onwards. They consisted of perhaps four floors, each floor being one room. The narrow windows provided protection; the family generally lived in the top floors for security reasons. Many were built with a grant of £10 (€12.5) in order to protect the Pale from the Irish. The Pale was the area around Dublin under the control of Dublin Castle, that is, English rule. There were many such castles built around Dublin and Meath including Ashtown Castle in the Phoenix Park. Many Irish chieftains adopted this idea and there are numerous tower houses around Ireland.

The twelfth century was a period of change in the Irish church. New religious orders like the Cistercians, Augustinians, Dominicans and Franciscans developed **abbeys** throughout Europe. St Malachy of Armagh introduced the Cistercians into Ireland in 1142 and they founded Mellifont Abbey. The Cistercians lived a very ordered life. The new abbeys were built on a square, with the church on the north side, the chapter house and sacristy on the eastern side, the kitchen and refectories on the south side, and store rooms, dormitories, etc. on the west side. All abbeys which date from this period are built to the same design. Within thirty years there were thirty-eight Cistercian abbeys in Ireland, e.g. Jerpoint in Co. Kilkenny, Boyle in Co. Roscommon. By the end of the twelfth century other orders had arrived in Ireland. The Augustinians built Ballintubber Abbey in Co. Mayo; the Dominicans built Sligo Abbey. The architecture had changed from the rounded Romanesque to the tall slender Gothic. Dublin's two cathedrals, Christchurch and St Patrick's, date from this period. Within the churches there are many fine examples of stone carving, for example, on tombs, effigies of knights and bishops, and baptismal fonts.

Fig. 12.7: Ballintubber Abbey

8. Tudor and Stuart Ireland, 1500–1700

By the time the Tudors had gained control of the English crown, in Ireland they controlled only the small area of the Pale. Peace in England allowed them the time to subdue the rest of their kingdom. The sixteenth century in Ireland was one of war, conquest and plantation, first in Leinster, then Munster and finally, at the beginning of the seventeenth century, in Ulster. Castles and tower houses were abandoned, and replaced by **Tudor mansions** like Ormond's Castle at Carrick-on-Suir and O'Brien's Leamanagh Castle in the Burren in Co. Clare. These houses were two and three stories high, with wide, mullioned windows and tall gables. Some of the settlers in the Ulster Plantation built fortified houses, for example Parkes Castle in Co. Leitrim and Donegal Castle.

War with continental Europe led to the building of a number of star-shaped forts around the coast. These included Charles Fort and James Fort built on either side of Kinsale Harbour, Co. Cork. Sir William Robinson, who designed Charles Fort in 1677, was also involved in designing the Royal Hospital at Kilmainham in Dublin. This was designed as a hospital for veteran soldiers. The hospital was located on the edge of Dublin city, and it offered peace to the recovering soldiers.

9. Georgian Ireland 1700–1800

The Williamite–Jacobite War ended at the Battle of the Boyne. This led to a period of peace and prosperity for the Protestant landlord classes. It resulted in the establishment of an Irish Parliament to rule Ireland, which occupied the building that is now the Bank of Ireland on College Green. The development of many public buildings designed by such famous architects as James Gandon, Thomas Cooley, and Richard Cassels – for example the Custom House, Four Courts, and City Hall – took place in Dublin. Many of these public buildings are still in use, and are also open to tourists.

Stately homes were designed for country estates. The best example of these **Palladian mansions** is Castletown House in Celbridge Co. Kildare, which was

Fig. 12.8: Castletown House, Co. Kildare

designed by Edward Lovett Pearce for William Conolly, the Speaker of the Irish House of Commons. Other examples are Strokestown Park House in Co. Roscommon and Russborough House, Co. Wicklow. These houses were usually designed around a large central block, and on either side wings extended to the servant's quarters. Strokestown Park House also had a gallery kitchen; this meant that the lady of the house never entered the kitchen; she lowered menus and instructions from the gallery that overlooked the kitchen. Many of these large houses were richly decorated with stucco (plaster) work. They had large ornamental gardens and parklands attached to them. Neo Classical designs were used for many houses at the end of the eighteenth-century, for example Emo Court, Co. Laois and Castlecoole, Co. Fermanagh.

The ascendancy built town houses for themselves in Ireland's cities and towns. Some of these were large town houses like the one Lord Leinster built for himself in Kildare Street, now Dáil Éireann. Others were in Georgian squares such as St Stephen's Green, Merrion Square and Parnell Square in Dublin. Georgian town houses were built not only in Dublin, but also in Cork and Limerick. They were built to uniform size and design, with the only differences being the doors and wrought ironwork. Many famous people lived in these squares; for instance, Daniel O'Connell, William Butler Yeats and Oscar Wilde all lived in Merrion Square, Dublin.

While the wealthy lived in their mansions and their town houses, most of the Irish peasants lived in small two- and three-roomed cottages. These were whitewashed with thatched roofs; they had small windows because of a tax on daylight. To overcome this problem many of the houses used half-doors, which could be opened into the kitchen to give light. The kitchen was in the centre with bedrooms on either side. Cooking was done on an open fire, and candles or oil lamps provided light. Different types of cottages were found in different parts of the country. Many examples of these cottages can be visited by tourists: Muckross Traditional Farms, Killarney, Co. Kerry; Bunratty Folk Park, Co. Clare; Pádraig Pearse's in Rosmuc, Co. Galway; and Hennigan's Heritage Centre in Swinford, Co. Mayo. In rural Ireland these types of houses are still lived in.

10. Nineteenth- and twentieth-century Ireland

The Act of Union in 1800 led to the decline of Dublin and some of its squares, for example Mountjoy Square. Many industrial buildings remain from this period. A wide variety of these have now been turned into museums; for example: in Dublin the Guinness Storehouse, and Jameson Whiskey Corner; Croom (corn) Mills in Co. Limerick; Newmills, corn and flax mills, in Co. Donegal. Ireland's oldest surviving windmill is located at Tacumshin Lake, Co. Wexford.

In 1845, Ireland's greatest tragedy hit in the form of potato blight. The Great Famine, or Gorta Mór, lasted from 1845 to 1849. One million people died of hunger, malnutrition and disease, while a further one million emigrated. The Famine

Museum in Strokestown Park House, Co. Roscommon uses the estate's documents from the period to relate how one estate coped with the famine. People who were destitute turned to the workhouse for help; the old workhouse at Dunfanaghty in Co. Donegal was opened as a museum in 1995. The Queenstown Story in Cóbh commemorates those who emigrated from Ireland in the century that followed.

Museums have also been established in the homes of famous Irish politicians who played a major role in Ireland's history. These included Daniel O'Connell who won Catholic Emancipation for Ireland in 1829 and whose home in Derrynane at Caherdaniel in Co. Kerry is now a museum in his memory. Charles Stewart Parnell played a major role in the Land League, and in the Home Rule Movement in the 1880s; his home at Avondale in Rathdrum, Co. Wicklow is now a museum. Pádraig Pearse leader of the 1916 Rising was not only a revolutionary, he was also a barrister and teacher, and his school at St Enda's in Rathfarnham, Dublin is a museum.

Transport has been used as a theme for developing new museums. Some have been developed in closed-down railway stations, like the one at Kiltimagh, Co. Mayo. Vintage cars can be seen in Buncrana Co. Donegal, and different types of vehicles at the Transport Museum in Howth, Dublin.

HERITAGE TOWNS

Under the Operational Programme for Tourism 1989-93, the idea of Heritage Towns developed. In 1989 Bord Fáilte launched 'Ireland's Heritage Towns'. At the beginning there were fifteen towns and these were to increase to twenty-three in the Operational Programme for Tourism 1993-99, but by 2001 there were thirty-four. The aims of the Heritage Towns were to

- Develop a wider range of more attractive products, particularly for cultural tourists.
- Provide better value for money for tourists; this was both in the price and quality of what the tourist were being offered.
- By better promotion, help Ireland to increase its market share in its main markets.

Towns that in the past were on the periphery of tourism areas would now become attractions in themselves and become part of Ireland's growing tourism industry.

The development of these towns involved careful planning and the provision of the following tourist facilities:

1. A number of conserved historic buildings were available for tourists to visit.
2. A theme was developed for the town that reflected its historic and cultural interests.
3. Since few tourists know much about Ireland's history, or a Heritage Town's

actual history, this then had to be presented to them as clearly as possible. A heritage centre was developed in the town to interpret and explain the historical development of the town.

4. Towns developed guided tours, tourist trails, or good signposting to historical sites. They produced a brochure which outlined the town's history, tourist sights and facilities.

5. Towns were encouraged to improve the streetscape, shop fronts, paving, street furniture, to reflect Ireland's traditions. Litter was removed, and flowers added to make the town's appearance more attractive.

6. Signposting was improved to help tourists find their way around the town.

7. Entertainment was developed in the town that linked into the town's theme, for example, traditional Irish music, drama, poetry readings, story-telling and art exhibitions. These often take place in the heritage centre so that it is used all year, and provides extra revenue for the heritage company.

8. Festivals were organised during the high season; some were linked with the heritage of the town.

9. A mix of hotels, guesthouses, hostels or self-catering accommodation, restaurants, pubs, craft shops etc., to suit a wide range of budgets was developed.

10. Good car-parking facilities and a traffic-management plan were put in place, to encourage tourists to visit.

These developments took place over time in conjunction with Bord Fáilte, the local authorities, the Regional Tourism Organisation (and later RATA) and community interests. A Heritage Town company was developed and worked with the various organisations, the tidy town committee, and the local historical or archaeological society in developing the town and its facilities. Funding was provided in 1989 to the tune of £14 (€17.5) million by the European Regional Development Fund. The local authority helped by improving signposting, providing car parks, repaving areas, improving street furniture, landscaping the town. Special funding for this came from the Department of the Environment.

Each town was developed around a particular theme. The main themes were Celtic monastic settlements, Viking towns, medieval towns; landlord-built, or planned towns; market towns and seaside towns.

- Medieval towns include Athenry, Co. Galway; Carlingford, Co. Louth; Dalkey, Co. Dublin; Kilkenny; Trim, Co. Meath; Youghal, Co. Cork.
- Planned towns include Abbeyleix, Co. Laois; Birr, Co. Offaly; Kenmare, Co. Kerry; Strokestown, Co. Roscommon; Westport, Co. Mayo.

Themes were developed for the Heritage Towns; for example, Cóbh the emigration town, or Tullamore the home of whiskey. Each has its own unique atmosphere and character.

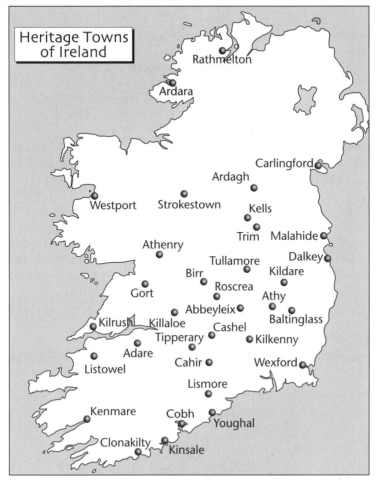

Fig. 12.9: Map of Heritage Towns in Ireland

Case study: Dalkey Co. Dublin; medieval Heritage Town

Dalkey is located eight miles south of Dublin city on the coast. It became a Heritage Town in 1998. The Dalkey Irish Heritage Town Company restored the castle and developed a heritage centre. In the same year it won Dublin Tourism's award for the best tourism product and service. Today it is Dun Laoghaire Rathdown's main tourism attraction and home to the rich and famous.

Dalkey comes from Deilginis or Island of Thorns; this refers to the island of Dalkey, which is just off the coast south of Coliemore Harbour. Dalkey developed as Dublin's main port during medieval times, when the port of Dublin suffered from silting. The waters off Dalkey allowed for deep-water anchorage. During this prosperous period seven castles were built; these were tower houses providing storage for wine and spices and houses for the wealthy merchants. The town had two gates and was walled. Within the town there was a church dedicated to St Begnet, who is now the patron saint of Dalkey. The building of Dublin's quays below Capel Street Bridge in 1610 led to the decline of Dalkey and it reverted to a fishing village. In the eighteenth century some prosperity returned as the local quarry was used to provide stones for the building of Dun Laoghaire harbour. Between 1844 and 1854 Dalkey had an atmospheric railway, which linked it with Dun Laoghaire. This train went downhill using gravity, but on the upward journey it used atmospheric traction, produced from the engine house located in the village. On the last part of the journey up to Dalkey, second-class passengers had to walk, while the third-class passengers had the pleasure of pushing the train up. A model of this train can be seen in the heritage centre. This train was replaced by the extension of the Dun Laoghaire line to Bray.

Dalkey also became home to many Victorians who built houses and villas in the area, because of its rural beauty, scenery, and its bathing. The Victorians built the Town Hall, which is attached to Dalkey Castle, and now provides a venue for plays, performances, and art exhibitions.

Dalkey has many literary connections. James Joyce taught there. George Bernard Shaw spent his summers in Torc Cottage. Maeve Binchy, Hugh Leonard and Bernard Farrell live there. In November the annual Dalkey Drama Festival takes place. The town has many other famous inhabitants including the singers Bono, Enya, and Chris de Burgh, and the racing-car driver Eddie Irvine. The town has a well-deserved reputation for fine food, with a range of good quality restaurants serving a variety of ethnic dishes.

Things for tourists to see in Dalkey include: Dalkey Castle and Heritage Centre, Archbold's Castle, St Begnet's Church, Bullock Castle and Harbour, Dalkey Hill, Sorrento Park, Shaw's Cottage, and the Vico Road.

Fig. 12.10: Dalkey Heritage Centre

Case study: Birr Co. Offaly; Georgian Heritage Town

Birr is one of Offaly's most attractive towns. It is located on the banks of the Camcor River, where it joins the Little Brosna. The earliest settlement here was in the sixth century, but Birr was not built until much later. In 1620 the Parsons family from the east of England were granted 1,000 acres, and took over the castle of the O'Carroll clan. During the seventeenth century the castle was besieged a number of times. Sir Laurence Parsons, the second Earl of Rosse, laid out the town of Birr and it was originally called Parsonstown.

The centre of Birr is its Castle, home to the Earls of Rosse for fourteen generations. The town contains a range of Georgian buildings including those of Oxmantown Mall and John's Place. These Georgian houses have beautiful fanlights, and those on St John's Place are set back from the road with trees and shrubs bordering it. Opposite the gate of the Castle is the Gothic Protestant Church, which was built in 1817, and once had the novelist Charlotte Bronte's husband A.B. Nicholls as rector. Pugin designed the Convent in the 1840s and there is an Irish round tower attached to it.

Fig. 12.11: Birr Castle

Birr Castle Demesne is famous for its gardens. There are sixty-two acres of grounds, and these include parkland, and a lake. Box hedges were planted in 1780 and are now the highest in the world. The sixth Countess of Rosse created the formal garden, using an Italian design. There are also woodlands, a waterfall and fountains. The gardens have many unusual trees and shrubs that come from all over the world, and are famous for their flowers in spring and autumn. The Castle itself was altered in the early 1800s, being both enlarged and given Gothic features.

The Earls of Rosse were very involved in science. The third and fourth Earls were both interested in astronomy. The third Earl built the world's largest telescope (Great Telescope) in 1845, which remained the largest until 1917, and this brought astronomers from all over the world to Birr. The fourth Earl discovered the temperature of the moon using the telescope. Sir Charles Parsons, the third Earl's youngest son, developed the steam turbine, which was used in warships. The wife of the third Earl, Mary Wilmer Field, was a pioneer in the field of photography. Another member of the family, Mary Ward, was an artist and naturalist. To commemorate these achievements, and those of other Irish scientists, a historic science centre has been opened in the Castle's old stables; this is known as The Galleries of Discovery. The Great Telescope has recently been restored.

Birr is fortunate that little urban development took place in the twentieth century, and that most of its history has been preserved. It was one of Ireland's first Heritage Towns. The town can hold its head high, for it has some of the best examples of Georgian buildings in the country. Since its development as a Heritage Town it has improved its services for tourists.

- Birr Heritage Centre, located in a miniature Greek-style temple, tells the town's history.
- A Walking Tour of Birr shows its main historic buildings.
- Birr Castle and Gardens; the Gardens are opened to the public, and the Castle is only open on special occasions, e.g. during Vintage Week.
- Emmet Square has one the oldest coaching inns in Ireland, and a Doric column.
- The Georgian Houses of St John's Place and Oxmantown Mall.
- The Riverside Walk, close to St Brendan's Catholic Church, and Pugin's Convent of Mercy.
- The nineteenth-century Courthouse and Bridewell, or jail.
- Birr holds a Vintage Week every August. Recitals are performed in Birr Castle when the 'Music Festival in Great Irish Houes' takes place
- Other tourist facilities include an equestrian centre, restaurants, hotels, guesthouses, craft centre, golf, and a tourist information centre.

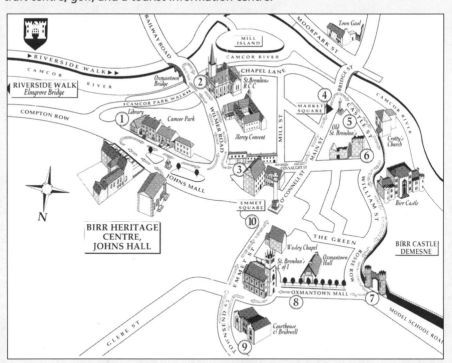

Fig. 12.12: Map of Birr, Georgian Heritage Town

The development of Heritage Towns as part of Ireland's tourism product has put Birr on the tourism trail, has helped increase visitor numbers and revenue, and has created employment.

The marketing group Heritage Towns of Ireland has many of the Heritage Towns as members. It is located in Cashel, Co. Tipperary. Its functions are:

- To promote its members at home and abroad by producing brochures, which are sent for distribution to Bord Fáilte's overseas offices, tour operators, and the Heritage Towns. It produces flyers that are available in local tourist offices and it operates an internet site.
- To attend trade promotions in Ireland and England.
- To co-operate together with Dúchas and Heritage Ireland.
- To provide workshops for training purposes.

In 1999 there were twenty-five members of the group, who paid an annual fee of £10,000 (€12,500) for promoting their town. This is about 12 per cent of the town's annual marketing budget. Many of the smaller towns are not members of this group.

REVISION EXERCISES

1. Explain the differences between conservation, preservation and reconstruction.
2. Look up the article 'Destroying the heritage that tourists come for' on the internet at *http/www.irish-times.ie* and make a note of other examples where our heritage is threatened.
3. Find examples of all different types of conservation when you visit historical attractions and museums.
4. Place the following in the correct chronological order:
   Georgian Period, Iron Age, Mesolithic Period, nineteenth and twentieth centuries, Normans, Bronze Age, Vikings, Tudor and Stuart Ireland, Early Christian Ireland, Neolithic Period.
5. In the case of each historical period named above, name the main type of building associated with each period, and give an example in each case.
6. Fill in the following blanks:

Historical Period	Type of Building	Example
	Stone Circle	
		Poulnabrone, Co Clare
Early Christian Ireland		
	Abbey	
		Parkes Castle, Co Leitrim
Georgian Ireland		

7. Draw a map of Ireland and on it place a few examples of each type of historical building that tourists can visit when on holidays here.

235

8. Explain the term Heritage Town.
9. List five features that Heritage Towns should provide for tourists.
10. Looking at the map, name the types of Heritage Towns that are located in your region.
11. Compare the tourist facilities that are offered at two Heritage Towns.

Assignments

1. Visit a range of historical sites, and (a) put them into their historical period, (b) explain in each case the amount of conservation that has taken place on the building, (c) find out about the people who lived in these buildings and what they were involved in, for example, literature, art, science or business, and (d) write up a report on each visit to a historical building.
2. Visit a Heritage Town and find out the following: (a) When it became a Heritage Town, and who administers it, (b) What is the history of the town? (c) How much work was involved in developing the town as a Heritage Town? (d) What facilities are available to the tourist, and are there future plans to increase those facilities? Write a report on your findings.
3. Carry out an audit of historical buildings in your area, and design a historical weekend break for a group of interested tourists.

References and further reading

B. de Breffney, *Heritage in Ireland*. Weidenfeld & Nicolson, 1980.
Bord Failte, *Heritage and Tourism: Development of Heritage Attractions in Ireland*. Bord Failte, 1992.
Buttimer, Rynne & Guerin, *The Heritage of Ireland*. Collins Press, 2000.
ENFO Briefing Sheets on 'History Around you', 'Medieval Dublin', 'Georgian Dublin', 'Victorian Dublin', 'Medieval Cork', 'Dublin Castles'.
P. Harbison, *Guide to National Monument*. Gill & Macmillan, 1975.
P. Liddy, *Dublin Be Proud*. Chadworth, 1987.
J. O'Brien and D. Guinness, *Great Irish Houses and Castles*. Weidenfeld & Nicolson, 1993.
J. O'Brien and D. Guinness, Dublin, *A Grand Tour*. Weidenfeld & Nicolson, 1993.
M. Robinson, N. Evans & P. Callaghan, eds, *Tourism & Cultural Change*. (J. Stock's article can be found in this book.)

CHAPTER 13

Genealogy Tourism

Genealogy is the study of a person's roots or family tree. It is normal when people research their family that they look at just one branch, either their father's family, or their mother's family, and in each case trace backwards using that surname. The origins of Irish surnames (i.e. the name of any person born in Ireland) may stretch back through many generations in Ireland, or may relate to someone who recently immigrated to Ireland. The intermingling of cultures in Ireland has created a large number of surnames. Many who look for their family history are tourists from North America, England, and Australia. Their ancestors may have emigrated from Ireland over the last three hundred years and they are the target market for this type of tourism. It is estimated that there are over 60 million people of Irish descent worldwide and these people are interested in discovering their Irish roots.

MIGRATION AND ITS INFLUENCE ON GENEALOGY

1. Immigration

The people of Ireland are not a homogeneous group; our ancestors arrived over a long period of time. As they came new ideas were introduced to the Irish culture and new names. Every period in history contributed to the development of Irish society and some of these influences make up the Ireland that we live in today.

The Celts arrived in Ireland about 500 B.C. and continued to rule until 500 A.D. without any major outside influence. They ruled through a system of king-groups that consisted of all people related through the same great-grandfathers. Celtic Ireland was one that lived by farming, with no towns. At this time there were few surnames, except the Eoghanacht of Munster and the Uí Néill of Ulster and these were the main sub-kings. People were known only by their first names.

The arrival of Christianity (fifth century) had a profound effect on Gaelic Ireland. New monasteries were set up, which became commercial and administrative centres, for example, Clonmacnoise and Armagh. At this time people had names that were not hereditary; for instance, Airt Mac Briain was Art the son of Briain, but Art's son Conor would be Conor Mac Airt, so each generation had a different surname. Hereditary surnames did not become common until after the eleventh century. Irish surnames are usually derived from the name of a person held in high esteem, e.g. Niall of the Nine Hostages, from a trade, or, rarely, from a placename.

Table 13.1: Examples of Gaelic names and their meanings			
Name	Origin	Name	Origin
O'Neill	Niall Glun Dubh	Clery/O'Cléirigh	cleireach or clerk
Duff	Dubh or dark	Mc Gowan	gabhan or smith

Over time clans' names were divided and subdivided; for example, Mahon O'Brien became Mac Mahons.

The Viking invasion began in 795 with an attack upon Lambay Island. From invader and plunderer the Vikings turned to settler and trader, building towns along the coast like Dublin and Wexford. Apart from building Ireland's first towns, they introduced names, for example Mc Loughlin and Mc Ivor.

The eleventh and twelfth centuries were periods of wars in Ireland as the kings from the five main areas vied with each other. These regions were Leinster or Laighin which was ruled by the Mac Murroughs from Ferns, Co. Wexford; Meath which was ruled by Malachy II from Tara who was a Southern Úi Néill; Connacht had two vying families, the O'Connors and the O'Rourkes of Bréifne (Sligo to Monaghan); Munster was ruled by the O'Briens, but the Mac Carthys were also powerful; Ulster had four kingdoms ruled by the O'Donnells, Mac Lochlainns, O'Carrolls and Mac Donlevys.

The Normans arrived in Ireland in 1166 with Robert Fitzstephen as their leader. Richard Fitz Gilbert, or de Clare, known as Strongbow, arrived later and quickly controlled Wexford, Waterford and Dublin. By the fourteenth century the Normans had introduced a system of counties; this was a copy of the Anglo-Saxon shire system. The counties they set up were Dublin, Carlow, Louth, Kildare, Meath, Cork, Tipperary, Kerry, Limerick, Waterford, Roscommon and Connacht. The names that the Normans introduced into Ireland were French names like de Burgo or Brugh which is now Burke, le Poer or Power, names with Fitz which comes from the French fils, or son of, for example Fitzgerald, Fitzmaurice. They also brought in names from Brittany like de Leon or Dillon, Le Breton or Brett, and Flemish names like Fleming, Roche or de la Roche and Wall or de Vale. Over time some of the Norman names were changed; for instance, the descendants of Piers de Birmingham became Mac Fheorais or Corish – this means the son of Piers.

The Tudor reign in Ireland was one when the English kings tried to establish their control of the country. King Henry VIII demanded that his Irish subjects recognise his power. His daughter Mary took the land from her Irish lords who were disloyal and rebelled; the first plantation of Ireland was in 1556 in Laois and Offaly. Queen Elizabeth planted Munster in 1586, and Ulster was planted in 1609. The defeat of the Irish at the Battle of Kinsale in 1601 led to the collapse of Gaelic society and had a major effect on Irish culture and traditions. In Ulster, Scottish Presbyterians were brought in to be tenants on farms, and introduced names like Ross, Kerr, Graham, Morrison and Stewart.

Rebellion in the 1640s in Ireland led to the English passing an 'Adventurer's Act'. This promised land to those who helped finance the suppression of the Irish. In 1649 Cromwell came to Ireland and after a series of massacres in Drogheda and Wexford forced the Irish to surrender. He then confiscated 11 million acres of land and gave this to 1,000 adventurers and 35,000 soldiers. About 25 per cent of these came and settled in Ireland. In 1689-91 the Williamite-Jacobite Wars were taking place with famous battles including the Boyne, Aughrim, and Limerick which led to more land being confiscated.

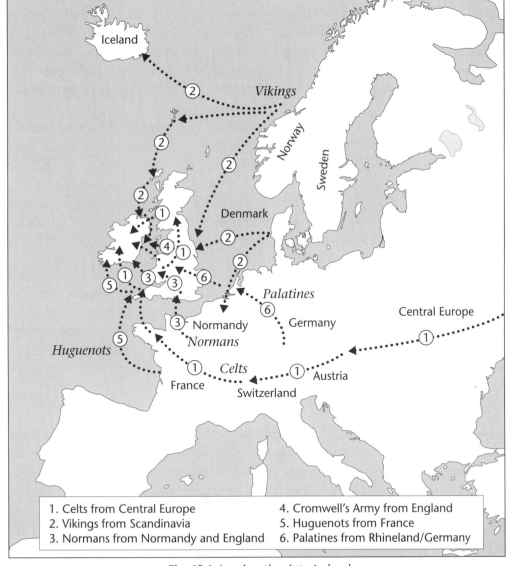

1. Celts from Central Europe
2. Vikings from Scandinavia
3. Normans from Normandy and England
4. Cromwell's Army from England
5. Huguenots from France
6. Palatines from Rhineland/Germany

Fig. 13.1: Immigration into Ireland

The change in the ownership of land between 1603 and 1691 showed that Catholic land ownership had fallen from 90 per cent to less than 14 per cent. Gaelic society collapsed and never recovered. Some parts of the old culture survived underground in poetry, music and folklore, but English ways dominated Irish life. O and Mac were dropped from surnames. English officials unused to Irish names either changed them to near sounding names (for example O'hArrachtáin became Harrington), or they translated them (for example Mac Gowan became Smith, and Giolla Easpaig became either Bishop or Gillespie). English names such as White or Black were also introduced.

In the eighteenth century two groups of Protestant refugees came to Ireland. The first were Huguenots from France who were fleeing the Catholic King Louis XIV. He had repealed the Edict of Nantes that promised religious toleration for Protestants in France. Many of the Huguenots set up textile industries in place such as Portarlington, Youghal, Lisburn. Huguenot names like Trench, Le Fanu, Maturin, or Blanc are still found in some of these towns. In 1709 large numbers of Palatines fled Germany as again war with Louis XIV drove them out of their homelands. Six hundred families came to Ireland. Some of these settled on land in Rathkeale, Co. Limerick, where there is now a Palatine Museum. The Palatines introduced names like Switzer, Ruttle, Bovenizer. There are currently over 10,000 names in the Irish phone directory that have Palatine origins.

The eighteenth century is the period when the Anglo Irish dominated Irish life. The Penal Laws forbade Irish Catholics from owning land or holding a profession and maintained Anglo-Irish power. It was also the time that architecture in Ireland flourished, when Georgian demesnes, towns and squares were built. Emigration to the colonies began, while immigration into Ireland declined.

Small numbers of people continued to come to Ireland in the last century, each bringing their own culture and enhancing Irish life. These include Italians, Chileans, Chinese, Vietnamese and the more recent refugees from Kosovo, Romania, Nigeria, and other parts of war-torn Africa. Our membership of the EU means that citizens from other EU countries can come and live here, and as the economy continues to boom, Ireland is attracting many of these people.

2. Emigration

Among the first to emigrate from Ireland were the Ulster Presbyterians. They left because of religious intolerance and economic oppression caused by the Penal Laws. They went mainly as indentured servants to the New England States. This emigration began from the 1720s and increased during periods of depression. Between the years 1770 and 1774 over 30,000 emigrated. Most left as families or even as whole communities, and when they settled in the new American colonies they continued their traditional way of life. These people described themselves as Scots-Irish. They influenced the culture, music, religion and way of life in the areas that they settled and played a major role in the American Revolution. This emigration is commemorated in the Ulster American Folk Park in Omagh, Co. Tyrone.

Catholics were not allowed to emigrate to America until after 1780 and the American War of Independence. Some Irish Catholics had been sent to the West Indies after 1655, to islands like Jamaica, Montserrat and Barbados, but most left soon after and went to America. People from Wexford and Waterford emigrated to Newfoundland in Canada. Irish convicts were sent to Australia from 1780 until 1861 for petty crimes and involvement in political crimes like the 1798 Rising. Irish convicts made up 20 per cent of the Australian population. In the late nineteenth century the New Zealand gold rush encouraged some Irish to emigrate there but only a small percentage of Irish emigrated to Australia and New Zealand. Irish Catholics who emigrated to the USA, Australia and New Zealand all suffered from discrimination in employment and housing.

Catholic emigration really began in the early decades of the nineteenth century. This was linked to the growth of population during this period, which brought increased poverty, as more people lived on smaller farms. They lived solely on the potato, and when poor weather led to bad harvests, there were food shortages and outbreaks of disease, for example typhus and cholera, which led to deaths.

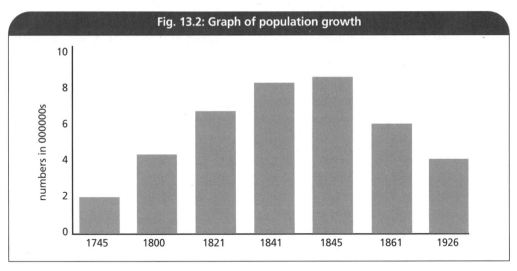

Fig. 13.2: Graph of population growth

Between 1815 and 1832 the main emigrants were from Ulster; after 1832 they were from the rest of Ireland. In the early years Belfast, Derry and Dublin were the main emigration ports, but as emigration increased, ports like Cork, Limerick and Sligo were used. In 1845 potato blight destroyed 40 per cent of the potato crop; the following year 80 per cent of the crop was destroyed. Large sections of the population were left destitute. Over 1 million died from starvation and disease. Many emigrated, some of them on coffin ships from the small ports of Westport, Killala and Kinsale. These ships were old and carried too many passengers, and provided insufficient food and water for them, resulting in death rates as high as 30 per cent. Between the years 1845 and 1855 nearly 25 per cent of Ireland's pre-famine population emigrated. They went to the USA (1.5 million), Canada (340,000), England (300,000), and Australia (70,000). Those who went to America settled in the ghettos of cities like Boston, New York and Philadelphia. They worked in poorly-paid jobs like building the railroads and canals, or faced unemployment, finding signs like 'No Irish need apply' when they went looking for work. Civil War and the industrialisation of the Northern USA created a demand for workers and soldiers; the Irish filled these jobs.

In Ireland after 1860 many Irish faced evictions. This became an even greater problem during the Land Wars of the 1880s. The practice of subdivision of farms ended and farms were handed down to one member of the family; the remainder emigrated. Emigration at this time was greatest among the Irish speakers from the western seaboard counties and it continued into the twentieth century, especially during bad harvests. It only stopped during the First World War and in times of depression abroad. Between 1845 and 1926 it is estimated that over four million people emigrated from Ireland. The areas that they emigrated to included the USA (three million), Britain (750,000), Canada (200,000), Australia and New Zealand (300,000), Argentina, South Africa and other countries (60,000).

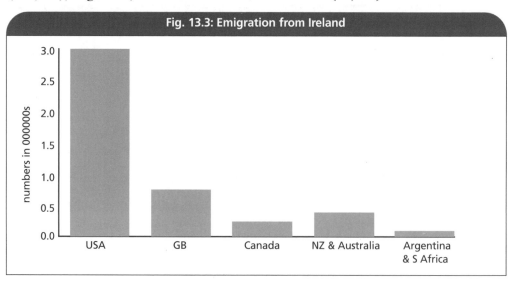

Fig. 13.3: Emigration from Ireland

During the 1950s, restrictions on emigration to the USA forced many Irish people to emigrate to England where there was a huge demand for workers to rebuild cities and factories after the Second World War. Depression in Ireland during the 1980s forced young Irish to emigrate to the USA and Britain. Economic development in the 1990s reversed this position, with many Irish returning home, and immigrants coming to Ireland because of job opportunities.

The situation in the North of Ireland was very different after 1921, as its population grew from 1.3 million to 1.5 million. This was due to industrialisation, better integration with the British economy, and more prosperity. There was a small flow of emigrations from Northern Ireland over the years, with Catholics going mainly to the USA, and the Protestants to Canada and Australia.

The effects of emigration on Ireland have been keenly felt.

- Some areas of Ireland have few inhabitants, deserted houses and villages, for example inland Connemara.
- Ireland has one of the lowest population densities in Europe. For example ours is one tenth of England's, our nearest neighbour.
- Irish language speakers fell from two million in 1851 to 70,000 in 1971.
- A positive effect has been the creation of large Irish communities abroad.

Bord Fáilte has put the effects of emigration to positive use in developing the Irish tourism industry.

SOURCES OF DATA FOR RESEARCHING GENEALOGY

There are two kinds of genealogical research: primary research and secondary research. Examples of primary research include looking up original documents such as birth certificates and death certificates, the census data, and finding gravestones. Secondary data involves using books, journals, and newspapers to get information on the family's history. Researchers of family history use both. For those who are interested in studying family history there are two organisations that they can join, the Irish Genealogical Research Society, and the Irish Family History Society. These groups hold lectures and produce journals and newsletters. There is also a magazine called *Irish Roots*, which deals with genealogy issues.

To begin research into one's family tree, the first step is to look at one's own family. This involves finding out information about parents, brothers and sisters, when and where they were born. The next step is to trace back to the previous generation and get information about grandparents, and their children. Again the information needed is the same: when and where they were born, where they live now, and whether they have family. If possible, information should be collected about a further generation back. This information can be collected perhaps from a great grandmother, or great grand aunt, who can provide details about their family, their brothers and sisters and their parents. Old people will gladly give this information. Some of the information required is very exact:

- Parish of origin, and religious denomination
- Date of birth, and place of birth, the street and town or townland and village
- Name of the ancestor who left Ireland, if the person searching is an emigrant Their parents, the place where they lived, date of marriage and place of marriage.

Old letters, photographs and family stories that have been handed down from one generation to the next are major sources of information. Once all this information has been collected and written down the first step of a family tree has been completed.

The next step is to decide whether or not to use a professional genealogical researcher. Irish Genealogy Limited is an organisation for a number of genealogical research companies, like the Irish Family History Foundation (IFHF). These carry out their research in genealogy centres around the country. The centres charge a fee for each document that they search for. They sometimes carry out a full genealogical search and provide a family history report. The Association of Ulster Genealogists and Record Agents and the Association of Professional Genealogists in Ireland carry out research in the National Archive and the National Library. These are independent professional researchers and usually get paid by the hour, with most family history research costing about £750 (€950). The Genealogical Office is a section of the National Library and staff there carry out research; they charge by the hour for their work.

People can do the research themselves; this involves using a range of sources. Family research is almost like being a detective, because researchers have to search through a range of information until they discover all the details of the family. Sources include the following:

- **Birth, marriage and death certificates** can be looked at in the General Register Office in Lombard Street East. These certificates will not only provide information about the person you seek, but also about the parents and witnesses.
- **Church records** on baptism and marriage will provide information on the parents, and perhaps other interesting items. Different denominations keep their records at different locations. For example Roman Catholic records are available in the National Library. The Church of Ireland records are held in the Representative Church Body Library in Churchtown. The Quakers, with records since the seventeenth century, have them available in the Friends' Historical Library in Donnybrook. Presbyterian records are in the Public Record Office of Northern Ireland on microfilm. Methodist records can be found in the Public Record Office of Northern Ireland on microfilm, in the Wesley Historical Society in Belfast. Jewish records are to be found in the Irish Jewish Museum off the South Circular Road in Dublin. Records are also kept at local churches.
- **Land and property valuation records** are available in the Valuation Office in Lower Abbey Street. This shows you who lived in a property since 1856 and can provide valuable information for the family historian. The registration of deeds, when land was purchased, is located in Henrietta Street in Dublin. Many Irish tenant farmers bought their land as a result of the Land Acts after 1881, and there are many properties registered there. Its records go back to 1708.

- **The 1901 and 1911 Censuses** are available in the National Archive and provide information on the population of the country. They were taken in April, and like census today provide a range of information. This includes the ages of the people in the house, their relationship to one another, literacy, and language spoken, i.e. English or Irish. Information is also given on the type and size of the house, and if it had land or sheds attached. The later censuses are not available for the public to use for research purposes. Earlier censuses are also not available because they were burnt during the fire at the Four Courts in 1922, although some remnants of the Census return for 1821, 1831, 1841, and 1851 are available. To assess this information you need to know the town, townland and village that people lived in.

- The **Griffith Valuation** in the 1850s lists all the properties in Ireland. It gives information on the size of the property, the occupier, and landlord. Townlands, town and streets are also important in looking up this information. This is available in the National Library and National Archive.

No. and letter of Reference on Map	Parishes, Townlands and Occupiers	Immediate Lessor	Description of Tenement	Content of Land	Net Annual Value Land Buildings Total		
					£ s d	£ s d	
	Brosna Glantanluska James Guiney	Ed. D Freeman	House, Office and land	A R P 194 2 34	30. 10. 0 33. 5. 0	2. 15. 0	
	John Daly Snr J. O'Connor	James Guiney	House, Office and land	87 1 19	3. 15. 0 7. 10. 0 8. 5. 0	0. 15. 0	

Table 13.2 Extract from the Griffith Valuation, 1856

(These figures are in pounds shillings and pence)

- The next major record that you can look up is the **Tithe Applotment Books 1830s**. These are available both in the National Library and National Archive. The Tithe Applotment Books give a list of the owners and occupiers of land, the land that they occupied, their rent and the 10 per cent or tithe that they had to pay to the Established Church, the Church of Ireland.

- **Transportation records** are available for those who were sent to Australia between 1788 and 1868. Irish descent is claimed by 25 per cent of Australians. Many of those who were condemned to transportation were sent because they stole a loaf of bread.

- **Wills** are also another source; these are to be found in the National Archive. However, only the very wealthy wrote wills, so this is not a major source of information for many genealogists.

- **Photographs** are also a source of information. Photography dates back to the 1850s, and many families had portrait photographs. Photographs can also be found in newspapers; there are many collections around the country, and some are published in books.
- **Newspapers** are on microfilm and in hard copy in the National Library. These include most Irish newspapers going back to the eighteenth century. Information from newspapers, particularly provincial newspapers, included death notices and in some cases details about the life of the person, the family, and who attended the funeral.
- **Books and historical journals** are sources of information. Edward Mac Lysaght has produced a series of books dealing with Irish surnames; these are called *Irish Families*, *More Irish Families* and *Surnames of Ireland*. There are also a number of books dealing with the topic of carrying out family research. These include *A Handbook on Irish Genealogy*, *Irish Genealogy: a record finder*, and *Tracing your Irish Ancestry*. For those who are carrying out research in the Cork-Kerry region O'Kief's *Coshe Mang, Slieve Lougher and the Upper Blackwater in Ireland* is a major source of information. It consists of fifteen volumes and is a collection of all material relating to birth, deaths, marriages, letters in the area. There are many historical journals, and local history societies pamphlets that provide information on local families, for example the *Journal of Cumann Luachra*, *Annagh Magazine* (from Ballyhaunis, Co. Mayo), and the *Donegal Annual*.

Case study: the Smyth family in Ballyhaunis, Co.Mayo

The Smyth family have lived in Ballyhaunis for over 150 years. John Smyth, who was born in Ballyhaunis but now lives in Dublin, carried out the research. He was born into the family home, which was originally bought by his grandfather in 1933. As a child he had heard stories of how the family was supposed to have come from Wicklow, and before that from Germany.

• To start his family history, John talked to his mother, to an aunt in England, and to one of the oldest inhabitants in Ballyhaunis who was a family friend. From this he found out about his father, Liam's, family, and his grandfather, J.T. There were thirteen children in Liam's family and Liam was the youngest. Many of them emigrated to England or the USA, and in fact Liam did not meet his oldest brother until he was thirteen because he had already emigrated before Liam was born. Most married and had their own families, so John had many cousins.

• The next step was to get information on John's grandfather J.T's family. There was a family **photograph** taken of John's great grandfather Pat with his wife and their thirteen children. John's grandfather J. T. was the oldest of the children. With help from older members of the family John was able to distinguish who the other members of the family were.

• The third step involved finding the **death certificate** of Pat Smyth, because John did not know the exact date of his death. For this he went into the General Register Office in Lombard Street, Dublin and for a small fee was able to search through the records.

> • He then went to the National Archive, and looked up the **Census** information for **1911**, and then **1901**. This gave him information about where the different Smyth families lived in Ballyhaunis. His grandfather J.T. was in fact married by 1911, and had four children, while some of his brothers and sisters had emigrated to the USA and Canada. His great grandfather Pat and great great grandfather John were both alive in the 1901 census. But by the 1911 census his great great grandfather John had died.
>
> • The next search involved finding the **death certificate** of John, which he found in the General Register Office. This was followed up by a visit to the National Library, were he looked up some of the **provincial newspapers**. *The Western People* had a big article on the funeral of John Smyth in Ballyhaunis, and it gave a list of the immediate family, cousins, nieces, in-laws etc.
>
> • Back in the National Library, John looked up the **Griffith Valuation** of 1856, and the **Tithe Applotment Book** of the 1930s. This revealed that the family lived in Ballyhaunis in 1856 where John Smyth rented three acres of land, but he did not live in Ballyhaunis in 1832. So where did he live before the 1850s?
>
> • Old family stories told that John was in fact from Wicklow, but what part? By looking up **grave inscriptions** in the National Library, he found out that there were three families of Smyths in Wicklow, two of which had died out. The remaining family lived near Blessington. The next step was to visit Blessington and find out if anyone knew anything about an old Smyth family from Blessington going back a hundred years ago. By coincidence, John met a woman who was a local historian and who turned out to be of Smyth descent. When he explained who he was, and what he was researching, he was asked a number of questions about the family, and the John Smyth who was supposedly from Wicklow. Both had similar **family stories** and in fact were related, very distantly. John Smyth left Wicklow after a prank involving sheep, for which he could have been accused of stealing, and fled to Mayo because he feared being transported to Australia. From this distant relation the family researcher got information about John's father, who was also John and who was born in 1799, and lived in Burgage. The small house that John Smyth lived in nearly 200 years ago still stands close to Blessington Lakes.
>
> • This is as far back as family researcher John Smyth has discovered. He still believes the family originally came from Germany, but there are few papers available that will prove his theory. The estate papers that he had hoped would provide some answers are lost, but given time perhaps he will solve the rest of the mystery.
>
> His family tree now encompasses seven generations, which is often as much as anyone can hope for. He has information on over 800 people, both alive and dead. Some of this information came from relations all over the world. His research into his family history inspired a family gathering in 1999.

- **Graveyards** are another source of information; headstone inscriptions give information about families. Some of the information from headstones can be found in the National Library, but more will involve visiting the graveyards and reading the headstones.

- **Estate papers** were information about rents paid by tenants, and payments to staff, etc., that landlords kept for their estates. Some of these are to be found in the National Library. The papers from Strokestown Park are on show in the Famine Museum in Strokestown.

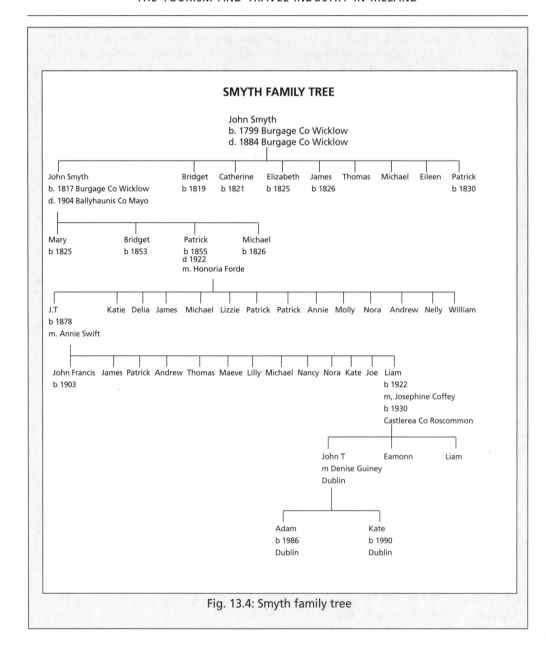

Fig. 13.4: Smyth family tree

CLAN GATHERINGS

Clans of Ireland are an organisation founded with the help of Bord Fáilte in 1990, but are now a voluntary organisation. They promote family clans worldwide, and have many members of Irish ancestry all around the world. In 1991 there were eighty-eight clan groups registered with the organisation. The central idea was to bring people of the same name and area of the country together at a clan rally. Many of these rallies are organised over a weekend. They bring together people whose ancestors are related. In 1992 the Irish Homecoming Festival was organised by both Bord Fáilte and the NITB. The aim of the festival was to promote family-history holidays in Ireland. It has been very successful and this type of tourism product is a growing area for Irish tourism.

Individual clans are involved in organising family gatherings. For example the Flannery clan held their clan rally in Dublin, and the Kavanagh clan gathering took place in Ferns, Co. Wexford in 2000. Clan gatherings have potential for repeat tourism as they occur every couple of years.

A clan gathering makes use of a large number of tourism products, including: accommodation for those attending; restaurants and banqueting facilities for the duration; transport to, and from Ireland, together with car rental and/or coaches to transport the visitors while they attend the gathering, or when they go on organised trips. Entertainment and guides are needed; guides provide information at the historical talks that take place during the gathering, and traditional entertainment is usually provided. These gatherings are more than just excuses for a 'wild weekend', their purpose is to inform those who attend about the history of the family, and their position in Irish society. These clan gatherings bring tourists and their money into Ireland in large numbers, and they satisfy a need that many emigrants have. Many people who attend come for a longer period than the gathering itself, and

Case study: the Cassidy clan rally

Historically the Cassidy family were physicians to the Maguire Clan who lived in Enniskillen Castle, Co. Fermanagh. Today they are still found in Fermanagh, but also all over Ireland, the USA and Australia. Every year Nuala Cassidy White organises the clan rally for the Cassidys. It takes place in Fermanagh, in small hotels close to Enniskillen, where the family originally came from. The rally takes place over a weekend, with clan members arriving on Fridays and often departing on the Monday. Events for the weekend include the following:

- A historical tour of the area involves a trip to Devenish Island on Lough Erne, where many of the Cassidy clan are buried. It also includes visits to historical attractions in the area, for example the Ulster Folk Park.
- A banquet is presided over by the life-long chieftain Sean Ó Casaide who is in his nineties. After the meal traditional Irish musicians entertain the clan members.
- The Devenish Summer School takes place the following day. This consists of a series of lectures on topics relevant to Fermanagh, for example archaeology, history, and culture. There are many writers in the Cassidy clan.
- During the clan rally of 2000, the Cassidy clan opened up access to an old Cassidy rath, which was located close to Cassidy Wood in Irvinestown, Co. Fermanagh. At the next clan rally it is planned to open up a holy well on Devenish Island and rededicate it to Saint Molaise. The water from the holy well is reputed to be a cure for sore eyes.
- Nuala Cassidy White is the genealogist for the Cassidy family in Ulster, and at each of the rallies she provides those who attend with information on their family history. She tries to bring together families who have been separated for generations. During the

last clan rally she reunited a family from Australia with their English and Irish relations. This policy of uniting families is special to the Cassidy clan.

After the gathering the clan members returned to their homes all over the world with new knowledge about their family roots. Approximately seventy Cassidys attend each rally. They are usually over thirty years of age, and most are from abroad; many of the American Cassidys are retired. Each year new members of the clan arrive to find out about the family and to attend the rally.

The organisation of the rally is left up to a small committee who are spread throughout the world. They keep in contact by email and a newsletter that is produced biennially. It takes about eighteen months to organise a rally. Funding is obtained through the International Fund for Ireland and the Millennium Lottery Award. This helps finance the marketing – production of brochures, tours, lectures. Bord Fáilte provides help with marketing, and the Clans of Ireland advertise the rally on their web page, and provide a link into the Cassidys' own web site (www.cassidyclan.org). In 2001 there was no Cassidy clan rally; it was postponed because of foot-and-mouth disease, and so 2002 promises a special rally. Peace is important to the success of all clan rallies in Ulster, because clan members, especially from America, do not travel if there is any violence.

spend the remainder of their time in Ireland sightseeing, meeting relations, and enjoying the country. Both Irish and overseas tourists attend these gatherings.

POTENTIAL FOR GENEALOGY TOURISM

There are over sixty million people abroad who claim Irish descent. Both the NITB and Bord Fáilte saw that tapping into their interest in genealogy was a way of developing tourism in Ireland. Genealogy was a growth area for tourism in the 1990s. In 1995 Bord Fáilte estimated that it was worth £10 (€12.5) million, and brought in 150,000 tourists to Ireland annually to trace their family roots.

Heritage centres

There are thirty-four heritage centres located all over Ireland, helping tourists trace their ancestors. They are members of the Irish Family History Foundation. Many of these centres are also linked to heritage sites, for example Strokestown, Co. Roscommon; Tagoat, Co. Wexford; the Brian Bórú Heritage Centre in Cashel, Co. Tipperary; the Kilkenny Archaeological Society in Rothe House, Kilkenny. All the records for each parish and other genealogical records in the county have been put on computer. These centres provide a valuable resource for tourists interested in discovering their ancestors.

Heraldry in Ireland

Tied in with the pursuit of genealogy is heraldry, which is the study and description of coats of arms. Heraldry is also a matter of whether people and families have the right to bear arms.

Fig. 13.5: Heritage Centre at Rothe House, Kilkenny

Coats of arms developed in the eleventh and twelfth centuries, when the knights of Europe were going off to war. In order to distinguish one knight from another, they put markings on their shields. These markings developed into coats of arms. The earliest were simple, consisting of two or three colours that divided up the shields, and either animals or symbols that were added later. These were the types that were brought into Ireland by the Normans; for example the de Burgos, de Clare and Fitzgerald families all have simple coats of arms. In the thirteenth century Anglo-Irish families had coats of arms developed for hereditary and personal use, such as on tombs, buildings, and seals for documents. Coats of arms were handed down within families, and the Office of Kings of Arms decided who was entitled to them. The English Crown set up the Office of Ulster King of Arms in Ireland in 1552. Anglo-Irish families sought coats of arms because they wanted to increase their social standing. Their coats of arms differed from those of the Norman families; they were much more elaborate in their designs.

Gaelic society had no tradition of coats of arms or heraldry, but they too developed their own coats of arms. Irish families used symbols linked to pre-Christian myths. For example the O'Neills used the Red Hand, which was linked to the Celtic Sun God, while families linked to Eoghanacht tribal group, such as Mac Carthy and O'Sullivan, used the stag. The difference between Gaelic society and Norman society was that the coat of arms belonged to people of the same name who lived in the same locality or sept, while within English and Scottish law a single family inherited the coat of arms.

In the early years the Office of Ulster King of Arms recorded, registered, and legitimised coats of arms. From the 1700s new peers started entering the House of Lords, and the Office of Ulster King of Arms recorded peerage succession. In 1783 the Chivalric Order of Saint Patrick was founded; its members coats of arms are on display in St Patrick's Hall in Dublin Castle. The Office was also responsible for the ceremonial aspect of state occasions.

The **Genealogical Office**, the successor of The Office of Ulster King of Arms, was founded in 1943. This office was concerned with heraldic rather than genealogical issues. Dr Edward Mac Lysaght was Ireland's first Chief Herald. His office granted arms to individual and corporate bodies. The office also studied the old Gaelic families, and researched the chiefs of these families. Today it is possible for Irish citizens to apply for a Grant of Arms, which can be displayed on a banner or shield and costs from €2,640 upwards.

The **State Heraldic Museum** was founded in 1909. It displays the range of uses of coats of arms in Ireland. They are used for instance on stamps, coins, notes, heraldic banners, heraldic china, corporate and county banners, bookbinding, and livery buttons. The museum is located in Kildare Street, Dublin.

Fig. 13.6: Coat of arms of the Cassidy family

Heraldic Achievements consist of three parts, the shield, crest and motto. The shield is the most important because it shows the coat of arms. There is often a wreath, and on this a helmet with the crest on top. The motto was underneath the

Fig. 13.7: Ulster American Folk Park, Omagh

shield in a scroll, and consisted of a slogan used in battle. Family mottoes often changed over time. The coat of arms does not need to include the helmet, mantling or wreath, but each has historical significance. The helmet reminds us of the wars in the Middle Ages which led to the development of coats of arms. The mantling refers to the cloak that the knights wore from their helmets and attached by a cord or wreath. The cloak protected their armour from the weather.

Many Irish families have coats of arms, and there are many companies that produce and sell these coats of arms to tourists and Irish alike. They are presented on glass and wood, as paper scrolls and on clothing. Such companies include Heraldic Artists Ltd, in Nassau Street, Dublin.

Historical attractions linked to emigration

There are a number of tourist attractions linked to emigration:

- The Ulster American Folk Park in Omagh, Co. Tyrone, tells the story of emigration to North America in the eighteenth and nineteenth centuries. It shows what life in Tyrone and in North America was like for emigrants. The visitors are shown some of the crafts and skills that the people used. It shows the houses of two emigrants who left Ireland for a 'better world'; these were Thomas Mellon, a Presbyterian who later became a judge in Pennsylvania, and John Joseph Hughes, who later became the Roman Catholic Archbishop of New York. Apart from tourists, the centre provides material for those studying emigration, history, and life in early America.
- The Queenstown Story, which is located at Cóbh Heritage Centre, tells the story of those millions who left there to seek a 'better life' in America. Some of those who left Cóbh, departed as convicts bound for Australia. Life aboard coffin ships is explained in the heritage centre. As the last port of call for the *Titanic* was Cóbh, a section of the museum is dedicated to this famous ship.

REVISION EXERCISES

1. Name in chronological order the main groups that immigrated into Ireland.
2. For each of the groups give an example of two typical types of names.
3. Each immigrant group contributed to the Irish way of life. Give an example of this.
4. Explain why emigrants left Ulster in the eighteenth century.
5. Why did the Irish population begin to rise in the eighteenth century?
6. Why did people emigrate in the nineteenth century?
7. What were the effects of emigration on Ireland?
8. Explain the term genealogy.
9. What groups will carry out genealogical research for tourists?
10. Give three examples each of primary and secondary data sources.
11. Explain the following: Griffith Valuation, Tithe Applotment and estate papers.
12. Explain the value of a clan gathering to the tourism industry.
13. Name the kind of events that take place at a clan gathering.
14. Explain the value of Genealogy to the Irish tourist industry.
15. Explain the work of the Office of Ulster King of Arms, the Genealogy Office, and The State Heraldic Museum.
16. Name a number of heritage attractions that have developed as a result of migration, and genealogy.

Assignment

1. (a) Research your family name from Mac Lysaght's books, and discover what period of history your name comes from. (b) Draw your family crest. (c) Carry out research into your family history, going back at least four generations.
2. Visit a heritage centre close to where you live and discover its work. Also visit at least one historical attraction that is linked into the theme of emigration.
3. Debate issues like emigration, immigration and the North of Ireland in the classroom, and discuss the impact of each on the Irish tourist industry.

References and further reading

Bord Failte, *Tracing Your Ancestors in Ireland*.

J. Watney, *The Irish Americans*. Pitkin, 1995.

J. Grenham, *Clans and Families in Ireland*. Gill & Macmillan, 1993.

E. McLysaght, *Irish Families*. Irish Academic Press, 1991.

E. McLysaght, *Surnames of Ireland*. Irish Academic Press, 1991.

E. McLysaght, *More Irish Families*. Irish Academic Press, 1996.

J. Ryan, *A Guide to Tracing Your Dublin Ancestors*. Flyleaf, 1998.

www.irishgenealogy.ie

CHAPTER 14

Irish Folklore

DEFINITION OF FOLKLORE

Folklore is the customs, beliefs and traditions of the ordinary people which have been handed down from one generation to the next, either by word of mouth or by example. They are rarely handed down in the written word, or as a result of formal education. The study of folklore only began in the nineteenth century, in England and Germany simultaneously. The Grimm brothers, famous for their fairy-tales for children, were folklore collectors and produced volumes of oral folklore and interpretations of German mythology. Others who were involved in the early study of folklore included Sir Walter Scott and Thomas C. Croker. After the discovery of medieval manuscripts such as the Book of Leinster, some of which were written in Latin and some in Gaelic and dating from the eighth century, there was great interest in finding out about Irish and Celtic folklore. During the 1880s and 1890s William Butler Yeats collected Irish tales and produced three books of Irish folk-tales and folklore. J. M. Synge lived on the Aran Islands for a period and drew inspiration from the life and language that he saw around him. He used this in his plays, for example, *The Playboy of the Western World*.

Some of the leading folklorists in Ireland in the twentieth century include Seán Ó Súilleabháin, Dáithí Ó hÓgáin and Kevin Danaher. Research into Ireland's folk customs and beliefs began officially in 1926 when the Folklore of Ireland Society was founded. In 1935 the Folklore Commission was founded and during 1937and 1938 it asked school children around Ireland to collect folklore from their grandparents and neighbours. The results are now stored in the Department of Folklore in University College Dublin, and consist of 1,128 volumes of stories. The Department of Folklore was set up in 1972, incorporates the work of the Folklore Commission, and is collecting Irish folklore, then classifying and storing it. It is also involved in teaching folklore to students. In 1980 and 1981 a similar programme was run in Irish city schools and was known as the Urban Folklore Project. These collections of folklore are available to the public at UCD.

When folklorists began collecting folklore originally, it was all painstakingly written down in copy-books. Later, when ediphone machines and tape recorders were developed, the old people told their stories and the information was recorded. Since 1980, with Government and EU funding, folklore is now collected using video and camcorders. Information is also kept on drawings, photographs, film, and manu-scripts. Most of the information (75 per cent) is in Irish, because many of those who kept the traditions longest lived in Irish-speaking areas of the country.

TYPES OF FOLKLORE

The eminent folklorist Seán Ó Súilleabháin in his book *A Handbook of Irish Folklore* identified fourteen areas of study within folklore. These are outlined below.

1. Housing and settlements

The old houses that were built in Ireland were built in harmony with the areas where they were located. The types of houses found in the lowlands of South Ulster, Leinster and East Munster were very different from the houses found along the west coast of Ireland. In the west the houses consisted of one large kitchen, with a room behind the fireplace, which was used by the older people, for their family mementoes and for laying out the dead. The kitchen itself was originally divid-ed into two parts by a drain, with the animals being kept in the lower end. Byre houses, as they were known, were common all along the west coast. In later years, many houses had walls built to form another bedroom. Houses were long and nar-row, only one room wide, and one storey high. The small towns of Ireland were lined with these small cabins and in order to get into the byre, or cowshed, behind the house, the cattle were brought in through the house. There are records of this happening in the nineteenth century in Co. Down, and in Co. Limerick in the early twentieth century. The tenants kept heaps of manure outside of the front door, to keep away the landlord's agent and to use on their potato crop. The advantage of keeping cows in the house was that they provided heat, and when they were warm they produced more milk.

The kitchen had two doors directly opposite each other, but usually only the front door was used unless the wind was blowing in the wrong direction. Irish people were very superstitious, and held various customs such as houses being only one room deep; spreading salt on the land; blessing the land with holy water; and visitors must enter and leave by the same door. Houses were made of both mud and stone. They were thatched with a variety of materials – oat, wheat and rye straw, flax, and reeds in Kerry where no straw was available. Along the west coast houses had their thatch tied down against the strong winds. In Donegal the ropes went both along the roof and over the roof, and stone pegs held the twine. Windows in these houses were small and usually faced away from the prevailing winds. Half-doors were devel-oped, which allowed light into the kitchen and at the same time kept out hens and other animals.

2. The way people made a living

Most of the people lived on the land and there are many references right through Irish customs and beliefs that relate to farming. For farmers the fertility of the land was very important and there were lots of customs to ensure that it remained fertile. The presence of fairy forts (often Celtic raths) and fairy wells on a farmer's land was considered lucky, and ensured that the land would be fertile. The land was sprinkled with salt before the crops were sown and with holy water either on Ascension Thursday or Whit Sunday. Harvest was a time of rejoicing, and dancing, singing and story-telling took place at this time. The last sheaf of corn was always placed on the kitchen beam and from these harvest knots were made. It was

Fig. 14.1: A typical thatched house

important when building the byre or the house that it was not located on a fairy passage, for it would bring illness to the animals. Farmers were always afraid of losing their milk, so they would not lend milk cans to anyone, or put milk into streams, in case they lost their 'milk luck'. Milk churns were protected by horseshoes placed underneath the churn. When butter was being made, it was the custom that anyone who came to visit had to turn the churn once; otherwise the cream would never become butter. On the poor farms in the west of Ireland work was done by hand, using spades and scythes and, for turf-cutting, the sleán. On larger farms in the south and east of the country horses pulled ploughs, reaper and binders, mowing machines, harrows, seeders, grubbers. These implements were used on many farms until the introduction of tractors in the 1970s.

Fishermen were also very superstitious. They would not go out fishing if they saw a woman or priest. Those who fished on the Shannon Estuary made pilgrimages to Scattery Island and brought stones from it when they went fishing because they believed this brought them luck. Also, they would never let a carpenter who made coffins make a boat because it was unlucky. Each group of craftsmen had its own set of customs. It was believed that the blacksmith had the power to cure diseases in both animals and humans, that he could also banish evil spirits and put curses on people.

3. Communications and trade

It is only since the nineteenth century that people began to travel long distances. Before that many people travelled less than twenty miles during their lifetime. Therefore people were afraid of travelling long journeys. They believed that people should travel eastwards on Mondays and westwards on Tuesdays and always carry salt and a piece of hazel to ward off the evil spirits. They also believed that if you forgot something, you should not return for it. American wakes took place when people were emigrating to the USA. The reason for this was that when most people left for America, they never came home again. The wake involved drinking, dancing and singing. Then as dawn arrived the family, friends and neighbours walked the emigrant down the road to see him or her off. Travellers placed themselves in the protection of God and St Colm Cille.

The Irish people since Celtic times lived in isolated farms, so they loved any type of gathering. The most popular gatherings were fairs. These were the Celtic substitute for towns, for on the date of the fair large numbers would gather to sell animals, to buy other goods that they did not produce themselves and to entertain themselves. Many of the fairs were linked to fighting, as rival groups came together. The Planter towns with their diamonds (squares) were used for fairs; the local castle overlooked them and this made sure that law and order prevailed. Weekly markets also took place until replaced by shops. The traditional Irish shop sold groceries to the front and had a pub at the back and many also sold hardware and clothes. Celtic gatherings often took place on hilltops and these are remembered in ballads. Among the most famous fairs were

- Donnybrook Fair, in Dublin. This took place on 26 August for a week; horses and black cattle were sold at it. It was also known for its bloodshed, brutality, debauchery and rioting and this led to its eventual closure.
- Puck Fair, in Killorglin Co. Kerry. This took place on three days in August; 10 August is Gathering Day, when the Puck or goat was brought by procession through the town before being put up on its platform to reign over the fair; 11 August is the Fair Day, when cattle and sheep were sold; 12 August is Scattering Day, when King Puck was removed from his throne and released to the Kerry mountains. It is believed that the Puck is revered because a goat warned the people of Killorglin of the arrival of Cromwell's troops and they were able to save themselves and their livestock.

- Ballinasloe Horse Fair in Co. Galway. This was held between 5 and 10 October. Horses were sold to army agents from countries as far away as Russia. During the eighteenth century 90,000 sheep and 12,000 cattle were sold to farmers from the lowlands of the east. It was also a time for local farmers to come together for fun and entertainment.

These large fairs took place because farmers did not have food for the animals during the winter months. Farmers also paid their rents at this time of the year. These were known as 'Gale Days'. At the early fairs goods were exchanged or bartered; later money was used. After the introduction of money, the old methods of bargaining, the rituals of noisy assessing of animals, hand-slapping, tight-lipped silences, etc., all continued. The seller of the animal gave back the purchaser a small amount of the money. This is known as 'the luck penny'; when it was not enough fights broke out.

Men proved their adulthood at fairs by showing their skill at buying or selling animals. Those who could not buy healthy animals, or sell animals at a profit, often became the butt of stories told by the seanchaí. Old clothes and boots were sold at Irish fairs in large quantities. Delph, wooden and metal vessels, sharp tools, beads and ribbons were also sold. The fairs also attracted beggars, gamesters, peddlers, entertainers like singers and fiddlers, matchmakers and troublemakers. Cock fighting and bull baiting took place at these fairs. Tents were set up for drinking, music and dancing and excesses in these often led to arguments and fights. Horse racing also took place.

4. The community

Life for many people in rural Ireland involved little money and there was little division of labour. When people needed work done, a meitheal was organised. The meitheal took place at harvesting time, haymaking, turf-cutting, etc. In return for the free labour the host would provide food and entertainment. At other times he too would help out his neighbours. Hiring fairs took place on St Brigit's Day. At these fairs wealthy farmers hired boys and girls to work in the house, the dairy and the fields and boys and girls as young as eight and ten would work until Hallowe'en. Those who were hiring the children out, bargained over the price of their hire, and when a deal was done, they got earnest money from the farmer and handed over the children's clothes to him.

Stations occurred twice a year, during Lent and autumn. This was when the Catholic priest visited a townland to say mass in a house and all the neighbours were invited. While the priest was there he collected the dues (money paid to the church by parishioners). After the mass, breakfast was served to all who attended and entertainment followed. It is thought that this practice developed during Penal times, when priests were on the run. The stations are still important in parts of Ireland.

5. All aspects of human life

Weddings and funerals were important in people's lives and there were many customs and superstitions linked with them. After the Famine many people emigrated and those who stayed in Ireland postponed their marriages. This resulted in women marrying at about twenty-eight, and men even older. Regardless of late marriages, families were still large. Being childless was considered a disgrace and there were many superstitions linked to it. It was believed that if a barren couple visited Diarmuid and Gráinne's bed (these were megalithic tombs all over the country), then their problem would be solved. Marriages were arranged matches, and involved dowries of cash or cattle. Often the dowry received on the marriage of the son was used as the dowry to marry off a daughter, and so on, with one dowry in fact leading to a number of marriages. Sometimes cousins married cousins, especially if it enlarged the farm.

There was an old custom of clothing boys in dresses like girls until they were about ten years of age. This was done to deceive the fairies who were always looking for healthy boys. The fairies would take the healthy boy and swap him for a sick baby or changeling. The idea of changelings came as a result of the higher death rates among baby boys.

There were many rites, omens and superstitions about death and burials. When a person died the clock was stopped, mirrors were covered and a bundle of straw put outside the house and set alight so that the neighbours would know of the death. In some areas when a person died, the doors and windows were opened to allow the person's spirit to escape. In Co. Sligo the bed of the dead person was brought outside the house and burnt. Travellers practise a similar custom today. There was a special way to lay out the corpse and a plate of salt and tobacco was placed on the corpse. Sometimes turf was put on the corpse; this was supposed to prevent the body from decaying.

Riddles, jokes, dancing, singing, and wrestling all took place at wakes. Matches (arranged marriages) were often made at wakes. Keening (from the Irish 'ag caoineadh'), when older women cried over the body, also took place; this is considered to be a very old Celtic practice. Drink, food, tobacco and clay pipes were supplied to the mourners. The wakes allowed the relatives to release tensions, and also allowed them to link with their ancestral spirits.

After the wake the coffin was taken to the graveyard and those who followed behind the coffin carried salt in order to ward off the spirits and protect themselves. Holy water was then sprinkled on the coffin, prayers said, and the grave filled in; unused pipes and white stones were placed on the grave.

6. Nature

This referred to the various mountains, rivers, trees and lakes in an area and the stories about them. The tops of mountains had significance for the Irish since Celtic times, because these were the places where people gathered for many of the festivals. St John's Eve is associated with bonfires on the tops of mountains even today. Croagh Patrick in Co. Mayo, the mountain that overlooks Clew Bay, is still a special mountain. Its pilgrimage is held on the last Sunday of July and this marks when summer ends and autumn begins; it is also the date of the old Celtic Festival of Lughnasa. It is believed that from Croagh Patrick, St Patrick banished all the snakes from Ireland.

The Celts worshipped wells, but after the arrival of Christianity they introduced the idea of holy water to tie in with the pagan traditions. There are 3,000 holy wells in Ireland, but only a small number of these have curing properties. Some holy wells were associated with lakes, for example, Gouganebarra, which is the source of the River Lee in Cork, and Lough Derg in Donegal, the location of St Patrick's Purgatory and the site of pilgrimages since the Middle Ages.

Trees like the mountain ash, elderberry, holly and whitethorn were all supposed to have magical properties. They were linked to the seasons of the year through their flowers and berries. Whitethorns that grew on fairy forts were considered to have special magical powers and under no circumstances were they cut down, or even their broken branches burnt, as to do so would result in bad luck.

7. Folk medicine

Old folk-techniques were used to heal illnesses until the twentieth century and many of these developed into modern medicines; about 25 per cent of the old cures are used in medicine today. Many of the old cures were based on herbs, and were successful; this is why they are now used in modern medicine. It was also believed that curses, fairies and spirits caused illness. Some families abstained from meat on St Stephen's Day to avoid illness.

- Pieces of white bread and bacon were kept in a damp place to develop mould; this was then put on sores that were difficult to heal. This is the origin of penicillin.
- Bread poultice was made to treat cuts that had gone septic; this involved soaking white bread in boiling water, placing it on the freshly-cleaned cut and tying it with a bandage. The poultice would draw out poisonous juice and the cut would clear up very quickly.
- Goose grease was used for chest infections. The goose grease was melted down and then stored until needed. When chest infections arose, the goose grease was rubbed on to the person's chest and then covered with paper before clothes were put on.
- For very bad cuts, where there was a lot of blood, moss was used to stop the bleeding.

- Poitín was usually found in most country households and it was used for a range of medicinal purposes, including being given to newborn lambs that were weak. Poitín was also rubbed on to the person to ease pain.

8. Annual festivals and patterns

There were many customs associated with different times of the year. Some of these were Christian festivals and others old Celtic festivals.

- **6 January** was the twelfth day of Christmas and known as Small Christmas. The holly and decorations were taken down on this day.
- **1 February, St Brighid's Day**, was an important pre-Christian festival. On this day no farm work took place. Shellfish were placed in the four corners of the house, to ensure that the house always had enough fish for the year. Rushes were collected and made into **St Brighid's** crosses; these were placed in the roof of the house and byre, to protect the family and animals.
- **17 March, St Patrick's Day**. The earliest people used to mark their arms with a charred stick in the shape of a cross, to commemorate St Patrick. Only after 1681 did people start wearing shamrock. The people sowed corn on this day. Later everyone went and had a drink to St Patrick. This was known as the 'pota Phádraig'.
- **Lent** was very important in the lives of Catholic Ireland. Weddings and dances were forbidden and people followed very strict fasting and abstained from meat and eggs during Lent. On Shrove Tuesday they ate up the last of the meat and eggs, making pancakes from the eggs. On Ash Wednesday turf ashes were blessed in the church and these ashes were spread on the land. On Palm Sunday the people wore sprigs of yew, and children collected eggs for their feast on Easter Sunday. Good Friday was considered a lucky day to plant potatoes, but milk could not be drunk, and blood could not be spilt.
- **1 May, May Day**, was another important festival in ancient Ireland, and it was the beginning of summer. The people brought flowers and green branches into their houses, and put them around the windows and doors. Few people went out on May Eve because the fairies moved between fairy forts, and people were afraid of meeting them. Farmers protected their animals, because they feared that their prosperity would be taken away.
- **24 June, Feast of St John**, was the old midsummer festival. On this night bonfires were lit; they still are in many rural parts of Ireland. Cattle were driven between the fires in order to protect them from harm. This was also the day when people went swimming and they drank the boiled juice of St John's weed (also known as St John's Wort) to make them healthier.
- **The Feast of Lughnasa** was celebrated either on the last Sunday in July or the first Sunday in August and was another ancient Celtic festival. Wild berries were

picked on this day and eaten. Today, the pilgrimage to Croagh Patrick in Co. Mayo takes place on this Sunday.

- **31 October, Halloween**, corresponds with the Feast of the Dead. Again the fairy forts were open on this night and people were afraid to be out. People prepared their houses for dead members of their families to return, and they lit candles in their windows. Colcannon was eaten; this is a mixture of potatoes, onions, cabbage or kale, and butter. People ate nuts and played games. The animals were brought in for the winter. This day was also known as Gale or Half-Gale Day, when rents were paid and servants who had been hired finished up their summer work and went home.

- **25 December, Christmas**, coincided with the winter solstice which was the ancient time for remembering the dead. Holly was used to decorate houses; Christmas trees were a German tradition and only introduced in the nineteenth century. A large candle was put in the kitchen window, in order to guide the Holy Family to shelter.

- **26 December, St Stephen's Day**, was the day when the Wren Boys visited houses. They wore masks, and went from house to house carrying a holly bush and a dead wren and singing:

> 'The wren, the wren, the king of all birds
> St Stephen's Day was caught in the furze . . . .'

As they moved from house to house they danced, played music, sang songs and collected money.

Patterns were local festivals and important social occasions. The people visited holy wells on these days. Dancing, drinking and eating took place at the patterns. Sometimes faction fights took place as rivals met at the patterns. Both the law and the Church tried to abolish these fights.

9. Popular beliefs and practices

There were all sorts of popular beliefs. Friday was considered a lucky day, and even today people often move into a new house on a Friday. To keep luck in a house, dust would not be swept out on a Monday. People believed all sorts of things protected them from harm; these included horseshoes, stones, four-leafed shamrocks, rowan trees, salt, religious objects, rings, certain types of money.

When people did wrong they expected that they would be punished, in particular for any of the following: cursing on Sundays; interfering with fairy forts; harming holy wells; harming birds and animals; telling secrets and lies; being dishonest; and serious crimes like murder. As can be seen from this list, people feared the Church and the fairies more than the law.

10. Mythological traditions

This covered the Devil, fairies, spirits, ghosts and púca. The Devil is feared in Ireland and it is believed that he is found in certain places in the country like the Devil's Bit in Co. Tipperary. He tries to control people's lives, and to buy their souls. There are a number of stories about people selling their souls to the Devil. To ward him off, people said prayers and used holy water. People blamed the fairies for any illogical problems. Fairies were also important to the Celts who believed that they were their dead ancestors, who lived on in the burial graves like Newgrange. It was believed that fairies lived in abandoned houses (lisses), moats, raths and hills. They believed that fairies moved house on the eve of the main festivals. People believed that the fairies played music, sang and danced, and that people had learnt music from them. It was also believed that the fairies led people astray at night. *Poitín*-makers always gave the first glass to the fairies. They did this by throwing it over their shoulder; if the fairies were dissatisfied they would help the police find the still. The fairies also helped people and this was referred to as being 'in with the fairies'. Their neighbours respected these people.

Spirits had an evil disposition; they were people who were being punished for evil deeds. They were usually found in a particular place. People used hazel sticks and holy water to banish spirits. Ghosts were less malicious and were only suffering a temporary punishment. They usually came back to their old homes, to visit their families, to help in times of trouble, or to take revenge. Sometimes mermaids married humans, especially fishermen, and the resulting children had webbed feet. The mermaid did not remain with the husband, but returned to the sea.

11. Historical traditions

Irish folklore shows a great interest in the past, the lives of saints, legends about names and placenames. People were interested in their family histories and most families had their own stories. The *seanchaí* came to visit and often told the histories of the people he called on. Some Irish families are able to tell their history right back to Adam. This was one of the most important aspects of both the file of Gaelic society, and the *seanchaí*. Many stories were also written about famous events in Ireland's history and told at the fireside. These included stories about Cromwell, Patrick Sarsfield, stories about rapparrees (robbers or highwaymen), the Rising of 1798 and the Famine. One such story is about Cromwell and his army when they were in Kilkenny and the origin of the 'Kilkenny cats'.

> When Cromwell had taken over Kilkenny, his soldiers decided to have a bit of sport. They hung two cats together from a pole by their tails, and let the cats fight, to see who would win. Instead the cats fought so hard, that when the soldiers returned to find the winner, all that was left of the cats were the two tails. The cats had eaten each other.

Irish was the spoken language of the people, and most of the stories the *seanchaí* told were in Irish. Most placenames in Ireland mean more in Irish than English, because they refer to the features of the countryside, or ancient buildings. The names of many Irish towns today are the Anglicised versions of the Irish names, not translations of the old Irish names. Most names in English have no real meaning. To find out the real meaning of placenames in Ireland, the Irish name must be studied.

Table 14.1 Irish place-names			
Irish	Meaning	English	Examples
Baile	Group of houses, or town	Bally	Ballyhaunis, Ballyfermot
Cill	Church	Kil/Kill	Kildare, Killarney
Ard	Height	Ard	Ardmore, Ardnacrusha
Gleann	Glen	Glen	Glencree Glencolmcille
Cluan	Meadow or Clearing	Clon	Clonmacnoise Clonakilty
Rath	Fort	Rath	Rathmines, Rathmore
Mainistir	Monastery	Monaster	Monasterboice, Monastereven

Between the ninth and twelfth centuries, poems were written about places, and each had a story attached to it. The Celtic sagas influenced some of these stories; one such story is about Dublin or Dubhlinn.

> There was once a poet called Dubh. Her husband had a lover, of whom Dubh was jealous, so she decided to kill her. When the lover went out in a boat, Dubh used her magic and drowned the husband's lover. Later a friend of the dead woman decided to avenge her death. Using a slingshot he hit Dubh and she fell into a pool. This is now known as Dubh's Pool or Dubhlinn.

This is an interesting story about Dublin, but in fact Dublin's old name is Baile Átha Cliath or the town on the ford of the hurdles.

12. Religious traditions

These relate to the various stories of Ireland's most famous saints like Patrick, Brighid and Colm Cille, and also of lesser-known saints, which tell of the various miracles that they performed, cures, and the way they fed the starving. There are many holy wells dedicated to these and other local saints.

> St Brighid wanted to build a monastery in Kildare. When she asked the local pagan

King for land he did not want to give her any, but he promised her he would give her as much land as her cloak would cover. By magic the cloak covered a very large area, that of the Curragh in Kildare. The King recognising that he had been beaten asked for the cloak to stop. St Brigit was granted the land, and the ruins of her monastery can still be seen in Kildare.

Another story about an Irish saint is that of St Moling who founded a monastery at St Mullins, Co. Carlow. His name means 'the holy leaper', and he got the name after he jumped a river in Kerry. His biography was written during the late medieval period in Irish and Latin. His story is as follows:

St Moling's mother began life in Luachair, where her brother-in-law made her pregnant. She fled the house and the child was born during a snowstorm. She intended killing the baby, but monks from St Brendan's monastery found them. The child was taken in and was brought up by the monks. He went to live with St Maodhóg, and then decided to set up his own monastery at Ros Broic. He was helped build the house by the Gobán Saor (a mythical figure) and they used a yew tree that had fallen down in Ros Broic. At the monastery Moling performed many miracles. He helped the local kings settle disputes. He helped the Leinster men to avoid paying tribute to the Kings of Tara. When the King realised that Moling had tricked him out of the tribute, he sent soldiers to kill him, but by a miracle they killed each other and Moling escaped. Later he became both a poet and prophet in Ireland, and Abbot of Ferns.

13. Popular oral traditions

Stories from the oral tradition were usually anonymous, but not the poetry and songs from the bardic schools. The numbers of stories that survive today are only a fraction of those that once existed; this is due to the destruction of the old Gaelic world in the seventeenth century, and the decline of the Irish language in the nineteenth. Those stories that survived were preserved by the *seanchaí*, who handed them down to later generations by telling them by the fireside. Tomás Ó Criomhthain and Peig Sayers of the Blasket Islands were both story-tellers, and they did much to preserve the folklore of the Blaskets.

The *seanchaí* is the person who tells the local tales, genealogies, stories of ghosts and fairies. These stories were told during the long winter nights between September and March. Most of the *seanchaí* were men, although there were some women like Eibhlin Ní Loingsigh from south-west Kerry who had learned the stories from her father and grandfather. The stories had all been developed over hundreds of years, but each story-teller used his own personality in the telling of the story, so that each story was unique. Seán Ó Conaill from Cill Rialaigh near Ballinskelligs was one such *seanchaí*. He had learned the stories as a child in the 1850s and 1860s listening to other story-tellers tell them by the fireside. He knew over 400 pages of stories, which were painstakingly written down in 1923 by a folklore collector when Ó Conaill was seventy years old. His stories included tales about heroes, sagas, mythological tales, religious tales, historical and fairytales, poetry and songs. All of these stories were told in Irish. Translations into English often meant that the flow of the language was lost and the story not as good. The *sean-chaí* told these stories by the light of the fire. He would begin his story when the right atmosphere had been achieved. His neighbours would come in and listen attentively to hear what came next. At the end of the tale, which was usually an hour long, anyone who questioned if it really could have happened, got the answer that 'There was magic in old times'. Such story-telling would go on until the early hours of the morning. Seán Ó Conaill learned his stories from his neighbours and from travelling beggars.

Folk-tales are better narrated than read. The advent of radio and television killed the art of story-telling. One of Ireland's best story-tellers was Eamon Kelly who died in 2001. He started off by telling stories on the radio and later put on one-man shows on stage. Many of his stories came from his native Kerry. The setting for story-telling is always that of the kitchen from the 1920s, with the large open fire, and all types of household utensils and furniture surrounding it. The story-teller also dresses like the old *seanchaí* of the past. The future of story-telling appears to be either in the theatre or on television.

There are many types of folk-tales found in Ireland. The main types are:

- **The Mythological Cycle.** These are the earliest tales from Ireland, and are the stories of the Tuatha Dé Danann and other people who lived in Ireland before the Celts. In these stories very strange things happen, like people turning into animals, and magic is commonly used. Among the most famous stories from this period are:
  (1) *The Children of Lir*
  (2) *The Tragedy of the Children of Tuireann*
  (3) *The Wooing of Étáin*

- **The Ulster Cycle.** These are the stories about the Red Branch Knights who lived at Navan Fort (Emain Macha) in Armagh. They include the characters of King Conchobor mac Neasa, Cú Chulainn, Ferdia mac Damain. The main stories are about
  (1) *Cú Chulainn*, the Hound of Culann
  (2) *The Táin Bó Cuailnge*, the Cattle Raid of Cooley
  (3) *Deirdre and the Sorrowful Tale of the Sons of Uisneach*.

- **The Fionn or Ossianic Cycle.** These stories are about Fionn mac Cumhaill, who led the Fianna, a band of brave warriors from Almu on the Hill of Allen, Co. Kildare. There are also stories about Oisín, Fionn's son, and Gráinne. The most famous of these stories are about:
  (1) *Fionn and the Salmon of Knowledge*

(2) *The Fianna*

(3) *Oisín and Tír na nÓg*

(4) *Diarmaid and Gráinne.*

- **The Historical Cycle or Cycle of Kings**. These stories involve real people, unlike most of the other tales, but many of their exploits are fictional. These are the stories about the kings of Tara, telling of Labhraidh Loinnsigh, Cormac mac Airt, Conn Céadchathach, and Niall Naoi-ghiallach. The most famous of these stories are:
  (1) *The Ears of Labraidh Loinnsigh*
  (2) *The Destruction of Da Derga's Hostel*
  (3) *Niall of the Nine Hostages.*

14. Sports and pastimes

From earliest times many sports were played, but they were not organised as we know them today. Athletics, martial skills and hurling are all referred to in the Celtic sagas. Hurling involved two teams (of any number of people). They used a brass ball and each team tried to get it into the opposition's hole or hit a stick with it, and defended their own hole or stick. Horse racing was also important and took place at the fairs. Hunting was popular, and people hunted birds, boar and deer. In the seventeenth century hunting foxes was introduced, and was very popular with the upper classes. People in towns and cities were more interested in cock fighting, dog fighting and bull baiting. Wrestling and boxing were developed in the seventeenth century. Bare-knuckle boxing was also popular, and one of the most famous Irish boxers was Dan Donnelly from Dublin. Between 1814 and 1819 he defeated three English champion boxers. The games of skittles, bowls and weight throwing were were also played.

The Irish also played board games such as *Fidhcheall*, like chess, and 'Black Raven' which later became backgammon. The Irish enjoyed feasting, and story-telling. The old Gaelic lords had poets to tell them stories and genealogies, and gleemen or crosains who were skilled acrobats and jugglers; they also recited humorous prose and verse. In the fifteenth and sixteenth centuries the English brought new sports like card playing and dice into Ireland. The Irish enjoyed playing cards, with some of them becoming professional gamblers. Stories developed about gamblers, including the one about a stranger who joined in a game of cards but turned out to be the Devil, who was after the souls of the gamblers. Playing cards for small bets was popular in the countryside, with people playing for a goose, or duck. Most of these games involved card-games such as Twenty-five, Forty-five, and One-hundred-and-ten.

The Irish spent much of their time making music, singing and dancing (see chapter 17).

There was little tradition of theatre in Ireland. The English folk drama called mumming was introduced into Leinster and Ulster. Mumming involved stories about saints and the Devil, and characters from history. They were performed in people's homes at Christmas time.

FOLKLORE AND THE TOURISM INDUSTRY

Some aspects of Ireland's folklore are available to tourists visiting Ireland.

Puck Fair still takes place during August in Killorglin. For the three days the Puck Fair provides free entertainment on the street, for twelve hours each day. The events include the coronation of King Puck and its associated parade, the horse fair, an Irish song competition, a busking competition, open air concerts, children's competitions, fireworks, street entertainers, dancing and music in pubs. Many of the traditional events of the Fair still take place, with newer entertainment also being provided. Over 100,000 people attend the Fair each year, and it earns over €2 million for the town, with visitors from America and Europe also joining in.

Ballinasloe Horse Fair takes place in October. The Fair in 2000 offered a range of activities including a horse-drawn display, steeplechasing, horse sales on the Fair Green, medieval jousting and horse stunts, sheep fair and sheep-dog trials, free entertainment and open-air theatre, music in the pubs, tug-o'-war competitions, an agricultural show and country fair, children's shows and busking competition. Some of these events have been taking place since the early nineteenth century, while some of the entertainment is more modern.

Siamsa Tire was started in 1967, and built its own theatre in Tralee in 1973 with two outreach centres at Finuge and Carraig. It is Ireland's folk theatre, and entertainment is based on Ireland's music, folklore, song and dance. The theatre has been developed in order to preserve our folklore for the future. Since 1998 Siamsa have a touring policy and take their entertainment around the country. Recent productions include *The Gobán Saor*, and *The Children of Lir*, both stories of early Irish mythology.

Ionad Árann on the Aran Island looks at life on the islands, the methods of building currachs, and fishing, collecting of seaweed for the land, crop growing, types of houses. It also provides information on history, folklore and geology of the islands.

Case study: Bunratty Castle and Folk Park

This is the most important tourist attraction linked to Irish Folklore. It is located in Co. Clare on the main Limerick–Shannon road. Thomas de Clare first built a castle on this site in the thirteenth century. It remained in de Clare hands until they were defeated in 1318 at Dysert O'Dea. The O'Briens owned the castle for the next 200 years. They rebuilt it a number of times, with The Great Earl Donagh O'Brien making major improvements, including introducing glass windows and cladding the roof with lead. After the wars of the seventeenth century the castle was confiscated from the O'Briens and awarded to an English family, the Studdarts, who lived there until the early nineteenth century. It fell into decay until it was bought and restored by Lord Gort in 1945.

- The castle consists of a rectangular keep with towers in each corner. The three floors of the castle are made up of the stable/store on the ground floor, the main hall on the first floor, which is where the medieval banquets take place today, and the great hall. At the top of the castle a spiral staircase leads to the battlements. The castle has been furnished with a range of sixteenth- and seventeenth-century furniture, paintings, Belgian tapestries, helmets and armour, which were mainly sourced in Europe.

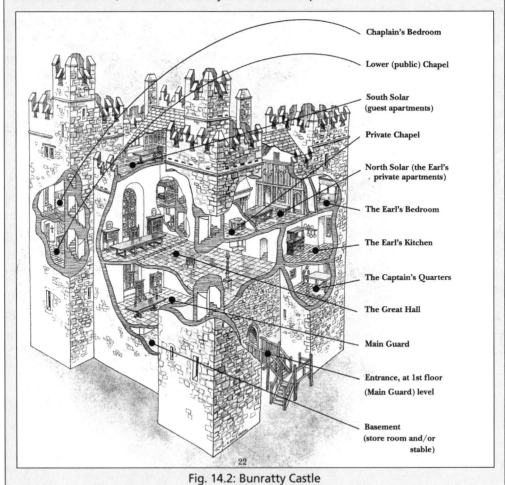

Chaplain's Bedroom

Lower (public) Chapel

South Solar
(guest apartments)

Private Chapel

North Solar (the Earl's
private apartments)

The Earl's Bedroom

The Earl's Kitchen

The Captain's Quarters

The Great Hall

Main Guard

Entrance, at 1st floor
(Main Guard) level

Basement
(store room and/or
stable)

Fig. 14.2: Bunratty Castle

• The Folk Park provides the tourist with a replica of Irish houses from around 1900. These houses have been carefully reconstructed. The Shannon farmhouse was built of clay and was thatched. It had a loft bedroom, and a parlour that was used for special occasions. The Cashen fisherman's house was also on the River Shannon, and this was a small two-roomed house. This house had a clay floor, which was common among the poor. The mountain farmhouse from the Sliabh Luachra area of Cork and Kerry, like the Shannon Farmhouse, used a loft to provide an extra bedroom. Their floors were covered with flag-stones to allow step- and set-dancing to take place. The Golden Vale house from Kilfinane was the home of a wealthy dairy farmer. The furniture was good quality and their parlour was wallpapered. These farmers had servants who worked on the farm and they slept in the loft. The kitchen was the centre of the home where most people lived and entertained their neighbours around the fire with songs, story-telling and talking.

The Moher farmhouse from the Burren area of north Clare was built from the local flag-stone; it was used to make walls, benches, cupboards, and the roof. The byre dwelling, which was common in west Mayo, shows the animals and the family living together, with a drain dividing the four cows from the remainder of the kitchen. Alcoves were added to provide a bed for the older couple in the warm kitchen. The labourer's house or bothán scóir was a one-room home for the landless peasant, who got half an acre to grow his potatoes, in return for working eighty days for the local farmer. This house had little furni-ture in it, perhaps some three-legged stools and a mattress on the floor.

The Loop Head farmhouse was made of stone and mortar, and whitewashed to make it waterproof. The thatched roof was roped to keep it down during the Atlantic gales. All of these houses are authentically furnished, animals are found around the houses particularly hens, and some have people explaining country skills like making brown soda bread.

• The village in Ireland began to develop during the late nineteenth century, because until this time most people were self-sufficient. From that time on the shopkeeper became more important in the local community. This village displays shops that were typical of the time; these include the pawnbrokers, the draper, the grocery and hardware shop, which

Fig. 14.3: The Village in Bunratty Folk Park

sold many imported goods, the post office, and the printer who made handbills, posters, newspapers, etc. The village also includes the Doctor's house, with the clinic where the Doctor performed minor surgery. The schoolhouse came from Belvoir in east Clare and is typical of the schoolhouse of the time, consisting of two rooms, one for the boys and the other for the girls. There are also terraced houses, which in the past were the homes of professionals, or well-off craftsmen who worked downstairs and lived in the upstairs rooms. Today a hand-knitter and photographer use these houses. There is also an old-fashioned public house. Pubs were not important for socialising until the end of the nineteenth century; before this people socialised in each others' homes. The new hotel and larger public house replaced the older more basic public house. At this time many shops had bars at the back of their premises, and this can be seen in Mac Namara's hotel and public house.

Fig. 14.4: Traditional water wheel in Bunratty Folk Park

• A range of other buildings can be seen in the Folk Park. These include the brightly painted travellers' caravans, the two water mills, the horizontal mill from Mashanaglas in Co. Cork, and the more traditional waterwheel mill. There is also a weaver's hut, and a blacksmith's forge. Bunratty House was the landlord's house; it is furnished in a Victorian style. In the stable yards there is a display of horse-drawn farm machinery including traps, ploughs, sprayers, hay cutters etc. The Regency walled garden has recently been restored. More recent additions to the Folk Park include the Church of Ireland church from Ardcroney and the Hughes brothers' house.
• The Folk Park also provides entertainment. The Castle provides its world-famous medieval banquets; the Barn holds nightly céilís and Mc Namara's pub often has entertainment. Old skills are practised in the folk park, such as thatching and whitewashing.

REVISION EXERCISES

1. What is folklore?
2. Why, do you think, was folklore important to the people?
3. Name the organisations which collected Irish folklore and describe how folklore was collected.
4. Name five areas of folklore, and give examples in each case.
5. Explain why you think Irish people were so superstitious, and give examples of superstitions.
6. Name four ancient festivals that are still celebrated today and the customs surrounding them.
7. Explain four different types of placenames, and give examples in each case.
8. Describe what a *seanchaí* does.
9. Name the different cycles of stories or folk-tales that come from Ireland. In each case give an example of a story. Organise a story-telling session that includes some of these stories.
10. Name some of the sports and pastimes that were popular in Ireland.
11. Describe how folklore has become part of the tourism industry, and suggest future development.

Assignments

1. By asking grandparents, research the customs of your local area, i.e. customs that are associated with different times of the year, old cures, old superstitions, etc.
2. Visit a local museum, and see the various implements that were used in farming, and discover the customs of the past.

References and further reading

E. Evans, *Irish Folk Ways.* Routledge, 1967.

Gibbons, *Hidden Connemara.* Connemara West Press, 1991.

M. Maclean, *The Literature of the Celts.* Senate, 1998.

D. O'hOgain, *Myths, Legends and Romance.* Prentice Hall, 1991.

D. O'hOgain, *The Hero in Irish Folk History.* Gill & Macmillan, 1985.

O'Suilleabháin, *A Handbook of Irish Folklore.* Education Company of Ireland, 1942.

O'Suilleabháin, *Irish Folklore and Tradition.* Education Company of Ireland, 1937.

O'Suilleabháin, *Storytelling in the Irish Tradition.* Mercier, 1973.

D. Smyth, *A Guide to Irish Mythology.* Irish Academy Press, 1988.

J.H. Delargy, *The Gaelic Storyteller.* Proceedings of British Academy, Vol. XXXI,

1945. Geoffrey Cumberlage London.

K. Danaher, *A Bibliography of Irish Ethnology and Folk Traditions*. Mercier Press, 1978.

D. O'Giollain, *Locating Irish Folklore*. Cork University Press, 2000.

S. O'Sullivan, ed, *Folktales of Ireland*. Routledge & Kegan Paul, 1966.

The Irish Folklore Commission. Comhairle Bhéaloideas Éireann 1979, Fact Sheet 4195, Folklore in Ireland. Department of Foreign Affairs.

Part 5
Cultural
Tourism

CHAPTER 15

Literary Tourism

Ireland has a strong literary tradition. Ireland's major writers include W. B. Yeats, George Bernard Shaw, Samuel Beckett and Seamus Heaney, all Nobel Prize winners for literature, and James Joyce, probably the world's greatest novelist. More books have been written about James Joyce than any other writer in the English Language, even Shakespeare. The Abbey Theatre Group travels the world performing Irish plays. Irish literature and Ireland have been brought before the world audience through Irish novels and drama. This has prompted satisfied readers to discover more about Ireland, and to come here as tourists. The majority of tourists who come to Ireland participate in some cultural activity, and quite a sizeable percentage participate in literary tourism.

Fig. 15.1: Postcard of Irish writers

GAELIC LITERATURE

In Celtic society the *file* was a very important person. He acted as poet, story-teller and historian to the nobles in society. At this time Gaelic was only a spoken language, and stories and poems were learnt during the poet's fifteen-year apprenticeship. The poet retold these stories. When Christianity arrived in Ireland in 432 A.D. it had an effect on Irish literature, because for the first time poetry, old tales and laws were written down. The *filí* told the stories to the monks who then wrote them down verbatim or adapted them in their own way. The earliest Irish books are the *Táin Bó Cuailnge* (*the Cattle Raid of Cooley*), and *Leabar Gabhála* (*Book of Invasions*); all three show European influences but are based on early Irish legends. The *filí* learned Latin rhythms from the monks, and used them in classical Irish poetry. Irish culture was not changed by the arrival of the Vikings in 795. In the tenth century old tales were written down in such books as the *Book of the Dun Cow*, and the *Book of Leinster*. Both these books were collections of poetry, legends, genealogies and histories from early periods. At the end of the twelfth century the position of the *filí* changed. They were no longer attached to monasteries, but to the houses of the nobles, Gaelic and Norman, instead. The stories that the *filí* told included the following:

- **The mythological tales** of the Fir Bolg and Tuatha Dé Danann, for example *the Wooing of Étáin*, in the *Book of Leinster*. They also told aisling or vision stories. Early monastic stories removed the druids, but the Normans found them great entertainment, and druids were reinstated.
- **The Ulster cycle**. This included the stories of Cú Chulainn, part of the *Táin Bó Cuailnge*. Another story was *Fled Bricrenn* (*Feast of Bricriu*). These were quite short stories, but allowed the *filí* room to expand on them, as they told their stories to a captive audience.
- **Tales of the Fianna**. They date from the seventh century in their oral form. During Norman times these stories were influenced by Norman romance literature, for example the story of Diarmaid and Gráinne. The longest narrative in Irish literature is the *Colloquy of the Ancients*, which tells the story of the leaders of the Fianna meeting with St Patrick.

These tales were important in Gaelic life right up to the demise of the old Gaelic society. In the nineteenth century Irish scholars reintroduced many of these stories through translations. During the Literary Revival, these stories played a major role; they influenced the writings of poets, novelists and dramatists, for example, Yeats's play based on the *Feast of Bricriu*, and Synge's *Deirdre of the Sorrows*. Austin Clarke was influenced by the stories of the Fianna when he wrote *The Bright Temptation*. Yeats and Lady Gregory wrote collections of Irish sagas and legends.

The earliest Irish poetry dates from the eighth century, and was written about nature, places, and saints. There were also lyric poems such as 'Deirdre's Lament'. Between the ninth and seventeenth centuries professional poets wrote classical Irish poetry. Irish poetry was very technical; there was very strict rhythm to each line, which had been influenced by both Latin poetry and hymns. This was taught in the bardic schools of the time. During the fourteenth century influences from French romance poetry began to affect Irish poetry. Poets travelled around the houses of noblemen writing and reciting poetry, and reciting folk-tales. This continued until the seventeenth century.

The seventeenth century in Ireland was a period of wars. The old Gaelic families who were patrons of the poets were dispossessed of their land, and many fled Ireland. Some of the poets left Ireland too, but those who remained taught in hedge schools or eked out a living by labouring. In Munster courts of poetry were held. Many poets including O'Carolan, Aodhagán Ó Rathaille and Eoghan Rua Ó Súilleabháin attended these. The theme of their poetry (laments) was the passing of the old way of life. One of the most important poets of this period was Brian Merriman from Clare, who wrote the satirical poem *The Midnight Court* in 1780. This poem was an attack against greed and convention. It was written in the language of the period.

The Irish language declined after the famine (1850). The national-school education that was provided at the time was through English, with no Irish or history taught in schools. This affected the amount of literature being produced in Irish. Douglas Hyde founded the Gaelic League to counteract this decline. Hyde collected Irish folk-tales and stories from Gaelic speakers in the west of Ireland, which he published in both English and Irish.

The tradition of writing in Irish was in poetry and folk-tales only. Irish poetry faced many problems in the early twentieth century; the Irish language had declined, and the poetry needed to be modernised. There was no tradition of writing novels or plays. The first novel in Irish was not written until 1894. It was *Séadna* by Fr P. O'Leary, the story of a shoemaker who sold his soul to the devil. Autobiographies were a very popular type of writing among Gaelic speakers. Those who produced such books included the three Blasket writers: Tomás Ó Criomhthain wrote *An tOileánach*, Peig Sayers *Peig* and Muiris Ó Súilleabháin *Fiche Bliain ag Fás* (*Twenty Years a-Growing*). Other novelists in Irish include Máirtín Ó Cadhain and Liam O'Flaherty. Modern Irish poetry has been developed using everyday speech, and in a lyrical form, by Máirtín Ó Direáin, Máirtín Ó Cadhain and Máire Mhac an tSaoi. More recently Michael Harnett and Nuala Ní Dhomhnaill have carried on the tradition of writing in the Irish language.

THE DEVELOPMENT OF ANGLO-IRISH LITERATURE

There are four major periods of development in Anglo-Irish literature, i.e Irish literature in the English language.

1. The Classical Period 1700–1880

This is the period of Anglo-Irish literature when writers were mainly from the gentry, and they represented this point of view in their writings.

- Jonathan Swift (1667-1745) was Dean of St Patrick's Cathedral. His writings often attacked the English Parliament because of their methods of governing Ireland, which was affecting the prosperity of the Irish Protestants. He wrote pamphlets, the most important the satirical *A Modest Proposal* that suggests, ironically, that poor Irish children should be sold for food so that their parents may survive. His most famous book is *Gulliver's Travels*, another work of satire.
- Oliver Goldsmith (1728-1774) wrote poetry, plays and novels. His most important poems were *The Deserted Village* and *The Traveller*. He lived in London most of his life and was an important Restoration dramatist producing such comedies as *She Stoops to Conquer*, and *The Good-Natur'd Man*. He also wrote the novel *The Vicar of Wakefield*. The inspiration for his writings came from his early life in Westmeath where his father was a vicar.
- Maria Edgeworth (1767-1849) lived in Longford where her father was a landlord. Her most famous novel, *Castle Rackrent*, is the story of the decline of an estate over four generations due to neglect, over-zealousness, gambling etc. She wrote other books dealing with this same theme including *The March to Kinsale, Ennui*, and *The Absentee*, which were written from the landlord's perspective.
- William Carleton (1794-1869) was a novelist whose background was of the Gaelic tradition, and whose family were dispossessed of their land. His education was in hedge schools where he was taught Irish folklore, which influenced his writing. Carleton's writings were about rural Ireland but from the perspective of the ordinary people he was often referred to as the 'peasants' novelist'. *The Black Prophet* was based on his own experiences during the Famine.
- Thomas Moore (1779-1852) was a poet who is most famous for his *Irish Melodies*; these were songs using Irish themes that he set to traditional airs. The Meeting of the Waters near Avoca, Co. Wicklow is linked to Moore's writings.
- Sir Aubrey de Vere (1788-1846) and Aubrey T. de Vere (1814-1902), father and son, were both poets. The father wrote sonnets. The son wrote poems based on historical events, for example 'The March to Kinsale'. He was influenced both by Irish history and by folklore. His poetry influenced many young poets during the Literary Revival.

- Edith Somerville (1858-1949) and Martin Ross (the pseudonym of Violet Martin, 1862-1915) were novelists. Although these date from a later period than the previous writers, their novels deal with themes that are similar. They wrote about the ascendancy class from their point of view, as can be seen in *The Real Charlotte* and *The Silver Fox*. They also wrote humorous stories centred on a Resident Magistrate; this later became a television series, *The Irish R.M.*

2. The Literary Revival 1880–1916

During this period Ireland was developing its national identity. This can be seen in the political events of the time, the Home Rule Movement, and the Land League. The GAA was founded to promote Irish games, and old Fenians like John O'Leary were influencing the younger generation. There was great interest in Irish legends, history, folk-tales, and the Irish language. In London Yeats, Douglas Hyde and other Irishmen published *Poems and Ballads of Young Ireland* to great critical acclaim. This encouraged writers to develop a new type of literature in Ireland that was based on Irish themes and folklore. Their work was written in the language of the ordinary people. Yeats, AE (George William Russell) and Douglas Hyde established the National Literary Society, to encourage literature on themes of Irish nationality, rebellion, and religion. Past experiences of famine, poor land tenure, the need to emigrate, and oppression by English rule made many of their works sad. They gave guidance to young poets of the period such as Padraic Colum and James Stephens. Not all Irish poets of this period were influenced in this way, for example Thomas MacDonagh and Francis Ledwidge.

- AE, as George Russell (1867-1935) was generally known, was a poet and visionary. During his lifetime he influenced many young poets, for example James Stephens.
- James Stephens (1882-1950) was a Dubliner whose background included life in an orphanage, and he later became a solicitor's clerk. He was both a poet and novelist. *The Rocky Road to Dublin*, and his adaptations of, for example, *Ó Brudair*, display his talent as a poet. His novels include *The Charwoman's Daughter* and *The Crock of Gold* and he produced a collection of Irish fairy tales.
- Francis Ledwidge (1891-1917) was from a labouring background in Co. Meath. He was involved in the Irish Volunteers, and was a supporter of James Connolly's Labour Movement. Encouraged by John Redmond he joined the British Army to fight on the Western Front (First World War). He wrote a number of poems about the Easter Rising, for example 'Thomas McDonagh'. His war poems were romantic, unlike many of the war poems at this time. He died on the Western Front.

The Literary Revival was involved in the founding of the Irish National Theatre.

(See Chapter 16.) Novelists who were linked to the Revival included James Joyce, Ireland's most important novelist, and George Moore. George Moore (1852-1933) wrote the very influential volume of short stories *The Untilled Field*. He was influenced by the work of Russian writers, for example Turgenev, who wrote about the landlord and peasant systems that operated in Tsarist Russia. Moore saw parallels with the Irish situation. Moore was involved with the Literary Revival for a period, but being a landlord and holding anticlerical attitudes made him unpopular. His trilogy *Hail and Farewell* was based on his involvement with the Revival. His best work is *The Lake*, which was set in his hometown of Ballinrobe, Co. Mayo.

3. After the Revival: 1920s–1950s

The 1916 Rising, and the period of unrest that followed, ended the Literary Revival. Many of the same writers continued writing but the emphasis of their writing changed; this was especially true of novelists. A period of disillusionment set in. This can be seen in the work of novelists like Kate O'Brien and Elizabeth Bowen, and among short story writers such as Frank O'Connor, Liam O'Flaherty and Sean O'Faolain. Literature now dealt with local events, and the characters all had limited horizons. Books that reflect this include O'Faolain's novels *A Nest of Simple Folk*, and *Bird Alone*. Liam O'Flaherty's *Skerrett*, deals with rivalry and a power struggle between the local parish priest and the local teacher. Life in the small Irish town is the theme of Kate O'Brien's *Without My Cloak* and Frank O' Connor's 'The Lucys'. O'Connor explores how a family copes with tensions in this environment. Many books written during this period were about war in Ireland. Elizabeth Bowen's *The Last September* deals with the reaction of the ascendancy to the War of Independence. Liam O'Flaherty's *The Informer* deals with the flight of a man from the IRA because he had informed on his friend.

There was also a certain amount of continuity with the past in the works of Daniel Corkery. His writings included what he considered were the three essentials of being Irish: religion, nationality, and land. These ideas are well illustrated in short stories in *The Hounds of Banba* and *The Stormy Hills*. Corkery's work influenced later writers like Bryan MacMahon and Francis MacManus. Francis MacManus wrote a number of historical novels set in the eighteenth century. He also wrote about the obsession with land, for example *This House was Mine*. Many newer writers found that Corkery's framework was too restrictive for their work. Austin Clarke remained influenced by folklore. There were also experimental novelists at work; these included Beckett, Joyce and Flann O'Brien.

The post-Revival period produced four short story writers. Themes included war in Ireland, and Irish society during this unsettled period.

- Sean O'Faolain (1900-1991) used the period between 1919 and 1923 as back ground for his first collection of stories, *Midsummer Night Madness and Other*

Stories. His later book of short stories, *A Purse of Coppers*, deals with the frustration of living in Irish society in the 1930s. O'Faolain's work is both humorous and sophisticated.

- Frank O'Connor (1903-1966) deals with Irish life in both a romantic and emotional way; this is seen in 'The Majesty of the Law' and 'Peasants'. He wrote satirical stories about urban Ireland. Some of his stories, like 'First Confession' and 'My Oedipus Complex', are stories about children. Many of O'Connor's stories were written to a formula, and lack the freshness or sophistication seen in O'Flaherty's or O'Faolain's writings.
- Liam O'Flaherty (1896-1984) wrote stories about rural Ireland, of courage, strength, and energy in coping with life. O'Flaherty was from the Aran Islands, and he was influenced by his experiences on the Islands. His books, including *Spring Sowing,* had thirty-two such stories.
- Mary Lavin (1912-1996) often deals in her stories with the shortcomings of people. 'The Will' depicts snobbery and petty mindedness, while in *The Becker Wives* living in a make-believe world, and in *A Single Lady* it is self-deception and its effect on other people's lives.

Autobiographies were also very popular, with W.B. Yeats, Sean O'Faolain, George Moore, Frank O'Connor, Austin Clarke and Sean O'Casey. Yeats was still producing his poetry, essays, and plays. He was considered to be the greatest 'Classical' poet of the times, and won the Nobel Prize for Literature in 1923. Samuel Beckett was one of the new poets; he lived in France and was influenced by life there. His poetry rejected materialism, and romanticism, and stressed the importance of the imagination and the consciousness of the individual; this can be seen in his *Collected Poems in English and French*. The following poets were also from this period:

- Padraic Colum (1881-1972) mainly wrote ballads about life in rural Ireland. He was influenced by the work of Douglas Hyde and his translations of old Irish love songs and religious poetry. 'She Moves through the Fair' was one of his ballads that became a folk song. Colum's most famous poems include 'The Drover' and 'The Old Woman of the Roads'.
- Patrick Kavanagh (1904-1967) was brought up on a small farm in Monaghan. Many of his poems were about rural Ireland, for example 'The Ploughman', *The Great Hunger* etc.
- Louis MacNeice (1907-63) was more interested in the work of Auden and the English modernist movement. He wrote lyrical poetry such as *Autumn Journal*. His later poetry became more meditative. The poems in *Autumn Sequel*, and 'Dublin' are among his best.

The effect of war on both England and Europe is reflected in the work of writers like Francis Stuart and Beckett. This period had a profound effect on each man.

Samuel Beckett spent the war in France with the French underground, while Francis Stuart lived in Germany.

- Samuel Beckett met James Joyce in Paris and was influenced by his writing. Like Joyce, Beckett had an absurd sense of humour, as can be seen in his novel *More Pricks than Kicks*. Among his best novels are *Molloy* (1947) and *Malone Dies* (1948) which are dominated by isolated characters who are victims of the human condition without the support of a concerned God. These characters reflect a despondency that was prevalent in Europe. Beckett also experimented with his writings, as seen in his novels, plays and poetry. He reduces language to its bare essentials, in order to focus on the innate meaninglessness of life.
- Francis Stuart (1902–99) first began writing poetry and later novels in the 1920s. While the novels he wrote in the 1930s showed promise, he couldn't make a living from writing, so in 1940 he went to Germany to lecture on English and Irish literature. His experiences during the war led him to write *The Pillars of Cloud* and *Redemption*, which dealt with the horrors of war in Germany. His novels now had a sense of realism they had previously lacked. In 1971 he wrote his autobiographical novel, *Black List: Section H*, again about the war in Germany, which started another period of successful writing for Stuart. While the war years in Germany played a major influence on Stuart's writings, it also made him a very controversial figure because of his pro-German stance.

4. Contemporary writing, 1950s onward.

Since 1950 there have been major changes in literature. The cultural and economic poverty of Ireland in the 1950s meant that many people emigrated. As the 1960s approached, outside influences began to encroach on Ireland. A more liberal and cosmopolitan society emerged with the advent of television (BBC and RTÉ), the easing of censorship restrictions and the creation of jobs. The ideas of new writers were more liberal and their writing more introverted, as they reflected on their past. This can be seen in the poetry of Thomas Kinsella, John Montague and Seamus Heaney, the novels of John Banville, Edna O'Brien and John McGahern, and the plays of Thomas Murphy.

- William Trevor (1928–) writes short stories, and is one of the world's best short-story writers. He has spent most of his life in England, but still he writes stories that are set in Ireland. He believes that today's world has been formed from the old class system that both corrupted and alienated people. Both Nationalist and Unionist traditions influenced him; these he inherited from his parents. Trevor's novel *The Children of Dynmouth* won the Whitbread Prize in 1976. The themes of his stories have included love, religious fanaticism, loneliness and alienation. In Ireland he is probably best known for *The Ballroom of Romance*, which he wrote in 1972. He comes from a long tradition of story-tellers, and holds that the writer must believe in both the story and its characters for it to be a success. An example of this is found in 'The Hill Bachelors'.

- Brian Moore (1921–) is from Belfast. He has written on many themes, including loss of religion, loneliness, the effects of success on people's lives. Such themes are found in *The Lonely Passion of Judith Hearne*, *An Answer from Limbo*. These books have been influenced by his life experience and are very realistic. His later works including *The Great Victorian Collection* are concerned with fantasy.

- John McGahern (1934–) from Leitrim has written a series of books that have developed from his experiences of love, death and separation, amongst them *The Dark* and *The Barracks*. John McGahern has also written short stories, collected in *Nightlines* and *Getting Through*. Characterisation is very important in all his novels.

- John Banville (1945–) has written short stories, for example the collection *Long Lankin*, and novels. His books are influenced by Nietzschean ideas, and are full of darkness and despair. His books include, among others, *Nightspawn*, and *The Book of Evidence*.

- Maeve Binchy (1940–) has written humorous short stories about life in London and middle-class Dublin, for example the collection *Central Line*. Themes of her books include illusions of romance, the relationship between adults and children, the success of people who are talented and capable. Her books include *The Lilac Bus*, *Circle of Friends*, and *Tara Road*. She is among Ireland's most popular novelists, and is known worldwide.

- John Broderick (1927–89) was originally from Athlone, and in his early books for example *The Waking of Willie Ryan*, *The Fugitives* he was critical of life in the Irish Midlands, its snobbery, hypocrisy and pretensions. In 1980 Broderick moved to England, and there he broadened the range of his work. These books have characters that are more sympathetically developed, for example *The Trial of Father Dillingham*, and *An Apology for Roses*.

- Roddy Doyle (1958–) is both a novelist and playwright. His first book was *The Commitments* in 1989, which was made into a film by Alan Parker in 1991. *The Snapper* and *The Van*, which completed the Barrytown Trilogy, followed. In 1993 he won the Booker Prize with *Paddy Clarke Ha Ha Ha*. His books are renowned for their humour and witty dialogue in the language of working-class Dublin.

Other important novelists from this period include Edna O'Brien, Benedict Kiely, Molly Keane, James Plunkett, Jennifer Johnston, Julia O'Faolain, Bryan McMahon, Thomas Kilroy, Colm Tobin, and Frank McCourt.

Since 1950, poetry has broken away from the strict format of that of the previous generations. It is rich in imagery and metaphor. There has been a prolific output of

Irish Writers

Frank McGuinness
Seamus Heaney
John Montague
Louis MacNeice
Patrick Mc Gill
William Carleton
Brian Moore
Brian Friel
Derek Mahon
Benedict Kiely
Michael Longley
Thomas Mc Donagh
John McGahern
W.B. Yeats

George Moore
Paddy Kavanagh
Douglas Hyde
Patrick McCabe

Mary Lavin
Maria Edgeworth
Oliver Goldsmith

Denis Johnstone
Richard B. Sheridan
Richard Murphy
Maeve Binchy
Padraic Colum
John Broderick
James Joyce
Jennifer Johnston
Thomas Murphy
Samuel Beckett
Thomas Kinsella
Liam O'Flaherty
Lady Gregory
Oscar Wilde
John M. Synge
G.B. Shaw
Thomas Moore
Brian Merriman
Sean O'Casey
Roddy Doyle
Edna O'Brien
Jonathan Swift
James Stephens
Bram Stoker
Kate O'Brien

Aubrey de Vere
Francis Mac Manus
John B. Keane
Michael Hartnett
John Banville
Thomas Kilroy
Bryan Mac Mahon
William Trevor
Peig Sayers
Elizabeth Bowen
Tomás O Críomhthain
Sean O'Faolain
Eogáin Ó Rathaille

Edith Somerville

Fig. 15.2: The geographical location of writers in Ireland

poetry in Ireland since 1980, a poetry that reflects the changes taking place in modern society. Major poets from this period include the following:

- **Thomas Kinsella** (1928–) has been influenced by a wide range of poets. His early poems like 'Baggot Street Deserta' were lyrical. Often his poetry deals with suffering and death, as in 'Cover Her Face', 'In Phoenix Park'. He has also produced poetry about significant events like the death of J.F. Kennedy.

- **John Montague** (1929–) refers to either love or loss in his poetry. This can be seen in *The Rough Field*. His poetry is expressed in a very clear way, as can be seen in 'The Trout'.

- **Seamus Heaney** (1939–) is from rural Derry, and has been influenced by the work of both Robert Frost and Gerald Manley Hopkins. Myths and the psychic are important to his work, as in 'Bogland', and 'Trial Piece', both of which stretch into the past and conjure up images of people long since dead. Since 1979 Heaney's work has become less complex, as in *Field Work*. He is Ireland's most important living poet.

Other important poets from this period include Richard Murphy, Derek Mahon, Brendan Kennelly, Eavan Boland, Michael Longley, Paul Durcan, and Michael Hartnett.

LITERATURE AND TOURISM

Writers come from every part of Ireland. This offers potential for literary tourism in every region. Many writers write about their local areas, and often fans of the writer want to visit the places they have read about. Summer schools and festivals have been established to study the work of many Irish writers. Organised summer schools attract large numbers of tourists. The tourists come for a weekend or a week, they stay in hotels, enjoy good food and drink; attend tours, lectures and readings of the works of the writer. This all creates employment within the tourism industry, and for academics. These summer schools start in February and run until November, so the term 'summer school' is a bit of a misnomer.

- **Oliver Goldsmith Summer School** takes place in Ballymahon, Co. Longford, in June. It examines Goldsmith's writings as poet, playwright, and satirist.
- **William Carleton Summer School** takes place in Clogher, Co. Tyrone. Carleton wrote novels during the Famine period, and was influence by the old Gaelic ways; these are all reflected in the summer school.
- **Oscar Wilde Summer School** takes place in Bray, Co. Wicklow during the middle of October. It includes drama, poetry evenings, readings by novelists, and a series of lectures linked specifically to Wilde, for example his school in Portora in Enniskillen, prison conditions when he was in Reading Gaol, and Wilde's links with Victorian Bray. Lectures, walks, and performances are all part of this summer school.

Other writers who have summer schools dedicated to their work include George Moore in Co. Mayo; J. M. Synge in Rathdrum, Co. Wicklow; Brian Merriman in Ennistymon in Co. Clare.

There are also summer schools dedicated to the art of writing. The most famous of these is **Listowel Writers Week** in Co. Kerry. This summer school usually attracts writers who give readings, lectures, and run workshops for aspiring writers. Theatre performances also take place. Listowel is the home of J. B. Keane and it has a rich tradition of literary activities. Other summer schools are: the Bard Summer School on Clare Island, Co. Mayo; General Humbert School in Ballina, Co. Mayo; McGill Summer School in Glenties, Co. Donegal, and the International Writer Course in UCG Galway.

There are a number of museums and cultural centres dedicated to writers around the country. **The Blasket Centre** is located at the end of the Dingle Peninsula, overlooking the Blasket Islands that stretch five kilometres off the south-west coast. The centre was built to the memory of the way of life and culture of these people. It

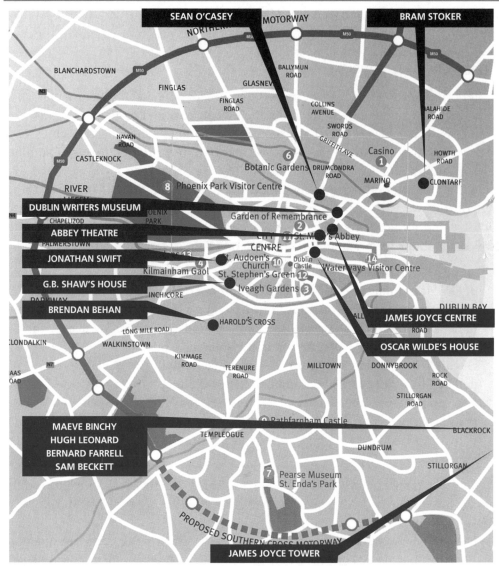

Fig. 15.3: Literary attractions in Dublin

is operated by Dúchas. It looks at a number of different aspects, the islands themselves, life in the harsh island environment, the literature that the island produced, and finally the abandonment of the island in 1953. At the beginning of the twentieth century, many academics went to the Blasket Islands to learn Irish; these include the Norwegian Carl Marstrander, and the Englishman Robin Flower. Flower has written a number of books on life in the islands.

These men also encouraged the locals to write stories about their lives. As a result three important books were written on the islands. **Tomás Ó Criomhthain** who wrote *An tOileánach* (*The Islandman*), was born on the Great Blasket Island in 1856, and lived on the island by both fishing and farming. At the age of forty he learned to write in Irish, and his famous book followed from this. **Peig Sayers** was born on the mainland, and did not move to the Island until 1873, when she married. She was a story-teller, and her story *Peig* was dictated to her son, who wrote down her words since she was illiterate. **Muiris Ó Súilleabháin** was born on the Island in 1904. He was encouraged to write by George Thomas, an English scholar who visited the Island. He wrote his story of growing up on the islands, *Fiche Blian ag Fás* (*Twenty Years a-Growing*). The Blasket Centre provides information about the other writers from the Blaskets.

There are a number of small museums located around the countryside, dedicated to the memory of local writers; these include The Paddy Kavanagh Museum in Monaghan, The Francis Ledwidge Museum near Slane, Co. Meath, and The Kerry Literary and Cultural Centre in Listowel.

Dublin city, a literary tourist destination

Through the centuries Dublin has produced a number of internationally-renowned writers. These have produced all forms of literature. There are many literary tourism activities in Dublin

- The **Dublin Writers Museum**, Parnell Square, is a museum dedicated to the work of Irish writers. Each display gives information about Irish writers and their most famous books. There is also a lecture room available, which is used for readings and other literary activities. On Bloomsday, 16 June, readings from Joyce's *Ulysses* take place there. A Living Writers Centre is next door, and this provides a setting for today's writers to meet and discuss their work.
- The **Dublin Literary Pub Crawl** is a walking tour that takes place at night, bringing tourists to many of the pubs that are linked with Irish writers. At each stop the actors read or perform from the books that are associated with the pub. They read and perform from Joyce, Flann O'Brien, Wilde, O'Casey and Brendan Behan. This is a very pleasant way to learn about Irish literature.
- **George Bernard Shaw House** is located in Synge Street. This dedicated museum is situated in Shaw's birthplace, and has information about the writer and his works. A Shaw Summer School is also organised for those who are interested in his works. Dublin Tourism manages the Shaw House as it does the Writers Museum.
- **The Wilde House** is located at 1 Merrion Square, and was the home of Oscar Wilde. This has restricted opening. An audio-visual presentation tells the story of Oscar, and a number of rooms display items belonging to Oscar's family.

Ireland's most important literary tourism sites are linked to Yeats, in Sligo and at Thoor Ballylee; and to James Joyce in Dublin.

Case study: W.B. Yeats and Co. Sligo

Fig. 15.4: William Butler Yeats

William Butler Yeats was born in Sandymount, Dublin in 1864. He is linked more with Sligo than any other part of Ireland, because he spent many of his summer holidays as a child there with his cousins and grandparents. He also drew on Sligo for inspiration for his poetry, and many of his poems are linked with the Sligo landscape. He began writing poetry in 1885; his early poetry was influenced by the English Romantic poets like Wordsworth, Keats etc. In 1886 he came under the influence of the Fenian John O'Leary, and this generated an interest in Irish history and folklore which also became an inspiration for his work. In 1888, along with Douglas Hyde and others, under the aegis of O'Leary, he published poetry in *Poems and Ballads of Young Ireland*; this book of was very successful in England. From this followed poems influenced by Irish mythology like *The Wanderings of Oisin*. Yeats fell in love with Maud Gonne in 1889, and wrote many love poems dedicated to her, along with the play *The Countess Cathleen*. He also produced his collection of poetry called *The Celtic Twlight*.

In 1894 Yeats met Lady Gregory and in 1897 they founded the Irish Literary Theatre along with Edward Martyn. This later became the Abbey Theatre. His friendship with Lady Gregory meant that he spent many summers on her estate Coole Park, near Gort, Galway. Yeats was a director at the Abbey between 1904 and 1939.

By 1910 Yeats had acquired a reputation as a major poet. In 1917 he married Georgie Hyde-Lees. During their early married years they lived in Oxford, but in 1922 Yeats returned to Ireland to become a Senator in the newly-formed Irish Free State. At this time he lived both in Merrion Square Dublin, and at Thoor Ballylee, Galway. In 1923 he won the Nobel Prize for Literature for his poetry. While living in Thoor Ballylee he wrote his collection of poetry known as *The Tower*, and *The Winding Stair and Other Poems*. In 1934 they moved to Rathfarnham in Dublin, and it was there that he had his collection of plays published. Yeats died in France in 1939, but it was not until the end of the war that he was buried at Drumcliffe churchyard, 'under Ben Bulben'.

Sligo is known as **Yeats' Country**, not only because he spent time there as a child, but also because he drew inspiration from the surrounding countryside for his poems. Yeats' poetry comes from three distinct periods:

1. His early poems were written between 1889 and 1904. Romanticism, French symbolism and, later, Irish folklore influenced these. Many of these were set in Sligo, around Lough Gill, e.g. 'The Lake Isle of Inishfree', 'The Song of Wandering Aengus', and 'The Fiddler of Dooney'. The Wanderings of Oisin are linked to Knocknarea, where the legendary Queen Maeve of Connacht is buried. The Glencar Valley and Ben Bulben were the inspiration for 'The Stolen Child'.

2. These are poems that Yeats wrote during middle age, (1904–25) and were linked with Coole Park. He published *Responsibilities and Other Poems*, and later *The Wild Swans at Coole*. He also wrote his poems about Ireland at this time, e.g. 'Easter 1916'.

3. In his last period, from 1926 until his death in 1939, many of his poems dealt with old age. 'In Memory of Eva Gore-Booth, and Con Markiewicz' was a poem written in memory of the two sisters who lived in Lissadell House, which Yeats had visited as a child. 'The Black Tower' was written a few days before his death and it is believed to be about Black Rock Lighthouse near Rosses Point. It is because of the many references to Sligo that tourists come to visit the area, to see Lough Gill, the Hazelwood, and Innisfree that are linked into the poem 'The Lake Isle of Innisfree'. They come to see Drumcliffe churchyard where Yeats is buried and to see Knocknarea, and Ben Bulben.

The **Yeats Summer School** is held each August in Sligo, where it attracts students, academics and tourists. The school provides lectures, field trips in the area, films and theatre. The local theatre, The Hawk's Well, is called after the play *At the Hawk's Well*, which refers to the area around Tullaghan Hill, close to Ballisodare. Yeats' old home at **Thoor Ballylee**, Gort, Co. Galway is a museum dedicated to the poet.

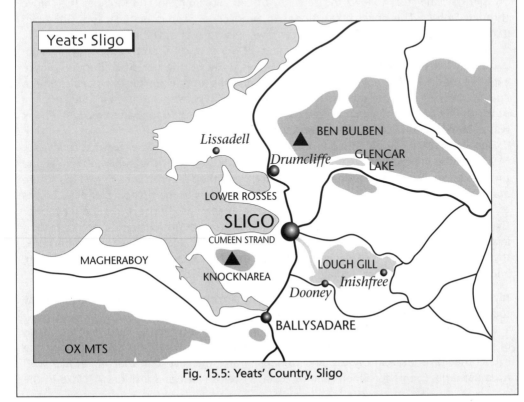

Fig. 15.5: Yeats' Country, Sligo

Case study: James Joyce's Dublin

James Joyce was born in Rathgar in 1882. He spent his young life moving house, as his father who liked to drink got further and further into debt. In all, he lived in fourteen houses in Dublin, each poorer than the previous one. The young Joyce was educated by the Jesuits in Belvedere College and later in UCD. After this he became a teacher, working in Dublin, Paris and later Trieste. He left Dublin for the Continent in 1904, eloping with Nora Barnacle. In his early years Joyce was an admirer of Yeats, but he moved away from Yeats and the Literary Revival because of the influence of the Church and nationalism on the movement. As a young man Joyce wrote poetry, for example 'The Holy Office', which satirised the Church, and *Chamber Music*, which was a collection of lyrical poetry. Joyce is best known as a novelist, and he used his experience of life in Dublin in all his books. Joyce's most famous short stories and novels are the following:

1. Dubliners is a series of short stories dealing with issues like frustration, alcoholism, inertia and conformity in Ireland; all of these, Joyce felt, were influenced by the Catholic Church.

2. Stephen Hero, and *A Portrait of the Artist as a Young Man*, deal with the development of the young man Stephen Dedalus and his maturity into an artist. This involves him leaving his home, church and country, not unlike Joyce himself.

3. Ulysses is considered one of the most important novels of the twentieth century. The story revolves around three characters, Leopold Bloom, his wife Molly who is unfaithful to him, and Stephen Dedalus who is looking for a father figure. The story takes place over an eighteen-hour period on 16 June 1904. It portrays many different aspects of life in Dublin on that day; the story follows the activities of Leopold, Stephen and Molly as they move through Dublin. The novel takes Bloom to Sandycove, Sandymount Strand, Glasnevin Cemetery, Duke Street, Eccles Street, in fact over a large area of Dublin. As events happen, the thoughts that are going through the minds of the characters, both consciously and subconsciously, are revealed to the reader. This is done by the use of soliloquies. Joyce experimented with the novel's style and form, and the story is similar to Homer's famous epic the *Odyssey*. Many academics have written about *Ulysses*. It is written in the language of the Dublin of the time, and is often considered easier to listen to than to read. The book was published in 1922, amid much controversy.

4. Finnegans Wake was published in 1939. It too was set in Dublin. The story has four parts; this forms the life-cycle of man. Joyce first deals with the life of the publican's family and their ancestors. Then he goes on to their children, and their dreams. Dreams and the future are dealt with in the third part, and then the story returns to the first part, and life begins to repeat itself. Joyce was influenced by the teachings of the Italian philosopher Giambattista Vico, who believed that civilisation went through four cycles, before returning to the start again. The rhythm and sound of the language is important to the book. Joyce loved to play with words, and he hoped that the book would make people laugh, and for this reason it is best read aloud.

Joyce's *Ulysses* is famous worldwide and brings many tourists to Dublin. There are many tourist activities that are linked to him and his writings. These include:

1. Bloomsday, 16 June. This is an event that is growing in significance. Each year thousands of tourists come to attend Bloomsday, many of them from America. The day follows the events that take place in *Ulysses*, and commemorates the first date that James had with Nora Barnacle. Events for Bloomsday take place over a week and includes A Wake in the

James Joyce Centre. *Ulysses* **by the Liffey** involves Joycean entertainment in the Docklands Area, river trips, readings, theatre, music and song. *Ulysses* **Bus Tour** visits a number of locations that are associated with Joyce, Sandycove's Joyce Museum, and a picnic on Sandymount Strand. It also visits the house where Joyce was born, and where he lived. David Norris, Joycean expert, performs his famous one-man show 'Do you hear what I'm seeing?' This is based on Joyce's works and life. Other events take place around the city, organised by Dublin public libraries, art galleries, etc.

Fig. 15.6: Statue of Joyce on Bloomsday

The first Bloomsday took place in 1954, to mark the fiftieth anniversary of the *Ulysses* day, in 1954. Many who participate in Bloomsday dress in Edwardian clothes for the occasion. Bloomsday itself starts off with the Bloomsday Breakfast. Readings take place to accompany the breakfast, which takes place in a number of venues in Dublin city including the James Joyce Centre. The Annual Bloomsday Lecture and Walking Tour takes place from the James Joyce Centre. The walking tour brings people through the North Inner City, where extracts from *Ulysses* are read and performed. Lunch is traditionally served in Davy Byrne's Pub in Duke Street. The Bloomsday Messenger Bike Rally starts from Findlater's Wine Vault, and many old bikes with appropriately-dressed cyclists make their way to the Mansion House to meet the Lord Mayor and continue on to the James Joyce Centre. A number of walking tours follow the journey of Leopold Bloom from O'Connell Street to Kildare Street. These are organised by a number of independent groups including the actors of the Balloonatics Theatre Company, who read and act out parts of *Ulysses*. Evening readings by contemporary writers take place at such venues as St Ann's Church, and the National Library.

2 **The James Joyce Annual Summer School**, organised by the Department of Anglo-Irish Literature, UCD. It was first held in 1988, and has been growing from strength to strength. It attracts large numbers of tourists from abroad, to lectures, workshops, field trips, etc.

3. **The James Joyce Cultural Centre**, located in North Great George's Street, in a restored Georgian property. It was opened on Bloomsday 1992, and is the centre for Joycean studies and cultural events. The Centre organises a range of walking tours, seminars, and workshops.

A reading group meets weekly to study James Joyce's writings. There are also performances based on Joyce's writings. A Joycean Film Festival takes place every February.

4. The James Joyce Tower, located in Sandycove Co. Dublin. Joyce lived in the Tower for a short period in 1904. The museum, which is dedicated to Joyce, exhibits his books and is managed by Dublin Tourism. The Tower is open during the high season (May to September).

5. Nora Barnacle House, is located in Bowling Green, Galway City. This small cottage was the home of Joyce's wife Nora and is open to the public during the summer months. It presents information about Nora, and the house has furniture that dates from the end of the nineteenth century.

REVISION EXERCISES

1. 'Gaelic literature was of two main types.' Explain this statement with examples.
2. Name a novelist from each of the periods of Anglo-Irish Literature, and give examples of work.
3. Explain the influence of Gaelic folklore on the writings of the literary revival.
4. Name poets from each of the periods of Anglo-Irish Literature, with examples of their work.
5. How did Irish writing change during the 1920s?
6. What changes took place in Irish writing after 1950?
7. Why are Yeats and Joyce so important to the Irish tourist industry?
8. Name tourist attractions that are linked to Irish literature.

Assignments

1. Select two novels or poems, one from the classical period (pre 1950), and one from the contemporary period (since 1950), and read them. When the books have been completed, prepare a report to include: (a) the image of Irishness that is portrayed, (b) the values and attitudes that are found, and how they have changed over time, (c) the qualities of the Irish people that are characterised, and how these qualities have changed, (d) how the traditions of Irish society have changed over time.
2. Visit a literary tourist attraction in your own area and write a report on it.

References and further reading

S. and T. Cahill, *A Literary Guide to Ireland*. Wolfhound.

R. Ellmann, *Four Dubliners*. Hamilton, 1986.

M. Harmon, *An Irish Studies Handbook for Anglo-Irish Literature*.

R. Hogan, ed, *Dictionary of Irish Literature*. Aldwych Press, 1996.

M. Stanley, *Famous Dubliners*. Wolfhound Press, 1996.

Irish Heritage Services, *Irish Writers*. Easons and Sons, 1986.

CHAPTER 16

The Arts as Tourist Attractions

The arts are defined by the *Encyclopaedia Britannica* as 'the use of skill and imagination in the creation of aesthetic objects, environments or experiences that can be shared with others'. This usually refers to the areas of art, drama and music. Irish art does not have the same reputation as Irish literature; none the less there is a strong tradition of art in Ireland. Irish art is found not only in art galleries but also at ancient monuments, abbeys, monasteries and museums. Ireland has a strong tradition of craftwork, and craft workers are located all over the country. Arts festivals take place in a number of centres. Recent developments in the arts make Ireland a good destination for cultural tourists.

DEVELOPMENT OF IRISH ART AND SCULPTURE

Irish art has developed over many thousands of years, but paintings date from the late seventeenth century. Inspiration for art often came from abroad, although frequently ideas were brought in, assimilated and then changed to meet Irish needs. Many designs that were developed in one type of art, were soon copied in another. This can be seen especially during the Early Christian period when similar designs are evident in metalwork, stonework and in manuscripts.

Neolithic, Bronze Age, and Celts

Fig. 16.1: Entrance stone at Newgrange

The earliest art found in Ireland consists of geometrical designs, that is, spirals, loops, zigzags, diamonds, squares and triangles. These can be seen on the large stones found at passage graves. One of the best examples of these can be seen on the entrance stone at Newgrange. It is thought that the designs on the stone are of some religious importance. The earliest type of metalwork was simple in design and decoration, and was made both of bronze and gold. Torcs and lunulae were produced and date from 1200 B.C. Torcs were necklaces formed from lumps of gold that were stretched and twisted, with the catch being simply small lumps at each end. The Gleninsteen Collar or Gorget is made of sheet gold, which is decorated with a rope pattern, and the end discs are decorated with circles and cones.

Later, metal objects were decorated with far more complex designs. The Celts moved away from simple geometrical designs and introduced designs that incorporated plants and animal heads. This can be seen in the Broighter Collar, which dates from Celtic times about 100 B.C. It is decorated with lotus birds and interlinking foliage. Ireland produced the best examples of gold work in Europe from this period. It is decorated with lotus buds and interlinking foliage. The metal decoration is repoussé work, the metal being hammered out from behind to create the design. Celtic metalwork at this time makes quite a lot of use of repoussé work, with stylised lotus-bud motifs and foliage, for example the Loughnashade trumpet, which is made of sheet bronze. The Celts also worked with red enamel, and this can be seen in pins and boxes found in Armagh.

Celtic artists also worked in stone, and their most important piece is the Turoe Stone. The design on the Turoe Stone is very similar to the Broighter Collar. It is thought that the Turoe Stone and its decoration have some religious significance. Art from this period can be seen at Newgrange Co. Meath; The National Museum, Kildare Street, Dublin; and Turoe Stone, Co. Galway.

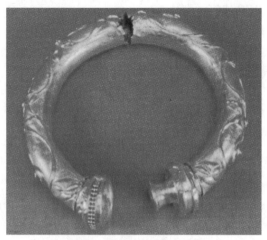

Fig. 16.2: The Broighter Collar

Early Christian Period

When Christianity arrived in Ireland, Celtic art had developed unhindered for nearly 1,000 years. There was some influence from Roman and Saxon Britain, which brought in some classical ideas and Germanic animal art. These foreign ideas were assimilated into the old traditions. Penannular brooches, which were decorated with animal heads, were introduced into Ireland in the second century, and were later to develop into highly-ornamented jewellery, for example the Tara Brooch. The new Christian monasteries fostered art and teaching. Early Christian art developed in three areas: manuscripts, metalwork, and stone crosses.

Art developed using the designs from the older Celtic art, such as spirals, interlacing stylised foliage from the old La Tène art, Germanic animals, and Celtic gods. Patterns found in this work were not regular, i.e. mirror images; this was done in order to keep interest alive in the work. Often spirals developed into animal motifs, and these did not have regular shapes either until the eleventh century; shortly after this the spiral was abandoned as a form of decoration. Irish art allowed the artist to use great imagination. Ideas for art came from folklore, for example tales of Tír na nÓg. Art from this period consisted of carefully worked out patterns. This included the interlacing of large animals, all of which were easily recognisable because they kept their shape. These major points can be seen in the important works of art of the period.

Manuscript production dates from the seventh century, and runs on until the tenth century. *The Book of Durrow* is the first important book with high quality illuminations; it is famous for its rich simplicity. This was produced in St Columba's monastery at Durrow in Co. Offaly. It consisted of the gospels, and was decorated in dark green, strong red and bright yellow colours, and interlacing of dark brown formed a frame for the illustrations of its double crosses, Evangelist symbols, and other decorations. The gospels were written in ancient Latin (vulgate), and they also used large decorated Irish letters (majuscule) to provide decoration at the beginning of the page or paragraphs. Birds were essential in the illuminating of Irish manuscripts. There were also a number of similar manuscripts. These are *The Book of Mulling* (St Mullins, Co. Carlow); the *Lindisfarne Gospels* (north-east England), the *Book of St Chad* (Lichfield Cathedral), the *St Gall Manuscript* (Switzerland).

The *Book of Kells*, which is often considered Ireland's most important treasure, dates from the early ninth century. It is comprised of four gospels, prefaces and summaries, and 340 vellum sheets. It is highly decorated with nearly every page having coloured illuminations. Some of the decoration consists of letters starting each paragraph being expanded into animals and humans of very unusual shapes. Other designs included leaf patterns, spirals and trumpets. Many colours are used in the decoration, while the Latin writing is in brownish-black ink. The Irish majuscule is more formal than in other manuscripts and the script is bold, well rounded, and looks as if it is printed. A number of pages are dedicated to portraits and gospel scenes; these use a variety of colours and shades of green, red, mauve, blue, brown and yellow. The pictures reflect the emotion of the situation. For example, the temptation of Christ shows the tension that exists between Christ and the Devil. Inspiration for the decoration came from the earlier Celtic period, with geometric designs, interlacing of plants, animals and man all appearing in the manuscript. This, like some of the other manuscripts, is on view in Trinity College Dublin.

Fig. 16.3: Illustration from the
Book of Kells

Irish monasteries produced many pieces of metalwork. These included chalices like the Ardagh Chalice and Derrynaflan Chalice, penannular brooches like the Tara Brooch, and also croziers, plaques, bells, etc. The Ardagh Chalice, which dates from the middle of the eighth century, is made up of a large cup and semi-spherical foot, both of beaten silver, which are joined by a bronze stem that is gilded and highly decorated. Most of the surface of the chalice is plain and this contrasts with the intricate panel of gold filigree, and the blue and red glass studs that decorate the panel. The names of eleven of the apostles are engraved in silver on the chalice. The panels are decorated with geometric, bird and animal interlacing in delicate gold filigree. Glass studs and filigree are also used beneath the handles and for the side roundels. The decoration makes a very impressive chalice, which can now be viewed in the National Museum Dublin.

The Tara Brooch that was found near the mouth of the Boyne, was originally used as a decoration on the clothes of kings and queens. It was cast in silver, and formed a closed ring, with a loose ornamental pin. It is decorated on both sides; on the front it has deep open panels, which are decorated with animals in delicate gold filigree. Amber and glass studs were also used to decorate the brooch, and copper was used to fill in some panels. Many of the designs on the Tara Brooch are similar to those of the Ardagh Chalice and it is believed that they could have been produced in the same workshop.

A number of important metalwork pieces date from the twelfth century. These include: the Lismore Crosier which is made of bronze and decorated with gold filigree, interlacing of animals and men, and coloured glass studs. The Cross of Cong, which once held the shrine of Jesus' cross, is made of oak, and is covered with bronze and gold. The centre of the cross has a large rock crystal, and here the relic was concealed. The cross is divided into panels decorated with intertwining animals and glass bosses. An animal's head joins the cross to its shaft; the cross was used during processions.

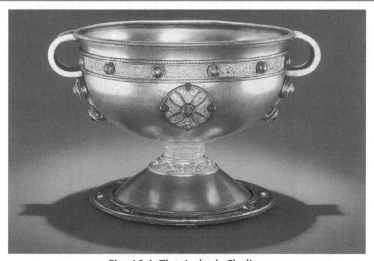

Fig. 16.4: The Ardagh Chalice

The earliest stone carvings involved simple crosses on slabs, and these were made in places such as Inishmurray in Sligo, and Glendalough. At the end of the seventh century standing stones began to change, and it is thought that the monks and people now used them as places of prayer. The earliest stones were engraved rather than carved; it is possible that they were also painted. The Carndonagh Cross is three metres high, and is decorated on both sides; on one side it has broad ribbons that are interwoven, while the other side has the figure of Christ surrounded by men and decorations. Typically of early high crosses, there is no circle through the Carndonagh Cross. High crosses date mainly from the eighth to twelfth centuries, and may have been influenced by the Eastern churches. The South Cross at Clonmacnoise has a panel of plants, on which are found birds and animals. Most high crosses have two types of decoration, the first consists of scenes from the old testament, for example Adam and Eve, Jonah and the Whale, Daniel in the Lions' Den, situations where sinners are looking for forgiveness and of course there is also the Crucifixion; the second are hunting scenes, horses, dragons, huntsmen. Some of these decorations can be seen on the Cross of Moone, Co. Kildare.

Two schools dominated high crosses in Ireland in the ninth and tenth centuries; the first was located in the North and included the monasteries of Ulster. The second school was known as the Monasterboice School and included its two crosses and also those in Clonmacnoise and Kells. These crosses are all in good condition. Muiredach's Cross in Monasterboice is seven metres high and made of blocks of sandstone. It stands east–west, and its panels tell a number of stories, for example Adam and Eve, Cain killing Abel, David and Goliath, Moses striking the rock, the adoration of the Magi, and the last judgement. The disk has interlacing decorations and some interlacing snakes and bosses decorate the area above and below the last judgement. The west side has only three panels; these are Christ being arrested, doubting Thomas, and Christ giving the key of the kingdom to St Peter and the laws to St Paul. The Crucifixion is on the arms of the cross. The theme is redemption.

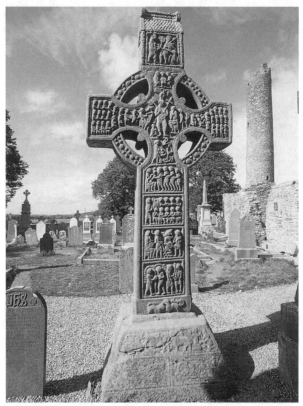

Fig. 16.5: Muiredach's Cross, Monasterboice, Co. Louth

The Georgian period

Following the great period of Irish Christian art, Ireland went through a time of unrest and war, which lasted until the Georgian period. During these years (1400–1700) Irish art was in decline and there are few major achievements. The return of peace and prosperity to Ireland after the Battle of the Boyne allowed Irish art to develop again. This was in the broad area of architecture, silverware, glassware, and furniture and, for the first time, painting. Art during the Georgian period was the preserve of the Protestant ruling class. Influences came from abroad, mainly from England, but also France, Holland and Italy. Ireland's prosperity encouraged the expansion of Dublin, with many new buildings being designed and built. The influences for these buildings were classical, and many of the architects came from abroad. These included:

- Thomas Cooley who designed the Royal Exchange (the City Hall)
- James Gandon who designed the Custom House, the Four Courts, the King's Inns.
- Sir William Chambers who designed some of Trinity College, Charlemont House, and the Casino at Clontarf
- Richard Cassels who designed the Dining Hall in Trinity College, Leinster House and Russborough House.

Irish architects included:
- Francis Johnston who designed the GPO, St George's Church, and buildings in Drogheda
- Thomas Ivory who designed the Blue Coat School, Blackhall Place.

These buildings were lavishly decorated inside. Italian craftsmen introduced the stuccowork (plasterwork), the most famous being the Francini Brothers. Later, Irishmen were trained in the trade. Classical symbols were used to decorate many of these magnificent buildings. Demand for fireplaces and furniture in these new buildings helped develop high quality craftsmen in these areas. Quality glass was produced in Waterford to adorn these houses.

In 1637 the Dublin Goldsmiths' Company was set up; many of its members were Dutch and Huguenot craftsmen who fled the wars in Europe. By 1700 Dublin craftsmen were producing a substantial amount of silverware (20,000 ounces per year was being registered in the assay office). Early eighteenth-century Irish silverware was very simple, with the minimum of decoration. In 1730 this silverware developed a rich rococo decoration and towards the end of the century was highly decorated. The influences on Irish silver came from both the Continent and England. Silverware development can be viewed at the Museum of Decorative Arts and History, Collins Barracks, Dublin.

The Duke of Ormonde (1619–89) was an important patron of the arts. He intro-

Fig. 16.6: Georgian silverware

duced such artists as James Gandy and Thomas Pooley to Ireland to produce portraits, and Francis Place who created drawings of Dublin. The Irish portrait painter Charles Jervas did most of his painting in London, including portraits of King George I and Jonathan Swift. He was influential on future artists. Many of them moved to London to paint. Early paintings in Ireland were predominantly portraits.

In 1731 the Dublin Society (this later became the RDS) founded a school of art to teach young Irish artists and sculptors. The school encouraged the development of landscape painting. The earliest landscape painters in Ireland came from abroad, including Joseph Tudor, and William Van der Hagen (who designed the tapestries *The Battle of the Boyne*, and *The Siege of Derry*, which are in the House of Lords, College Green, Dublin). George Barret was Ireland's most important landscape artist by the mid eighteenth century. His work included *Powerscourt Waterfall*, which portrayed the landscape in a very natural way. Francis Wheatley, from London, painted arcadian landscapes, for example *Salmon Leap at Leixlip with Nymphs Bathing*. He also produced portraits and historical paintings, for example *View of College,*

Fig. 16.7: Malton's view of Trinity College

with a Meeting of Volunteers. Wheatley also helped James Malton who produced views of Dublin in watercolour and etchings. Other important artists of the time were Nathanial Hone the Elder (*The Piping Boy*) and his son Horace, a painter of miniatures.

Dutch sculptors John Van Nost and Simon Vierpyl developed sculpture during the eighteenth century in Ireland. Both of them produced busts and statues for Trinity College. Vierpyl trained Edward Smyth, one of Ireland's most important sculptors at this time. Smyth worked with Gandon, producing the statues and River God heads for the Custom House.

The peace that encouraged art during the Georgian period ended in the 1790s; the Act of Union in 1800 destroyed Ireland's prosperity, and art went into decline.

Nineteenth- and twentieth-century art

Since the nineteenth century painting and sculpture have dominated Irish art. Most of the artists of the nineteenth century spent a lot of their time living abroad, in London, France or Italy where their art was influenced by popular developments. There was a movement towards landscape painting and away from 'topographical records' of earlier periods. Irish landscape artists included:

Fig. 16.8: Foley's statue of Burke
outside Trinity College

- James Arthur O'Connor (1792–1841). He was Ireland's first major landscape painter. The Dutch landscape painters influenced his work. For a period he lived in Westport where he produced many paintings of the area, including *View of Westport House*. He was famous for the light that he created in his pictures, as in *The Poachers*. After 1820 O'Connor lived in London, and later on the Continent. He produced work in watercolours, ink and wash, and oils. O'Connor produced paintings of famous tourist attractions in Co. Wicklow.
- John Danby (1793–1861). He worked in both watercolours and oils, producing many fine landscapes including *The Temple of Flora*. Danby is famous for his sunsets, for example *Sunset at Bight of Exmouth*. Some of his paintings were influenced by mythological themes; one of the best of these was *Liensford Lake Norway*. Danby's paintings can be seen both in the Tate Gallery in London, and the National Gallery of Ireland.

Many Irish artists worked in London where their work was famous. William Mulready produced both portraits and landscapes. His works included *Bathers Surprise*, and *Last in*. Daniel Maclise painted portraits of Charles Dickens and Walter Scott, among many others. He also painted narrative pictures such as *The Falconer*, and *The Marriage of Princess Aoife and Strongbow*. He was involved in the production of wall paintings, e.g. *Wellington Meeting Blucher* and *Death of Nelson* in the Houses of Parliament in London.

The most important nineteenth-century sculptor was John Foley (1818–74). He produced many important pieces, including the statues of Oliver Goldsmith and Edmund Burke (outside Trinity College), and the O'Connell Monument in O'Connell Street, Dublin. As the best sculptor in the British Isles he produced a section of the Albert Memorial in London, along with Pat McDowell from Belfast. John Hogan (1800–58) studied in Italy and was Ireland's most important neo-classical sculptor; his work included the statue of Father Mathew the temperance priest.

The Celtic Revival dates from the 1880s. Irish art was not going in any one direction during this period. Instead a number of important artists dominated the period and they were being influenced by different trends from abroad. New developments had taken place in paints, which allowed artists to work out of doors with oils. Many Irish art students went to France where art colleges were free. Art colonies in Pont Aven, Grez sur Loing, Barbizon, attracted many of these students and there the artists learned new techniques and painted. The most important Irish artists from this period included the following:

- Nathaniel Hone the Younger (1831–1917) was influenced by French art. He worked with Jean François Millet at Barbizon. Hone was more interested in naturalist painting; he produced many paintings of sea, and sky, for example *Rocks at Kilkee*. His landscape paintings of Ireland were dominated by his attention to the skies, as can be seen in *Pastures at Malahide*. A large number of Hone's works were donated to the National Gallery of Ireland; today only a small percentage of these are on display. Hone was professor of painting in Dublin and influenced many future generations of Irish artists.

- John B. Yeats (1839–1922) was influenced by the English Pre-Raphaelite painters and produced both street scenes, for example *The Bird Market*, and portraits for which he is famous. His best paintings are those of his friends and his sons William and Jack. Most of his portraits are of the upper body, and his best features are eyes, which capture the sitter's human qualities.

- John Lavery (1856–1941), from Belfast, studied in Glasgow and Paris, and later in Grez sur Loing. His open-air style produced such paintings as *Under a Cherry Tree*. He also produced portraits of Winston Churchill, John McCormack and his own wife, Hazel, who was used as a model for Ireland's bank notes.

- Walter Osborne (1859–1903), studied in Belgium, where he learned both impressionism and outdoor painting. He produced landscapes, paintings of gardens, for example *Apple Gathering in Quimperlé*, and street scenes, for example *St Patrick's Close*. These can be seen in the National Gallery of Ireland. Osborne enjoyed painting landscapes but he had financial problems and turned to painting portraits in order to make a living. He was a excellent portrait painter, particularly of women.

- Roderick O'Conor (1861–1940) studied and lived in Pont Aven, France, the home of both Van Gogh and Gauguin. His best landscapes were produced there,

Fig. 16.9: Walter Osborne's *A Cottage Garden Uffington*

including his impressionist paintings of the 1890s, for example *Field of Corn, Pont Aven*. His colours became very distinctive during the early years of the twentieth century and his range of style also expanded. His important paintings include *A Young Breton Girl* and his self-portrait. While O'Conor produced paintings of expert colour, light and space, he lacked great innovation in his work, and did not achieve a worldwide reputation like his friends Renoir or Gauguin.

• Jack Yeats (1871-1957) began by painting watercolours of race meetings, circuses and fairs in Devon and Norfolk, for example *Waiting with its Bright Sunlight*. Like his brother William, he found inspiration during the years spent in Sligo. When Jack Yeats returned to Ireland from England he worked as an illustrator. Later he worked in oils. Yeats, unlike other artists, did most of his painting in Ireland, and from 1920 he developed his art to include new mediums and techniques. These paintings were very expressive because of his use of strong

Fig. 16.10: Paul Henry's *In the West of Ireland*

colours and his bold paint strokes. He often painted horses, for example *There is a Night*. Yeats's later work became more abstract. Jack Yeats is considered Ireland's most important artist, and his work is on display in the National Gallery of Ireland.

- William Orpen (1878–1931) trained in Dublin and London. He painted landscapes and portraits, for example *A Bloomsbury Family*, and *George Moore*; and nudes, for example *The Model*. Between 1904 and 1914 Orpen's drawings and paintings dominated the art scene in Dublin. During World War I Orpen became a war artist and his work from this period is in the Imperial War Museum in London. Orpen taught art in Ireland in the 1920s and controlled the RHA (Royal Hibernian Academy).

Many other Irish painters, for example Garstin and Forbes, went to the continent and later Cornwall to study art and became part of the Newlyn School of realist painters.

The stained-glass movement in Ireland developed in the twentieth century. Behind its growth were Sarah Purser (1849–1943) and Edward Martyn, who set up the Glass Tower which brought in craftsmen from England to train Irish stained-glass artists. Ireland produced three important stained-glass artists: (a) Harry Clarke (1889-1931) whose work can be seen at Honan Chapel in Cork and in the Hugh Lane Gallery (*The Eve of St Agnes*). His work was very distinctive because of his use of colour. Clarke also worked as an illustrator of books. (b) Michael Healy (1873-1971) was more traditional in his stained-glass work. *His Last Judgement* can be seen in Loughrea Cathedral. (c) Evie Hone (see below).

Students of Osborne dominated art in Ireland during the 1920s. It was a period of realism for Irish painters, and art movements that were occurring in Europe had little or no impact on Ireland. The RHA was conservative in its outlook. Many of the paintings were nationalistic and romantic, and were chiefly landscapes of the west of Ireland, as can be seen in the work of Paul Henry, Seán Keating, Charles Lamb and Maurice MacGonigal. Of these Paul Henry (1877-1958) is the most famous, for his landscapes of the west, many of which featured cloud-filled skies, peat bogs, mountains and lakes, for example *Killary Harbour*. Some of his paintings have fishermen or labourers in them, for example *Launching the Currach*, and *The Turf Cutters*. Many of Henry's paintings were used to promote Ireland as a tourism destination. Maurice MacGonigal painted country fairs and landscapes, for example *Early Morning Connemara*. Seán Keating's paintings represented a romantic view of Ireland, for example *An Aran Fisherman and his wife*. Charles Lamb painted landscapes and portraits, for example *A Quaint Couple*.

Evie Hone and Mainie Jellet introduced modernism to Ireland. Both women had studied in Paris, first under Lhotes and later Gleizes, where they learned about cubism. While artistically they moved in different directions, they came together in 1943 and set up the Irish Exhibition of Living Art. This was set up in opposition to the RHA, and allowed artists who painted in these new styles the means of exhibiting their work. Jack Yeats supported them. Modernist artists included the following:

- Mainie Jellet (1896-1943) learned cubism in Paris, and produced abstract paintings that were dominated by segments of colour and light. Many of the subjects of her paintings were religious, for example *Deposition*. Apart from painting she also taught art.
- Evie Hone (1894-1955) studied in Paris, and produced stained-glass work. She was Ireland's most important stained-glass artist. Her best work is in the Chapel of Eton College, in Government Offices in Merrion Street, and in Kingscourt Church, Co. Cavan.
- Louis Le Brocquy (1916-) studied on the continent and was influenced by the work of Degas and Manet. Themes for his paintings include prisoners and travellers. He worked in oils and designed tapestries. From 1956 Le Brocquy studied the physical and psychological aspects of man; paintings from this period include a portrait of Samuel Beckett.

Since the 1960s Irish art has become more internationalist. The NCAD (National

College of Art and Design) is modernist in outlook. This has resulted in more varied work, with abstract art being balanced by figurative art. The Rosc Exhibition, which started in 1967, brought international art to Dublin. The Francis Bacon Exhibition took place in the Hugh Lane Gallery. Artists were welcomed to Ireland with tax-free schemes. The Irish Museum of Modern Art was established in the Royal Hospital Kilmainham, Dublin and this brings worldclass exhibitions on a regular basis. The New Irish Expressionist artists include Brian Maguire, Patrick Graham and Michael Mulcahy; other leading artists include Robert Ballagh and Conor Fallon. Art continues to develop, but many of the new artists prefer to be at the centre of world art and to work in New York, London or Berlin.

REVISION EXERCISES

1. Name the types of designs found on the large rocks at Newgrange.
2. What was a torc?
3. What kind of designs were used by the Celts on the Broighter Collar?
4. What were the main areas of Irish Christian art?
5. What types of decorations were used in the production of *The Book of Durrow*?
6. What are the main features of the *Book of Kells*?
7. Where can the *Book of Kells* be seen?
8. What are the main decorations on the Ardagh Chalice?
9. What kind of a brooch is the Tara Brooch?
10. What similarities of design are found in the Cross of Cong and the Ardagh Chalice ?
11. Explain the designs of early stone crosses like the Carndonagh Cross.
12. How did Muiredach's Cross at Monasterboice differ from the earlier crosses?
13. Where did the influence for Georgian architecture come from?
14. Name a famous building designed by the following architects: (a) James Gandon, (b) Francis Johnston, (c) Sir William Chambers, (d) Richard Cassells.
15. What were the different stages in the development of silverware design in the eighteenth century?
16. Name other quality products that were important during the Georgian period.
17. Name early Irish artists in the following areas:
    (a) portrait painting, (b) landscape painting, (c) sculpture, (d) etching.
18. Name Ireland's earliest landscape painters, with examples of their paintings.
19. Name John Foley's most famous sculptures.
20. What Irish painter worked with some of the great Impressionist painters?
21. Name Ireland's best-known portrait painter and some of his work.
22. Who were Ireland's leading artists during the Celtic revival?
23. Who were Ireland's leading stained-glass artists?
24. Who were the important landscape painters during the 1930s?

25. Who were the leaders of the modernist movement in Ireland?
26. Name some of Ireland's modern artists from the end of the twentieth century.
27. Who is Ireland's most famous artist? Name some of his paintings.
28. Name venues where Irish art can be seen.

THE INFLUENCE OF THE IRISH THEATRE AND CINEMA ON TOURISM

Irish theatre has gone through five distinct periods of development.

1. Early Irish theatre (1660s to 1900)

Ireland had no tradition of theatre until the middle of the seventeenth century. During the Restoration period a number of theatres were founded in Dublin, including Smock Alley Theatre, Crow Street Theatre, and the Music Hall in Fishamble Street where Handel first performed the *Messiah*. During this period there were many famous Irish dramatists including Goldsmith, Sheridan, Farquhar and Congreve. They produced comedies and satire. One of the first Irish dramatists to write plays based on Irish themes was Dion Boucicault, who wrote melodramas such as *The Colleen Bawn* and *The Shaughraun*. At the end of the nineteenth century two Irish playwrights, Oscar Wilde and George Bernard Shaw, dominated the theatre.

- Oscar Wilde (1854–1900) worked as a playwright in London and wrote four very famous plays, *Lady Windermere's Fan*, *A Woman of No Importance*, *An Ideal Husband* and *The Importance of Being Earnest*. He was a master of satirical comedy. He also wrote children's stories, such as 'The Selfish Giant' and *The Happy Prince*, and he wrote the novel *The Picture of Dorian Grey* which raised much controversy when it was published. At the height of his career he was arrested and imprisoned for homosexual offences; this resulted in his writing *The Ballad of Reading Gaol*. After his release from prison he went to the Continent where he lived in poverty.
- George Bernard Shaw (1856–1950) is considered to be the greatest dramatist in the English language since William Shakespeare. His earliest writings, which included novels and newspaper articles, were not successful, but from 1894 he started writing a large number of plays. These were performed in England, Ireland and the USA. In 1904 he wrote *John Bull's Other Island* for the newly-formed Abbey Theatre and when it was performed in England it was an instant success. His play *Heartbreak House* was produced on Broadway New York in 1920, and this enhanced his reputation even further. In 1925 Shaw was awarded the Nobel Prize for Literature. Among the many plays that he wrote was *Pygmalion*, which was adapted into the film *My Fair Lady*.

2. The theatre revival (1890 to 1920s)

In the 1890s Yeats, Lady Gregory and Edward Martyn began to plan their Irish theatre. There were a number of commercial theatres in the city; of these only the Gaiety and the Olympia remain today. The new theatre was intended to be a literary theatre. At this time there were neither the playwrights, actors nor audiences for such intellectual plays, but this did not deter Yeats from trying to create a new type of dramatic tradition. The Fay brothers, William and Frank, became involved with Yeats and his friends to form the Irish National Theatre Society. The main playwrights to emerge from this stage of the Abbey's development were Lady Gregory, Yeats, Synge, and O'Casey. The plays from this period have a sense of Irishness that is tied in with nationalist Ireland. The characters in the plays live within communities that are well defined; this is seen in the tenement life in O'Casey's *Juno and the Paycock*, or in rural Ireland in Synge's *The Playboy of the Western World*.

- Lady Gregory (1852-1937) was a main force behind the Irish dramatic movement between 1896 and 1932. She wrote over thirty plays, many comedies, for example *The Rising of the Moon*. Many of the characters and the language that she used in her plays were based on those of the people of south Galway. She also wrote miracle plays, plays for children, and historic plays like *Kincora*, based on Brian Boru. She helped young writers during this period, and many visited her home, Coole Park Gort, Co. Galway.
- Yeats (1864-1939) wrote twenty-five plays for the theatre. In the early period (1894-1904) he wrote morality and fantasy plays, such as *Cathleen Ni Houlihan*. Later he was influenced by Irish folklore, which included *On Baile's Strand* and *Deirdre*; these were written in verse. From 1916 he produced Noh plays, which brought together a balance of narrative, acting, lyric, music and movement. *The Dreaming of the Bones* and *At the Hawk's Well* are examples of Noh drama.
- John Millington Synge (1871-1909) originally studied music in Germany, and, later, literature in France. When he came in contact with Yeats in 1896 he was advised to visit the Aran Islands. Synge went to the Aran Islands each summer between 1898 and 1902. These visits influenced him to write *In the Shadow of the Glen* and *Riders to the Sea*, which were produced by the Irish National Theatre Society in 1903 and 1904 respectively. When the Abbey opened in 1904 Synge became involved. In 1907 *The Playboy of the Western World* was first produced there, causing a riot. He wrote a number of plays and was writing *Deirdre of the Sorrows* when he died. His death was a major blow to the Abbey because he was its most important writer.
- Sean O'Casey (1880-1964) was a self-taught man, who was involved with the Labour movement and wrote articles for *The Irish Worker*. He began by writing short plays for the Abbey, and was encouraged by Lady Gregory to continue

writing. In 1923 the Abbey produced *The Shadow of a Gunman*, which was very successful. *Juno and the Paycock* followed this. His plays were a combination of tragedy and comedy. In 1926 *The Plough and the Stars* was produced at the Abbey, but was met with riots. It is thought to be his best play. In London *Juno and the Paycock* won the Hawthornden Prize. In 1928 *The Silver Tassie* was rejected by the Abbey, and was later produced in London. O'Casey lived in England and wrote a number of plays through the 1930s. In 1939 he began his autobiography, which took six volumes and was eventually finished in 1954. O'Casey was the main playwright in the Abbey during the 1920s, and Ireland's most important until 1950.

3. Period of Abbey decline (1920s to 1950s)

During the period 1926–51, Lennox Robinson and George Shiels dominated the Abbey's work. There were few outstanding plays from this period, except M.J. Molloy's *The Visiting House*. Frank O'Connor adapted some of his short stories for theatre and Austin Clarke wrote verse drama, for example *The Sun Dances at Easter*. But the new director of the Abbey, Ernest Blythe, was more interested in developing the Irish language at the Abbey rather than verse drama or quality theatre. This change in policy had an adverse effect on the Abbey, which went into a period of decline during the 1940s and 1950s.

In 1928 Mícheál Mac Liammóir and Hilton Edwards began producing for the Dublin Gate Theatre Company. They presented quality drama from all over the world. These were first performed in the Peacock, for example *Peer Gynt* in 1928, and later in 1930 they set up the Gate Theatre, which was shared with Longford Productions. The Gate produced plays by Sheridan, Goldsmith, Shaw and Wilde. This situation continued until 1958. As the Abbey declined, the Gate replaced it and became the centre of Irish international drama; this was due to the work of both Mac Liammóir and Edwards. Mac Liammóir attracted new playwrights such as Denis Johnston.

- Denis Johnston (1901–84) had been rejected by the Abbey but was welcomed by the Gate. His plays included *The Old Lady Says 'No!'*, which was first performed in 1928. In 1931 Johnston joined the board of the Gate Theatre. He now wrote more plays for the Gate, *The Moon in the Yellow River*, which won international recognition and *The Dreaming Dust*. During the Second World War he was a war correspondent for the BBC and after the war worked in television. In 1958 the Abbey produced *The Scythe and the Sunset*.
- Samuel Beckett (1906–89) wrote plays as a relaxation from the writing of his novels. Metaphysics was central to his plays. The plays look at the chaos of people's lives, and their inability to cope with them. The characters in his plays are trapped by the situations they find themselves in, whether it is the two tramps

waiting for Godot, or Hamm and Clov who have physical disabilities in *Endgame*, and who cannot part from each other. Beckett provides what is known as total theatre: the integration of speech, acting, lighting, into the design of his play. Beckett's plays are very complex, and often too abstract for the audiences to fully understand them. He won the Nobel Prize for Literature in 1969.

- Brendan Behan (1923–64) with his play *The Quare Fellow* and autobiography *Borstal Boy* began working in the theatre during this period.

4. The second revival (1950s to 1980s)

Ireland was modernising during these years, and there was much tension between traditional ways of doing things and the new ways. This created a period of conflict, which produced many classical works within the theatre. This is shown in the work of Brian Friel, John B. Keane, and Thomas Kilroy. The world that these playwrights operate in is more complex. Friel's *Philadephia, Here I Come!* is dominated by the split personality of Gar O'Donnell. Hugh Leonard's *Da* has Charlie. Tom Murphy's approach is slightly different, using two characters that are two halves of one person. In all these plays the conflict and contradictions that exist can be played out to show the reality of Irish life.

DUBLIN THEATRE GUIDE		
ABBEY THEATRE Tel: (01) 878 7222 8pm Mat Sat 2.30pm	**BLACKWATER ANGEL** a new play by Jim Nolan	"It's a hugely courageous undertaking.. a deeply serious work of soul-raking, big stage literature" (The Guardian) Tickets: £18.50, £15, £10.
ANDREWS LANE THEATRE FINAL PERF Tel: (01) 679 5720 8pm	**LOCO COUNTY LONESOME** by Pat McCabe	WINNER The Edinburgh Herald Angel Award, London Times Critic's Choice. "A stunning piece of storytelling" (Edinburgh Ev News) "Entertainingly brash" (London Times) Tickets: Mon/Tues Specials £1; Wednesday – Saturday: £14.
FOCUS THEATRE FINAL PERF Tel: (01) 676 3071 8pm	Irish Premiere of **LIPS TOGETHER, TEETH APART** by Terrence McNally	"interesting and exciting piece of work... the acting was very strong" (Rattlebag, RTE) "uncompromising intensity" (Irish Times) Directed by Paul Keeley, Designed by Robert Lane. £10 & £7 Conc.
GATE THEATRE LAST WEEKS Tel: (01) 874 4045/874 6042 8pm	**PORT AUTHORITY** Written & directed by Conor McPherson	Irish premiere starring Stephen Brennan, Éanna MacLiam, Jim Norton. "entertaining, moving and exceptionally well-told. It deserves to be seen" (Sun. Business Post) "They are superb" (Sun. Independent) Tickets £15, £17.
LAMBERT PUPPET THEATRE May Sat/Sun Tel: (01) 280 0974 / 280 1863 3.30pm	**HANSEL & GRETEL and THE 3 BILLY GOATS GRUFF**	Lambert Puppet Theatre presents another classic double bill for children of all ages. Every Saturday and Sunday in May. Tickets: £6.
NEW THEATRE East Essex St. Temple Bar Tel: (01) 670 3361 8pm	Irish Premiere of **THE ENTERTAINER** by John Osborne	Ronan Wilmot as Archie Rice. "Wilmot plays Archie Rice with an unnerving core of lost brutality" (Emer O'Kelly, Sunday Independent) Monday to Saturday 8pm. Tickets: £10 – £5.
PAVILION THEATRE Dun Laoghaire Tel: (01) 231 2929 Tues 15 –Sat 19 May 8pm	**WIRED TO THE MOON** by Maeve Binchy	Presented by Fishamble Theatre Company. Adapted and directed by Jim Culleton. "huge creative energy... very comical" (Irish Times) "gently hilarious... excellent" (Sun. Indept.) Tickets: £14 (£10 conc.)
PAVILION THEATRE Dun Laoghaire Tel: (01) 231 2929 Sunday 20 May 7pm	**THE FAMILY** Presented by Mwldan Theatre/Opera Cocktail/Pavilion Theatre	The Irish premiere of this hilarious musical romp through the confused and crazy world of Greek mythology. Comedy, drama, great singing and wonderful music from Monteverdi and Rossini to modern day and new original work by Andrew Wilson Dickson. Tickets: £14 (£10 conc.)
PEACOCK THEATRE Tel: (01) 878 7222 8.15pm	**THE MEMORY OF WATER** by Shelagh Stephenson	Winner of the Olivier Award for Best New Comedy in 2000. Cast includes Dawn Bradfield, Jane Brennan, David Herlihy, Ruth McCabe, Marion O'Dwyer, Mark O'Regan. Low price previews £8 Thurs 24 – Mon 28 May.
PROJECT Space Upstairs Tel: 1850 26 00 27 8pm	Rough Magic presents the Irish Premiere of **DEAD FUNNY** by Terry Johnson	"You'll die laughing" (I. Times) "A wonderful play and an excellent production" (Rattlebag, RTE) With Míche Doherty, Janet Moran, Kate O'Toole, James Wallace & Mal Whyte. Directed by Lynne Parker. £12/£6
PROJECT Space Upstairs TODAY ONLY Tel: 1850 26 00 27 2pm	**PLAYS⁴** Rough Magic presents a public reading of AMONGST BARBARIANS by Michael Wall	Cast includes Nathalie Armin, Barbara Brennan, Jonathan Chan-Pensley, Garret Keogh, Fergal McElherron, Kate O'Toole, Robert Price, Karen Scully and Harmage Singh Kaliral. Directed by Conall Morrison. £5/£3

Fig. 16.11: Theatres in Dublin

- Brian Friel (1929–) has produced both short stories and plays. His first, most famous play was *Philadelphia, Here I Come!* It deals with the emigration of a young Donegal man who does not know his own mind, and who must come to terms with his conflicting thoughts. Other plays by Friel include *The Loves of Cass McGuire*, and *Dancing at Lughnasa*, which is probably his greatest play. It was considered the most important play in the Abbey since *The Plough and the Stars* and toured extensively. It has now been made into a film with Merril Streep in the leading role.

- John B. Keane (1928–), from Listowel in north Kerry, has produced many humorous stories and plays about rural Ireland. His plays include *Big Maggie*, *Moll*, and *The Field*. *The Field* was first performed in the Olympia Theatre in 1965 and tells the story of one man's love for the land and what he is prepared to do to keep what he thinks is rightfully his. *The Field* is internationally known because it was made into a film in 1990 staring Richard Harris. Keane has also written novels, for example *The Bodhrán Makers*.

Other important playwrights include Bernard Farrell and Hugh Leonard.

5. The third revival (end of 1980s–)

The third revival continues to include the work of Friel and Murphy. Drama is created by the use of language, since many of the older conflicts no longer exist, or only exist in isolation. Some of the plays deal with dramas that exist within isolated groups around the country. This can be seen in Frank McGuinness's *Observe the Sons of Ulster Marching Towards the Somme*, which looks at Ulster Protestantism and its role in the First World War. Brian Friel's *Dancing at Lughnasa* deals with a house of single women, and how that life falls apart on the return of their missionary brother. Conor MacPherson's *The Weir* deals with the lives of rural bachelors in an increasing urban society. Today many of Ireland's playwrights are doing similar work in the creation of drama through language, as Synge and Yeats did earlier.

There has been a major expansion in the number of theatres all over Ireland, with many large towns and cities getting new theatres. These theatres are a mixture of commercial theatres (which offer concerts, plays and light entertainment like pantomimes at Christmas) and more serious theatres that are available to travelling theatre groups. Tourists are an important audience for many of these theatres during the high season.

Irish Cinema

In 1896 the Star of Erin Theatre in Dame Street, Dublin, showed 'The Lumière's Cinematographhé'. This introduced Ireland to the world of cinema. James Joyce set up the first cinema in Dublin, called the Volta, in 1909. Many more cinemas followed and by 1930 there were 265 cinemas in Ireland. Over the last 105 years there have been dramatic changes in the cinema, first with the introduction of 'talkies', colour, and more recently of videos and computers. Cinema reflects the political, social and cultural history of Ireland and the world. For many years successive Irish

Governments saw the cinema as a threat to our culture and our morals. Strict censorship dominated Irish cinema.

The Irish film industry has gone through a very chequered history. In 1916 the Film Company of Ireland was set up and produced such films as *The Colleen Bawn* in 1920 and *The Dawn* in 1936. During the 1940s and 1950s British and American film companies produced most of the films that were made in Ireland. The best of these was *The Quiet Man*. There was no studio in Ireland, so all the inside scenes for these and other films were shot in British studios. In 1957 Ardmore Studios were built to rectify this situation, and the first film that used the facilities was *Shake Hands with the Devil*. In 1961 RTÉ was set up, and this created work for both film technicians and actors. In 1981 the Irish Film Board was set up; it provided funding for new filmmakers. Films like *Angel* by Neil Jordan and *Pigs* by Cathal Black resulted, but the funding was stopped in 1987. Many other filmmakers emerged at this time, including Joe Comerford, Thaddeus O'Sullivan, and Pat O'Connor. From 1989 Jim Sheridan and Noel Pearson made a series of films that won Oscar nominations; this put the Irish film industry on the international stage. The films were *My Left Foot* in 1989, *The Field* in 1990, and *In the Name of the Father* in 1993. In 1993 the Irish Film Board was re-established, and this helped provide finance for such films as *Circle of Friends* (1995). The Government also introduced tax incentives to encourage foreign films to be made in Ireland; this resulted in *Braveheart* (1995) and *Saving Private Ryan* (1998) being filmed here. Recent attempts to develop the industry have resulted in the production of many new films.

The themes of Irish films fall into five categories:

1. Romantic Ireland: Most of these films were produced by film makers from outside of Ireland, who are nostalgic about Ireland, or who were influenced by the writings of the Literary Revival movement (1880–1916) such as Yeats and Synge, or the paintings by Paul Henry and Seán Keating, or Bord Fáilte's images of Ireland. Films that fall into these categories include *The Quiet Man*, *Far and Away* (1992), and *Circle of Friends* (1995).

2. Adaptations of Irish literature to film: Many of Ireland's finest writers have had their work adapted for films. These include the writings of James Joyce – *Ulysses* (1967), *A Portrait of the Artist as a Young Man* (1977), *The Dead* (1987), Synge's *The Playboy of the Western World*, and more recently Samuel Beckett's plays including *Waiting for Godot*, and *Endgame*.

3. Ireland and violence: Ireland's violent history has been depicted in its films since the 1920s with such films as *Irish Destiny* (1926), *The Dawn* (1936), *The Plough and the Stars* (1936), and more recently *Michael Collins* (1996). These films dealt with the War of Independence and the Civil War. The Troubles in Northern Ireland have been the background for a number of recent film's like *Cal* (1984), *The Crying Game* (1992), and *In the Name of the Father* (1993).

4. Rural Ireland: Cinema, like drama and literature, has been influenced by Ireland's countryside. It tends to reflect the harshness of the land, its rolling hills, or the love of the land. These varied themes are seen in *Men of Aran* (1934), *The Field* (1990), and *Into the West* (1992).

5. Urban Ireland: Cities have been an important theme in world cinema since it was first invented. However, few films made in Ireland used this theme until the influence of Roddy Doyle's books in the 1990s. These books are centred in Dublin, for example *The Commitments* (1991), *The Snapper* (1993). *My Left Foot* (1989) is also about life in Dublin. Many recent films are set in urban locations and deal with psychological themes like *Guiltrip*. This shows the new, more confident Ireland that has emerged in the 1990s.

Irish films are so popular that Bord Fáilte has brought out a booklet that links Irish locations with films. These include Dublin, which was the location of *Educating Rita*, filmed in Trinity College; *The Commitments*, some of which was shot on the DART. Kerry was the location of films like *Ryan's Daughter*, filmed on Dingle Peninsula where a village was actually built near Dunquin for that purpose. In Cork, Youghal was the setting for *Moby Dick*, filmed by John Huston. Wicklow has been the location of many films, including *Dancing at Lughnasa*, and *Excalibur*. The latter filmed in Powerscourt Gardens. *Braveheart* was filmed on the Curragh and at Trim Castle. The west has attracted dramatists, artists and film makers. John Ford filmed *The Quiet Man* in Cong, Co. Mayo. Leenane in Co. Galway was the location of *The Field*. Monaghan was the location for Neil Jordan's film *The Butcher Boy*, based on Pat McCabe's novel depicting life in the 1960s there. Shane Connaughton wrote *The Playboys* and *Run of the Country* about his hometown of Redhills Co. Cavan, where both films were made. *Circle of Friends* was made in Inistioge and Thomastown, Co. Kilkenny. The beaches of Wexford were the location for Speilberg's *Saving Private Ryan* which was an Oscar success.

The small screen also has produced programmes in Ireland like Pat O'Connor's *Ballroom of Romance* set in Mayo, *Father Ted* filmed in Co. Clare, and *Ballykissangel* located in the Vale of Avoca, Wicklow. Tourists are attracted to these film locations, thereby creating a boost for the tourism industry. Film crews making these films use a range of tourism facilities, e.g. accommodation, catering, entertainment and leisure facilities etc. A crew of 250 worked on *Saving Private Ryan*, and they stayed in accommodation between Rosslare and Gorey in Co. Wexford.

Ten per cent of tourists chose Ireland for their holidays because of the images they had seen of Ireland on film. The top seven films that influenced tourists to come to Ireland on holidays were: *The Quiet Man* (1982), *Ryan's Daughter* (1970), *The Commitments* (1991), *Far and Away* (1992), *In the Name of the Father* (1993), *Braveheart* (1995), and *Michael Collins* (1996).

ARTS ATTRACTIONS AND FESTIVALS

A number of major art galleries are located in the major cities.

- **The National Gallery of Ireland**, located in Merrion Square, Dublin, was set up in the 1860s. It holds the national collection of Irish painting from the seventeenth century, portraits by Orpen, landscapes by O'Connor, subject paintings by Osborne, etc.; work by stained glass artists like Evie Hone, and the Yeats Gallery. The European Masters include: the Italian School with paintings by Titian, Carravaggio, and Rubens; the French School with painters such as Claude; nineteenth-century landscape painters; Impressionists, for example, Monet; early twentieth-century artists like Picasso; Dutch seventeenth-century masters like Vermeer and Ruisdale; Spanish artists like El Greco and Goya; and British portraits by Reynolds. The Gallery holds exhibitions, for example the annual Turner Exhibition of Watercolours, organises lectures, workshops, drawing classes, guided tours, concerts and piano recitals for visitors to the gallery.

- **Hugh Lane Municipal Gallery**, Charlemont House, Dublin was set up in 1908, and was the first modern art gallery in these islands. It was the dream of Hugh Lane to establish the Gallery. He sought both financial and political support for it and was promised paintings from many sources. When the original gallery was set up in 1908 it was located in Harcourt Street, and the artists it had on show were the best of English (Constable and Whistler), French (Corot, Manet, Degas, Pissaro and Renoir) and Irish (Jack, and John Yeats, Hone, Lavery, Osborne and Orpen). Impressionist paintings dominated the exhibitions. Lane wanted a permanent location for his gallery; his attempts were thwarted at every stage. This led to the paintings being given to The Tate in London. A row ensued between the Dublin Municipal Art Gallery and The Tate over Hugh Lane's will. Lane drowned on the *Lusitania* in 1915. He wanted the Government in Ireland to build a Gallery within five years of his death; his paintings were only given a permanent home in 1993. The dispute over his will lasted until 1960, and then it was decided to alternate the Lane paintings between the two galleries. The Gallery has a range of international and Irish works, Impressionist paintings, stained-glass work by Harry Clarke and Evie Hone, traditionalists like Seán Keating, modernist painters like Mainie Jellet, and contemporary Irish art. The Gallery also holds exhibitions of Irish art, for example Brian Maguire's neo-expressionist works (2000), and Francis Bacon (2001). Like other Galleries it provides guided tours, lectures, etc., for tourists.

- **Irish Museum of Modern Art (IMMA)** was established in the Royal Hospital Kilmainham in May 1991. The Duke of Ormonde constructed the hospital in 1660 for ex-soldiers. William Robinson, using a classical layout, designed the building. The Museum displays both permanent and temporary exhibitions. The art collection consists of works produced in the twentieth century, from 1940 onwards. Some were donated, others bought, while others were on loan. The works include William Scott's *Candle and Card*, John Bellany's *Candle Woman of the North Sea*, plus 600 more that can be viewed in the West Wing. IMMA also has a policy of introducing works by established international and Irish artists. Annual events include The Nissan Art Project. A number of exhibitions take place simultaneously, each lasting about twelve weeks. Tours of IMMA art are undertaken to regional arts centres. The Museum was extended in March 2000, to house new work.

- **The Temple Bar Cultural Centre** was set up in 1991 as part of Dublin's European City of Culture. It was redeveloped in two phases. Phase One involved developing five local cultural organisations, five new cultural centres in Temple Bar, and three newly-formed cultural organisations. Phase Two involved residential development around the Fishamble Street area. Over £40 (€50) million of Government funding went into the area. The cultural centres include the Arthouse, Temple Bar Gallery and Studios, The Ark which is a centre for children's culture, Gaiety School of Acting, National Photographic Archive, Gallery of Photography, Irish Film Centre, Designyard which is run by the Craft Council of Ireland, Project Arts Centre, Temple Bar Music Centre, and Dublin's Viking Adventure and Exhibition. Meeting House Square is an open area that is used for concerts, films and other activities. A number of bars offer traditional music entertainment. Nearly 2,500 jobs have been created in the cultural and services areas of Temple Bar.

- **Derek Hill's Glebe House and Gallery Co. Donegal** was the home of Derek Hill, the English artist who died in July 2000. He loved the people of Ireland and the country. He painted on Tory Island, and developed the Tory Island School of Painters, providing them with lessons, and encouraging them to paint. His house is located on Lough Garton, and he bequeathed it to the Irish State, along with his paintings. The house is now opened to the public, where guided tours are given. Large selections of paintings are on view including Hill's own collection of paintings, his own landscapes and seascapes, and those of the Tory Island School, for example James Dixon. This is popular with both tourists and locals, and is an added bonus to the culture of Donegal.

Other art galleries include The Crawford Municipal Art Gallery in Cork, The Chester Beatty Library in Dublin Castle, The Hunt Museum in Limerick, the Sirius Arts Centre in Cóbh.

- **The Kilkenny Arts Festival** takes place in August, in a number of venues that include Kilkenny Castle, the Kilkenny Ormonde Hotel, the Watergate Theatre, Kells Priory, and Rudolf Heltzel Gallery. The Festival involves a number of different activities. Music includes classical, traditional and jazz. Films are shown. Theatre includes plays by famous writers such as Samuel Beckett, or Eugene

McCabe, readings by, for example, Brendan Kennelly. Visual art includes works by Irish, English and international artists and sculptors.

Other arts festivals take place in Galway, which is the country's largest, Sligo and elsewhere.

- **The Dublin Theatre Festival**, which takes place during October, offers three weeks of theatre from all over the world. This is very popular both with the citizens of Dublin and visitors. Other parts of the country also offer theatre festivals, for example Donegal's Errigal Arts Festival.

- **Film festivals** take place in Dublin in April, Galway Film Fleadh in July, Cork Film Festival in October, Foyle (Derry) Film Festival in November and Cinemagic (Belfast) in December. Murphy's sponsor the Cork Film Festival. The Cork Film Festival began over forty-five years ago. Its aim is to promote new film talent nationally and internationally. The programme includes features, documentaries and workshops. The venues for the festival include the Cork Opera House, Kino Cinema, Triskel Arts Centre and the Gate Multiplex. There are three main awards, The Jameson Award, Best Irish Short Film Award, Claire Lynch Award for the best Irish Director of Short Films. Some new films receive their world premiere at the Cork festival, for example *Peaches*. Documentary films are also important. The festival takes place over eight days.

- A number of **summer schools** for those interested in arts and crafts take place. These include: The Irish School of Landscape which takes place between January and October, and operates in Connemara, Wicklow, Donegal and Down; The O'Neill's Burren Painting Centre which has been operating for twenty-seven years, and runs courses in the Burren and on the Aran Islands from April to August; Tapestry and Weaving Course which takes place in Glencolmcille, Co. Donegal and operates between June and September. The Achill Island School of Painting takes place over two weeks of the summer and is in its thirty-fifth year.

- There are groups of **craft workshops** all over the country, where Irish craft workers can be seen at work and where it is possible to buy their products. The best-known of these is the Kilkenny Design Workshop in the former stables of Kilkenny Castle. Other centres are found in Spiddal, Co. Galway, and Donegal Craft Village. There is usually a range of crafts available, often including pottery, textiles, jewellery, paintings. Quality Irish products are produced by large industries, for example Waterford Glass, Irish linens, Donegal Tweeds, Lainey Keogh knitwear and by smaller producers such as potters, goldsmiths and silversmiths. These quality goods are sold in such shops as Kilkenny Design, Blarney Woollen Mills, and Avoca Handloom Weavers. The production of quality items for tourists is good for the craft industry and it has expanded to meet this demand.

REVISION EXERCISES

1. Name a playwright from each period together with an example of that playrights work.
2. Who made most of the films in Ireland during the 1940s and 1950s? Give examples of films.
3. What encouraged the growth of the film industry in the 1980s? Give examples of films.
4. What are the main themes of Irish films? Give examples with films. Name some locations of Irish-made films and television shows.
5. Research the role of the Irish Film Centre.
6. Name the major art galleries in the country.
7. Name the main arts festivals, cinema festivals, and theatre festivals that take place around the country.
8. Explain what the Temple Bar area has to offer cultural tourists.
9. List locally-produced quality crafts.

Assignments

1. Working in groups, research the work of the artists that are named in the above section.
2. Make a collection of postcards or pictures of works by Irish artists that is representative of all the major periods in the twentieth century.
3. Visit a local art gallery, and see how many of the above-mentioned artists' work you can find on view in the gallery.
4. Look up information about theatres in your local area, and choose a play that you feel is suitable for tourists to view. You need to explain the reason for making your choice. Then attend the play you have chosen. Afterwards, compile a report about the play you have seen, and about the theatre you have visited.
5. Through plays of different periods explain the different ways in which the characteristics of Irishness are portrayed.
6. Name as many films as possible that were made/set in Ireland and then answer the following questions: Where is the film set? What is the main theme of the film? What is the overall impression of Ireland from the film?
7. Visit some of the tourist attractions like the art galleries, or craft villages mentioned above and see what they offer tourists.
8. Look up the internet and research the festivals, theatre, cinema or arts. Write a report on what you have discovered.

Recommended and further reading

B. Arnold, *A Concise History of Irish Art.* Thames & Hudson, 1977.

F. Henry, *irish Art in the Early Christian Period* (to 800 AD). Methuen, 1965.

F. Henry, *Irish Art (800–1020 AD)*. Muthuen, 1970.

G.O. Simms, *The Book of Kells*. Dolmen Press, 1982.

B. Fallow, *Irish Art 1830–1990*. Appletree, 1994.

H. P. F. Wallace, *A Guide to the National Museum of Ireland*. Townhouse, 2000.

E. Kelly, *Early Celtic Art*. Country House, 1993.

M. Bourke, S. Bhreatnach-Lynch, *Discover Irish Art at the National Gallery of Ireland*. National Gallery of Ireland, 1998.

H. Pyle, *Yeats, Portrait of an Artistic Family*. Merrell Holberton, 1997.

Images and Insights – Hugh Lane Municipal Gallery of Modern Art, 1993.

S.B. Kennedy, *Irish Art & Modernism* 1880–1950. Institute of Irish Studies, 1991.

Rockett, Gibbons, Routledge and Hill, *Cinema and Ireland*. Routledge, 1998.

A. Flynn: *Irish Film, 100 Years*. Kestral Books, 1996.

B. McIllroy, *Irish Cinema, An Illustrated History*. Anna Livia Press, 1988.

Hainsworth, Hill, McLoone, eds, *Border Crossing Film in Ireland, Britain and Europe*. Institute of Irish Studies.

CHAPTER 17

Irish Entertainment and the Tourism Industry

Irish music is popular all over the world and this attracts tourists to Ireland. Irish artists perform concerts on television and radio, produce albums, and have millions of fans. A wide range of music is played in Ireland – classical, jazz, rock, pop, country and, of course, traditional which is unique. Bord Fáilte research has found that approximately 70 per cent of tourists come to Ireland because traditional music is important to them. The popularity of Riverdance has introduced millions of people to Irish dance and has been good publicity for Irish tourism. Music is presented to the tourist in a range of situations, in formal concerts, at cabarets and medieval banquets, in tourist attractions and at sessions where musicians gather.

Music and performing arts attract large numbers of tourists: (a) 46 per cent of overseas tourists go to pubs to hear traditional music played; (b) 24 per cent of tourists go to pubs to hear popular music played; (c) 3.5 per cent go to a concert; (d) 20 per cent attend festivals; (e) 14.5 per cent go to a disco or nightclub.

This level of interest in the music and entertainment industry has resulted in major investment through the operational programmes for tourism. This has provided new venues, for example, singing pubs entertainment in historic buildings, festivals, and tourism products such as the Rock and Stroll Guide, the Dublin Musical Pub Crawl, The Hot Press Irish Music Hall of Fame.

ORIGINS OF TRADITIONAL IRISH MUSIC, DANCE AND SONG

Seán Ó Riada described traditional music as 'untouched, unWesternised and orally transmitted music'. Irish music is not European, but is influenced by Eastern music. This can be particularly heard in *sean-nós*. The main difference between Irish and European music is: Irish music moves in circles, with patterns repeated, as is evident in reels and jigs, while European music generally starts and grows towards a climax and then resolves itself towards the end, rather like a graph.

The earliest music in Ireland was the music of harps, pipes and fiddles. In pre-Norman Ireland the harp was used by the *fili* to accompany their poetry as they entertained their lord and chieftain. The most famous of the harpists was Turlough O'Carolan (1670-1738), a blind harpist who was influenced by the Italian music of the late seventeenth century in his compositions of harp music, for example *Planxty Irvine*. He produced and published his songs in 1720. At the end of the century a Great Harp Festival took place in Belfast (1792) and there the last of the harpists met to play their music. Edward Bunting attended this event. He wrote down the music, but unfortunately not the words. Within a short period these men were gone and their tradition of harping lost for ever. The music of the people was divided in the eighteenth century between *sean-nós* songs in Irish, and sentimental ballads that were introduced from England. Ballad singers sang at fairs around the country. Irishmen like Thomas Moore wrote Irish airs during this period, for example *The Meeting of the Waters*. Itinerant dancing masters taught dancing in the cottages and preserved the art of dancing.

Traditional music was dealt a number of blows in the latter half of the nineteenth century. The first was the Famine, which resulted in the death of many musicians and dancers. The decline of the Irish language led to the loss of many *sean-nós* songs. Many musicians left Ireland and emigrated to America. The cities where the Irish lived became centres of thriving Irish music and dance. Many Irish musicians performed in Vaudeville music halls.

The early twentieth century was no different, with emigration attracting many of Ireland's finest musicians. Michael Coleman (1891–1941), the Sligo fiddler, was one of these. He went to the USA in the early twentieth century. He made a living from his music, performing on radio and producing albums. This made his Sligo style of playing well known in America, and later in Ireland.

Fig. 17.1: Michael Coleman Centre, Gurteen, Co. Sligo

Irish music during this period was played in people's homes, and it was played so that people could dance to it. Rarely was it played for people to listen to. The foundation in 1926 of Radio Éireann (which became RTÉ) promoted traditional music in Ireland, with many musicians performing their music. At about the same time Céilí Bands were formed. The 1935 Public Dance Hall Act, which forbade house dances, encouraged the development of Céilí Bands, the best known of whom were the Kilfenora and the Tulla Céilí Bands. This type of music remained popular until the 1950s.

In 1951 the Pipers Club in Thomas Street founded Comhaltas Ceoltóirí Éireann and that year the first Fleadh Cheoil was held in Mullingar. Its aim was to encourage traditional songs, music and the Irish language. In the early 1960s Seán Ó Riada, a musician, composer and broadcaster with Radio Éireann, founded Ceoltóirí Chualann. He introduced new ideas into traditional music; for instance, bringing together groups of musicians playing a variety of different instruments. Before this, musicians played in céilí bands, in twos, or individually. He revived the music of O'Carolan and promoted the playing of the bodhrán. A number of the musicians who played in Ceoltóirí Chualann went on to become members of the Chieftains, Ireland's best-known traditional group. The increased interest in folk music in the USA and UK helped create an interest in traditional music during the 1960s and in ballad groups, for example The Clancy Brothers and Tommy Makem. These three separate events helped the revival of Irish traditional music. From the 1970s the music industry grew, with many traditional, folk/traditional and solo artists emerging. A number of these became international stars for example Dé Danann, Clannad, Altan, Dolores Keane, Martin Hayes.

The **Instruments** most associated with traditional Irish music are the following:

- **Uilleann Pipes**. This is a very sophisticated and complex instrument which was developed during the eighteenth century. It is made up of the chanter which plays the melody; the leather bag which is filled by a bellows that the piper puts under the arm and provides the air for the pipes; drones, of which there are three – bass, tenor and treble; and regulators which provide the harmony for the pipes – there are thirteen regulator keys; the piper also wears a leather pad on the right knee on which rests the chanter and when the piper plays a low *d* note the chanter is lifted. The piper uses all of these parts of the pipes to produce his tunes, as well as adding ornamentation. Famous pipers include Séamus Ennis, Leo Rowsome, Paddy Moloney, Liam Ó Floinn.

- **Fiddle**. This is the most popular instrument played in the country, but it is played in a number of different regional styles. The Donegal style is a 'loose style of fiddling' which was influenced by Scottish fiddle playing. The Sligo style was promoted by Michael Coleman and has a rapid, flowing style, which uses slurring and lots of ornamentation. The Sliabh Luachra fiddlers of north Kerry lean harder on the bow and this produces a coarser tone with a strong rhythm.

Other distinctive styles are found in west Clare, east Clare, and elsewhere. Famous fiddlers include Michael Coleman, Denis Murphy, Junior Crehan, Frankie Gavin, Martin Hayes, etc.

- **Flute**. A wooden flute is used in Irish music; this produces a rich, warm tone. There are regional differences in the way it is played. Sligo flute playing breaks up phrases irregularly, and uses little ornamentation, while Clare flute playing uses longer phrases with a rolling, ornamented style. Famous flute players include John McKenna and Matt Molloy.

- **Tin whistle**. This is a very popular instrument and very cheap to purchase. The most popular whistle is the D whistle because it allows the player to play in a session. Many tin whistle players also play either the flute or pipes. Famous whistle players are Micho Russell, Willie Clancey, Paddy Moloney, Mary Bergin.

- **Accordion**. This was introduced to Ireland during the 1920s from Germany. It is a single action instrument, which means that when the button is pushed and drawn out it produces two notes. An early form of the accordion was the one-row melodeon, which had ten buttons and twenty notes, and the music was achieved by push and draw method. The melodeon was very suitable for dance music because of its rhythmic style of playing. It is mainly the two-row button accordion that is used today and it is played in two styles. The first is the older 'push and pull' style that is usually played on C/C-sharp accordions. The second is the technically more difficult style, which involves using both rows, with rolls and triplets being formed by moving between the rows; these use B/C accordions. An accordion is often referred to as a 'box'. Famous accordion players include Paddy O'Brien, Joe Cooley, Mairtín O'Connor, and Sharon Shannon.

- **Concertina**. This is a reed instrument like the accordion and the main type of concertina used in traditional music is a double action German one. This instrument is very popular in Co. Clare. It produces a pleasant tone that sounds good with fiddles. Famous concertina players include Mrs Crotty, Noel Hill, and Michael O'Rathaille.

- **Other instruments** that are used in traditional music: The **harp** is no longer played in the traditional way with the fingernails pulling upwards; instead it is played with the tips of the fingers pushing downwards in the Classical style; the old tradition was lost in the nineteenth century. The **bodhrán** is a goatskin drum. It is beaten with either a stick or the hand, and the inside of the skin is pressed outwards to achieve different tones; it is used for accompaniment, and helps control the rhythm in a session. The **tenor banjo** was introduced into Ireland by travelling American-Irish 'Minstrels' during the late nineteenth century, and was adapted to Irish needs to play traditional music. Both the banjo and the **mandolin** are used to play the melody. The latest instrument for playing Irish music is the **bouzouki**, which is used for accompaniment.

Fig. 17.2: Irish traditional music is played on these instruments

Irish music consists of two types:

- Tunes played for dancers. This consists mainly of jigs, reels and hornpipes which were introduced into Ireland from Scotland and the Continent. Irish music is full of variation, with the melody repeated but never played exactly the same way twice, because the musician introduces ornamentation. Musicians learn traditional music by listening to other musicians, and in this way the music has been handed down from one generation to another. Tunes were first written down in 1720, when O'Carolan published his tunes. Traditional musicians do not look at notes when they play.

- *Sean-nós* singing, the 'old style' of singing, which is unaccompanied.

Dancing

There are three categories of Irish dancing:

1. Step dancing was taught by the old dancing masters who went from house to house. They taught reels, jigs and hornpipes. It is believed that the original use of the reel was for the male dancer to impress the woman he fancied. Since many of the houses where these dances took place only had mud floors, people danced on the flagstone hearth, or on the half door. Modern dancing teachers, who taught intricate dances that involved high kicks and special steps, soon replaced these itinerant teachers. Irish dancers always dance with the lower parts of their bodies, while their upper parts remain very stiff and straight. A number of reels are still taught by these modern dance teachers. Students start off with the easy reel, then they progress to jigs, and then to the hard reel. Later hornpipes are taught.

Most students of Irish dance are young children, and their dancing prepares them

326

for competitions, eventually aspiring to the World Irish Dancing Championships, which usually occur during the Easter holidays in Ireland. The World Irish Dancing Championships attract thousands of competitors each year, and all over the world there are tens of thousands learning Irish dancing. In Ireland alone over 10,000 children learn Irish dancing. Girls who participate in competitions wear dresses embroidered with Celtic designs, with their hair in ringlets, and boys wear kilts with knee socks, and a jacket with a shawl attached by a brooch. In the past dancers wore their normal clothes. Step dancing is taught solely for competition and this often lacks the enjoyment of other types of dancing.

2. Set dancing is the traditional dancing of the people, and occurred at house dances and at crossroads on warm summer nights. Sets consist of eight people who stand opposite each other, and dance in a group. Sets are usually comprised of five to seven parts, each having a slightly different series of movements, and each part is played to different types of music, that is, in polka-, jig-, or reel-time. Sets are very similar to French quadrilles. These dances were popular during the Napoleonic wars, and it is thought that they were introduced to Ireland by soldiers returning home. Sets were very popular in Clare and Kerry, but during the 1930s the tradition nearly became extinct, because of the development of parochial dancehalls and céilí bands. There are many types of set dances; in some cases in the past they were only danced in their local area; for example Ballycommon set was danced around Ballycommon, Co. Tipperary. Pat Murphy, in *Toss the Feathers*, identifies sixty-four different sets, the most popular being the Caledonian Set, Clare Lancers Set, Sliabh Luachra Set.

The formation of Comhaltas Ceoltóirí Éireann (CCÉ) helped in the revival of set dancing; many dances were organised at fleadhs. In the 1970s the GAA and Comhaltas set up a competition for set dancers. This competition encouraged the revival of old sets and this revival of set dancing led to new céilí bands being formed, for instance the Shaskeen. The 1980s and 1990s saw the development of workshops for set dancing all over the country, set up by dancing teachers like Connie Ryan and Joe O'Donovan. Summer schools, like the Willie Clancy Summer School in Miltown Malbay Co. Clare, played an important role in the revival of set dancing. Following the Willie Clancy Week, classes were set up the length and breadth of the country to teach set dancing. Their success meant that the old traditional sets have been preserved for future generations, and that those who take part have good fun and exercise too.

3. Céilí dancing: The Gaelic League first set up céilí dancing in London, and they were very much influenced by Scottish céilís. Céilí dancing involves group dancing; these can range from four people to sixteen. The céilí dances were developed from jigs, reels and hornpipes. They became common in rural Ireland, and céilí bands were developed to play at these dances. Céilí bands usually included four fiddles, two flutes, a piano, drums, accordion and sometimes a concertina. Among the most famous céilí bands are the Saskeen and Kilfenora. Céilí dancing is not as intricate as set dancing. Céilí dances include 'The Walls of Limerick' and 'Seige of Ennis'.

Singing

Ireland has two traditions of singing:

1. *Sean-nós* singing means the 'old style' of singing, and is unaccompanied. The themes of the songs are varied, from birth, to marriage, to death, and everything else in life. Songs are generally improvised but in a particular style. The singer sings in an even tone. Emotion is never shown by raising or lowering the voice. Instead the singer will either add or take away ornamentation. Most *sean-nós* songs are very long with many verses. In order to keep the listeners entertained, the singer will sing each verse in a different way, by either adding grace notes to already existing notes (melismatic), adding a separate high note that will change the phrase (intervallic), or lengthening or shortening notes in order to change the rhythm (rhythmic). All of these changes are known as ornamentation. Each region has its own type of ornamentation. The areas important for *sean-nós* singing are: (a) Connacht, for example singer Sean 'ac Dhonnach and the song *Donnachadh Bán;* (b) Munster/Ring Gaeltacht, for example singer Nioclás Tóibín and the song *Róisín Dubh*; (c) west Munster including west Cork area of Ballyvourney, for example singer Pádraig Ó Tuama and the song *Amhrán Phead Bhuí*. Today there are a number of *sean-nós* singers including Iarlath Ó Leonard from Coolea Co. Cork, and Antaine Ó'Farachain who sings in a Connacht style. *Sean-nós* singing was originally in Irish, but after the famine it became more common to sing in English.

2. Ballads were originally introduced to Ireland from England. Like the *sean-nós* songs they told a story, but they are a very different style of singing. Ballads were made popular in Ireland by balladeers singing and selling their songs at fairs, on the street etc. Many of the ballads of Ireland have political themes, for example 'The Boys of Wexford', which is about the 1798 rebellion. Some ballads celebrate more recent events, like Christy Moore's 'Lisdoonvarna' which was a song about the music festivals that occured there during the 1970s. Ballads from Ireland were sung by many famous Irish singers e.g. the Clancy Brothers in the 1960s, the Fureys and Davy Arthur, the Dubliners and all of these singers had a large following on the Continent towards the end of the twentieth century. For many Europeans Irish singing means ballad singing, with few of them having ever heard *sean-nós*.

The popularity of traditional music and dance is due to several factors. **Comhaltas Ceoltóiri Éireann** is the main group involved in the promotion of traditional music. It was formed by The Pipers' Club in 1951 in Mullingar. Among those involved in its formation was the famous piper Leo Rowsome. The aims of CCÉ are:

to re-establish the uilleann pipes and the harp in Irish music; to promote Irish dancing and the Irish language; to bring all Irish traditional musicians closer together. In
order to achieve these ends CCÉ has 400 branches in Ireland, Japan, Australia, the
USA and the UK. The branches organise classes in musical instruments, dancing,
singing and the Irish language. They prepare children and adults for the Fleadh
Cheoil competitions. These take place at local (county), regional (provinces) and
finally at the all-Ireland Fleadh in August. About 10,000 musicians compete in fleadhs
in Ireland, the UK and USA. CCÉ are also involved in organising other festivals like
the Fleadh Nua which takes place in Ennis in May, and the Fleadh Amhrán agus
Rince in Ballycastle, Co. Antrim in June. CCÉ members organise three concert tours
annually that visit the USA, Britain, and Ireland. They have regional centres where
Irish music is promoted and played at sessions, concerts, and céilís; these include
Cultúrlann na hÉireann in Dublin, Cois na hAbhna in Ennis, etc. They create an interest in Irish music wherever they play and this attracts tourist to Ireland. The Fleadh
Cheoil in Enniscorthy, Co. Wexford in 1999 attracted over 200,000 tourists to the
town for the weekend, while the Scoil Éigse provided classes for 600 aspiring traditional musicians, dancers and singers.

Fig. 17.3: Musicians in Comhaltas Ceoltóiri Éireann

Riverdance began on 30 April 1994 during the ten minutes intermission of the
Eurovision Song Contest. The music was composed by Bill Whelan, and was performed by an eighty-five-piece orchestra. The dancers were led by Michael Flatley
(an Irish-dancing champion) and Jean Butler, both of whom are Irish American.
Three hundred million viewers all around the world watched the performance on
that night. Those who saw it in the Point were overwhelmed by the performance,
and gave a dozen standing ovations. The Riverdance single entered both the Irish
and UK charts. It was decided to produce a two-hour show. The new show brought
in other elements of dance such as flamenco dancers from Spain, Moscow Folk

Ballet and African-American tap-dancers, gypsy musicians and gospel singers. The show was organised for the Dublin Point Depot and the first show was a complete sell-out. After the success in Dublin the show moved to the Apollo Theatre in London in June 1995, and again opened to record crowds. After 151 shows in London, the show moved to New York, where it played in the Radio City Music Hall. Again it was a success. This led to the development of a second team of musicians, singers and dancers, which allowed one group to perform in Europe and the other in America. Everywhere, they played to full-house audiences. A third team went on the road in Australia on St Patrick's Day 1997, and they play there and in Asia.

Three troops still perform Riverdance. Over the years there have been a number of changes in the musicians and dancers involved in Riverdance. Other shows like Lord of the Dance have been developed and all this has helped to promote Ireland abroad. Many members of foreign audiences who have seen and enjoyed Riverdance, have come to Ireland as tourists to discover the cradle of this ancient dancing tradition. Riverdance, apart from promoting Ireland, has also developed a renewed interest in Irish dancing.

CLASSICAL MUSIC

Classical music holds a less prominent position in Ireland than it does in other European countries. The reasons for this are historical. European music developed in Renaissance Europe, and was associated mainly with Austria and France. In these countries the monarchs provided patronage for the musicians who composed operas and symphonies for their entertainment, and music for their dances. In Ireland classical music flourished in the eighteenth century. During this time music halls were opened, like the New Music Hall in Fishamble Street (where Handel performed the *Messiah* for the first time in 1742), the Crow Street Music Hall, and the Theatre Royal in Smock Alley. The Anglo-Irish aristocracy encouraged orchestras and chamber music. This continued until 1800.

As the Parliament moved to England after the Act of Union, so too did the aristocracy, and the musicians were forced to as well. During the nineteenth century important Irish musicians worked abroad; for example **John Field** (1782–1837), a pianist and composer of nocturnes and piano concertos, lived in St Petersburg in Russia, in the court of the Tsars. **Michael Balfe** (1808–70) was a baritone singer and wrote operas; these included *The Rose of Castile* and *The Bohemian Girl*.

Ireland has produced many international opera singers but most lived abroad. **Michael Kelly** (1764–1826) lived in Vienna and was a friend of Mozart's. He wrote operas for Drury Lane Theatre in London. **Catherine Hayes** (1825–61) was a favourite of the La Scala Opera in Milan, and travelled through North and South America and Australia performing Irish ballads, airs and European opera. **John O'Sullivan** (1878–1948) trained in Paris, and did most of his singing in France and Italy. **John McCormack** (1884–1945) was Ireland's most important opera singer and tenor. He played in many of the world's most famous opera houses. He studied in Italy and made his debut in Savona in 1906 under the name Giovanni Foli. Between 1908 and 1914 he performed in Covent Garden. At twenty-three he was the youngest tenor to play a major role in Covent Garden in London. The same year he performed *Faust* in Dublin. Within two years he had played at the Manhattan Opera House in New York. His singing made him a favourite with American audiences. He sang in many operas including *La Traviata*, *La Bohème* and *Carmen*, until in 1924, at the age of 40, he decided to end his opera-singing career. Instead he concentrated on making records and performing concerts. His concerts still contained arias and duets from his favourite operas, but they also included Victorian ballads like 'Kathleen Mavourneen', 'Somewhere a voice is calling', and his most famous song 'I hear you calling me'. Financially McCormack was very successful. He returned to live in Athlone, and there is now an exhibition in the Athlone Castle in his memory. Ireland has produced many other opera singers over the years. They include Margaret Burke Sheridan, Ann Murray, Veronica Dunne, Bernadette Greevy, Virginia Kerr, Patricia Bardon, Regina Nathan, Frank Patterson, Finbarr Wright.

Classical music in Ireland developed through the nineteenth century with the setting up of societies like the Dublin Musical Society that operated from 1876 to 1902. This and other societies organised choral and orchestral recitals. Since 1922 the development of classical music in Ireland has been through broadcasting, Radio Éireann (RTÉ), the development of the orchestra, and the teaching of music in schools, e.g. the Royal Irish Academy of Music (RIAM), and the Municipal School of Music in Dublin. Classical music recitals and concerts took place in a number of venues around Dublin and classical musicians played in the theatres and cinemas.

The development of a symphony orchestra went through many stages over sixty years (1926–1986). It began as a quartet in 1926. In 1937 the orchestra played public performances. First these were performed in the Gaiety, later in the Mansion House, and finally they were moved to the old La Scala Opera House, which was in Princes Street and is now part of Penney's of O'Connell Street. In 1946 the Minister of Post and Telegraphs was interested in music, and he wanted to set up both a proper concert hall in Parnell Square, and to establish a new Dublin orchestra that would rival those of Paris or London. By 1946 the Radio Éireann Orchestra had sixty-two members, and had a Light Orchestra of twenty-two players. In 1948 the orchestra became the RÉSO (Radio Éireann Symphony Orchestra) with musicians from all over Europe – Italy, France and Germany. Many of these musicians taught in the music schools, and the Secretary of the Department of Post and Telegraphs, Léon O'Broin, hoped to set up a conservatoire of music in Dublin. A change of Government in 1948 changed the policy of the RÉSO with cut-backs occurring. Public concerts were stopped and instead studio concerts with music lovers attending were broadcast live from Phoenix Hall twice weekly.

The RÉSO was involved with the Dublin Grand Opera Society's Spring and Winter

Seasons, which were held in the Gaiety Theatre Dublin, the Cork Opera Season, and the Wexford Opera Festival. They began performing children's concerts in 1951 and shortly afterwards the RÉSO went on tour around Ireland. These early children's concerts developed into Music in the Classroom, and 'Music for Fun' concerts. The Radio Éireann Choral Society was set up, and performed with the RÉSO until 1984, when it was replaced by Cór Radio Éireann. A training programme was introduced for young musicians; this eventually developed into the Irish Youth Orchestra. By 1953 public concerts were again taking place in Dublin and regional towns. The Dublin concerts were organised in the Gaiety Theatre on a Sunday night. Pressure to set up an orchestra in Cork resulted in the formation of the RTÉ String Quartet (later Vanburgh Quartet) there in 1956.

The Orchestra held an annual competition for young Irish composers (O'Carolan Prize). Composers such as Brian Boydell and Seán Ó Riada produced work for the Orchestra. During the 1960s there were plans to build a concert hall to commemorate John F. Kennedy's visit to Ireland. It was to be sited in Beggars Bush in Dublin, but it took twenty years for it to become a reality. In 1967 the Orchestra began to travel abroad to play concerts, first to England, then later to the Continent. Over the first twenty-five years of the Orchestra, classical music was brought to the people of Ireland through radio, television and public concerts. The popularity of television during the 1960s led to the closure of many cinemas around Ireland; this deprived the orchestra of venues for regional concerts.

The location of the National Concert Hall was decided in 1981; this was in the Examination Hall of UCD in Earlsfort Terrace. The NCH was opened on 9 September 1981 with a special concert. The opening of the NCH meant that a full programme of concerts was now able to take place, including lunchtime concerts during the summer months.

The RTÉSO (Radio Telefís Éireann Symphony Orchestra) produced a number of soloists like Veronica Mc Sweeney (pianist), John O'Conor (pianist), Geraldine O'Grady (violinist), Hugh Tinny (pianist), Barry Douglas (pianist), and James Galway (flautist). These classical musicians are all now internationally renowned and perform concerts all over the world.

RTÉ organised a number of festivals over the years. (a) The Dublin Festival of Music and the Arts (1969), which later became the Festival of Music, involved operas, concerts, and recitals, and its aim was to attract tourists to the city. (b) The Dublin International Organ Festival was organised for the first time in 1979, and it was repeated every four years. (c) In 1988 the first Dublin International Piano Competition took place. The pianist John O'Conor managed this competition from its inception, and is among the best piano competitions in the world. The final stages of the competition involves the competitors playing concertos with the Orchestra. (d) The first Proms started in 1989; this is a very popular series of concerts. (e) The Adare Festival was inaugurated in the 1990s, and provided a series of concerts with the NSO (National Symphony Orchestra), similar to the Proms. (f) The Association of Irish Composers developed the Accents Festival in order to concentrate on new music. All of these festivals continue to make classical music more accessible to Irish people.

The Dublin Grand Opera Society was the main source of opera in Dublin until it evolved into Opera Ireland in 1996. Opera Ireland has two seasons only, at which two major operas are performed. They also provide master classes for young opera singers, organise lunchtime performances and took part in the Summers Diversions Festival in Temple Bar Dublin in 2001 (the L'Altro Mondo – a combination of modern dance music and opera). International opera singers come to Dublin to perform in venues such as the RDS and the Point Depot. Placido Domingo and Kiri te Kanawa are among those who have sung there. The NSO performed alongside these international stars. Cork and Belfast are the only Irish cities with opera houses. Opera Ireland would like a dedicated opera house built in the new Dublin Docklands. Ireland has many talented opera singers, but most of these have to live abroad as there is limited work in Ireland.

The National Symphony Orchestra was formed in 1990 with ninety-five members, and it has been very successful. In 1992 it moved in a new direction, by signing a recording contract with Naxos/Marco Polo Company, and they produced a number of CDs. Many of the recordings involved the music of Irish composers like Brian Boydell's violin concerto, Gerard Victory's *Ultima Rerum*, Philip Martin's harp concerto, Gerald Barry's orchestral work. They also made live recordings of operas like *The Demon* by Rubinstein from the Wexford Opera Festival. Now Irish people are able to support their own orchestra and composers by buying their works on CD. In 1993 the University Concert Hall was opened in Limerick, and this is another venue for Irish concerts. The development of the classical music radio station Lyric FM is benefiting those involved in classical music.

A number of choirs provide recitals and concerts in Dublin and around the country. Many of these, like the Culwick, and Our Lady's Choir, perform Handel's *Messiah* in Dublin at Christmas. At other times of the year, other choirs including Cór na nÓg, the RTÉ Philharmonic, Dublin University and Guinness, perform recitals. The Cork Choral Festival, which takes place over Easter, provides a venue for many of these choirs to perform, along with choirs from abroad.

Over the years there has been an enormous growth in the amount of classical music available in Dublin and Ireland. This has been helped by (a) the establishment of the National Concert Hall; (b) the production of albums by the NSO; (c) the NSO concerts abroad. Education in music is still carried on by the RIAM, and The Chatham Row School of Music, introducing classical music to young people, and creating future audiences. Ireland is still waiting for a conservatoire where young musicians can learn music to the highest level. One is planned for the music centre in the University of Limerick.

june at a glance

main auditorium

Fri 1st Sat 2nd	RTÉ Concert Orchestra The Music and Songs of Andrew Lloyd Webber	8pm
Tues 5th	"Magical Mystery Tour!" Stage Door Theatre School	8pm
Fri 8th	NCH/The Sunday Business Post International Orchestral Series Royal Liverpool Philharmonic Orchestra	8pm
Sat 9th	Joaquín Rodrigo Commemoration Concert	8pm
Tues 12th	National Symphony Orchestra Lunchtime Concert Series	1.05-2pm
Tues 12th	Geraldine O'Grady & Oonagh Keogh Violin Duo	8pm
Wed 13th	Music by Philip Carty Orchestra of St. Cecilia	1.15-2pm
Thurs 14th	ESB National Children's Choir Sean Creamer, director	8pm
Sat 16th	National Symphony Orchestra 'The Planets'	8pm
Sun 17th Mon 18th	ESB National Children's Choir Sean Creamer, director	8pm
Tues 19th	National Symphony Orchestra Lunchtime Concert Series	1.05-2pm
Tues 19th	The Hibernian Orchestra 20th Anniversary Concert	8pm
Wed 20th	An Evening with Rosemary Clooney & Michael Feinstein	8pm
Fri 22nd	National Symphony Orchestra Piotr Folkert, piano	8pm
Sat 23rd	RTÉ Concert Orchestra Rattlebag Listeners' Choice	8pm
Sun 24th	RTÉ Concert Orchestra Music for Fun	3.30pm
Tues 26th	National Symphony Orchestra Lunchtime Concert Series	1.05-2pm
Tues 26th	Stairway to Paradise A tribute to the songs of George Gershwin	8pm
Fri 29th	National Symphony Orchestra Romeo and Juliet	8pm

john field room

Fri 1st	Michael O'Toole, guitar	1.05-2pm
Wed 6th	Cavalli: L'Egisto Royal Irish Academy of Music Opera Studio	7.30pm
Thurs 7th	Ralph Sutton, 'stride' piano	8pm
Mon 11th	Children for Children Soundfest	8pm
Fri 22nd	Mozart: Bastien, Bastienne	1.05-2pm
Sat 23rd	Anna Livia "Coffee Concert"	11am-1pm
Mon 25th	Sempre Verdi Italian Cultural Institute Choir	6.30pm
Wed 27th	Soirée Francis Poulenc	8pm

Fig.17.4: Programme of concerts for June 2001 at the National Concert Hall, Dublin

CONTEMPORARY MUSIC

The showbands, who played cover versions of songs and travelled around the country playing in dance halls, introduced contemporary music in Ireland. One of Ireland's major international stars is **Van Morrison** who started in the 1950s with the Monarch Showband. He disliked travelling and doing covers, so he soon left to form the group Them in 1960. These were both musically and commercially a success, but the group soon split up, and Van set off on his solo career in 1967. His first album *Blowin' Your Mind*, was produced in New York. Since then his mixture of Celtic, country, jazz and gospel has resulted in a series of albums that stretch over thirty-five years. Among the best are *Astral Weeks* (1968), which brought him to the attention of the rock world. Since the late 1980s he has worked with other artists, like the Chieftains on the *Irish Heartbeat* album, and Georgie Fame on *A Night in San Francisco*. After thirty-five years in the music industry Van Morrison still has a lot to offer his fans, both live on stage and on his albums.

The other great name from the 1960s was **Rory Gallagher** (1948-95); he was one of Ireland's best blues and rock musicians. He began his career with a band called Taste, but by 1971 had become a solo artist producing a series of albums – *Rory Gallagher* in 1971, for instance, and *Live in Europe*. During the same period he was involved with Jerry Lee Lewis working on the *London Sessions '72-73*, and *London Revisited*. Gallagher is best remembered for his live shows, and he produced many live albums e.g. *Irish Tour in '74*, and *Stage Struck*. This talented musician died in June 1995.

The 1970s saw the emergence of rock groups like Thin Lizzy, Boomtown Rats, and Horslips, and singers like Christy Moore, Paul Brady and Elvis Costello. **Thin Lizzy** was formed in 1969 with Phil Lynott as its lead singer. They entered the UK charts in 1975 with their album *Fighting*, this was followed up with the album *Jailbreak* in 1976, which broke through the US market. They followed this up with further albums. Lynott died in 1986 at the age of thirty-four.

Horslips merged Irish folk and rock music. Their 1972 album *Happy to Meet, Sorry to Part* won them international recognition. Irish mythology influenced the music of their following albums. Unfortunately internal disagreements led to poorer albums, and eventually the group broke up in 1980. Horslips were the most successful and influential group of the 1970s in Ireland. The **Boomtown Rats** with Bob Geldof were an important punk band in the 1970s, but while they made an impact on the UK market they never made it in the USA. Bob Geldof is most famous for his role in organising Live Aid and Band Aid in 1985, which brought together the major music acts of the period, and raised millions for charity. The Boomtown Rats broke up in 1986, and Geldof started a solo career.

Christy Moore is a balladeer who was involved in such groups as Planxty and Moving Hearts. Later he embarked on a solo career. His songs have had political themes and sporting themes. Christy Moore has a large following all over the world. **Paul Brady** was also involved in Planxty, and later played in a duo with Andy Irvine. He first played folk music, but in 1981 he turned to rock music with his album *Hard Station*. Brady writes songs for singers worldwide, including Bob Dylan and Tina Turner. He has developed an international reputation as a songwriter rather than a singer. **Elvis Costello** came to the music scene in 1977 with his own type of punk rock (punk/reggae) album *My Aim is True*. Many other types of music have influenced Elvis Costello's work including Motown and pop in the mid-1980s. His biggest US hit came in 1983 with *Punch Clock*. Elvis Costello is of Irish descent. His real name is Declan Mac Manus, and his work has been influenced by Irish music. He appeared on the Chieftains' 1991 album. Costello is a renowned songwriter with many artists covering his songs. His album *All this Useless Beauty* in 1996 consists of many of these songs.

The 1980s brought Ireland's most important band to the scene, that is **U2**. They have been described as the 'biggest band in the universe bar none', and they are considered to be on a par with the other greats of the rock business, the Beatles, and the Who. Their early music, including the album *War*, showed freshness when compared with the pop that was all the rage in the early 1980s. The ideas for the music came from their religion and left-wing politics. *War* reached number one in the UK, and *Unforgettable Fire* in 1984 brought them on to the international stage. *The Joshua Tree* in 1987 reached number one worldwide, something unique for an

Irish band. Other albums followed and were successful worldwide. Their latest album is *All That You Can't Leave Behind*. U2 have lived in Ireland, and have encouraged the growth of a music industry here. Prior to the success of U2 there were few recording studios in Ireland; there are now many, and both domestic and foreign musicians come here to record. The Artists and Writers Dispensation from Income Tax Act has been an incentive for many musicians to come and live in Ireland, and it has encouraged successful Irish musicians to remain living here.

Other musicians from the 1980s include Chris de Burgh, the Saw Doctors, Clannad, Enya, the Pogues and the Waterboys. **The Pogues**: Shane Mac Gowan is first generation Irish and was influenced by both traditional Irish music and ballads; this can be seen in many of his albums, where he blended punk and traditional music together. The Pogues produced a number of albums like *Red Roses for Me* in 1984, and toured Ireland, the UK and America. Mac Gowan is a very talented song-writer, and he went on to form the Popes after leaving the Pogues.

The 1990s have seen a major growth in the Irish music industry, from rock bands, to boy bands, and to major solo artists like Brian Kennedy and Sinéad O'Connor. Ireland won the Eurovision Song Contest and made the millions of viewers in Europe aware of Irish pop music and musicians. **The Divine Comedy** with Neil Hannon produced their first album in 1990. The music is very distinctive, and the influences came from ELO, and Scott Walker. His second album won critical acclaim in 1993. Other albums reached the indie Top Ten. **The Cranberries** from Limerick was formed in the early 1990s. In 1993 they produced their album *Everyone else is doing it, so why can't we?* which reached number one in the UK and Europe. Their second album was a hit in twenty-five countries, they won the MTV song of the year award, and their album was the best European seller for 1994. They continue to be successful in the UK and US market. **Brian Kennedy** from Belfast became success-ful in 1990, when he released his album *The Great War of Words*, and he supported Suzanne Vega on her UK tour. He has worked with other artists, such as Sweetmouth, and with Van Morrison. He has produced a number of albums, and toured with Clannad. **Sinéad O'Connor** has fame both in the UK and USA both for her music and her controversial ideas. Her early albums consisted of cover versions but her later work shows that she is extremely talented as a songwriter. This is par-ticularly evident in her *Universal Mother*. Her songs reflect both Irish traditional music, and rock and roll. She is Ireland's biggest female singer. Other bands include Ash, and the Corrs.

Boyzone were founded in 1993 with five boys from Dublin, and was the first of the Irish boy bands. Many in the music industry did not expect them to do well, but were surprised when Boyzone's début single reached number two in 1994, and later they won an award for best new act. Their records were covers of classic songs like *Father and Son*, or *Words*. Their records have all reached number one in the charts. **Westlife**, another boy band from Ireland, is managed by Louis Walsh and Ronan

Keating. Their first five singles all entered the UK charts at number one. Having been successful in the UK, they have tried to spread their music to the US market, and in April 2000 did a tour of the USA. **Samantha Mumba** is the latest singer to come from Ireland. She has risen to fame in Ireland and the UK. She is now launching her career on the US market.

Jazz music is performed at a number of venues in Irish cities. Among the most famous jazz musicians in Ireland is **Louis Stewart**, who is one of the world's best jazz guitarists. He began his career in a showband, but loved jazz music and decided to move into jazz. He formed a jazz trio in Dublin, but later moved to London. This helped him win a major award at the Montreux Jazz Festival. He worked with Ronnie Scott during the 1970s and this brought him in contact with such greats as Sam Getz, Bill Evans, and Cedar Walton. He has played in New York, where he is greatly appreciated by jazz lovers. Recently there has been a growth of interest in jazz in Ireland.

Blues music has produced such artists as Don Baker and Mary Coughlan. **Don Baker** is best known for his harmonica playing. **Mary Coughlan** won recognition for her singing of old classics at the Cork Jazz Festival in the 1980s. Her most recent performance has been for her *Lady Sings the Blues* concert, which deals with the songs of Billie Holiday.

Country music is very popular in rural Ireland. The most famous of Ireland's country singers is **Daniel O'Donnell**, from Kincaslagh in Co. Donegal. Daniel O'Donnell has a large following, with many fans in Ireland, Britain and the United States. Many of his albums are covers of songs of artists from the 1970s, gospel songs, etc. His albums include *Morning has Broken*, *I Believe*, and *Daniel O'Donnell's Greatest Hits*.

MUSICAL TOURIST ATTRACTIONS

Music festivals and summer schools occur in a number of locations, right through the summer. These attract both international and domestic tourists, with students of the summer schools coming from Japan, Germany, America and England. Some of these people have Irish connections, but many come to learn traditional music because they love it and want to learn to play, sing or dance.

- **All Ireland Fleadh** occurs at the end of August and is the culmination of a number of local fleadhs for the many competitors who attend. These competitions take place at many different venues in the town, and cover all traditional instruments, céilí bands, grúpaí ceols, singing, etc. But for many who attend the fleadh it is the sessions in the bars, the music on the streets, and the drink and craic that attracts them. The Fleadh is Ireland's largest traditional music festival, and in 1999 it attracted over 200,000 people over the weekend. Serious Irish music lovers often attend Scoil Éigse, which comprises classes run by CCÉ in the week before the Fleadh. The Fleadh, unlike other festivals, does not take place in the same town every year; in 2001 it took place in Listowel, Co. Kerry.

- **Willie Clancy Festival** occurs during the first week in July in Miltown Malbay, Co. Clare. It started in 1973, and attracts thousands of students each year. They attend workshops, lectures and concerts. Sessions occur in the local pubs, and by the end of the week many of the small villages that surround Miltown are also packed with musicians and lovers of Irish music. This is the biggest traditional music summer school in Ireland.

- **Performance Music Centres** are located at Siamse Tire in Tralee Co. Kerry, Brú Ború, in Cashel Co. Tipperary, Cois na hAbhann in Ennis Co. Clare and Culturlann na hÉireann in Dublin. Concerts, set dancing céilís and sessions take place at these centres.

- **Rock Festivals** at Slane have attracted over 80,000 fans to listen to major groups like U2, or Robbie Williams. There are a number of concerts organised throughout the year at locations like the RDS, The Point, and Smithfield. Some of these are outdoor locations for summer concerts, and they attract major musical acts from all over the world.

- **The Hot Press Irish Music Hall of Fame** in Dublin is a museum of Ireland's major stars from the world of traditional, rock and pop music. Visitors can learn about Ireland's major musicians like Rory Gallagher, Van Morrison, U2, Showband and Punk eras, club culture. The diversity and size of the Irish music industry can be appreciated. There are many items to see in the Memorabilia Room, which were donated by famous Irish musicians. There is the opportunity to buy videos and CDs on these artists. There is also the HQ music venue, for live performances, and late-night clubbing. The Irish Music Hall of Fame is now being relocated.

- **The Wexford Opera Festival** started in 1951 and takes place over eighteen nights in the second half of October. The aim of the festival is to perform rare or neglected operas. The performers mainly come from Russia, the USA and Italy. There are usually three operas performed, along with choral concerts, recitals, and extracts from opera scenes. At the Wexford Festival in 2000 the operas were *The Maid of Orleans* by Tchaikovsky (1881); *If I were King* by Aldolphe Adam (1852); and *Conchita* by Riccardo Zandonai (1911). The festival takes place in The Theatre Royal, White's Hotel, St Iberius Church and Rowe Street Church. Since 1995 the Festival has been a sell-out, with all 10,000 seats sold. The festival is important to tourism in Wexford, because 85 per cent of those who attend the festival are tourists.

- **The Cork Jazz Festival** occurs over the October Bank Holiday weekend. It is among the most popular festivals in the country, and attracts large numbers of tourists. It began in 1978 in order to generate tourism during the newly-organised October public holiday, and it has been very successful. Over the years it

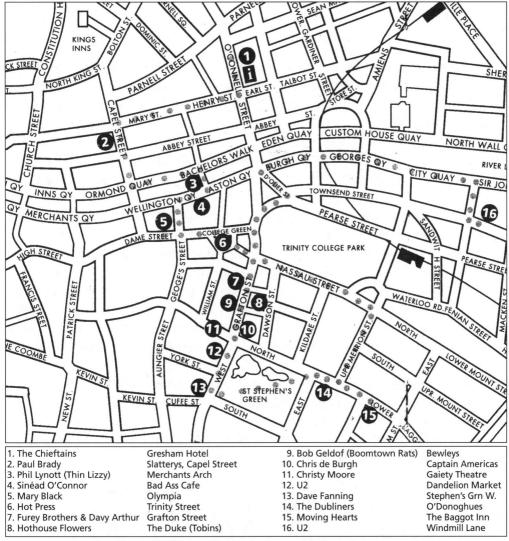

1. The Chieftains	Gresham Hotel	9. Bob Geldof (Boomtown Rats)	Bewleys
2. Paul Brady	Slatterys, Capel Street	10. Chris de Burgh	Captain Americas
3. Phil Lynott (Thin Lizzy)	Merchants Arch	11. Christy Moore	Gaiety Theatre
4. Sinéad O'Connor	Bad Ass Cafe	12. U2	Dandelion Market
5. Mary Black	Olympia	13. Dave Fanning	Stephen's Grn W.
6. Hot Press	Trinity Street	14. The Dubliners	O'Donoghues
7. Furey Brothers & Davy Arthur	Grafton Street	15. Moving Hearts	The Baggot Inn
8. Hothouse Flowers	The Duke (Tobins)	16. U2	Windmill Lane

Fig.17.5: Rock and Stroll map of Dublin

has attracted international stars like Ronnie Scott, BB King, Ella Fitzgerald, George Melly, Dizzie Gillespie, and Louis Stewart. Other Irish acts that attend the Festival include Don Baker, Paddy Cole, The Stargazers, and Mary Stokes Blues Band. Many different types of music are on offer, including jazz, jump, and jive and blues music. There are often up to 100 bands located in fifty venues, for example the Opera House, the Metropole, hotels, and bars. A Guinness Jazz Trail operates which names the best venues that are offering jazz and blues music. Over 40,000 visitors attend the weekend festival, which is worth millions to the tourist industry.

CULTURAL IMPACT OF TOURISM

Culture (including the arts, literature and historical buildings) can benefit from tourism. It impacts in a number of ways:

- Tourists often visit historical buildings, archaeological sites etc. In order to attract large numbers of tourists these sites are preserved through a programme of restoration. The buildings maintain our heritage for future generations and allow our children to learn about their past. Recently restored buildings include Kilkenny Castle and Castletown House.

- The restoration of historical buildings has led to the development of crafts that were becoming extinct. FÁS teach trainees fine stuccowork, cabinet making, and dry-stone walling etc. These old crafts will now be preserved for the future. In Clonegal, Co. Carlow the Carlow Town and County Amenity Trust have restored two weaver's cottages. The main mover behind this restoration was the County Council's conservation officer. The restoration was funded under the urban and village renewal scheme. The cottages had been vacant for over fifty years, and the restoration work was 'slow and intricate'. The renovated cottages are now being used as an arts and crafts centre and a residence for an artist/craft worker. Since weavers originally used the cottages, a new spinning-wheel and loom were made for the cottages. These restored cottages will add to Carlow's tourism product.

- Tourists visit galleries, museums, theatres, concert halls, and all benefit from the money they spend. This extra spending means that many of these venues remain open. Large numbers of tourists attend, for instance, the Abbey, or Siamse Tíre in Tralee. Tourism is very important to the many festivals that take place around the country. The Wexford Opera Festival is just one of many that survives because of the large numbers of tourists attending.

Fig. 17.6 Young Irish traditional musicians in Grafton Street, Dublin

- Development of quality crafts in Ireland (see chapter 16).
- Irish culture, in the form of traditional music, is very popular with tourists and locals. All around the country there are traditional musicians and ballad singers playing in pubs and entertaining tourists. Where this has revived an interest in Irish music among young people, then the country has benefited from tourism. Where commercialism is the driving force behind these young people playing music, the quality of their music suffers. Those who are involved in traditional music organisations, particularly Comhaltas Ceoltóiri Éireann, believe that any change away from the traditional ways of playing is in fact destroying our heritage. Others believe that for a tradition to live on into the future it has to evolve; otherwise it dies. When the market rather than art dictates development, Irish music does not benefit.
- In Ireland tourists are provided with examples of Irish culture at such venues as Jury's and the Burlington Hotel, where cabaret nights have taken place for the

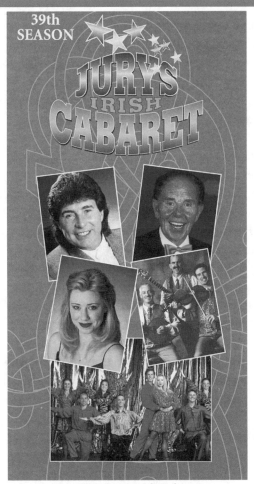

Fig. 17.7: Jury's Irish Cabaret

last thirty years or more. The tourists are provided with samples of Irish music, step dancing, Irish singing with traditional ballads, airs etc. Jury's Cabaret is very popular with American audiences, and during the low season it tours in the USA. The question of whether this is of benefit or has a negative effect on tourism is hotly contested by those who manage these Cabarets.

- Too many tourists can also put a culture under threat. This is particularly true in Gaeltacht areas of the country like Dingle and the Aran Islands. These areas are trying to preserve the Irish language as a living language. When large numbers of tourists come to an area, the local people too become less bilingual than they would wish and speak more English rather than Irish. At present the Aran Islands are a popular destination for tourists. They attract 150,000 tourists each year. This puts these small islands under great pressure from overcrowding and the need to speak English, and it places a threat on their traditional way of life.

REVISION EXERCISES

1. Describe traditional Irish music.
2. How did Irish music change over time?
3. Name the main instruments used in traditional Irish music, and a musician associated with each.
4. Name the three categories of Irish dancing and give examples of types of dances in each case.
5. Explain *sean-nós* singing.
6. How do ballads differ from *sean-nós* singing?
7. Explain the Sliabh Luachra musical traditions.
8. Compare and contrast the regional variations that occur in Irish music or singing.
9. Explain how CCÉ has developed traditional music in Ireland and abroad.
10. Describe the phenomenon of Riverdance.
11. Explain why you think tourists like traditional Irish music.
12. Give three names that Ireland's orchestra was known by.
13. Name three venues where Ireland's orchestra have played over the years.
14. Name three opera singers who have come from Ireland.
15. Name three soloists from Ireland, and the instruments that they play.
16. Name three Irish composers, and works they have composed.
17. Name three choirs that put on concerts in Ireland.
18. Name three festivals that involve classical music.
19. Look up your local newspaper, and contact your RTA to find out where your local classical concert venue is located, when the next concert or recital is taking place, and if classical music festivals take place in your region.
20. Explain the attraction of classical music to tourists.

21. Name the major rock stars through the different decades; and give an example of albums.
22. Name a musician from each of the other main types of popular music.
23. Locate on a map of Ireland the homes/birth places of Ireland's main contemporary musicians.
24. Explain the attraction of Irish contemporary musicians to tourists visiting Ireland.
25. Name three major festivals of Irish music from the different genres of music.
26. Name three places where tourists can find out about the Irish music industry.
27. Based on information from your Regional Tourism Authority, name the locations where tourists can sample the different types of music in your area, and give a list of local music festivals.
28. Explain the importance of Irish music entertainment to the tourism industry.
29. Explain the impact of tourism on culture.

Assignments

1. Visit and sample venues that offer music entertainment, be this a concert, a session or a music interpretive centre. Follow up the trip by writing a report of your experience.
2. Carry out research into musical performers, classical, traditional, rock, and jazz. Your research is to include researching the artists, and also listening to them perform on CD, television, or live; then make a tape of different types of Irish music.

References and further reading

C. Carson, *Pocket Guide to Irish Traditional Music*. Appletree, 1986.

P. J. Curtis, *Notes from the Heart*. Torc, 1994.

T. Clayton Lea and R. Taylor, *Irish Rock*. Gill & Macmillan, 1992.

A. Fleishmann, *Music in Ireland – A Symposium*. Cork University Press, 1952.

D. Hickey, *Stone Mad for Music*. Marino, 1999.

C. Larkin, *The Guinness Who's Who of Folk Music*. Guinness, 1993.

P. Murphy, *Toss the Feathers*. Mercier, 1995.

P. O'Kelly, *The NSO of Ireland*. RTÉ, 1998.

S. O'Riada, *Our Musical Heritage*. Dolmen Press, 1982.

F. Vallely and C. Piggott, *Blooming Meadows*. Townhouse, 1998.

F. Vallely, *The Companion of Irish Traditional Music*. Cork University Press.

M. Prendergast, *Irish Rock*. O'Brien Press, 1987.

G. Norris, *A Musical Gazette of Great Britain and Ireland*. D. Charles, 1981.

www.operaireland.com

Part 6
Other Aspects
of the
Travel Industry

CHAPTER 18

The Travel Industry

The travel industry refers to the channels of distribution of the tourism industry. It is comprised of three parts: tour operators, ground handling agents and travel agents. The Irish Travel Agency Association and the Incoming Tour Operators Association are the organisational bodies of the travel industry that look after their interests.

TOUR OPERATORS

Tour operators are involved in organising inclusive tours for outgoing tourists. They organise package holidays which they then wholesale to travel agents. These package holidays are to destinations located outside Ireland, for example Spain and other Mediterranean areas, USA, Mexico and Thailand. Accommodation is organised in hotels, self-catering apartments, B&Bs, caravans or tents. Catering is provided in hotels. This can mean full board, half board, or breakfast. All-inclusive holidays may mean most or all food and drink at the hotel are paid in advance. Transport is organised on chartered or scheduled flights, on ferries, or by rail or coach. At the destination, transport is also organised to bring the tourists from the airport to their accommodation. The company usually has a holiday representative, or courier, at each resort to care for their customers. Activities may also be included on all-inclusive holidays, for example water sports, kiddies clubs, entertainment.

Anyone who organises a package holiday from Ireland must hold a tour operator's licence under the Transport Act 1982. These licences are issued by the Department of Trade and Public Enterprise, Transport Section. In order to be issued with a licence, a tour operator must provide:

1. An application form two months in advance of trading as a tour operator
2. Audited accounts of the company
3. Financial projections for the business to be generated by the tours
4. Copies of brochures, booking conditions, etc. that the company will use
5. Arrangements for a bond, either with cash, through the banks or an insurance company
6. Competent and experienced employees
7. An annual fee which is based on the turnover of the company, and which is paid annually.

Provided the Department is satisfied with the information provided by the tour operators, they will be issued with a licence for one year. The bond to be paid is worked out at 10 per cent of the projected turnover from the sale of package holidays in the year. A tour operator company hoping to earn €3.75 million from sales must pay €400,000 into the Travellers' Protection Fund. This is to ensure the protection of the customers' money, before and during their holiday. This Act was introduced in 1984 after a number of tour operators and travel agencies collapsed, leaving passengers stranded abroad and other customers losing their money.

A variety of package tours are organised by tour operators involving different types of holidays, and to different destinations. These include: (a) summer sun holidays, (b) winter sun holidays, (c) winter ski holidays, (d) short-break holidays, (e) long-haul destinations, (f) cruises, (g) group escorted tours, (h) special-interest packages, (i) conference and incentive tours. Fourteen countries offer tours to Ireland; most of these are from Europe (Austria, Belgium, Britain, Finland, Iceland, Italy, Norway, Spain, Sweden and Switzerland). The long-haul holidays come from the USA, Australia, New Zealand and Japan. They offer a range of holidays to Ireland including group escorted tours, short-break holidays, special interest and/or golfing packages, conference and incentive tours.

Organising an inclusive tour is a very risky business, as plans are made two years in advance of the holiday actually taking place. It must be organised carefully in order to minimise the risk and have a broad appeal to tourists.

1.   The destinations/resorts are chosen on the basis of their popularity, climate, customs. Then the tour operator must decide how many seats and hotel rooms they will be able to sell each week during the holiday season (April to October).

2.   The tour operator must look at the purchasing of flights. They must decide whether to charter an aeroplane, or just book a block of seats on a plane, either on chartered or scheduled flights. The company must decide on the airline company they will use, which are often either Irish, or from the country they are flying to. The tour operator must look at the times of flights. Once this is decided, the cost is negotiated with the chosen airline. Payment can be made on a 100 per cent guarantee basis, which means that the tour operator pays for the seats whether they are used or not; these are the cheapest seats. The other method is on a release basis; this means that if the tour operator does not sell the seats by a certain date, then they are returned to the airline. The reductions on these seats are not as great because the risk is being shared.

3.   The tour operator must then decide on the accommodation mix. This means they must decide whether to use hotels, and if so, what grade, or to use apartments. Usually the company will decide on a mix, in order to appeal to the largest number of people. They will have to decide on the location of the accommodation, whether close to the beach or to the night-life. The tour operator must also settle on the

meal options that the hotel will offer. In deciding the type of accommodation, the tour operator must look at the target market, whether couples, families, or groups, all of which have different requirements, and travel at different times of the year. After the tour operator have decided on the accommodation, they negotiate the price with the hoteliers and apartment owners.

4. The next step is to organise coach transport between the airport and hotels.

5. With all costs known, the tour operator now works out the retail price for each holiday. This has to take into account the number of children, free places. It also takes seasonal factors into account. During the high season (July and August), demand will outstrip supply, so the tour operator will maximise profits by charging high prices. During the shoulder and mid season (June and September), prices will be lower. During the low season (April, May and October), the tour operator will be trying to encourage purchases with special offers.

6. The tour operator now prepares the brochure. The brochure describes the resorts and the accommodation with its location and facilities, and gives information on flights and prices, days and times of departure. The information must comply with the EU Directives on Package Travel and Tours 1992. These brochures are prepared fifteen months in advance.

7. Because tour operators must pay for hotels, airlines, brochures, etc. in advance, they need money in as quickly as possible. This is why when customers are booking holidays they must pay a deposit. They also have reductions for early booking. Full payment for the holiday is made eight weeks in advance of the departure date. When flights and hotel rooms have not been sold within a week of departure, then the tour operator will offer them at reduced rates, or as special offers. There are usually no special offers available during the high season.

8. Bookings are made at the reservation department of the tour operator, or through travel agents using computers. When the booking is made the customer must complete and sign the booking form and pay the deposit. These are then sent off to the tour operator.

Budget Travel is a major Irish company that organises tours to the Mediterranean and to other exotic destinations. Other important tour operators include Falcon, Joe Walsh, and Panorama.

Case study: Budget Travel

Gillian Bowler founded Budget Travel in 1975, in a basement office in Baggot Street, Dublin. Her previous experience in the travel trade was in London, and she came to Dublin to set up her new office. She introduced many Irish people to the exotic experience of Greece for the first time. During that first year she sold 200 seats. Many of her early package holidays involved flights with one night's accommodation, which appealed to backpackers who wanted to visit the Greek islands. Sales rose quickly. During the late 1970s and 1980s the tourist trade was cut-throat; many tour operators collapsed, leaving tourists stranded abroad. Budget introduced a bonding in order to win public confidence in the company and it succeeded. By 1983 the Irish travel market was growing, with 200,000 Irish people travelling abroad annually. Budget offered this growing market 'better places, better prices, real choice and value for money'. Budget Travel had now grown into a national brand that offered quality holidays at unbeatable prices. By 1984 it carried over 25,000 passengers, had earned over £8 (€10.1) million, and was in Ireland's top 500 companies.

In 1987 Granada PLC bought Budget Travel, and this provided the company with the finance to expand its operation to new destinations. In 1990 Budget Travel bought the Aer Lingus travel company Blue Skies, and expanded its holidays to become Ireland's number one tour operator. Long-haul destinations to Florida and Jamaica were added to its package tours. The Independent Travel Agents voted Budget the best tour operator, offering the best value for money, and giving the best service during the 1990s.

In 1996 Thomson Holidays bought Budget from Granada. Budget continued to trade under its old name and with its old management. As part of Thomson it now used Britannia Airlines to expand its range of long-haul holidays. During 2000 Budget Travel took over 340,000 Irish tourists on a range of holidays, to sun destinations in the Mediterranean, on cruises, long-haul and winter-sun holidays. It employs nearly 300 staff and remains Ireland's number one tour operator.

In 1995 Budget opened its Travel Shops, a retail section of the company. It now operates twenty-seven shops throughout Ireland, making it Ireland's leading travel agency chain. It has succeeded because it is an innovative and flexible market lead company which has maintained its personal touch and approach through its twenty-six years of operation. Budget Travel will continue to change with future trends so that it will be successful into the twenty-first century.

Fig. 18.1: Budget Travel

GROUND HANDLING AGENTS OR INCOMING TOUR OPERATORS

Ground handling agents usually work for the medium or small tour operators, providing them with a range of services at the destination. The ground handling agent provides expertise on destinations, and can negotiate with the local tourism producers better than small tour operators. The knowledge of the local market means that they know new hotels, for instance, or those offering the best value. Often the agent will negotiate for a number of different tour operators from different parts of the world, but never for operators that compete in the same market. When they are negotiating for large numbers of hotel rooms for a number of tour operators, they get better deals and cheaper rooms, due to bulk buying. The agents also organise taxis or coaches to transfer tourists from the airport to the hotels. They may also organise an excursion programme to visit the major tourism attractions. This may be part of the package holiday or an optional extra. The company may organise specialised programmes for individual groups, and put together itineraries for them. By using a ground handling agent the small tour operator cuts down on costs and the risks that this business incurs.

Case study: Silverdale's Ireland

Silverdale's Ireland is a small company operating as an incoming tour operator for the last forty years. Its main business areas are as follows:

(a) Ground handling agent for a large British coach operator; they organise accommodation, coach transport, guided tours etc for their three escorted trips to Ireland. These include a Dublin city four-day break programme, and weekly tours around the south and south west of Ireland, for which there are two different routes.

(b) Organising conference, meeting and incentive trips for business people mainly from Scandinavia, but also from Argentina and the USA. Such trips are often for small groups, about thirty business people who come over a three- or four-day period. These trips often involve a short conference followed by tours around Dublin's tourism attractions and entertainment.

(c) Organising larger conferences, for example the Spar Managers Conference, which took place last September. This conference involved 130 delegates. Silverdale organised hotel accommodation, meals, a banquet, airport transfers, sightseeing, the actual two-day conferences, city tours and horse-racing at Leopardstown.

Silverdale has operated for forty years, although the present management has only recently bought it. The company is a member of the ITOA, and SITE. The advantage of being a member of these organisations is that the company can attend conferences run by them. During April each year the ITOA holds a marketing conference or trade fair which brings together tourist suppliers (sellers) and incoming tourism operators in Ireland (buyers) for the benefit of both groups. At these fairs prices are decided for the following year. The lead-in time for organising these trips varies from as long as two years to as short as two months. Trips that arrive in October are usually organised during the previous April. The high season for many meetings and incentive trips is from March to June, and October/November. Most of these trips take place in Dublin (60 per cent), with the remainder being based in cities like Galway, Limerick or Kerry, all of which are accessible by air.

The Incoming Tour Operators Association (ITOA) was set up in 1987. It represents thirty-seven members of the tourism business in Ireland. These companies are involved in creating packages, and promoting Ireland to the main markets abroad. They promote mainly three main types of holidays: (a) business holidays, for example Incentive Conference Ireland; (b) language holidays, for example ATC Language and Travel Ltd.; (c) leisure holidays, for example Experience Ireland Holidays. They organise hotels, coach transport, and excursions in Ireland. They work together with the major tour operators in Ireland's major markets (the USA, Britain, Europe, Australia and Japan) putting together holiday arrangements for the tour operator's clients in Ireland. Staff members must include people who are fluent in foreign languages, so that they can deal competently with foreign tour operators. Some of the companies also provide coaches, drivers and guides for incoming package tours.

The ITOA works closely with Bord Fáilte so that the best service is provided for these package tourists, and in order to maximise the benefits to the tourism providers in Ireland. The ITOA has a code of conduct for its members, which states that they must be working towards the growth and development of the Irish tourism industry, and they must also have a good reputation within the industry. The ITOA provides insurance for its members in cases where the company collapses. It organises annual workshops for its members. These bring together the tourism providers and incoming tour operators, and allow them to negotiate for the benefit of all (incoming tour operators, tourism producers, the overseas tour operators, and the customers). Over £3.6 (€4.5) billion has been invested in the tourism industry; this has improved the tourism product greatly. The numbers of new three-star hotels means that there is now a plentiful supply of hotels for package holidays at all the major destinations. The ITOA works together with the Council of the Convention Bureau of Ireland in order to increase the numbers of conference and incentive travellers coming to Ireland. But as this area of the business rises, it will create a greater demand for four- and five-star hotels, and investment in this area needs to be increased. The ITOA is involved with the ITIC's 'People and Places' programme in order to improve the quality of service to tourists. The ITOA represents companies such as Irish Travel Partners, O'Mara Travel, Delaney Marketing, Abbey Tours and Brendan Tours, all important players in this market.

TRAVEL AGENTS

Travel agents are the retailers in the travel trade. They sell a range of products to customers, and provide advice to customers on the destination that best suits their needs. Travel consultants provide information on timetables for a range of transport, fares and brochures. There are 362 travel agents in Ireland and many of these are small companies employing fewer than ten people. In recent years larger travel companies have been established in Dublin, and they have many branches located in shopping centres, and on main streets. The larger chains include Budget Travel Shops and Sunway Travel.

In order to operate as a travel agent, the company must acquire a travel agency licence. Like a tour operator's application for a licence, the travel agent must provide audited accounts and financial projections, and employ competent and experienced travel-trade workers, including staff that hold IATA certificates. The Department of Trade and Public Enterprise, Transport Section issues a licence provided it is satisfied with the company and they have paid their bond. The bond is set at four per cent of projected income from the sale of their products. All travel agents pay a bond in order to protect their customers in case the company goes out of business.

The success of a travel agency depends on its location and its experienced staff. Most travel agents are located on busy streets in towns and cities, or in shopping centres because they are able to avail of a good passing trade. Experienced staff is important because it is they who handle enquiries and turn them into sales. Staff employed in travel agencies must have good computer skills, particularly on computer reservation systems like Sabre, Worldspan, and Amadeus. Over 80 per cent of Irish Travel Agents use the Galileo system.

A range of jobs is available in travel agencies; these include travel consultants, receptionists and accounts clerks. Travel consultants deal with the customers, and are required to discover customer needs. Once this has been done they can then advise their customers on the possible solutions to those requirements. In order to do this consultants must know what is available in their brochures. They must also know how to access information on the computer system to find other solutions, availability, and prices. Ongoing training is provided for staff on the newest computerised reservation systems. The most common queries that arise in travel agents regard the availability of flights, and which is the most suitable package holiday for the customer's requirements. Checking flights to the destination required, examining the fares and availability on the computer system easily solves queries about flights. This information is then presented to clients who make their choice based on availability, times, company and fares.

Package holiday selection is more complex, because there is a range of information about each resort that the consultant must know. This includes general information, for instance about the weather, local customs, or closeness to the airport, and more specific information about the accommodation; the location, facilities and cost. This information is built up over years of experience, by reading brochures, books and manuals, by visiting some of the resorts and through education programmes. When the customers are happy with their holiday they will return to the travel agency and purchase further holidays. When the travel consultant gets the advice wrong, then the holiday can turn out to be a nightmare, and complaints follow when the customers return.

The staff in travel agencies have to deal with complaints. Complaints from holidays are due to these factors:

- Customers select the wrong product; this is probably their own fault if they have not taken the good advice offered by the travel consultants.
- Customers have experienced poor delivery of the product, for example tickets arriving late, customers not being told to check up return flight times. These are the fault of the travel agents.
- Customers have experienced poor quality service in the hotel, on the airline, by the courier. All of this is the fault of the tour operator. The information in brochures, for example facilities and standard of accommodation, must always be correct under the Trades Description Act.

There are three stages of complaints. First, customers complain to the company. If they do not get satisfaction at this level, the second stage is to go to arbitration. If the problem still is not solved then the case will go to court. While travel agency staff need to know how to deal with complaints, most customers have enjoyable holidays and there are few complaints.

The types of products that are normally sold by travel agents include the following:

- Package holidays are sold from a range of tour operators, to a range of destinations, and for various lengths of time. Brochures are available for potential customers to take and decide on which holiday suits them most. The trained travel consultants can also advise their customers on the resorts that best suit their needs, a lively resort for young adults, or quieter resorts for families and couples. Popular brochures are available from Falcon, Budget, JWT, for long-haul, short-break and cruise holidays. Long-haul and cruise holidays are usually for the wealthier end of the market. Both of these markets are growing in importance, and this can be seen in the number of companies offering these types of holidays direct from Dublin. In the past long-haul holidays and cruises were only on offer from UK tour operators.
- Travel agents sell airline tickets to a range of destinations. Using a computer system like Galileo, travel consultants can check on availability of flights, book the flights and provide their clients with airline tickets. Travel agents who display the IATA (International Air Transport Association) sticker are agents for selling airline tickets for their members.
- Hotel accommodation is sold around the world by travel agents. By subscribing to the Hotel & Travel Index or a CRS system, travel consultants can find a hotel that best suits the needs of their client. This is done on the basis of the location of the hotel whether in the airport, city centre, or on the beach. The price range, star rating, and facilities are also relevant. These can be booked, and hotel vouchers provided.
- Car hire is sold. The major car-hire firms have offices located in most cities in the world, and the travel agency can provide information about the types of cars

that can be hired, the cost, and the restrictions on driving in their chosen destinations.

- All travel agents sell insurance. Customers going on holidays take out insurance to cover death, hospitalisation, lost baggage, curtailment and cancellation of holidays. All travellers are encouraged to obtain insurance policies, but they do not have to purchase it from the tour operator or travel agent. Travel agents make higher commissions on insurance than other types of sales.

- Business travel and company accounts are a very profitable area of business for travel agents, as the business people purchase tickets for flights, hotel accommodation, and car hire when they travel. Often these companies are purchasing first class tickets and five-star accommodation, so the level of commission is very high. The kind of service that business companies require from travel agents is different from the service that holiday-makers want. They need credit, because accounts will be paid monthly. Reliability in the delivery of tickets and travel documents is also important. Some travel agents only serve business travellers because they operate differently, and it is a lucrative business for those who are experts in delivering the right service.

- Some travel agents sell coach, rail and ferry tickets, but often these are not an important area of business for them. CIÉ Tours International are the main travel agents in Dublin who sell rail tickets for railway companies abroad. Often people book directly with ferry companies, but it is possible to do this through a travel agent. Some travel agents make bookings for West End theatres in London and provide theatre vouchers. A number of travel agents also sell travellers cheques, for example American Express.

- Travel consultants provide a range of information on passport, visa, and health requirements.

Travel agents are paid for these sales by commission from the companies. The level of commission varies with the type of sale, from 30 per cent for insurance to 7 per cent for airline tickets.

Some travel agents organise inclusive tours, for example football weekends to the UK, or short city breaks to the UK and Europe. Companies who organise such trips must hold a tour operator's licence.

The Irish Travel Agency Association (ITAA) represents travel agents in Ireland. This was founded in 1970, when the Alliance of Irish Travel Agents, and the Irish Provincial Travel Agents joined together. The ITAA membership is made up of 370 travel agents and twenty tour operators, who operate all over the country. Their members are all licensed and bonded according to the 1982 Transport Act, 1995 Package Holidays, and Travel Trade Act. To become a member of the ITAA the travel agent must employ only qualified staff; this ensures that all customers get the highest quality of customer service, and their advice is sound and unbiased. Every member of the ITAA displays the membership sticker in his or her window. The

Case study: Colette Pearson Travel

Colette Pearson set up her small travel agency in 1994 in South William Street in Dublin. She had spent many years in Australia, South-East Asia and the Pacific Islands, and on her return to Ireland she worked in an Irish travel agency and established their long-haul section. Using this experience, she set up her own travel agency. Today her successful travel agency specialises in tailor-made long-haul and adventure holidays. Many of these holidays are to Asia, Africa, South America, Australia, and round the world tours. Her work involves advising customers of their travel needs, making bookings, looking after accounts, issuing tickets.

(a) A typical trip that she organises is the overland trip from Nairobi in Kenya to Dar-es-Salaam in Tanzania. This trip travels overland on a Mercedes truck with a small group (maximum 16), and camping or staying in lodges. The trip visits Safari parks to see Africa's endangered wildlife and climbs part of Kilimanjaro – Africa's highest mountain. Trips can last from three to twenty-six weeks and are geared at the most adventurous tourists. These holidays use scheduled flights, and her clients may link up with some specialised tour operators like Exodus, Imaginative Traveller and Adventure Bound. She is the general sales agent in Ireland for these companies.

(b) She also provides her clients with important information about passport, visa, health and vaccination requirements for their trips. She sells insurance to her customers and ensures that they are adequately covered, as repatriation costs from these out-of-the-way parts of the world are very expensive.

(c) Her travel agency sells scheduled flights all over the world. Availability of flights is checked using her Sabre GDS system.

Colette Pearson Travel is a member of the IATA and the ITAA, which is essential for it to carry out its business. The travel agency is advertised in the Yellow Pages, in the Irish Independent and Evening Herald (as The Real Wizard of Oz and Round the World Tours), in editorials in the newspapers, and by word of mouth. Many clients are repeat customers who are satisfied with the holidays that the travel agency has organised for them.

main reasons that customers can be confident about booking through ITAA travel agents are because they: (a) are Government bonded and licensed; (b) provide professional independent advice; (c) are experts in the use of new technology, for example computer reservation systems, the internet; (d) provide the customer with the best possible value in travel services.

The European Confederation of Travel Agents Association (ECTAA) is the European-wide grouping for travel agents, which the ITAA is represented on. It is also represented on the Universal Federation of Travel Agents Association (UFTA).

REVISION EXERCISES

1. Describe the work of tour operators.
2. Describe the work of incoming tour operators.
3. Name the products that travel agents sell.
4. Explain what the following initials stand for: ITAA, IATA, ITOA, ECTAA and UFTAA.

Assignment

Students are asked to collected brochures for three different types of holidays, analyse them and produce a report on the resorts, destinations, access, amenities etc provided.

References and further reading

C.J. Holloway, *The Business of Tourism*. Longman, 1998.
G. Syratt, *A Manual of Travel Agency Practice*. Butterworth & Heinemann, 1995.
CERT: *Tourism & Travel in Ireland*. Gill & Macmillan, 1997.
Department of Public Enterprise, Transport (Tour Operators and Travel Agents) Act 1982. Government of Ireland, 1995.

CHAPTER 19

Information Technology in the Tourism Industry

THE GROWING IMPORTANCE OF TECHNOLOGY

Over the last thirty years information technology has been growing in importance for the tourism industry. It now plays an important role in the distribution of goods for a whole range of tourism products, for example airline tickets, hotels and car hire. There are three major areas of information technology: Central Reservation Systems, Global Distribution Systems, and the internet.

CENTRAL RESERVATION SYSTEMS (CRS)

CRS were the first systems to be developed. **Airline companies** needed a system to control their seat reservations, flight schedules, crew schedules, so they were the original users of CRS. The systems were developed 'during deregulation of the airline industry' when it was essential that tight control be kept on the business. The CRS consists of a large central computer with a database that has all the information on flights, seats, fares and classes. The database is available to travel agents who are linked to it, and this allows them to make airline bookings and produce tickets. As well as linking airlines to travel agents, the CRS can link airlines to each other. The information between airlines uses a global communication network, in Europe this is SITA, the Société Internationale de Télécommunication Aéronautiques.

When using a CRS, the travel agent must make contact with SITA (Société Internationale de Télécommunication Aéronautiques). The speed at which information flows between the CRS and the travel agent depends on the type of user connection with the system provider. The agent can use CRS off-line or on-line. The most basic link is known as 'availability and phone', whereby the travel agent checks availability by computer, but in order to book must telephone the airline company's reservation desk and talk to them. The most advanced link is known as 'direct connect availability', which links the travel agent directly into the airline's CRS, where they can check availability on the flight, and then book as many seats as they require. The airline CRS will then send the travel agent the passenger name record (PNR) locator. A PNR is given to everyone who books a seat with an airline. All these CRS systems use common commands so that it is relatively simple for travel agents to access the information. Each travel agent is given a city code, and when they contact the CRS they will be given information about flights from the closest airport. When the travel agent has checked the fares and availability of flights, and has then booked the flight and payment is made, the next step is providing the tickets. There are four ways of producing tickets: (a) Manually writing out the ticket using a metal plate which is very similar to the old visa card voucher; (b) OPTATs, that is off-premises transitional automated tickets; these are often known as BSP tickets and are issued by the IATA. They are printed using an impact printer and continuous paper, and produce seven copies. (c) ATB tickets which are single cards that have a magnetic strip attached and this can be read by a computer at the airport. (d) Electronic ticketing which involves no paperwork. An electronic image of the ticket is produced instead, with all the information about the flight. Within a period of less than fifteen years we have moved from manually-produced tickets to e-ticketing, which shows the extent of the impact of IT on the travel industry. It is also expected that by 2010, 60 per cent of tickets will be sold by e-ticketing, but it will not totally replace the old hard-copy airline tickets that travel agents produce. Other information is also available on airline CRS; these include hotel and car-hire availability, rates and reservations. This allows the travel agent to sell a range of tourism products to customers.

Hotel companies also use central reservation systems, but the level of computerisation depends on the size of the hotel. The use of computerisation in hotels has only become evident since the late 1980s. Before this everything was done manually. Hotels may opt to develop an in-house system, but these are expensive and tend to be found only in large hotel chains. It is possible to buy a software package from a computer firm that specialises in the production of packages for the hotel.industry. The third alternative is to use a computer company to look after all your IT needs and outsource the business. These last two alternatives are known as using property management systems. There are in fact a number of systems that hotels can purchase:

- Property management systems hold all the information about the hotel, its facilities, bedrooms, guest details and tariffs. They are used to check in guests, produce invoices, accounts, and records of payment as the guest departs. They also record whether rooms are in use, or have been cleaned. This information is provided to the receptionist and manager.
- Reservation systems keep up-to-date on room availability.
- Self-service kiosk system allows guests to check in and out without using the front desk; they use swipe cards instead. This allows business clients to save time, but it will never replace the personal touch that the front desk provides.
- Food and beverage systems are used to control food-stocks required for menus and costing from suppliers.
- Point of sale systems create bills, and method-of-payment cards are linked to an authorisation system and to the accounts department.

- A sales and marketing system includes customer data that have come from the reservation system. This information can be used in future direct-marketing campaigns. Back office systems look at accounts and the hotel's income and expenditure, and are supported by the hotel's financial accounting system.
- In-room systems allow guests to have access to the internet for e-mails and for teleconferencing. Guest rooms may have internet points, power sockets for PCs and faxes.

These systems have helped hotels to be run more efficiently. Travel agents have access to some of these hotel systems, but it is only since the development of GDS systems that they have successfully been able to tap into the hotel CRS, and increase the number of sales.

GLOBAL DISTRIBUTION SYSTEMS (GDS)

Global Distribution Systems link several CRS to a mainframe computer that has a large database. GDS sell a range of travel products, including airline seats, car hire, and hotel rooms. There are four major GDS systems: Galileo, Amadeus, Sabre, and Worldspan. The GDS system contains a switch that allows the computer to link into different suppliers and to different travel agents. Most of the GDS systems were set up and owned by airline companies, because they were the first to computerise their own businesses. At present 80 per cent of all bookings in the USA are made through GDS systems; fewer are sold in Europe because travellers make fewer flights and more use of other types of transport and holidays. Information on availability, fares and prices must be supplied in an unbiased manner. For this reason airline companies will often provide flight information on the international market with the GDS, but supply their domestic market with their CRS.

Galileo is located in sixty-six countries, with 33,000 locations. It is linked into 500 airlines, 208 hotel chains that operate 37,000 premises around the world, and forty-seven car hire firms. Galileo was set up in 1991, by joining United Airlines' Apollo system, and the Swiss-based Galileo International, which had been set up by British Airways, KLM, Swiss Air and Covia. It is now owned by these airlines along with Aer Lingus, Austrian Airlines, Olympic, TAP, Alitalia, US Airways, and Air Canada. Its large mainframe computer is located in Denver, USA, and deals with sixty-six million messages per day. Travel agents and tourism suppliers are linked to the computer using high-speed communication lines, which are linked to nodal points in a web system to prevent downtime, i.e. the computer not operating for any period of time.

Galileo is Ireland's main GDS system; it operates in over 80 per cent of travel agents' outlets. All of these travel agents have PCs with special software that runs on Windows. The most recent development is Edifact Select, which allows Galileo to integrate with in-house systems of tour operators and air consolidator. Focal Point and OLE Select help to link the PC to the Galileo computer via a server that stores all the agencies' data. The PC systems using Galileo are linked into ticket printers either for OPTAT tickets, or ATB tickets, invoice and itinerary printers and a general printer. The Galileo software only gives access to the GDS system; for other work, travel agents require other software programmes. Training is provided for travel agents' employees by Galileo Ireland on their system. The core functions of Galileo include the following:

1. Flight availability on over 210 airline can be checked, both for direct and indirect flights.
2. There are over two billion fares available on Galileo's database; these are updated three times daily. The fares are displayed with the cheapest flights first.
3. The flight is then booked. Information is collected about the flight, the passenger, and the travel agency booking the flight. This is then sent to the Galileo database, and from there to the airline's CRS.
4. The next stage is to produce airline tickets based on the information from three databases, i.e. fares, availability, and booking file.
5. Seating on the aeroplane can be chosen in advance. Customers can choose either the type of seat they require, for example non-smoking window seat, or the number of the seat.
6. Clients' files are also kept on the database, and they can be useful when a client returns to book a new flight.
7. A queuing system controls the workflow of the business and increases its efficiency. Queues operate within the travel agency, between the travel agency and Galileo, and between Galileo and the suppliers. Any changes in flights, times etc., are put on to the queue, which the travel agency accesses.
8. RoomMaster is the hotel booking service that Galileo provides. The 37,000 hotels are linked either directly or indirectly to the Galileo system. Using the Galileo Spectrum CD, which is a map system that shows the location of all the hotels, customers can choose the most suitable hotel. RoomMaster allows the travel agent to check availability, and rates, and to make a booking.
9. CarMaster allows travel agents using Galileo to reserve cars all over the world. All the major car companies, such as Hertz and Avis, can be hired at 15,000 locations worldwide.
10. Galileo's Information System provides general information about consulates, and customer services. Using TIMATIC travel agents can also access information on countries, visas and health regulations. The system also provides information on how to encode and decode codes used by airports, airlines and countries.
11. Galileo Productivity helps travel agents to improve their operations. It gives them access to old records, which they can then use for marketing purposes.

Galileo is very successful in helping travel agents to provide a better service to their customers. Most of the smaller independent travel agents and airlines use this system.

Fig. 19.1: Galileo

Worldspan was formed in 1990 by TWA, Abacus, Northwest and Delta. Their computer is located in Atlanta USA, and they handle 1.2 billion enquiries every month. Worldspan operates in forty-five countries at 15,000 offices, providing booking facilities for 414 airlines, forty car-rental companies, 29,000 hotels, and for thirty-eight special travel service suppliers that include tour operators and cruise operators. Worldspan's business has grown enormously since 1990 and this is because

1. It provides a customised product for its customers
2. Its business is aimed at both the leisure and business market, unlike other GDSs.
3. It makes increasing use of the internet, and allows direct links into their GDS system.

Worldspan offers four levels of services to its airlines: direct contact into the airline CRS, direct sell, direct access, and direct response which is the most basic level and involves the airline getting back with a PNR. Worldspan also links travel agents with the major hotel chains' CRS and into Hotel Reservation Systems like Thisco.

The travel agent is linked to Worldspan's computer in Atlanta in order to find out availability, fares and tariffs, and to make the booking. To find out about non core-services suppliers, travel agents reach a localised database using the X25 network. Such services include most of the major ferry companies, railway companies providing domestic services in Europe, the Eurostar service and international services in North America on Worldspan.

The core functions of Worldspan include:

1. Profiles of passengers, usually given as PNRs
2. Checking of airline schedules and availability
3. Airline fares
4. Airline reservations
5. Worldspan Hotels Select, allows the travel agent to make hotel reservations
6. Worldspan Car Select allows the travel agent to organise car hire bookings
7. Queues for information on PNR, changes in flight details and messages between the airline and travel agent

8. Production of tickets and other travel documents. Tickets are usually ATB2, e-tickets or satellite ticket printing which allows tickets to be printed in different offices or countries.

9. Other information systems including Worldspan Traveller Supplies, Travel Guides.

Travel agents are able to use their PCs with Worldspan for Windows software. It includes a number of applications including management information (Compass), which allow travel agents to review their performance, or to forecast the future. Commercial World is a package to help business travellers. E Travel is also aimed at the business traveller, and gives them direct access to the Worldspan Network, which allows them to make bookings directly.

Travel agents with multiple outlets use Worldspan. These can access the system by leasing a data line and using a Worldspan gateway server. Worldspan can then be linked into the company's own local area network. Smaller, independent travel agents can access Worldspan using a modem and PC to DialLink. Tour Operators use the World Solutions programme to link them with travel agents and other non-air suppliers. Worldspan is increasingly being used on the Irish market.

Air France, Lufthansa, and Iberian airways set up **Amadeus** in 1987. In 1997 it was the world's largest GDS system. It was located in 117 countries, at 39,000 locations. It provides information on 440 airlines, 35,000 hotels, and fifty-five car-hire firms. Its major offices are located in a number of cities in Spain, France and Germany. The large mainframe computer is able to cater for thirty million transactions per day. The company also has national marketing companies in every large country where they operate; this is to help local travel agents and local suppliers. The largest of these looks after the North American, Central American and Caribbean region. All of the top US travel agency chains use Amadeus.

Sabre, the Semi Automated Business Research Environment, developed from American Airlines CRS that was set up in 1976. In 1995 Sabre became separated from American Airlines, although American Airlines is a major shareholder. Sabre has four sections:

1. Sabre Computer Services runs the computer and data-processing service.
2. Sabre Decision Technology provides software to airlines and airports.
3. Sabre Travel Information Network sells Sabre products to travel agents and travel suppliers.
4. Sabre Interactive develops new technology for the system.

Sabre's mainframe is located in Dallas/Fort Worth and it earned $2.6 billion in revenue in 2000. The mainframe is linked to 4,540 airlines, 53,000 hotels, 54 car hire companies and 59,000 travel agents in over forty-five countries.

Like Worldspan, a range of products other than airlines, hotels and car hire can be accessed; these include cruise operators, railways (SNCF), Eurostar, ferry companies, and tour operators. Sabre provides a number of products:

- Sabre Travel Marketing and Distribution allows travel agents and travel management companies to organise sales of airline, car hire, cruises and package holiday's products.
- Get There allows business companies and suppliers to use the Internet to make reservations; this reduces cost all around and makes the system very efficient.
- Travelocity.com is Sabre's online travel agency; during 2000 it sold over fourteen million tickets on airlines earning over $2.5 billion.
- Airline Solutions is a package used by airline companies to improve their efficiency in areas of scheduling flights and crews, tariffs and planning.
- Sabre Technology Innovations involves developing new technology to deal with the transportation and travel industry, continuing the role it adopted nearly forty years ago.

Travel agents who install the Sabre GDS system pay for it by renting the equipment. The equipment includes the PC, ticketing printers and software. A monthly fee pays for these. The travel agent also pays a booking fee; this decreases with the number of bookings made per month. Offices that make a large number of bookings using the system may in fact cover the monthly equipment rental fee. Other GDS systems operate similar payment systems.

THE INTERNET

Commercial development began in the USA in the 1990s, with sales amounting to $2 billion, but this rose to over $60 billion by 2000. Sales are greatest in the areas of travel, computer and entertainment. By 2017 the US Government expect that 20 per cent of all tourism and travel sales will be done over the internet. Use of the internet is much greater in the USA than in Europe, but numbers are growing all the time.

For a company to get on the internet, they must set up a web site. In developing a website, first the site name must be decided, the home page designed, and links to other sites organised. The aim of the web site is to get as many people to visit the site as possible, to keep them interested and then to turn those visits into purchases. The home page must download in less than ten seconds or the client will get bored and move on to a different site. When the company intends to sell directly to customers over the internet, it must set up a computerised reservation system. Specialised IT companies set up internet booking systems. Selling on the internet is best suited to companies who can accept credit cards, require the minimum amount of delivery, and can sell to any place in the world. A successful site can receive e-mails from visitors. A database of all visitors to the site is kept, along with a record of customers' purchases. The company will use the database for future direct-marketing activities.

Companies that intend to use the internet to sell products must consider the use of Search Engines. A search engine like Yahoo or Google will allow users to search for different types of businesses just by typing in the topic that they require. Legal issues can arise when sellers and buyers of goods on the internet are from different countries, because contracts may not have the same binding agreements when a dispute arises. Booking fees are not paid when the consumer books directly on the internet with the service provider; if a GDS system is used then fees are charged, which must remain competitive with travel agents' fees. Travel agents must decide which is the best GDS system to use, because for financial reasons they are not able to join them all.

There are many different types of travel services on the internet:

1. Intermediaries: include travel services on the internet, and gobal distribution systems that are now accessed through the internet. These include Expedia and Worldspan.
2. Supplier sites like British Midland, Ryanair, Aer Lingus, Jury's Doyle Hotels
3. Business travel companies like American Express's AXI
4. Tourism organisations like Bord Fáilte's Gulliver, British Tourism Authorities' site.

1. Intermediaries

Expedia is Microsoft's travel agency on the internet, which was set up in 1996. It is found at *http://expedia.msn.com*, and since its inception has sold millions of dollars' worth of air tickets, hotel rooms and car hire per week. Its business has been growing by 20 per cent per year. It first sold on the domestic US market but later expanded internationally to Europe and Australia. It uses Worldspan to check the availability of flights, and has negotiated its own airfares, which are displayed along with scheduled fares. Customers can then book using the flight wizard, and either pay by credit card directly or by giving details over the telephone. The tickets are prepared and sent to the customer by a local travel agent. Other services include the Hotel Wizard for hotel bookings, Car Wizard for car-hire bookings, and Hotel Pinpointer, which locates hotels on maps and helps visitors find them. When this web site was first opened many people came on to the site as curious visitors; they were soon replaced with clients making bookings.

Worldspan at *http://www.worldspan.com* provides three services on the internet:

1. Gateway Plus which is a service to travel agents to get access to the internet
2. A system for consumers to get access to their GDS by providing an interface browser
3. Information to help travel agents and tour operators to set up web sites.

By having access to the Worldspan system those who use the internet can book their complete range of travel products.

2. Supplier sites

British Midland was the first airline company to set up an internet site in 1995. They are found at *http://www.iflybritishmidland.com*. They were set up because increasing competition was forcing them to reduce costs, and flights booked through a GDS system were costing £4 (€5) per flight, no matter the price of the ticket. They also found that travel-agency commission was eating into their costs, so they were looking for a new way to distribute their tickets; the internet was the answer. Problems arose when the site was first set up. For example British Midland had to find a way to distribute tickets in other countries, and there were security problems until encryption technologies improved and protected payments over the internet. Their product is known as Cyberseat, and it provides information about British Midland flights, routes, timetables, and has a simple three-step booking system. Passengers who use the internet in the past used travel agents, so British Midland are now making savings on commission, which they pass on to their customers with lower fares.

Other supplier sites include: Aer Lingus (*www.aerlingus.com*), Ryanair (*www.ryanair.ie*), Ryan Hotels (*www.ryan-hotels.com*), and Jury Doyle Hotels (*www.jurydoyles.com*).

3. Business travel companies

American Express AXI set up its business travel services on the internet domestically in the USA in 1997, and internationally in 1998. It offered a range of services to business people and companies. These include the setting up of a travel policy for companies, which it then helps to operate. It helps the company plan trips for their executives, and arrange all the reservations. Tickets and boarding cards are prepared. Payments and expenses are organised, often using the company's American Express card. It also negotiates prices for the company with hotels, airlines and car hire. This is a complete package that is provided by American Express AXI for its corporate clients. It also supplies management with a profile of their travel patterns, which can be useful for planning future company activities. Companies who use AXI are already customers of American Express's business travel services. The company benefits from using this system because it reduces their travel costs but American Express also benefits because the company is tied into the American Express range of travel products, which creates employment and profits.

4. Tourism organisations

Ireland's national tourism board, Bord Fáilte, won awards at the Tourism and Technology Conference in Edinburgh in 1997 for its website. Bord Fáilte is found at *http://www.ireland.travel.ie* and provides a range of information about low-cost accommodation and B&Bs. It also gives details about events, various activities, attractions and accessibility. The search engine allows tourists to obtain information about different parts of Ireland, i.e. each county. It allows the user to compose his or her own itinerary around Ireland, and to create a customised brochure to fit his or her needs, which includes maps and accommodation and which can then be downloaded and printed out.

Gulliver Ireland

*The **Swift** Way to Get Away*

Fig. 19.2: Gulliver

GULLIVER

This is Ireland's travel information system on the internet, and it provides the database for the Bord Fáilte site, but it in fact pre-dates the internet. Bord Fáilte and the NITB developed Gulliver during 1990 and 1991 as a joint venture. Funding came from the International Fund for Ireland, EU development grants, and two tourism organisations. It came into use during the 1993 tourist season. The Gulliver system consisted of a database of all tourism products in Ireland, for example approved accommodation, attractions, events, leisure facilities, maps. Most accommodation providers were small, with fewer than thirty bedrooms. Each supplier was grouped into the appropriate tourism-sector type, for example approved accommodation, transport. In order to be listed on Gulliver, the tourism supplier had to pay a fee, which also gave them access to the on-line booking system. The suppliers had to pay a commission of 10 per cent of each booking on-line. Gulliver could be accessed by tourists through the regional tourism authorities and tourism information centres, information areas at airports, ferry terminals, railway and coach stations in Ireland. Abroad, Gulliver was available at Bord Fáilte offices, and through the main GDS at travel agents. The people who required access to this information were inbound tourists. They could access information about Ireland, 365 days a year, and twenty-four hours a day. This information allowed tourists to plan their holidays in Ireland in advance; they were able to prepare itineraries, and book all their accommodation on-line.

This seemed like an ideal way to advertise Ireland abroad to the travel trade;

unfortunately a number of problems arose. These included delays in downloading information during the peak summer seasons. The cost of establishing dedicated Gulliver lines was very high and few overseas offices installed the system. Resistance came from the small tourism providers who did not like the Minitel system, and did not use it on a regular basis, resulting in high costs. Many suppliers abandoned the system altogether and updated information for the computer system by phone or fax. New technology was developed during the 1990s including the internet, CD Roms, and multimedia, none of which was used by Gulliver; this resulted in the system becoming obsolete shortly after it was set up. In 1996 Gulliver was updated by Bord Fáilte, Microsoft Consulting Services, Internet Business Ireland, Gulliver Tourism Information and Reservation network, and Flexicom. It was also decided that the Gulliver system should be run as a commercial operation, and the tourist boards reduced their holdings. Fexco took over 74 per cent of Gulliver (1997) on a public and private partnership venture.

The new updated system allowed both producers and buyers to be linked to Gulliver's database in a number of ways: (a) through Gullink, Gulliver's own system, (b) using a PC system and Lilliput software, (c) using the old Minitel system or Faxlink. Whether using the internet or the call centre, access to Gulliver is inexpensive for the potential tourist; it is only the cost of a local phone call. Queries can be answered within seconds, and confirmations of bookings also are done rapidly. Tour operators are able to contact Gulliver automatically to make reservations. Small Irish tourism businesses use PCs or the FaxLink, to contact Gulliver. FaxLink uses a preprinted fax form, which is similar to a lottery ticket. The information is electronically scanned into the Gulliver system. Using Gullnet, accommodation providers can check on reservations, alter tarrifs, update details of their premises, and send messages to Gulliver's marketing groups. Gulliver members who own web sites can be linked into Gulliver. A multilingual call centre using free phone numbers also operates seven days a week, and is linked into the Gulliver system to answer queries and make reservations. Minitel systems are still used in France, which is one of Ireland's main inbound markets. Elsewhere, Gulliver has set up self-service kiosks in airports, ferry ports etc. The amount of information on Gulliver has also expanded, with route planners, calendar of events being available. The new Gulliver system which is linked with the Bord Fáilte site provides incoming tourists with all they need to know about Ireland, and the opportunity to book on-line, making it one of the best tourist sites on the internet.

THE FUTURE OF THE TRAVEL TRADE AND THE INTERNET

There are different types of travellers, some of whom are prepared to use the internet, while others prefer to stay with the more conventional methods of booking travel products.

- Frequent travellers are often business people, or are visiting friends and family. These people use the same routes and services over and over, and many of them request the same low-fare flights each time; they would benefit from using the internet.
- Independent travellers are people who organise their own trips rather than going on a package tour. They do not use the services of travel agents. These travellers tend to check prices out on the internet before travelling, and many will choose to buy on the internet because flights are cheaper.
- Package holiday-makers are often people who go to identikit resorts in the Mediterranean. Many are looking for cheap packages, and this information is available on the internet.
- Business people, travelling to different cities, and staying in different hotels, require advice from travel agents, and most will not use the internet for this reason.
- Infrequent travellers make little use of travel services, so they require advice and guidance in choosing a holiday; travel agents provide this service to these customers.

Three of these different types of travellers will choose to use the internet service that best suits their needs, opting to use either an internet travel agent, GDS, a product provider, a specialist business travel agent or a national tourism organisation. Some of the travellers will continue to use travel agents, but the type of service that these travel agents will be providing for them will have to change, if travel agents are going to survive the onslaught of new technology.

The new travel agents will need to

- Offer a quality consultancy advice service, from a well-trained staff
- Make more use of the internet for their own sales, to keep up-to-date about destination, suitable packages and other products
- Offer highest-quality service to business people, with the provision of up-to-date advice, and a prompt delivery of airline tickets and hotel vouchers
- Accept the new technology. Some of these new internet travel services make use of local travel agents to provide and deliver tickets; this is a new area for business expansion for travel agents. The companies that accept the new technology readily can find new opportunities for expanding their business; it is only those who oppose it that will be left behind and face closure.

Web sites of other internet travel businesses include:
www.travelweb.com
www.travelocity.com
www.marriott.com
www.hotelbook.com

www.visitbritain.com
www.DiscoverNorthernIreland.com

REVISION QUESTIONS

1. Explain the following abbreviations: CRS, SITA, PNR and GDS.
2. How does a CRS system operate?
3. Name two companies which have CRS systems.
4. How have computer systems helped hotels run more efficiently?
5. Name the four main GDS systems.
6. Write about the GDS system that you are most familiar with.
7. What kind of information do all the GDS systems provide?
8. Explain the value to the travel industry of using the internet.
9. Describe the types of travel companies that use the internet. Give examples.
10. Describe the different types of travellers who might use the internet.
11. How does the internet pose a threat to the tourism and travel industy?
12. How can the travel industry overcome this threat?
13. Explain how Gulliver operates today.

Assignments

1. Look up all the internet sites that are referred to here, especially the Irish tourism industry sites, to see the services that they offer, and then write a report on your findings.
2. If you are doing travel as part of your studies, carry out an in-depth study on the GDS system that is used in the travel agents where you do work experience.
3. Research the Bord Fáilte web site to collect information on Ireland's tourism industry.

References and further reading

G. Inkpen, *Information Technology for Travel and Tourism*. Longman, 1998.
Galileo Information Sheet. Galileo Information: www.galileo.com.
Gulliver Information Sheet. Gulliver.
www.sabre.com.
www.amadeus.com.
www.worldspan.com

CHAPTER 20

The Future of Ireland's Tourism Industry

It is impossible to predict the future as far as any aspect of the economy is concerned; all the Government can do is put plans in place that will help the tourism industry to expand. Government investment since 1989 has amounted to €1.27 billion. This has improved the quality of hotels, the provision of all-weather attractions, and the accessibility of Ireland from abroad. Unexpected events can alter plans. The arrival of foot-and-mouth disease, first in England and later in Ireland in spring 2001, resulted in the close down of most events in Ireland for two months. Severe restrictions were imposed on movement in the countryside, and poor advance bookings during these vital spring months resulted in major losses for the tourism industry. Predicted losses in March 2001 were £500 (€625) million. The survival of many small, family-run tourism enterprises during the poor tourism season of 2001 is difficult to predict. The downturn in the USA and Japanese economies at the beginning of 2001 affected the amount of money that tourists from these countries had to spend on holidays. The knock-on implications of these events affected the Irish tourism industry. The Government took some action, for example extra funding for marketing, to try to minimise the impact of these events on the tourism industry.

The World Tourism Organisation expects that tourism will grow astronomically over the next twenty years. The expectation is that overseas tourists will grow from 563 million in 1995 to 1,602 million in 2020, that is an annual growth rate of 4.3 per cent. Since the events of 2001 in New York these figures have been revised downwards. The WTO expects the growth of tourism figures to be affected seriously in the short term, but growth will return to earlier predictions in the long term. It is expected that the major change that will occur in outbound tourists will be the growth of the Chinese market. China will then be ranked fourth in the world after Germany, Japan and the USA. Domestic tourism will also grow, particularly outside Europe and the USA, and the ratio of domestic to international tourism will remain 10:1. Problems in the South-East Asian and Far East economies in the late 1990s caused a downturn in tourism and travel from these countries; it is expected that by 2010 these economies will be back on track, and spending on tourism will rise again.

Within the world tourism market, Europe will continue to receive the largest numbers of tourists, but their market share will drop from 59 per cent to 45 per cent. Long-haul holidays will become more important in Europe, increasing from 18 per cent of holidays to 24 per cent. Ireland as part of Northern Europe along with the UK, Denmark, Norway, Sweden, Finland and Iceland had growth rates above the European average, and this is expected to continue because short break holidays and European trips will keep on rising. The other major change that is expected to take place is that the numbers of Asians visiting Europe will be higher than those visiting from America.

The major influences at work on the tourism industry will include the following:

- It is expected that economies will continue to grow, and that China, Brazil, Russia and India will increase their wealth. The Euro harmonisation means that in most EU countries the same currency is being used, and those who offer good value for money will attract large numbers of tourists.
- Technology will improve both transport and communication (information technology).
- Globalisation will occur with more large companies, including those in the tourist industry, influencing the economies of many countries, and reducing the control of individual governments on their countries.
- People will be more aware of the effects of industry, tourism, and other influences on their environment, society and culture.
- There will be fewer political barriers and more deregulation of transport; both will encourage more people to travel further and more often.
- The environment that people work in will become more stressful, leading people to want to 'get away from it all', and increasing the demand for second homes or rural tourism holidays.

Trends in the twenty-first century will include the following:

- Beach resorts will remain popular in southern Europe and the eastern Mediterranean.
- There will be strong growth in special-interest holidays; this is an area that Ireland can focus on.
- City-based tourism will also grow; this will be encouraged by the interest in cultural and historical activities. Ireland can develop this in cities other than Dublin.
- Eco-tourism will become more important, for example whale and dolphin watching.
- The ownership of many hotels will be in the hands of large US groups. This trend is already occurring in Ireland.
- Business tourism will move away from the luxury hotel market as companies become more conscious of value for money.
- There will be an increase in residential tourism and timeshares that offer high standards of facilities and equipment.

- Long-haul destinations will become more attractive.
- Tourism will become more competitive, and tourists will demand more from their tourism products. This will mean only those who provide the best quality of service, for the best value, will be able to survive in the future. Irish tourism will be required to offer value for money, especially now that the Euro is in use.

These trends can be looked on as a threat to Irish tourism, or the industry can see them as an opportunity to develop new products and so benefit from these future trends. The Irish Government has developed plans which they expect will generate tourism growth within the economy.

THE STRATEGY FOR TOURISM DEVELOPMENT 2000– 2006

The aim of this plan is to make Ireland a 'desirable holiday destination for discerning high-spending international tourists.' This will be achieved by

- Developing products to fill gaps in the market
- Marketing to encourage tourists to come to Ireland during the low season
- Training for women returning to work and early school leavers to join the tourism industry
- Access to Ireland, especially on an all-year-round direct ferry service from the continent.

There will be less EU finance available for investment so those in the industry will have to increase their own levels of finance to upgrade their facilities, training and marketing. The Government plans to see all development for the tourism industry within the boundaries of 'sustainable tourism'. (See Chapter 2 for more details on the Strategy 2000–2006.)

Deregulation of the coach and bus business

Since August 2000 the Department of Public Enterprise has produced a new policy for changing the way coach and bus companies operate in Ireland. This is part of the National Development Plan that will operate between 2000 and 2006. The main parts of it will involve the following:

Radical changes to the bus system within the greater Dublin area

This will involve, first, allowing Bus Éireann and Dublin Bus to operate services within each other's areas. They will also become independent companies. Then Dublin Bus is going to be sold off into private ownership. This will done with the agreement of the Trade Unions involved. Dublin Bus will sub-contract their services to private operators. This will lead to private bus operators being granted licences on bus routes in the Dublin area. A bus regulatory body will be set up for the greater Dublin area, and their job will be to licence buses, organise competitions for franchises on different routes between private operators and Dublin Bus, and allocate subsidies as the need arises. They will only monitor the service being provided by the different companies to make sure it is up to standard. The old 1932 Act will be amended, and the regulatory body will be given the power to grant and terminate licences; they will also establish an integrated ticketing scheme. They expect franchising of routes in Dublin to begin by 2004 and be completed by 2007.

Major investment in Dublin's bus network

This is essential because of the congestion in the city caused by cars. There is a need to reverse the trend of Dublin's citizens travelling by car instead of bus.

Table 20.1: Growth in Dublin's a.m. peak-hour journeys				
Am Peak hour trips	1991	1997	2016 Minimum change	2016 DTO Strategy
Public Transport	62,000	69,000	172,000	312,000
Car	110,000	181,000	316,000	176,000
Total	172,000	250,000	488,000	488,000
Courtesy of Department of Public Enterprise				

Major investment will have to take place in the public transport system, otherwise the average speed on the road will be 8kph, reduced to a crawl! This will involve investment in light rail, suburban trains, and a new metro. There will be an increase in the number of bus services, including orbital (around Dublin, rather than just into the city centre), and local routes, which may feed rail services in the future. It is also intended to increase the number of Quality Bus Corridors, and purchase 525 extra buses to provide these new services. The enhanced bus services will be part of an integrated service, which will allow passengers to move between buses and between buses and trains.

Revitalising the railway network

The railway system will be broken into two areas. The Railway Infrastructure Company will look after the tracks and signals. There will be major investment in this area to bring the tracks up to modern requirements. This company will remain in the ownership of the State. The Railway Operating Company will look after the provision of trains. This will either be sold off to the private sector, or the Government will franchise the railway operations. A Railway Safety Authority will be established to ensure that all safety regulations are adhered to.

Deregulation of the bus market outside Dublin

It is hoped that this market will be changed but as yet the actual plans have not been drawn up. These plans will be available by 2003.

Changes in the way our internal transport system operates will have a bearing on our tourists who use the present rail and coach transport.

SPORTS TOURISM

Since 1998 the Irish Government has taken an active role in developing sports tourism in Ireland; this is known as the International Sports Tourism Initiative. It has taken the form of providing funding to attract major sporting events to the country. At present €3.15 million per year is available to major events to locate in Ireland. So far they have managed to attract the first stage of the Tour de France (1998), the Cutty Sark Tall Ships Race (1998), the World Cross-Country Championships (2002), the Special Olympics (2003) and the Ryder Cup (2005); other events are being planned. The Sports Tourism Advisory Group (STRAG) approves events that are entitled to funding, all the major tourism bodies are represented on this, for example the Department of Tourism, Bord Fáilte, ITIC, Aer Lingus. The Government is also planning to spend over €563 million (some say €1.1 billion) on its new sports complex at Abbotstown, Dublin. The site, which is 500 acres, is located north west of the M50, close to Blanchardstown. The complex will offer a range of sporting facilities, including:

- An 80,000 seated stadium which will be used for soccer, rugby internationals and athletic events.
- A 15,000 seated indoor arena which will be used for a variety of events, including concerts.
- A velodrome for cycling races.
- A sports hall for indoor events like volleyball or indoor soccer.
- Tennis courts set in walled gardens.
- A golf academy where young golfers can improve their skills.
- An aquatic centre or fifty-metre pool large enough for international galas.
- Outdoor sports-fields for a range of field games.
- A sports science facility.

Many of these sporting facilities do not exist in Ireland at the moment, which will mean that they will attract new international events to Ireland.

Apart from the sports complex approximately 175 acres of the site will be parkland, which both locals and tourists can enjoy strolling around. There will also be a large artificial lake which will attract wildlife. These facilities will create a 'people's park', which will become a 'destination attraction in itself'. Other facilities that will enhance the sports complex will include bars, restaurants, shopping, leisure facilities, hotels, one of which will be located in the old Abbotstown House, and at a later

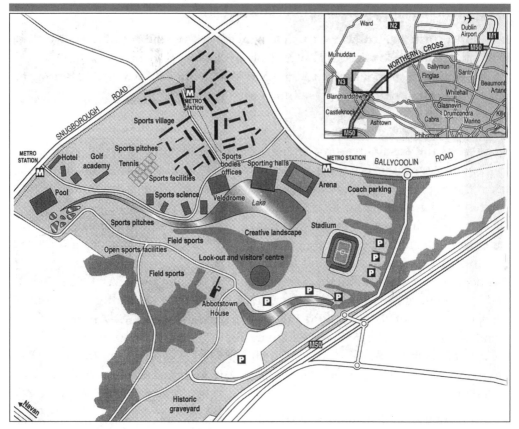

Fig. 20.1: Plan of new sports complex

stage a sports village. Adequate car parking, coach parking, public transport, for example metro, and railway stations would be provided. These new sports facilities would attract large numbers of both domestic and international sports followers to Ireland. However, escalating estimates of costs of this project, and political opposition are putting the complete project in jeopardy. It is likely that a scaled down version of the plan will be developed.

LONG-HAUL TOURISM

In the past long-haul tourism to Ireland meant visitors from the USA, Australia and New Zealand. Most of these tourists were of Irish descent, and lived in Irish communities. Bord Fáilte has successfully tapped into these markets over the years, with the arrival of large numbers of tourists from these source destinations. While direct flights operate from the USA, Australian and New Zealand holiday-makers usually come via London. This creates extra expense, takes longer and is inconvenient.

More recently in the 1990s, Ireland has tapped into the Japanese market, again with success. The type of Japanese tourist who comes to Ireland is very different, because there are no ancestral links with this market. These are part of the groups of Japanese tourists who travel to Europe to see its scenery and history, and to play golf. Go to any part of Europe, whether the slopes of Mont Blanc in France, the Habsburg castles in Austria, or the cafés of Paris, and there are thousands of Japanese tourists. The Irish are now tapping into this market. In the last year or two, the recession in the Japanese economy has affected the numbers of tourists visiting Europe, but once the economy picks up again, these numbers will rise. Many tour operators from Japan now run package holidays to Ireland, encouraged by the work of Bord Fáilte.

The latest markets for development by Bord Fáilte are the South American markets. During the late nineteenth and the twentieth centuries, large numbers of Irish, (mainly from the Midlands) emigrated to Argentina, Chile and Brazil. There are large numbers of Argentineans of Irish descent (over 300,000), known as the Argentinian Diaspora. These included the founder of the Argentinean navy, Admiral Brown from Foxford, Co. Mayo; the liberator of Chile Bernard O'Higgins; the Santo Patricio of the Mexican army. Irish families in South America are both influential and wealthy, and are able to afford long-haul holidays.

There are flight connections between Buenos Aires and Madrid or London daily and these can link easily with flights into Dublin. It only takes thirteen hours to fly between Buenos Aires and London. Long-haul holidays from South America have been growing, and are set to expand in the future among the wealthier groups within these societies. South-American tourists on their first trip to Europe usually visit the main city destinations like Paris, London, Venice, and Rome which are often considered the home of culture. After these cities have been visited, the tourists are looking for new destinations offering something different, and this is where Ireland has the appeal, with its scenery, people and culture. Ireland is a fashionable destination at present, and Bord Fáilte are trying to cash in on this popularity to increase the numbers of tourists from these new markets.

Since 1997 tour operators from South America have been including Ireland in their package holiday programmes. During May 2001, many tour operators from Mexico, Argentina, Chile and Brazil came to Dublin for a Bord Fáilte workshop to meet Irish tourism providers, and to sample our hospitality. This in turn will generate more tourists from these countries in future years. Bord Fáilte also operated a web site in Spanish and Portuguese for these tourists, because of the level of interest that they have shown in Ireland as a holiday destination. Bord Fáilte expect that this market is about to take off, and that in future years Ireland will be a popular long-haul destination.

Eastern Europe and Russia are all linked to Ireland directly by air, through flights by Aeroflot, CSA, etc. This makes access easy for these markets. The population in this area is very large, and while only a small percentage of the population is wealthy enough to enjoy long-haul holidays, it is this market that Bord Fáilte wants to develop. The removal of the Berlin Wall in 1990 eased travel restrictions in Eastern Europe, and travel has grown. Ireland has much to offer wealthy Eastern European tourists, for example luxury five-star hotels, leisure centres, and quality craft shops. As tourism increases in Eastern Europe Bord Fáilte hopes to benefit from this expansion.

SHORT CITY-BREAKS

Short city-breaks are holidays that last for fewer than five days and they usually occur in the low season. In 1989 eighteen per cent of tourists took such breaks; since then the numbers have grown, and this growth is expected to continue. The popularity of these types of holidays is due to increased leisure time, greater prosperity, and improved accessibility especially from the UK. Most tourists taking short city-breaks are on second holidays. UK tourists come to Dublin to enjoy the culture, entertainment, shopping and to visit friends. Irish tourists also go on short breaks, but within Ireland, often making use of special offers in hotels around the country. Sixteen per cent of domestic tourists on short breaks in Dublin visit the capital for concerts and sporting events. Dublin is a popular destination for short-break holidays; 75 per cent of foreign tourists to Dublin (3.1 million overseas tourists) are on short breaks. Large numbers of these tourists are from the UK, and many are young travellers. They find that Dublin is a hospitable and friendly destination, with plenty of activities to entertain them.

Tour operators only organise a small number of short-break holidays, and this is mainly in the US market. Travel agents and the use of the internet are more important in the organisation of these trips. Booking through the internet will continue to grow in importance for those organising short-break holidays. Many of the tourists use special offers on the internet to encourage them to visit Dublin. Overcrowding is a disincentive to the growth of short breaks to Dublin, while at the same time cities like Cork, Limerick and Galway are waiting to offer them to UK and European markets. Improved access by air will allow Ireland's other cities to come on stream to the short-break holiday market, and it is these destinations that will benefit most in the twenty-first century. The World Tourism Organisation expects that city destinations will continue to attract large numbers of tourists.

RESIDENTIAL TOURISM

Residential tourism refers to the ownership of second homes by tourists. Historically the very wealthy have always owned holiday homes; in the eighteenth-century the gentry had their country homes (Palladian Mansions) and town houses (Georgian Squares). It is only as the wealth of the general population has increased that more and more ordinary people can afford second homes. They range from mobile homes to luxury villas with swimming pools. Often they are converted cottages, timeshare apartments, or, more recently, residential villages. Holiday homes are popular with both domestic and international tourists, in Ireland, Spain, North America and other parts of Europe. Greater prosperity and more leisure time have encouraged people to buy second homes. Some people buy these homes as a form of investment, or for their future retirement. The roar of the Celtic Tiger has encouraged many people to purchase holiday homes in Ireland, and, since the changes in taxation on second homes, abroad in Spain, Florida and even on some of the Caribbean Islands.

Residential tourism for many Irish people began with mobile homes at seaside resorts in the 1970s. Other popular destinations were west Cork, Kerry and Connemara where people bought old cottages, or bought sites and built bungalows. Residential tourists like their holiday homes to be located close to the sea, lakes or rivers where they can indulge in many different water sports. In 1996 a Government tax-incentive scheme was put in place to redevelop old seaside resorts. This encouraged investment in many resorts, such as Kilkee, Westport and Courtown. It was hoped that investment would be in the hotel and guesthouse sector; instead, residential villages and apartments were built for investors, and for holiday homes. This had major consequences on the environment in many cases, Courtown in Wexford being among the worst affected. In June 2000 the Government introduced stamp duty on second houses of 9 per cent, which discouraged Irish people from buying holiday homes in Ireland; they bought them abroad instead. The rural renewal scheme, which is operating in Longford, Leitrim and surrounding counties, provides tax relief on some houses in these areas. This shows that the ownership of holiday homes is still popular among the Irish, and that this type of tourism will continue into the future.

Studies that have taken place in the last twenty-five years among people who own holiday homes have found that the owners use them for weekends and for holidays. Distance influences the amount of use that is made of the holiday home. Holiday homes offer different things to different people:

- A holiday home provides a different, more leisurely way of life, where they do not have to think of time, and where they can relax and do very little, take exercise, read, walk, talk.
- Returning to the holiday home year after year provides them with reassurance because they are so familiar with the area.
- Older holiday homes can be owned by several generations of families, and this provides a sense of continuity.
- Most holiday-home owners are from urban areas, and no matter how often they return to the holiday home they still remain outsiders.
- Sometimes those who own these holiday homes are well off, and they form distinct communities in an area. These new communities want to keep the area

for themselves; they put up 'Private, Keep out' signs, or attempt to stop further development in the area.

- Some people purchase these second homes for investment purposes, but most do not.

Often those who buy holiday homes abroad find that they have little in common with the locals; this is because they are from different classes, speak different languages, and perhaps have different values and attitudes. When outsiders are purchasing holiday homes, it may push up the value of houses in the locality, and this may prevent locals from buying houses in the area. When this occurs resentment may build up between the locals and the outsiders. In some areas of Ireland, for example Clare, outsiders are now restricted from building new houses in tourist areas in order to prevent the proliferation of holiday homes. Second homes in residential villages cause the urbanisation of many rural resorts. There are advantages to these types of homes because they bring investment into an area, create jobs in the building industry, and during the high season increase trade for shops, restaurants and entertainment. Most local people prefer all-year-round residents to seasonal visitors, because they create more demand for services, which allows businesses to thrive. The success of residential tourism very much depends on gradual development rather than rapid expansion with large numbers of tourists coming into an area and taking it over.

In spite of the problems associated with residential tourism it is set to continue to grow, well into the twenty-first century. Ireland's domestic residential tourists will continue to buy second homes, perhaps at a slower rate than they did in the period 1996–2000. Internationally, we will still attract Dutch and German tourists to the quieter scenic areas of the country. As long as Ireland offers tourists a pollution-free environment and slower pace of life, then it will continue to attract residential tourists.

The tourism industry must continue to offer tourists the friendliness, hospitality etc. for which we are famous, and then we can expect the industry to expand for many years into the future.

IMPACT OF TOURISM ON SOCIETY

The tourism industry **impacts on society** in many ways, both beneficial and negative. These are some of the effects:

- Inter-cultural understanding takes place because locals meet tourists from many parts of the world in their local pubs, hotels and other venues. The more we come in contact with other cultures, the more we understand them, and the less we fear them. It is from ignorance that fear and racism develop. When tourists arrive in large numbers they often affect local attitudes to tourists, because the tourists appear to dominate the area. It is better that tourism should develop and grow in a sustainable way.

- Community co-operation may be fostered by the development of tourism, for example tidy town competitions.
- In west Donegal the people have come together to set up an eco-powered community centre. It has a wind turbine that generates electricity, and runs a reed-bed Puraflow sewage system. This has been paid for by EU Interreg funding, the International Fund for Ireland, Leader, and Donegal County Council. The local community and co-operative society have raised money for the project. The centre provides tourist information, a café and souvenir shop, an events and sports hall, meeting and conference rooms, and sauna rooms. This is an example of a community joining together to develop a tourist attraction, which is of benefit to the environment and economy of the area. Another good example of communities uniting to develop tourism can be seen in Ballyhoura Country (see rural tourism, chapter 11).
- Community co-operation may involve setting up arts festivals and home-coming festivals. Most of these are initially set up to benefit the local people, by organising musical events, putting on plays, exhibiting art. Some of these festivals have been very successful and now attract large numbers of tourists, which benefit local pubs, hotels and B&Bs.
- Where mass tourism occurs people leave their traditional jobs to work in the tourist industry. This often leads to a breakdown in the way of life of the people. This effect is more marked in some traditional societies, for example Spain in the 1960s, Greece and Turkey. The Irish tourism industry expanded during the 1990s, with many of the businesses being small family-run ones; this means that it is less likely to cause a breakdown in society among those involved in it. Many countries like Tunisia, and the Dominican Republic have allowed the development of tourism behind closed doors, in special resorts. The tourists come into limited contact with the locals, so they cannot influence the locals' way of life. By the same token the tourists never meet the locals or find out about the customs of the country that they are visiting.
- Tourists often attract criminals because they are considered to be wealthy. Many countries have problems with crime against tourists. For example Dublin has a reputation for bag-snatchers, and Prague has a reputation for pickpockets. Crime was rising so much in O'Connell St, Dublin that a Garda Station was established there. CCTV operates in both O'Connell Street and Temple Bar to allow the Gardaí to monitor the activity of criminals, drunks and crowds. This has helped reduce crime in these areas. A victim support scheme exists to help tourists who are victims of crime in Ireland.

Crime also takes place in the countryside as this article from the *Irish Times* of Wednesday 31 December 1997 shows.

Criminals target tourists in isolated beauty spots

With Co. Waterford's tourism planners aiming to increase visitor numbers by at least 5 per cent next year, they and Gardaí are wrestling with a new problem that is a depressing reflection on the times we live in.

Crime against tourists has spread from the cities to some of the country's isolated beauty spots. Last autumn a number of motoring visitors who made their way into the valley where Mahon Falls is located became unexpected victims.

The visitors, who left their cars and went walking in the beauty spot, deep in the heart of the Comeragh Mountains, returned to find that their luggage and other belongings had been stolen. The occurrence of several such incidents in a short period indicated the visitors were being specifically targeted.

The problem was debated at this month's meeting of Waterford County Council, and there were suggestions warning signs might have to be erected at lay-bys and car parks in such locations, which attract thousands of visitors every year. The main danger time appears to be around the beginning and end of the season, when few visitors are around and occasional cars are left unattended.

He said it was acutely disappointing to hear of this trend in popular tourist locations and there would have to be efforts to stamp it out as speedily as possible.

The car break-ins are believed to have been carried out by non-locals, and there must be a lesson for the tourist authorities in other counties with scenic attractions, as the gang or gangs responsible are likely to operate a 'hit-and-run' strategy, targeting each beauty spot only for a brief period.

This new phenomenon is all the more disturbing for the South East region as the regional tourism authorities have concentrated on regenerating growth in activity holidays in the years ahead.

A marketing co-operative for walking and cycling tourism operators in Carlow, Kilkenny, South Tipperary, Waterford and Wexford was set up by South East Tourism earlier this month.

The region's tourism executives believe there is great scope for increasing the south-east's share of this niche market, which is worth more than £50 million annually to Ireland. But the very remoteness, which attracts visitors to the mountainous areas, may also, it seems, facilitate a new trend in opportunist crime.

Tourism is expected to grow in the areas of sports tourism, residential tourism, short breaks and long hauls in the future. The World Tourism Organisation expects that tourism will treble over the next twenty-five years, and it is up to the Irish tourism industry to meet the needs of these new tourists.

REVISION EXERCISES

1. How does the World Tourism Organisation expect tourism to change in the next twenty years?
2. Name five of the major influences of change on the tourist industry.
3. What five main tourism trends will prevail over the next twenty years?

4. Describe how the bus and coach industry will change in Ireland.
5. Describe how sports tourism will develop tourism in Ireland.
6. What kind of long-haul tourists will come to Ireland in the future?
7. What type of short-break tourists come to Dublin?
8. How will short-break holidays develop in the future?
9. Describe the advantages and disadvantages of residential tourism.
10. Describe the impact of tourism on society.

Assignments

1. Choose one of the six types of tourism dealt with above, and study how this type of tourism is affecting your area at the moment, or will in the future.
2. Carry out an audit of your local area under the following headings:
   - The benefits from tourism on (a) the environment, (b) culture, (c) society.
   - The negative effects of tourism on (a) the environment, (b) culture, (c) society.
   - Taking into account the benefits of tourism to the economy (chapter 5), do you feel that the benefits of tourism outweigh the negative effects? Explain briefly why you have reached this conclusion.

References and further reading

Bord Failte, International Sports Tourism Initiative.
World Tourism Organisation, Tourism to the Year 2000. WTO, 1991.
World Tourism Organisation, Tourism Vision 2020. WTO, 1998.

Glossary of Terms

Access Transport: transport for tourists entering Ireland, usually by air or ferry

Aer Lingus: Ireland's national airline

Aer Rianta: Ireland's airport company

AEWA: Agreement on African Eurasian Migratory Water-birds

Agri-tourism: tourism facilities provided in agricultural areas by farmers, eg farmhouse accommodation

AIPCO: The Association of Irish Professional Conference Organisers

Air consolidators: also known as air brokers. These act as intermediaries between aircraft owners and tour operators in securing the best deals for chartering aircraft

A la carte menu: individually-priced items on a menu; this type of menu offers the greatest choice

Alluvial fan: a build-up of material deposited by a river on the floor of a valley

An Taisce: Ireland's National Trust, which seeks to preserve buildings of historic importance

APEX: Advance Purchase Excursion Tickets: special cheap airline tickets

Balance of trade: the difference in value between imports and exports

Basalt plateau: formed from a flow of lava exposed to the air which cooled slowly

BES: Business Expansion Scheme, a system of raising finance for investment in tourism businesses by providing tax incentives

Bonding: acts as insurance for customers in the event of tour operators' and travel agents' businesses failing

Bord Fáilte: Ireland's national tourist board

BSP: Bank Settlement Plan: a clearing system for IATA ticket payments

Bus Éireann: Ireland's national bus service

Carrier: transport companies, e.g. airlines, ferries, coaches

CERT: Council for Education, Recruitment and Training for the tourism industry in Ireland

Charter flights: flights organised for a group, often by a tour operator: they can easily be changed if the plane is not full

CIÉ: Córas Iompar Éireann, the semi-state body that deals with rail and bus transport in Ireland

CITES: (Convention on International Trade in Endangered Species). International trade in endangered animals and plants is prohibited under this agreement

CRS: Central Reservation Systems, used by airports and hotels

DART: Dublin Area Rapid Transit

Deregulation: opening up of controls: allows market forces to decide the level of service

Direct income: income earned directly from tourists' spending in hotels, restaurants and tourism attractions

DIT: Dublin Institute of Technology

DMC: Destination Management Company

Domestic tourists: tourists who travel within their own countries

Drumlins: oval-shaped hills, formed by glaciers, made of boulder clay

Dúchas: Government department which looks after Ireland's natural and man-made heritage

EC: European Community

Economies of scale: as production increases the cost of each unit gets cheaper

Eco-tourism: watching animals (including birds, whales, dolphins) in their local habitat A growing area of tourism

ECTAA: European Confederation of Travel Agents Associations

EEC: European Economic Community, now referred to as the EU

ENFO: Environmental Information Service, Andrew Street, Dublin

EPA: Environmental Protection Agency

ERDF: European Regional Development Fund: aid provided to underdeveloped regions

EU: European Union

Eurostar: Train service between the Continent and England using the Channel Tunnel

Exchange rate: the relationship between our currency and other foreign currencies

Excursionist: day-tripper

Fauna: wildlife, animals, birds

FETAC: Further Education and Training Academic Council

Fifth freedom: allows an airline from one country to land in another, pick up/drop off passengers, and continue on to its destination,

Flora: vegetation, trees, flowers

Foreign exchange earnings: the money that overseas tourists spend in Ireland including money earned by airlines and ferries

Galileo: GDS system developed by United Airlines and Galileo International, now owned by eleven airlines including Aer Lingus

GDS: Global Distribution System, used by travel agents to make airline bookings

Genealogy: the study of a person's ancestors or family tree

Glaciated valley: a steep-sided valley with a flat floor, dug out by a glacier: often referred to as a u-shaped valley

GNP: Gross National Product, the total of services and products of a country in any one year

Ground handling agent: a company providing services to a tour operator at a holiday destination: they are paid a fee for their service

GSH: Great Southern Hotels, operated by Aer Rianta

GSR: Great Southern Railway

Gulliver: Ireland's computerised tourist information and reservation system

Half board: accommodation that provides breakfast and one other meal

IAA: Irish Aviation Authority

IATA: International Air Transport Association

ICC: International Conference Centre, Dublin

Identikit resorts: offer sun or ski holidays in many different countries but all resorts are similar

IHF: Irish Hotel Federation

IMMA: Irish Museum of Modern Art, located in the Royal Hospital, Kilmainham, in Dublin

Incentive travel: travel organised by employers as a reward for hard work

Indirect income: income earned by suppliers to hotels and the tourist industry

Internal transport: transport within a country, usually road, rail, rivers and canals

International tourism: tourists who travel abroad

International tourists: tourists from overseas

Invisible export: tourism is an invisible export, it earns foreign income for the economy

Iarnród Éireann: Ireland's national railway company

InterReg: Inter-regional harmonised transEuropean co-operation. This promotes cross border transnational co-operation

ITAA: Irish Travel Agents Association

ITIC: Irish Tourist Industry Confederation

ITOA: Irish Incoming Tour Operators Association

Karst area: an area of limestone, which is porous, weathered and worn down by water into unusual landforms

Liberalisation: the deregulation of the airline industry in Europe

Load factor: the number of passengers on an airplane required to cover expenses

LoLo: a system of loading freight on to ferries

£sd: pounds, shillings and pence, pre-1970 currency 1£ = 20 shillings: 1 shilling = 12 pennies

LUAS: Dublin's new light rail system

Machair: sandy plains found behind sand dunes

Market share: the amount of the market that is controlled by the company within the market place

Marketing mix: the four Ps – product, price, place and promotion

Meanders: the s-shaped bends found in slow-moving rivers in flat areas and often close to the sea

NCH: National Concert Hall

NHA: Natural Heritage Area

NITB: Northern Ireland Tourist Board

NSO: National Symphony Orchestra

OECD: Organisation for Economic Co-operation and Development

Operational Programme for Tourism: Government planning for the tourist industry 1989–94 and 1995–99

OPW: Office of Public Works

Package tour: a holiday that includes flight, accommodation and transport, organised by a tour operator, and sold through a travel agent at a fixed price

PMS: Property Management System

PNR: Passenger Name Record, used by airlines

PR: Public relations, a form of promotion in the marketing mix

PRSI: pay-related social insurance paid by all workers as a percentage of earnings

Product life-cycle: each product goes through a cycle of birth, growth, maturity, saturation and decline A marketing person will apply different strategies at each stage of the life-cycle

QBC: Quality Bus Corridors

REPS: Rural Environmental Protection Schemes

RTA: Regional Tourism Authority

Ria: a river valley drowned by rising seawater

RoRo: Roll on, Roll off, a term used for trucks loading freight on ferries

RTESO: Radio Telefís Éireann Symphony Orchestra

Rural tourism: tourism organised in, and offering facilities associated with, the countryside, eg accommodation on farms, farm visits, walking, fishing

Sabre: Semi Automated Business Research Environment GDS

SAC: Special Area of Conservation

Scheduled flights: operate on specific routes, to strict timetables regardless of the numbers flying on each flight

Self-catering accommodation: apartments, cottages, caravans etc in which guests look after their own catering and housekeeping

Serviced accommodation: catering and housekeeping are provided, eg hotel

SITE: the Society of Incentive and Travel Executives

Solution lakes: formed by the action of water in limestone areas

SPA: Special Protection Area

Sustainable tourism: this is the tourism for the future It will develop in harmony with the local area and will have no negative impact on the environment, society and culture

SWOT: strengths, weaknesses, opportunities and threats used in marketing to develop a company's business plan

Table d'hôte: fixed-price meal in a hotel or restaurant with limited choice for each course

TIC: Tourist Information Centres are found in Northern Ireland

TIM: Tourism Income Multiplier

TIO: Tourist Information Offices

Tour operator: organises package holidays

Tourism revenue: the money earned from tourists both overseas and domestic

Tourist: a person who stays more than twenty-four hours away from home

Tourist destination: an area that draws tourists because of its historical, geographical or cultural attractions

Travel agent: retails travel products, eg package holidays, flights and car hire, to the public and is paid by commission

Turlough: a lake that dries out in summer and fills up during winter rains Common in limestone areas of the west of Ireland

UFTAA: Universal Federation of Travel Agents Associations

Utell: an agency that represents hotels worldwide, providing them with a reservation system over the internet

VAT: Value Added Tax, paid on all goods and services

VFR: Visiting Friends and Relations

WTO: World Tourism Organisation